Advanced Intelligence Systems and Innovation in Entrepreneurship

Sanjay Misra
Institute for Energy Technology, Norway

Amit Jain
Amity University, Jaipur, India

Manju Kaushik
Amity University, Jaipur, India

Chitresh Banerjee
Amity University, Jaipur, India

Yudhveer Singh
Amity University, Jaipur, India

A volume in the Advances in IT Personnel and Project Management (AITPPM) Book Series

IGI Global
PUBLISHER of TIMELY KNOWLEDGE

Published in the United States of America by
IGI Global
Engineering Science Reference (an imprint of IGI Global)
701 E. Chocolate Avenue
Hershey PA, USA 17033
Tel: 717-533-8845
Fax: 717-533-8661
E-mail: cust@igi-global.com
Web site: http://www.igi-global.com

Library of Congress Cataloging-in-Publication Data

Names: Misra, Sanjay, 1971- editor. | Jain, Amit, 1977- editor. | Kaushik, Manju, 1979- editor. | Banerjee, Chitresh, editor. | Singh, Yudhveer, 1981- editor.
Title: Advanced intelligence systems and innovation in entrepreneurship / edited by Sanjay Misra, Amit Jain, Manju Kaushik, Chitresh Banerjee, Yudhveer Singh.
Description: Hershey, PA : Engineering Science Reference, [2024] | Includes bibliographical references and index. | Summary: "The book provides rigorous research on the formation and implementation of effective strategies and business plans, as well as current studies on the nature, process, and practice of entrepreneurship and innovation in the development, implementation, and application of information technology worldwide"-- Provided by publisher.
Identifiers: LCCN 2023043689 (print) | LCCN 2023043690 (ebook) | ISBN 9798369307908 (hardcover) | ISBN 9798369307915 (ebook)
Subjects: LCSH: Information technology--Management. | Technological innovations. | Entrepreneurship.
Classification: LCC HD30.2 .A3425 2024 (print) | LCC HD30.2 (ebook) | DDC 658.4/038--dc23/eng/20240108
LC record available at https://lccn.loc.gov/2023043689
LC ebook record available at https://lccn.loc.gov/2023043690

This book is published in the IGI Global book series Advances in Computational Intelligence and Robotics (ACIR) (ISSN: 2327-0411; eISSN: 2327-042X)

British Cataloguing in Publication Data
A Cataloguing in Publication record for this book is available from the British Library.

All work contributed to this book is new, previously-unpublished material.
The views expressed in this book are those of the authors, but not necessarily of the publisher.

For electronic access to this publication, please contact: eresources@igi-global.com.

Advances in IT Personnel and Project Management (AITPPM) Book Series

ISSN:2331-768X
EISSN:2331-7698

Editor-in-Chief: *Sanjay Misra*, Institute for Energy Technology, Halden, Norway,
Ricardo Colomo-Palacios, Østfold University College, Norway

MISSION

Technology has become an integral part of organizations in every sector, contributing to the way in which large enterprises, small businesses, government agencies, and non-profit organizations operate. In the midst of this revolution, it is essential that these organizations have a thorough knowledge of how to implement and manage IT projects as well as an understanding of how to attract and supervise the employees associated with these projects.

The **Advances in IT Personnel and Project Management (AITPPM)** book series aims to provide current research on all facets of IT Project Management including factors to consider when managing and working with IT personnel. Books within the AITPPM book series will provide managers, IT professionals, business leaders, and upper-level students with the latest trends, applications, methodologies, and literature available in this field.

COVERAGE

- Cost-Effective Methods for Project Management
- Performance evaluation
- Outsourcing of IT Projects
- Project Sponsorship
- Measuring Project Success

IGI Global is currently accepting manuscripts for publication within this series. To submit a proposal for a volume in this series, please contact our Acquisition Editors at Acquisitions@igi-global.com or visit: http://www.igi-global.com/publish/.

The Advances in IT Personnel and Project Management (AITPPM) Book Series (ISSN 2331-768X) is published by IGI Global, 701 E. Chocolate Avenue, Hershey, PA 17033-1240, USA, www.igi-global.com. This series is composed of titles available for purchase individually; each title is edited to be contextually exclusive from any other title within the series. For pricing and ordering information please visit http://www.igi-global.com/book-series/advances-personnel-project-management/77666. Postmaster: Send all address changes to above address.

Titles in this Series

For a list of additional titles in this series, please visit:
p://www.igi-global.com/book-series/advances-personnel-project-management/77666

Futuristic Technology Perspectives on Entrepreneurship and Sustainable Innovation
Sanjay Misra (Department of Applied Data Science, Institute for Energy Technology, Halden, Norway) Amit Jain (Amity University, Jaipur, India) Manju Kaushik (Amity University, Jaipur, India) and Chitreshh Banerjee (Amity University, India)
Business Science Reference • copyright 2023 • 255pp • H/C (ISBN: 9781668458716) • US $250.00 (our price)

Handbook of Research on the Role of Human Factors in IT Project Management
Sanjay Misra (Covenant University, Nigeria) and Adewole Adewumi (Covenant University, Nigeria)
Business Science Reference • copyright 2020 • 616pp • H/C (ISBN: 9781799812791) • US $325.00 (our price)

Project Portfolio Management Strategies for Effective Organizational Operations
Luca Romano (PMI Central Italy Chapter - CUOA Business School, Italy)
Business Science Reference • copyright 2017 • 388pp • H/C (ISBN: 9781522521518) • US $200.00 (our price)

Handbook of Research on Leveraging Risk and Uncertainties for Effective Project Management
Yuri Raydugin (Risk Services & Solutions Inc., Canada)
Business Science Reference • copyright 2017 • 504pp • H/C (ISBN: 9781522517900) • US $275.00 (our price)

Managing Project Risks for Competitive Advantage in Changing Business Environments
Constanta-Nicoleta Bodea (Bucharest University of Economic Studies, Centre for Industrial and Services Economics, Romania) Augustin Purnus (Technical University of Civil Engineering Bucharest, Romania) Martina Huemann (WU-Vienna University of Economics & Business, Austria) and Miklós Hajdu (Budapest University of Technology and Economics, Hungary)
Business Science Reference • copyright 2016 • 348pp • H/C (ISBN: 9781522503354) • US $210.00 (our price)

IGI Global
PUBLISHER of TIMELY KNOWLEDGE

701 East Chocolate Avenue, Hershey, PA 17033, USA
Tel: 717-533-8845 x100 • Fax: 717-533-8661
E-Mail: cust@igi-global.com • www.igi-global.com

Table of Contents

Detailed Table of Contents

This book chapter explores the dynamic interplay between advanced intelligence systems and the realm of entrepreneurship, shedding light on the transformative potential and implications of these technologies for innovation. In an era marked by unprecedented technological advancements, the fusion of artificial intelligence, machine learning, and data analytics has ushered in a new paradigm for entrepreneurship. This chapter provides a comprehensive examination of the multifaceted relationship between advanced intelligence systems and the entrepreneurial landscape, elucidating the ways in which these innovations are reshaping traditional business models, driving novel opportunities, and catalyzing disruptive change.

This chapter delves into the profound transformations that entrepreneurship has undergone in the era of artificial intelligence (AI). As advanced AI systems continue to disrupt industries and redefine business landscapes, entrepreneurs are faced with both unprecedented opportunities and challenges. Through a historical lens, this chapter traces the evolution of entrepreneurship in the age of AI, exploring the ways in which AI technologies have shaped and continue to shape entrepreneurial

With recent technological breakthroughs, AI is developing as a revolution for mankind, and it has obvious potential advantages in a number of areas. The potential to improve the educational outcomes and experiences of children with exceptional needs by incorporating AI in special education is significant. The theoretical foundations of using AI in special education have been examined in this study and how AI technologies could enhance learning outcomes and promote inclusion. This study aims to further the understanding of how AI may successfully help students with special needs while simultaneously addressing the practical difficulties involved with its implementation. In conclusion, integrating AI into special education has enormous potential to enhance the educational results and experiences of kids with exceptional needs. The use of AI-driven technology may help special educators as well as persons with special needs by enabling real-time feedback and evaluation, individualized education and rehabilitation services, and training tailored to each individual's requirements.

Several authors have researched and published articles clarifying sustainability and how large businesses participate in sustainability initiatives. On the other hand, there is a dearth of published research on the factors that motivate small and medium-sized enterprises (SMMEs) to engage in environmentally friendly business practices. To fill this void, this chapter presents the results from a study on the factors that influence SMMEs to engage in sustainable practices. Normative pressures have a greater influence when leading entrepreneurs to engage in sustainable practices. Interestingly isomorphic forces impact SMMEs in their pursuit of sustainability similarly to large corporations. From a managerial perspective, this chapter urges the micro, small, and medium-sized enterprise sector to place a greater emphasis on information exchange to accommodate the growing demand for businesses to become involved in sustainable development. In addition, entrepreneurs need to be more aggressive in encouraging internal innovation towards sustainable practices.

The present chapter is an attempt to revive the ancient communication skills and techniques and its influence on the relationships; it is by no means a suggestion that technology is less significant. The long hours given to mobiles have put a negative impact on the human relationships. The use of AI techniques has now become an everyday thing which certainly shall, at a point of time, be dangerous for the critical and mental growth of humans. Excessive use of technology has a negative impact.

Many historically significant documents are only accessible in paper record form, making text recognition a crucial problem in the arena of digital image processing. Text recognition techniques primarily aim to convert paper documents into digital files that can be easily managed in a database or other server-based entity. Size, colour, font, orientation, backdrop complexity, occlusion, illumination, and lighting all make text identification more difficult in photos from real-world settings. Variations in writing style, several forms of the same letter, linked text, ligature diagonal, and condensed text make Urdu text identification more difficult than with non-cursive scripts. To separate the spatial correlation and appearance correlation (DSSAC) of the mapped convolutional channel, the suggested intelligent model employs the deep separable convolutional layers in place of the conventional design in the U-Net. To achieve cursive region, capture, the research offers a model called DSSAC-RSC.

With its unprecedented ability to harness collective intelligence Web 2.0 has ushered possibilities in digital entrepreneurship. Digital entrepreneurship has occupied an indispensable place in the business industry as it has a dynamic approach to engross customers on online platforms and to promote their products and services. Over the years, access to digital technology has played a major role in empowering women to do business.The famous women entrepreneurs of Nykaa, Zivame, Limeroad and Sugar Cosmetics have paved a way for entrepreneurial development that features each kind of new digital business, and an analysis of how those traits determine the success factors of women entrepreneurship. In the panorama of entrepreneurship, the function of women has been evolving step by step over the years. One place wherein their effect has been specifically noteworthy is virtual media entrepreneurship. This chapter delves into the arena of girls' entrepreneurs within the virtual media area, brands like Nykaa, Zivame, Limeroad and SUGAR Cosmetics.

Evangelos Vasileiou, University of the Aegean, Greece
Elroi Hadad, Shamoon College of Engineering, Israel
Aikaterini Chalkiadaki, University of the Aegean, Greece

This paper examines the usefulness of Wikipedia pageviews as indicator of the performance of stock prices. We examine the GameStop (GME) case, which drew the investors' and scholars' attention in 2021 due to the Short Squeeze (SSQ), and its skyrocketing price increase since 2021. We use the daily number of pageviews of Wikipedia pages for COVID-19, GME, and SSQ as explanatory variables for the period 31/12/2018-30/3/2022. The results show strong statistical evidence that increased number of Wikipedia pageviews for COVID-19, which represents the fear of the pandemic, has a negative impact on the GME performance. Moreover, the findings show that the increased interest in information regarding the short squeeze, as expressed by the increased number of pageviews of the relative Wikipedia page, is positively linked with the GME price. This approach holds the potential to yield benefits not only for entrepreneurs within the finance sector but also across various other fields. It serves as a valuable proxy for gauging the demand for goods, services, and/or overall interest in a market.

Mahsa Amiri, Faculty of Economics, Universidade do Algarve, Portugal
Célia M. Q. Ramos, School for Management, Hospitality and Tourism (ESGHT), Research Center for Tourism, Sustainability, and Well-Being (CinTurs), Universidade do Algarve, Portugal

Nowadays, making the right business decisions is crucial for companies. With the enhancements in connectivity, data accessibility has been expanding rapidly.

Information is meaningful, data and business intelligence (BI) turn data into information to support the decisions of persons or companies with the purpose of efficiency and effectiveness increasing. However, selecting the right BI system which can be adopted perfectly by a business is an important issue which still needs further studies. The given study comprises the literature review which focuses on BI and analytics, and it continues to study the structure of a BI system and the effects such systems may cause. The findings contribute to a better comprehension of BI and more efficient feedback from BI systems by choosing the right ones. The future collaboration between BI and artificial intelligence (AI), also BI and sustainability goals, are further given topics in this study

This chapter will delve into the dynamic landscape of event management and how artificial intelligence (AI) is revolutionizing the overall event experience. AI technologies have left no area untouched, and, similarly, event planners and event entrepreneurs have also integrated AI in every phase of seamless event execution. Through a comprehensive exploration of AI-driven tools and technologies in the realm of event management, the chapter aims to shed light on how AI is reshaping the entire process of event design, delivering a personalised touch to its attendees thus influencing the nature of engagement strategies. The chapter aims to provide the readers with a holistic understanding of the transformative potential and responsible use of AI in creating unforgettable event experiences. The researcher also employs qualitative research method and seeks the perception of seasoned event professionals related to the topic to further add to its relevance and significance.

The future may be unknown and uncertain, but there are still opportunities to make money by anticipating it. The request of AI and ML to stock market prediction is one such opportunity. Artificial intelligence may be used to generate accurate forecasts before investing, even in a dynamic environment like the stock market. The stock

of crop losses in farming because of competition with crops. This figure can be lowered with effective weed detecting technology. One of the most important areas of AI, known as deep learning (DL), is revolutionizing weed discovery for site-specific weed management (SSWM). In the past half a decade, DL methods have been used with both ground- and air-based technology for weed documentation in still images and in real time. According to the latest findings in DL-based weed detection, developing methods that aid precision weeding technologies in making informed decisions is a priority. Over the past five years, deep learning algorithms have been successfully incorporated into both ground-based and aerial-based systems for the purpose of weed identification in both still picture and real-time scenarios.

Preface

We are delighted to present this edited reference book, *Advanced Intelligence Systems and Innovation in Entrepreneurship*, which brings together the expertise and insights of distinguished contributors in the field. As Editors, we have sought to curate a comprehensive collection that explores the intersection of entrepreneurship, innovation, and information technology (IT).

In today's dynamic and unpredictable economic landscape, the role of information technology in shaping successful enterprises cannot be overstated. The importance of a well-defined IT strategy, balancing daily operational needs with future development, is highlighted throughout this volume. The advent of advanced intelligence systems, powered by artificial intelligence (AI) and machine learning techniques, adds a new dimension to the capabilities of businesses in terms of reasoning, problem-solving, and decision-making.

The chapters in this book delve into the multifaceted relationship between entrepreneurship and technology. From the imperative of innovativeness and risk-taking in entrepreneurial ventures to the crucial role of IT in determining a company's capacity for innovation, the discourse extends to the transformative potential of futuristic technologies. Entrepreneurship and sustainable innovation emerge as essential components in the global pursuit of a socially responsible and environmentally conscious future.

The need for organizational restructuring, coupled with the incorporation of innovative IT tools, is a recurring theme. Studies worldwide have demonstrated the positive correlation between IT utilization and the intensity of entrepreneurial activity, emphasizing the ongoing evolution of restructuring efforts in response to the demands of the present and the potential of future technologies.

Furthermore, the book explores the influence of digital technologies on the conception and development of new entrepreneurial initiatives. The emerging technological paradigm underscores the power of cooperation and collective intelligence in building robust and enduring ventures. Green entrepreneurship, social networks, sustainability entrepreneurship, and the role of intellectual property rights in fostering innovation are additional areas covered in this comprehensive volume.

The concept of intrapreneurship, which empowers employees to function as entrepreneurs within an organizational structure, is examined alongside the transformative impact of information and communication technology (ICT) on various facets of business operations. A forward-looking exploration of emerging technologies, such as blockchain, artificial intelligence, and machine learning, adds depth to the discussions.

The proposed book is intended for a diverse audience, including Ph.D. scholars, researchers, faculty members, undergraduate and postgraduate students, industry professionals, entrepreneurs, intrapreneurs, policymakers, and various specialists. The thematic chapters cover a range of topics, including digital entrepreneurship, computational algorithms, green entrepreneurship, intellectual property, advanced intelligent systems, smart innovation, and IT strategy.

We believe this collection will serve as a valuable resource, offering readers up-to-date, comprehensive, and rigorous research-based articles. The aim is to facilitate a deeper understanding of effective strategies, business plans, and the intricate nature of entrepreneurship and innovation within the realm of information technology, fostering global insights and collaborative knowledge exchange.

Chapter 1: Advanced Intelligence Systems and Their Impact on Innovation in Entrepreneurship

Authored by Amit Singh and Swapnesh Taterh from Amity University Rajasthan, India, this chapter explores the dynamic interplay between advanced intelligence systems and entrepreneurship. It sheds light on the transformative potential and implications of technologies like artificial intelligence, machine learning, and data analytics for innovation in the entrepreneurial landscape. The comprehensive examination reveals how these innovations reshape traditional business models, drive novel opportunities, and catalyze disruptive change.

Chapter 2: The Evolution of Entrepreneurship in the Age of AI

This chapter, co-authored by Amit Singh, Swapnesh Taterh, Uddalak Mitra, and Yudhveer Singh, all affiliated with Amity University Rajasthan, delves into the profound transformations that entrepreneurship has undergone in the era of artificial intelligence (AI). Offering a historical perspective, the authors trace the evolution of entrepreneurship and explore how AI technologies have shaped and continue to shape entrepreneurial endeavors. The chapter highlights key trends, strategies, and ethical considerations essential for entrepreneurs navigating this AI-driven landscape.

Chapter 3: Envisaging Dynamics of Entrepreneurship in view of Modern-day Innovation and Advancements - A Contemplating Phenomenon

Authored by K. Madhu Kishore Raghunath and Chandra Sekhar Patro from GITAM University and Gayatri Vidya Parishad College of Engineering (A), India, this chapter focuses on the influence of AI on entrepreneurial effectiveness. It assesses AI determinants, identifies key strategies for digital transformation, and explores the benefits and challenges of AI in entrepreneurship. The authors highlight the generativity of AI, indicating its potential as a fundamental innovation in the entrepreneurial toolkit.

Chapter 4: AI-Enabled Industrial Applications

Khaja Kamalapuram, Maria Joseph, Abhishek L., and Jahir Pasha M. collaborate on this chapter to provide insights into AI-enabled industrial applications and their potential benefits for businesses. The authors discuss how AI, as a contributing factor to the fourth industrial revolution, can enhance economic growth, streamline tasks, and improve human performance. They explore the automation of tasks, decision-making support, and optimization in interconnected supply chains through real-time data, while acknowledging the challenges and the potential impact on the workforce.

Chapter 5: AI in Special Education: Emerging Trends and Challenges

In this chapter, SUYESHA SINGH and Paridhi Jain from Manipal University Jaipur, India, explore the potential benefits of incorporating AI in special education. The authors examine the theoretical foundations of using AI technologies to enhance learning outcomes and promote inclusion for children with exceptional needs. The study aims to deepen the understanding of how AI can assist students with special needs and address the practical challenges involved in its implementation.

Chapter 6: Sustainable Warriors Unleashed - Unravelling the Triggers of Eco-Enthusiasm in a Developing Nation's SMME Community: Sustainable Entrepreneurship

Thembelihle Pita and Nigel Chiweshe from UKZN, South Africa, address the dearth of research on factors motivating small and medium-sized enterprises (SMMEs) to engage in environmentally friendly practices. They present findings from a study on normative pressures and isomorphic forces influencing SMMEs in adopting sustainable practices. The chapter emphasizes the need for information exchange and internal innovation in the SMME sector to meet growing demands for sustainable development.

Chapter 7: Technology and Communication: Technically Leading Towards Fictional Connections

This chapter, authored by Parul Mishra from Amity University Rajasthan, delves into sustainability initiatives by large businesses and their impact on small and medium-sized enterprises (SMMEs). The chapter highlights the influence of normative pressures and isomorphic forces on leading entrepreneurs to engage in sustainable practices, encouraging information exchange and internal innovation in the SMME sector.

Chapter 8: Urdu Cursive Word Recognition Using Advanced Intelligent Model of Optimized Deep Learning Model

Asha V, Uma N, Balasubramanian Prabhu kavin, and Gan Hong Seng contribute to this chapter, which addresses the challenges in recognizing Urdu cursive words. The authors present an intelligent model called DSSAC-RSC, incorporating Deep Separable Convolutional Layers to separate spatial and appearance correlations. This model aims to enhance the recognition of Urdu cursive words in images, overcoming the complexities posed by variations in writing style, fonts, and other factors.

Chapter 9: Shattering the Glass Ceiling of Women Entrepreneurship in the Digital Retail Landscape

Authored by Pallavi Mishra and Tanushri Mukherjee from Amity University Rajasthan, this chapter explores the role of digital technology, specifically Web

2.0, in empowering women entrepreneurs. The authors analyze the impact of digital entrepreneurship on various businesses, with a focus on influential women entrepreneurs in the digital retail landscape, such as Nykaa, Zivame, Limeroad, and Sugar Cosmetics. The chapter offers insights into how digital technology has shaped and continues to influence women entrepreneurship.

Chapter 10: A Wikipedia Narration of the GameStop Short Squeeze

Vasileiou Evangelos, Elroi Hadad, and Aikaterini Chalkiadaki examine the GameStop Short Squeeze case in this chapter, assessing the usefulness of Wikipedia pageviews as an indicator of stock prices. The authors analyze the impact of increased pageviews related to COVID-19, GameStop, and the Short Squeeze on stock performance. The findings provide valuable insights for entrepreneurs, scholars, and various fields, serving as a proxy for gauging market interest and demand.

Chapter 11: Potential of Business Intelligence and Analytics on Performance of Tourism and Hospitality Companies

Mahsa Amiri and Célia Ramos, affiliated with the Universidade do Algarve, Portugal, delve into the crucial role of Business Intelligence (BI) in decision-making for tourism and hospitality companies. The authors explore the structure and effects of BI systems, shedding light on their potential collaboration with Artificial Intelligence (AI) and sustainability goals. This chapter contributes to a better understanding of BI and its future implications for efficient decision-making in the tourism and hospitality sector.

Chapter 12: AI Unleashed - Transforming Event Experiences and Engagement: AI Technology reshaping Event Design delivering a personalized touch to Event Attendees

Tanushri Mukherjee and Pallavi Mishra from Amity University Rajasthan examine the transformative impact of AI on event management in this chapter. The authors explore how AI technologies are revolutionizing the entire event experience, from planning to execution. They provide a comprehensive overview of AI-driven tools and technologies, emphasizing the personalized touch AI brings to event design and its influence on attendee engagement.

Chapter 13: Development of Intelligent System for Stock Market Prediction Using Enhanced Deep Learning Technique with Banking Data

Manjunatha B, Revathi V, Balasubramanian Prabhu kavin, and Gan Hong Seng contribute to this chapter, presenting an Enhanced Bidirectional Gated Recurrent Neural Network (EBGRNN) for stock market prediction. Focusing on three prominent banks - HDFC, Yes Bank, and SBI, the authors evaluate real-time datasets from the National Stock Exchange (NSE) of India. The study aims to offer insights into predicting stock price trends using Enhanced Deep Learning techniques.

Chapter 14: Ensembled Time Series Deep Learning Framework for Stock Market Prediction

Lakshmipriya Balagourouchetty, Nidhi Singh, and Jayalakshmy S explore the competency of ensembled sequential learning elements in predicting stock market trends. The authors assess long short-term memory (LSTM), bidirectional long short-term memory (BiLSTM), and gated recurrent unit (GRU) with different depths and combinations. The chapter highlights an ensemble prediction model using BiLSTM-LSTM and BiLSTM-GRU, demonstrating improved performance and accuracy in stock market trend forecasting.

Chapter 15: A Smart Innovative Pre-Trained Model Based QDM for Weed Detection in Soybean Field

Gunapriya B, Arunadevi Thirumalraj, Anusuya V S, Balasubramanian Prabhu kavin, and Gan Hong Seng present a chapter on precision farming using Artificial Intelligence (AI) for weed detection in soybean fields. The authors highlight the role of deep learning algorithms in ground and aerial-based systems to identify and manage weeds effectively. The chapter emphasizes the significance of integrating AI into precision weeding technologies to make informed decisions and optimize agricultural practices.

As editors of this meticulously curated reference book, *Advanced Intelligence Systems and Innovation in Entrepreneurship*, we find ourselves immensely gratified by the comprehensive exploration undertaken by our esteemed contributors. The amalgamation of diverse perspectives, scholarly insights, and practical applications encapsulated in the chapters underscores the pivotal nexus of entrepreneurship, innovation, and information technology (IT).

In an era defined by rapid technological evolution, the chapters collectively emphasize the critical role of information technology in sculpting contemporary enterprises. The intrinsic connection between a well-defined IT strategy and the sustainable development of businesses resonates throughout the volume. The infusion of advanced intelligence systems, driven by artificial intelligence (AI) and machine learning, ushers in a new era where businesses harness the power of reasoning, problem-solving, and decision-making on unprecedented scales.

The chapters explore the intricate relationship between entrepreneurship and technology, dissecting themes ranging from innovativeness and risk-taking to the fundamental restructuring of organizations. The discourse extends beyond immediate concerns, reaching into the transformative potential of futuristic technologies, paving the way for a socially responsible and environmentally conscious future.

The collaborative effort of our contributors touches upon the global landscape of entrepreneurship, showcasing studies that highlight the positive correlation between IT utilization and entrepreneurial activity. The profound insights provided are not only reflective of current demands but also serve as a foresight into the potential of future technologies.

Digital technologies take center stage in shaping and nurturing new entrepreneurial initiatives, with an emphasis on cooperation, collective intelligence, and the pivotal role of intellectual property rights. Additionally, the chapters delve into contemporary concepts such as intrapreneurship and the transformative influence of information and communication technology (ICT) across various business facets.

The thematic diversity of the book caters to a broad audience, spanning Ph.D. scholars, researchers, faculty members, undergraduate and postgraduate students, industry professionals, entrepreneurs, intrapreneurs, policymakers, and specialists. From digital entrepreneurship and computational algorithms to green entrepreneurship, intellectual property, advanced intelligent systems, smart innovation, and IT strategy, each chapter provides a unique lens through which to understand the intricate nature of entrepreneurship and innovation in the realm of information technology.

We extend our gratitude to the contributors who have enriched this volume with their research, bringing to the forefront the symbiotic relationship between innovation and entrepreneurship. It is our sincere hope that this collection serves as a catalyst for continued exploration, collaboration, and inspiration in the ever-evolving realm where entrepreneurship and technology converge. May the ideas presented herein spark new dialogues, inform strategic decision-making, and contribute to the ongoing narrative of innovation shaping the future of entrepreneurship.

Sanjay Misra
Institute for Energy Technology, Norway

Chapter 1
Advanced Intelligence Systems and Their Impact on Innovation in Entrepreneurship

Amit Kumar Singh
https://orcid.org/0000-0002-1325-7329
Amity University, India

Swapnesh Taterh
https://orcid.org/0000-0003-2770-8829
Amity University, India

ABSTRACT

This book chapter explores the dynamic interplay between advanced intelligence systems and the realm of entrepreneurship, shedding light on the transformative potential and implications of these technologies for innovation. In an era marked by unprecedented technological advancements, the fusion of artificial intelligence, machine learning, and data analytics has ushered in a new paradigm for entrepreneurship. This chapter provides a comprehensive examination of the multifaceted relationship between advanced intelligence systems and the entrepreneurial landscape, elucidating the ways in which these innovations are reshaping traditional business models, driving novel opportunities, and catalyzing disruptive change.

INTRODUCTION

In today's fast-paced and technology-driven world, the relationship between advanced

DOI: 10.4018/979-8-3693-0790-8.ch001

intelligence systems and innovation in entrepreneurship has become increasingly intertwined. The emergence of advanced technologies, such as artificial intelligence (AI), machine learning, natural language processing, and robotics, has revolutionized the way entrepreneurs' approach problem-solving, decision-making, and product development. This chapter explores the profound impact of advanced intelligence systems on innovation in entrepreneurship, highlighting the opportunities they present, the challenges they pose, and the potential for transformative growth. Advanced Intelligence Systems have had a profound impact on innovation in entrepreneurship, transforming the way businesses approach problem-solving, decision-making, and product development. These cutting-edge technologies, including artificial intelligence (AI), machine learning, and data analytics, enable entrepreneurs to leverage vast amounts of data and extract valuable insights to drive informed and data-driven decisions (Al Suwaidi et al., 2020). With predictive analytics and advanced algorithms, entrepreneurs can identify market trends, consumer behavior patterns, and untapped opportunities, empowering them to develop innovative products and services that cater to specific customer needs. Moreover, AI-powered automation streamlines operations, optimizing efficiency and freeing up valuable time for entrepreneurs to focus on strategic planning and creative ideation. The integration of Advanced Intelligence Systems has not only enhanced the overall innovation process but also fostered personalized customer experiences, leading to improved customer satisfaction and loyalty. As these technologies continue to advance, entrepreneurs who embrace and harness their power are better positioned to drive disruptive innovation, gain a competitive edge, and shape the future of entrepreneurship in an increasingly dynamic and technology-driven business landscape (Almazrouei et al., 2021).

THE RISE OF ADVANCED INTELLIGENCE SYSTEMS

The rise of advanced intelligence systems marks a transformative era in human history, propelled by the remarkable progress in artificial intelligence, machine learning, and data analytics. These cutting-edge technologies have unlocked unprecedented capabilities, allowing machines to mimic human intelligence, learn from vast amounts of data, and make autonomous decisions. Advanced intelligence systems have permeated various aspects of our lives, revolutionizing industries such as healthcare, finance, transportation, and entertainment. With their ability to process information at unparalleled speeds and uncover hidden insights, these systems have empowered businesses, governments, and individuals alike to make data-driven decisions, solve complex problems, and drive innovation to new heights (Ahmad et al., 2020). As the journey of technological advancement continues, the impact of advanced intelligence systems is set to reshape the world, opening limitless opportunities, and ushering in a future defined by unprecedented possibilities.

Artificial Intelligence (AI)

AI is the cornerstone of advanced intelligence systems. It refers to the ability of machines to perform tasks that typically require human intelligence, such as learning, reasoning, problem-solving, and decision-making. Machine learning, a subset of AI, allows systems to improve their performance through learning from data without explicit programming. Artificial Intelligence (AI) has emerged as a catalyst for innovation and disruption in the realm of entrepreneurship. This transformative technology has revolutionized the way entrepreneurs approach business challenges, empowering them to make informed decisions, optimize processes, and create novel solutions (Chien et al., 2018). AI provides entrepreneurs with invaluable tools such as predictive analytics, natural language processing, and machine learning algorithms that can sift through vast amounts of data, identify patterns, and forecast trends. These capabilities enable entrepreneurs to gain a deeper understanding of their target markets, anticipate customer needs, and develop products and services that are more aligned with market demands. Moreover, AI-driven automation streamlines operations, reducing costs and freeing up resources to focus on creativity and strategic growth. As AI continues to evolve, entrepreneurs who embrace this technology have a competitive edge, unlocking untapped opportunities and driving their ventures towards a more efficient, customer-centric, and innovative future (Daradkeh et al., 2022).

Data-Driven Decision Making

The proliferation of big data and the advent of advanced analytics have empowered entrepreneurs to make data-driven decisions. AI can process vast amounts of data at unprecedented speeds, extracting valuable insights and patterns, which were previously impossible to identify. Data-driven decision-making using AI has become a game-changer for businesses across various industries. With the exponential growth in data availability, AI technologies, such as machine learning and predictive analytics, have enabled organizations to extract valuable insights from vast datasets and transform them into actionable intelligence. By leveraging AI algorithms, businesses can identify patterns, trends, and correlations that would be otherwise difficult for human analysts to detect (Masa'Deh et al., 2021). This empowers decision-makers to make well-informed choices based on empirical evidence rather than intuition alone. Data-driven decision-making using AI enhances efficiency, minimizes risks, and maximizes opportunities for growth and innovation. Moreover, it enables businesses to respond swiftly to changing market dynamics, adapt to customer preferences, and deliver personalized experiences that lead to improved customer satisfaction. As AI technologies continue to advance, organizations that embrace data-driven decision making will thrive in a highly competitive landscape, establishing themselves as pioneers in their respective domains (Nespeca et al., 2018)

THE ROLE OF ADVANCED INTELLIGENCE SYSTEMS IN ENTREPRENEURIAL INNOVATION

The role of advanced intelligence systems in entrepreneurial innovation is nothing short of transformative. These cutting-edge technologies, including artificial intelligence (AI), machine learning, and data analytics, have revolutionized how entrepreneurs approach innovation and problem-solving. By harnessing the power of data and sophisticated algorithms, advanced intelligence systems enable entrepreneurs to make data-driven decisions, gain valuable insights into market trends and customer behavior, and identify untapped opportunities. These systems streamline processes through automation, freeing up time and resources for creative thinking and strategic planning. Moreover, AI-powered tools foster personalized customer experiences, leading to enhanced customer satisfaction and loyalty. As entrepreneurs increasingly adopt advanced intelligence systems, they gain a competitive edge, drive disruptive innovation, and unlock new possibilities, propelling their ventures towards success in today's dynamic and technology-driven business landscape (Turban et al., 2011).

Idea Generation and Validation

AI-powered tools, such as natural language processing and sentiment analysis, help entrepreneurs analyze market trends, customer feedback, and social media interactions to generate and validate new business ideas. This accelerates the innovation process and reduces the risk of pursuing unviable concepts (Kunduru et al., 2023)

Product and Service Innovation

Advanced intelligence systems enable entrepreneurs to create innovative products and services that cater to specific customer needs. For instance, AI-driven personalization and recommendation engines provide customers with tailored experiences, fostering loyalty and driving sales.

Process Automation and Efficiency

Entrepreneurs can leverage AI and robotics to automate repetitive and time-consuming tasks. This allows them to streamline operations, reduce costs, and focus on higher-value activities, such as strategic planning and creativity.

Market Research and Customer Insights

AI-powered analytics provide entrepreneurs with in-depth market research and customer insights. Entrepreneurs can understand their target audience better, identify emerging trends, and anticipate customer preferences, facilitating agile and customer-centric innovation.

CHALLENGES AND CONSIDERATIONS

While the role of advanced intelligence systems in entrepreneurial innovation is promising, it also presents various challenges and considerations that entrepreneurs must navigate. One key challenge is the ethical use of data and AI algorithms. Ensuring data privacy, transparency, and avoiding bias in AI decision-making are crucial to maintaining trust with customers and stakeholders. Additionally, the integration of advanced intelligence systems may require significant financial investments and expertise, especially for startups and small businesses (Giuggioli et al., 2023). Entrepreneurs must carefully assess the potential returns and resource requirements before adopting these technologies. Human-AI collaboration is another consideration as entrepreneurs balance automation with the preservation of human jobs and creativity. Addressing these challenges requires a thoughtful approach to technology implementation, coupled with continuous learning and adaptation to harness the full potential of advanced intelligence systems while safeguarding against potential risks and ensuring responsible innovation (Alqahtani et al., 2023).

Ethical and Social Implications

As entrepreneurs adopt advanced intelligence systems, ethical considerations become crucial. Issues related to data privacy, AI bias, and job displacement should be addressed responsibly to ensure a positive and inclusive impact on society.

Resource Constraints

Implementing advanced intelligence systems may pose financial and resource-related challenges for entrepreneurs, particularly for startups and small businesses. Ensuring access to affordable and scalable AI solutions is essential for widespread adoption.

Human-AI Collaboration

Entrepreneurs must navigate the delicate balance of human-AI collaboration. Integrating AI into workflows without alienating employees requires effective change management and training programs.

FUTURE TRENDS IN ADVANCED INTELLIGENCE AND ENTREPRENEURIAL INNOVATION

The future of advanced intelligence and entrepreneurial innovation promises to be dynamic and transformative, with several trends shaping the landscape. Explainable AI is expected to gain prominence as businesses seek transparency in AI decision-making to build trust with customers and comply with regulations. Collaborative innovation networks will emerge as entrepreneurs recognize the value of collective intelligence and cross-industry collaborations to tackle complex challenges and drive breakthrough solutions (AK Singh et al., 2023). Additionally, AI is poised to play a pivotal role in sustainability and social impact efforts, as entrepreneurs leverage its capabilities to develop eco-friendly products and address pressing global issues. As AI technologies continue to evolve, entrepreneurs will witness a rise in augmented creativity, where AI becomes a creative partner, inspiring novel ideas and optimizing artistic endeavors. Overall, the future trends in advanced intelligence and entrepreneurial innovation hold great potential for fostering responsible, inclusive, and sustainable business practices, driving societal progress, and creating new avenues for growth and success (Zhang et al., 2023).

Explainable AI

As AI systems become more sophisticated, the need for explainable AI arises. Entrepreneurs will seek transparency in AI decision-making to build trust with customers and stakeholders. It is a critical area of research and development within the field of artificial intelligence that aims to provide transparency and comprehensibility to the decision-making process of AI models. Unlike traditional AI algorithms that operate as "black boxes," Explainable AI seeks to unravel the

intricate inner workings of AI systems, allowing humans to understand how and why a particular decision was made. By providing clear explanations and insights into the factors influencing an AI's output, Explainable AI addresses the challenge of AI interpretability, making it easier for users, businesses, and regulatory authorities to trust and accept AI-based decisions. This growing emphasis on Explainable AI is not only crucial for gaining insights into complex AI models but also for ensuring ethical and accountable deployment of AI technologies across various domains, fostering human-AI collaboration, and enabling a more responsible integration of AI into society (Taherdoost et al., 2023)

AI for Sustainability and Social Impact

The application of advanced intelligence systems in sustainable business practices and social impact initiatives will be on the rise. Entrepreneurs will leverage AI to develop solutions that address environmental and societal challenges.

AI Ecosystems and Collaborations

Entrepreneurs will increasingly participate in AI ecosystems and collaborations to access shared resources, talent, and knowledge. Collaborative networks will foster innovation and drive transformative breakthroughs (Taherdoost et al., 2023).

CONCLUSION

The integration of advanced intelligence systems has redefined the landscape of entrepreneurship, catalyzing a wave of innovation across industries. By harnessing the power of AI and other advanced technologies, entrepreneurs can make data-driven decisions, enhance customer experiences, and pioneer groundbreaking solutions. However, they must address ethical considerations, overcome resource constraints, and foster human-AI collaboration to realize the full potential of advanced intelligence systems in driving entrepreneurial innovation. As AI continues to evolve, entrepreneurs must remain adaptable and forward-thinking, embracing the possibilities that advanced intelligence presents to create a better and more prosperous future.

REFERENCES

Ahmad, S., Miskon, S., Alkanhal, T. A., & Tlili, I. (2020). Modeling of business intelligence systems using the potential determinants and theories with the lens of individual, technological, organizational, and environmental contexts-a systematic literature review. *Applied Sciences (Basel, Switzerland)*, *10*(9), 3208. doi:10.3390/app10093208

Al Suwaidi, F., Alshurideh, M., Al Kurdi, B., & Salloum, S. A. (2020, September). The impact of innovation management in SMEs performance: A systematic review. In *International conference on advanced intelligent systems and informatics* (pp. 720-730). Cham: Springer International Publishing.

Almazrouei, F. A., Alshurideh, M., Al Kurdi, B., & Salloum, S. A. (2021). Social media impact on business: a systematic review. In *Proceedings of the International Conference on Advanced Intelligent Systems and Informatics 2020* (pp. 697-707). Springer International Publishing. 10.1007/978-3-030-58669-0_62

Alqahtani, M. (2023). Artificial intelligence and entrepreneurship education: A paradigm in Qatari higher education institutions after covid-19 pandemic. *International Journal of Data and Network Science*, *7*(2), 695–706. doi:10.5267/j.ijdns.2023.3.002

Chien, C. F., Wang, H. K., & Fu, W. H. (2018). Industry 3.5 framework of an advanced intelligent manufacturing system: Case studies from semiconductor intelligent manufacturing. *Management Review*, *37*(3), 105–121.

Daradkeh, M. (2022). Innovation in Business Intelligence Systems: The Relationship Between Innovation Crowdsourcing Mechanisms and Innovation Performance. [IJISSS]. *International Journal of Information Systems in the Service Sector*, *14*(1), 1–25. doi:10.4018/IJISSS.302885

Giuggioli, G., & Pellegrini, M. M. (2023). Artificial intelligence as an enabler for entrepreneurs: A systematic literature review and an agenda for future research. *International Journal of Entrepreneurial Behaviour & Research*, *29*(4), 816–837. doi:10.1108/IJEBR-05-2021-0426

Kunduru, A. R. (2023). Effective Usage of Artificial Intelligence in Enterprise Resource Planning Applications. *International Journal of Computer Trends and Technology*, *71*(4), 73–80. doi:10.14445/22312803/IJCTT-V71I4P109

Masa'Deh, R. E., Obeidat, Z., Maqableh, M., & Shah, M. (2021). The impact of business intelligence systems on an organization's effectiveness: The role of metadata quality from a developing country's view. *International Journal of Hospitality & Tourism Administration*, *22*(1), 64–84. doi:10.1080/15256480.2018.1547239

Nespeca, A., & Chiucchi, M. S. (2018). The impact of business intelligence systems on management accounting systems: The consultant's perspective. In *Network, Smart and Open: Three Keywords for Information Systems Innovation* (pp. 283–297). Springer International Publishing. doi:10.1007/978-3-319-62636-9_19

Popovič, A., Puklavec, B., & Oliveira, T. (2019). Justifying business intelligence systems adoption in SMEs: Impact of systems use on firm performance. *Industrial Management & Data Systems*, *119*(1), 210–228. doi:10.1108/IMDS-02-2018-0085

Singh, A. K., Taterh, S., & Mitra, U. (2023). An Efficient Tactic for Analysis and Evaluation of Malware Dump File Using the Volatility Tool. *SN Computer Science*, *4*(5), 457. doi:10.1007/s42979-023-01844-8

Taherdoost, H., & Madanchian, M. (2023). Artificial Intelligence and Knowledge Management: Impacts, Benefits, and Implementation. *Computers*, *12*(4), 72. doi:10.3390/computers12040072

Turban, E. (2011). *Decision support and business intelligence systems*. Pearson Education India.

Zhang, H., Gao, S., & Zhou, P. (2023). Role of digitalization in energy storage technological innovation: Evidence from China. *Renewable & Sustainable Energy Reviews*, *171*, 113014. doi:10.1016/j.rser.2022.113014

Chapter 2
The Evolution of Entrepreneurship in the Age of AI

Amit Kumar Singh
https://orcid.org/0000-0002-1325-7329
Amity University, India

Swapnesh Taterh
https://orcid.org/0000-0003-2770-8829
Amity University, India

Uddalak Mitra
Siliguri Institute of Information Technology, India

Yudhveer Singh
Amity University, India

ABSTRACT

This chapter delves into the profound transformations that entrepreneurship has undergone in the era of artificial intelligence (AI). As advanced AI systems continue to disrupt industries and redefine business landscapes, entrepreneurs are faced with both unprecedented opportunities and challenges. Through a historical lens, this chapter traces the evolution of entrepreneurship in the age of AI, exploring the ways in which AI technologies have shaped and continue to shape entrepreneurial endeavors. It also highlights key trends, strategies, and ethical considerations essential for entrepreneurs navigating this AI-driven landscape.

DOI: 10.4018/979-8-3693-0790-8.ch002

INTRODUCTION

The rise of artificial intelligence has ushered in a new era for entrepreneurship. As AI technologies have matured, entrepreneurs have been presented with innovative tools and opportunities to create and scale businesses in previously unimaginable ways. This chapter explores the evolution of entrepreneurship in the age of AI, providing insights into how these transformative technologies have influenced the entrepreneurial landscape. In the age of artificial intelligence (AI), entrepreneurship stands at the threshold of unprecedented transformation (Colleoni et.al, 2023). The fusion of human ingenuity and machine intelligence has given birth to a new era of business innovation. With each passing day, entrepreneurs are confronted with a landscape that is both exhilarating and challenging, as AI technologies continue to evolve and redefine the rules of the game. This chapter embarks on a journey through the remarkable evolution of entrepreneurship in the age of AI, tracing its historical roots, examining its present dynamics, and charting a course towards a future where AI is not just a tool but a driving force behind entrepreneurial endeavors. As we delve into this transformative narrative, we will explore how AI has become a catalyst for innovation, empowered data-driven decision-making, disrupted markets, and necessitated ethical considerations—all while offering entrepreneurs unparalleled opportunities to shape the future of business (Giuggioli et.al, 2023).

THE EMERGENCE OF AI-ENABLED ENTREPRENEURSHIP

This section provides an overview of the early adoption of AI in entrepreneurship, showcasing pioneering startups that harnessed AI for novel solutions. It discusses how the convergence of big data, computational power, and machine learning catalyzed the growth of AI-driven entrepreneurial ventures. In the annals of entrepreneurship, there exists a chapter that is being continuously rewritten, a chapter that unfolds with the relentless advancement of technology. It is a chapter that tells the story of how, in the age of artificial intelligence (AI), entrepreneurship has evolved into a realm where innovation knows no bounds. The emergence of AI-enabled entrepreneurship represents a pivotal moment in this ongoing narrative, one that has forever altered the way businesses are conceived, nurtured, and propelled to success. This section embarks on a journey through this pivotal transformation, shedding light on the pioneers, the technologies, and the groundbreaking ideas that have catalyzed the fusion of entrepreneurship and AI (Audretsch et.al, 2001). From the birth of early AI startups to the current landscape of machine learning-driven enterprises, we explore the origins of this remarkable convergence and the profound impact it continues to exert on the entrepreneurial ecosystem.

AI AS A CATALYST FOR INNOVATION

Here, we delve into the ways in which AI has fueled innovation across industries. Case studies and examples illustrate how entrepreneurs leverage AI to develop disruptive products and services, and how traditional industries are undergoing digital transformation. In the ever-evolving landscape of entrepreneurship, innovation has long been the lifeblood of progress. However, in the age of artificial intelligence (AI) (Brynjolfsson et.al, 2004), innovation takes on a new dimension, where machines endowed with cognitive abilities collaborate with human ingenuity to push the boundaries of what is possible. AI, in all its algorithmic elegance, emerges not only as a tool but as a catalyst, fundamentally altering the entrepreneurial landscape. This section delves into the dynamic realm of AI as a catalyst for innovation, examining how AI technologies have ignited the spark of creativity, disrupted traditional business models, and unlocked unprecedented opportunities for entrepreneurs. Through compelling case studies and illuminating examples, we navigate the terrain where AI-driven innovation thrives, reshaping industries, and redefining the very essence of entrepreneurship itself (Chesbrough et al., 2006).

DATA-DRIVEN DECISION MAKING

AI's role in enhancing decision-making processes is examined in this section. It explores how entrepreneurs leverage AI-powered analytics to make data-driven decisions, optimize operations, and gain a competitive edge. In the age of artificial intelligence (AI), where information flows abundantly and data accumulates at an unprecedented rate, decision-making has become a finely tuned art. This chapter explores the pivotal role that data-driven decision-making plays in the entrepreneurial landscape, where AI systems serve as invaluable partners in the quest for informed choices. From startups to established enterprises, entrepreneurs are harnessing the power of AI-driven analytics to transform raw data into actionable insights, revolutionizing how they navigate challenges and capitalize on opportunities. In this section, we delve into the methodologies, technologies, and real-world applications that empower entrepreneurs to make smarter decisions, optimize their operations, and achieve a competitive edge. As we navigate the intersection of data and entrepreneurship, we will uncover how data-driven decisions have become a cornerstone of success in the AI-driven business world (Davenport et al., 2007).

AI AND MARKET DISRUPTION

This section analyzes how AI technologies have disrupted traditional markets and created new opportunities for entrepreneurs. It examines the strategies employed by startups to challenge established players and introduces the concept of "platform entrepreneurship." The winds of change have swept through industries far and wide, leaving in their wake a trail of market disruption and innovation. At the heart of this transformative storm lies artificial intelligence (AI), a technological juggernaut that has redefined the rules of engagement for entrepreneurs and businesses alike. This section unravels the compelling narrative of AI as the catalyst for market disruption, reshaping traditional industries while birthing entirely new ones. We explore the strategies, the success stories, and the profound implications of AI-driven entrepreneurship in a world where the status quo is continuously challenged. Through illustrative case studies and insightful analysis, we embark on a journey that reveals how AI has become not just a tool but a driving force, propelling entrepreneurial ventures towards uncharted horizons and reimagining the very foundations of markets and industries (Drucker et al., 1985).

ETHICAL CONSIDERATIONS IN AI ENTREPRENEURSHIP

As AI becomes increasingly integrated into entrepreneurial ventures, ethical considerations come to the forefront. This part explores the ethical dilemmas associated with AI, including issues of bias, transparency, and privacy, and emphasizes the importance of responsible AI use. As entrepreneurs harness the remarkable potential of artificial intelligence (AI) to innovate and disrupt, a critical dimension of this journey comes into focus: ethics. In the rapidly evolving landscape of AI entrepreneurship, where algorithms hold sway and data flows ceaselessly, it is imperative to pause and deliberate on the ethical implications that accompany this newfound power. This chapter delves deep into the complex and nuanced ethical considerations that entrepreneurs must grapple with when integrating (Kurzweil et al., 2005) AI into their ventures. From addressing issues of bias and transparency to safeguarding privacy and ensuring responsible AI use, we navigate the ethical terrain that underpins AI entrepreneurship. Through compelling insights, real-world examples, and thought-provoking discussions, we shed light on how entrepreneurs can chart an ethical course in the AI-driven business world and build ventures that not only innovate but also uphold the highest standards of social and moral responsibility (McKeown et al., 2017).

SCALING AI-DRIVEN VENTURES

Scaling an AI-driven venture presents unique challenges. This section discusses the strategies entrepreneurs use to overcome these challenges and offers insights into securing funding, building teams, and expanding markets. Scaling a business has always been a formidable challenge in the entrepreneurial journey, and in the age of artificial intelligence (AI), this challenge takes on a new dimension. As AI technologies continue to evolve and shape industries, entrepreneurs who harness these innovations find themselves in a unique position to accelerate growth and expand their ventures exponentially. This section explores the strategies, intricacies, and considerations that underpin the process of scaling AI-driven ventures (Shane et al., 2008).

From securing funding in a competitive landscape to building teams equipped to navigate the complexities of AI, we delve into the critical elements that determine whether an AI-driven venture can transition from startup to industry leader. By drawing on real-world examples and expert insights, we provide a roadmap for entrepreneurs seeking to unlock the full potential of AI, seize market opportunities, and navigate the challenges inherent in scaling AI-driven ventures. Whether you are a seasoned entrepreneur looking to leverage AI or a newcomer to the field, this chapter offers a comprehensive guide to scaling your AI-powered business successfully.

COLLABORATIVE ECOSYSTEMS IN AI ENTREPRENEURSHIP

Collaboration and ecosystem building are vital in the AI entrepreneurship landscape. This chapter examines how entrepreneurs, academia, and industry partners come together to foster innovation in AI. In the dynamic realm of entrepreneurship driven by artificial intelligence (AI), the notion of "going it alone" has given way to a more collaborative and interconnected approach. AI entrepreneurship thrives within a rich tapestry of partnerships, alliances, and ecosystems, where innovators, researchers, businesses, and investors converge to collectively shape the future. This chapter delves into the intricate web of collaborative ecosystems that play a pivotal role in nurturing and propelling AI-driven ventures (Tapscott et al., 2006).

From innovation clusters and research hubs to startup accelerators and industry partnerships, we explore the various facets of these collaborative environments. Through case studies, success stories, and insights from experts in the field, we unveil the advantages of participating in these ecosystems. Whether it's accessing resources, gaining market insights, or fostering innovation through cross-disciplinary collaboration, entrepreneurs in AI are finding new avenues to thrive. As we navigate the landscapes of collaboration in AI entrepreneurship, we discover how working together becomes a catalyst for transformative ventures that push the boundaries of possibility. This chapter serves as a compass for entrepreneurs seeking to navigate and leverage the rich collaborative ecosystems in the AI-driven entrepreneurial world (Tapscott et al., 2006).

THE FUTURE OF ENTREPRENEURSHIP IN AN AI-POWERED WORLD

Looking ahead, this section explores the future trends and potential disruptions that AI may bring to entrepreneurship. It discusses emerging technologies such as quantum computing and their potential impact on the entrepreneurial landscape. As we stand at the precipice of a new decade, the future of entrepreneurship is inextricably intertwined with the relentless advance of artificial intelligence (AI) (Venkatraman et al., 1997). The symbiotic relationship between entrepreneurship and AI is evolving at an unprecedented pace, reshaping industries, redefining business models, and posing both exhilarating opportunities and formidable challenges. In this chapter, we embark on a forward-looking journey, exploring the future of entrepreneurship in a world where AI is not just a tool but a transformative force. We begin by examining the emerging trends in AI, from quantum computing to neural network architectures, and their potential to revolutionize the entrepreneurial landscape. We delve into the disruptive potential of AI in sectors yet untouched and discuss the strategies that forward-thinking entrepreneurs are employing to position themselves at the forefront of these changes (Ak Singh et al., 2023). Additionally, we explore the profound societal impacts of AI-driven entrepreneurship, from job displacement to new opportunities for social entrepreneurship and global problem-solving. Ethical considerations, responsible AI use, and regulatory frameworks take center stage as we ponder the ethical dimensions that entrepreneurs must navigate in this AI-powered world.

Through expert insights, real-world examples, and speculative glimpses into the future, this chapter offers a panoramic view of what lies ahead for entrepreneurs in an AI-powered world. It challenges readers to envision the possibilities, anticipate the disruptions, and embrace the innovations that will shape the entrepreneurial landscape for years to come. For entrepreneurs and innovators alike, the future beckons with boundless potential, and this chapter serves as a compass to navigate the exciting and transformative journey ahead (Ak Singh et al., 2023).

CONCLUSION

In closing, this chapter underscores the profound impact of AI on entrepreneurship and highlights the need for entrepreneurs to adapt, innovate, and address ethical considerations in this dynamic AI-driven world. It encourages entrepreneurs to embrace AI as a powerful tool for realizing their visions and shaping the future of business. This chapter provides a comprehensive overview of the evolving relationship between entrepreneurship and AI, offering valuable insights and guidance for both seasoned and aspiring entrepreneurs as they navigate the exciting and ever-changing landscape of AI-driven innovation.

REFERENCES

Audretsch, D. B., & Thurik, A. R. (2001). What's new about the new economy? Sources of growth in managed and entrepreneurial economies. *Industrial and Corporate Change*, *10*(1), 267–315. doi:10.1093/icc/10.1.267

Brynjolfsson, E., & McAfee, A. (2014). *The Second Machine Age: Work, Progress, and Prosperity in a Time of Brilliant Technologies*. W. W. Norton & Company.

Chesbrough, H. (2006). *Open Innovation: The New Imperative for Creating and Profiting from Technology*. Harvard Business Press. doi:10.1093/oso/9780199290727.001.0001

Davenport, T. H., & Harris, J. (2007). *Competing on Analytics: The New Science of Winning*. Harvard Business Review Press.

Drucker, P. F. (1985). *Innovation and Entrepreneurship: Practice and Principles*. Harper & Row.

Giuggioli, G., & Pellegrini, M. M. (2023). Artificial intelligence as an enabler for entrepreneurs: A systematic literature review and an agenda for future research. *International Journal of Entrepreneurial Behaviour & Research*, *29*(4), 816–837. doi:10.1108/IJEBR-05-2021-0426

Illia, L., Colleoni, E., & Zyglidopoulos, S. (2023). Ethical implications of text generation in the age of artificial intelligence. *Business Ethics, the Environment & Responsibility*, *32*(1), 201–210. doi:10.1111/beer.12479

Kurzweil, R. (2005). *The Singularity Is Near: When Humans Transcend Biology*. Penguin.

McKeown, P. (2017). *Competitive Intelligence Advantage: How to Minimize Risk, Avoid Surprises, and Grow Your Business in a Changing World*. John Wiley & Sons.

Shane, S. (2008). *The Illusions of Entrepreneurship: The Costly Myths That Entrepreneurs, Investors, and Policy Makers Live By*. Yale University Press.

Singh, A. K., & Taterh, S. (2023). Exploring the Significance and Obstacles of Adopting Futuristic Technology Perspectives for Entrepreneurship and Sustainable Innovation. In Futuristic Technology Perspectives on Entrepreneurship and Sustainable Innovation (pp. 1-10). IGI Global. doi:10.4018/978-1-6684-5871-6.ch001

Tapscott, D., & Williams, A. D. (2006). *Wikinomics: How Mass Collaboration Changes Everything*. Penguin.

Teece, D. J. (2010). Business Models, Business Strategy and Innovation. *Long Range Planning*, *43*(2-3), 172–194. doi:10.1016/j.lrp.2009.07.003

Venkatraman, N. (1997). The Concept of Fit in Strategy Research: Toward Verbal and Statistical Correspondence. *Academy of Management Review*, *22*(4), 853–854.

Chapter 3
Envisaging Dynamics of Entrepreneurship in View of Modern-Day Innovation and Advancements:
A Contemplating Phenomenon

K. Madhu Kishore Raghunath
https://orcid.org/0000-0002-8134-5718
GITAM University, India

Chandra Sekhar Patro
https://orcid.org/0000-0002-8950-9289
Gayatri Vidya Parishad College of Engineering, India

ABSTRACT

Digital technologies are changing the essence and extent of entrepreneurship. A distinctive characteristic of digitization is its ability to automate tasks that demand a lot of human labour. Contemporary innovations in artificial intelligence (AI) are making it possible for computers to perform activities that would typically need human intellect, such as processing vast unstructured data sets using sophisticated, adaptive algorithms. This has prompted entrepreneurs to consider the generativity of AI, indicating that the technology may represent a fundamental innovation to the instruments that they develop with, in addition to a way to achieve cost and productivity gains. Thus, the purpose of the chapter is to assess the influence of AI determinants on entrepreneurial effectiveness, identify the key strategies for successful digital transformation, benefits and challenges of AI on entrepreneurship.

DOI: 10.4018/979-8-3693-0790-8.ch003

INTRODUCTION

Entrepreneurship has touched and improved many lives by becoming a cult in the modern young generation. The art of entrepreneurship is now the most learnt and followed phenomenon among schools and universities around the world. Modern-day entrepreneurship is completely different from what traditional entrepreneurship ever was (Ransbotham et al., 2020). Oztemel and Gursev (2018) stated that traditional entrepreneurs mostly relied on established rules and practices and explored the opportunities around them to grow and sustain, whereas modern-day entrepreneurs are more innovative and creative with constant access to the best of technology and artificial intelligence (AI).

Development started with industrialisation and behind every Industrial Revolution there were a group of people who were entrepreneurs within themselves but were working in an organisational setup, things went on well and then there was a stage where the Industrial Revolution became a generic phenomenon and economies needed something that could address very niche and specific problems in modern societies (Balasubramanian et al., 2022). This gave rise to the entrepreneurial phenomenon among nations which filled the significant gaps within the economies of different countries and revolutionised the startup culture (Lindebaum et al., 2020; Raisch & Krakowski, 2021).

According to Schlick et al. (2014), artificial intelligence as a tool for innovation which was a distant dream earlier has now become the daily entity of interaction for individuals as well as inventors. Artificial intelligence is a broad term that refers to a technology or software that involves human-like activities involving planning, organising, problem-solving and decision-making. Entrepreneurial activities undertaken by entrepreneurs in the present generation have led them to use technology at every step of their enterprise from idea generation to product development. The impact of AI is rising day by day presumably at every nook and corner of the world enabling faster, more flexible and more efficient processes with better quality goods and services.

Artificial intelligence is already a pro in performing many tasks in areas like copywriting, scheduling, organising and decision-making concerning many functional areas in the organisation for effective forecasting of cashflows. AI has become a candidate for excessive use as it helps new founders speed up research and bridge societal gaps. It is also claimed that 40% of startup entrepreneurs fail due to their inability to understand and use historical databases for predicting future demand and supply of products. Shepherd and Makchrzak (2022) opined that the combination of entrepreneurship and AI was always destined and the only thing in doubt is the outcome of the combination, it can be good, the way of making the decision-making process easier or can be a bad outcome leading to complete unemployment or the third outcome where the good outcome is made better and bad outcome is considered as an opportunity to find new avenues (Chalmers et al., 2021). While researchers have understood a lot about entrepreneurship and artificial intelligence, these two components still need to be worked upon to find the future directions.

ARTIFICIAL INTELLIGENCE AND ENTREPRENEURSHIP

Artificial intelligence (AI) systems are envisaged to bring major changes in various industries such as health care, education, transportation, customer services, marketing, HR, banking financial services etc. Speaking of AI in all the above industries leads to the changes to be brought in by the startups and entrepreneurs themselves. Entrepreneurs have been making giant strides in the world of business and lately, there seems to be a slowdown in the way the operations are executed but now that AI has come into its prime form, AI can change the dynamics of the race that all entrepreneurs are into (Balasubramanian et al., 2022). It is also posited that as AI is a distinctive phenomenon to human intelligence, entrepreneurs using artificial intelligence are predominantly important in organizational decision-making (Raisch & Krakowski, 2021; Roundy, 2022). Moreover, AI is the only entity which can help entrepreneurs improve their decision-making systems, and enhance the quality of decisions in terms of their effectiveness and efficiency (Kraus et al., 2020).

According to Chalmers et al. (2021), Contemporary entrepreneurs value AI significantly as it helps in manoeuvring through strategic gateways for organizations that face business hurdles affecting their productivity and efficiency. In this technological era of advancements, AI further plays a strategic role in performing difficult tasks and solving complex problems. Moreover, this AI revolution also encapsulates. AI also is the magical hat that can keep modern-day organisations afloat and stay competitive and AI coupled with blockchain networking enhances entrepreneurial security and envisages transparency within business processes (Treiblmaier, 2018). The interaction between AI and entrepreneurs are becoming more and more and areas like machine learning, natural language processing, deep learning and artificial neural networks are used now to automate daily regular activities to dedicate the human resource in pursuit of new opportunities and ventures (Berger et al., 2021; Lévesque et al., 2022; Rojas & Tuomi, 2022; Chalmers Townsend & Hunt, 2019; Roundy, 2022).

AI does a great job when it comes to the new venture creation process and helps young and old entrepreneurs to develop, design and scale their companies to the next big thing in the world of AI, creating new opportunities and introducing new products and services with most innovative and credible outcomes (Dinhand & Thai, 2018; Elia et al., 2020). In the present generation, AI is integral to the Internet of

Things (IoT) and it is also considered a dominant research area with its application delving into different industries and entrepreneurial ventures which will lead to human-computer interaction to improve the accuracy and robustness of decision-making (Azuma ct al., 2021).

Eventually, AI till now has been a great boon to humanity, which not only improves organisational performance but also develops them using AI-based solutions. This AI phenomenon has been the greatest entrepreneurial opportunity in the history of civilization (Iansiti & Lakhani, 2020). Jussupow et al. (2021) also published that human decision-making as a part of entrepreneurship includes an array of contexts where paraphernalia of AI is used to make the process proof (Meissner & Keding, 2021). This statement was further supported by Giuggioli & Pellegrini (2023), who mentioned that the disruptive potential of AI is having a major positive impact and influence on entrepreneurship.

AI and entrepreneurship at present are bonded strongly and it will remain the same for the coming few generations (Iansiti and Lakhani, 2020). With AI and entrepreneurship being a bonded phenomenon, there is also a dire need to study the impact of AI determinants on entrepreneurship. In light of the above statement, the present study will evaluate the significance of AI on entrepreneurship effectiveness in terms of its key variables such as automation, data analysis, customer service, predictive analysis and personalisation for small business entrepreneurs and large company entrepreneurs. The study will also put forth the strategies for the successful implementation of AI in business organisations and workplaces.

OBJECTIVES

1. To study and analyze the impact of various determinants of artificial intelligence on entrepreneurial effectiveness.

CONCEPTUAL FRAMEWORK

AI has the potential to revolutionize the way businesses operate, from automating repetitive tasks to providing insights on various issues of various dimensions. In the present study, authors will comment upon the performances of various determinants of AI namely, the automation, data analysis, customer service, predictive analysis and personalization component. The framework as shown in Figure 1 shows the flow of the study.

Implementation of AI is the replication of human intelligence that can be envisaged to think and learn like human beings, which involves analysis of vast amounts of

Figure 1. Conceptual framework

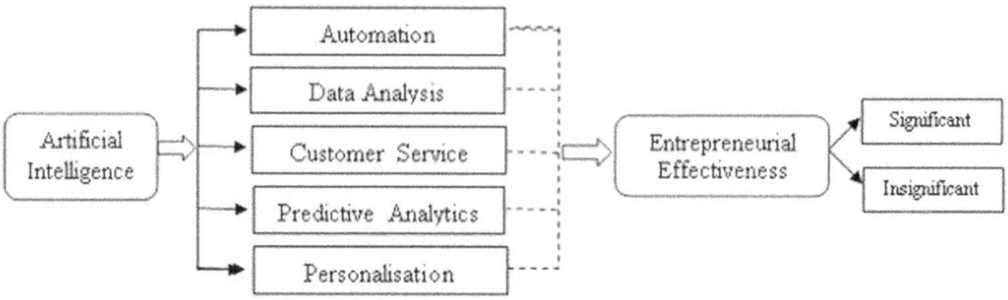

data, building patterns and making strategic decisions. Implementation of AI in entrepreneurship is mostly observed in terms of the following:

1. **Automation:** The core competence of AI in entrepreneurship comes in the form of automating repetitive tasks which require less human supervision and helping manpower to concentrate on complex objectives requiring closed human intervention.
2. **Data analysis:** In addition to the automation of processes the next best contribution of AI in any organisation or enterprise is to analyse large sheets of data develop strategic patterns and further provide insights that otherwise are beyond human observation.
3. **Customer Service:** Artificial Intelligence presence has made it easier to reach large audiences by the way of chatbots and voice bots to listen, interpret and solve the queries of various individuals by providing them with apt and relevant information (Ughulu, 2022).
4. **Predictive analytics:** Artificial intelligence also helps in predicting future patterns and trends by analysing the current and past data with the help of a score. Where a higher score indicates a high probability of occurrence of an event and vice-versa (Kumar & Garg, 2018).
5. **Personalisation**: Personalisation refers to tailoring customised support to individual specific needs, where they have access to information to make the best use of it according to need. AI can analyse customer data to provide personalized recommendations and offers, increasing customer satisfaction and loyalty (Carr, 2010).

METHODOLOGY AND HYPOTHESES

The required data was collected from both secondary and primary sources. The secondary sources of information are used from reputed journals, magazines, newspapers, internet sources, books, and websites of small and large business enterprises. The primary data sources are collected through an online survey, using a structured questionnaire with closed-end questions. The questionnaire was sent through email communication to various small companies and large business entrepreneurs operating in the state of Andhra Pradesh. The questionnaire was validated and data was collected on a five-point scale. To assess the association between the determinants of artificial intelligence (AI) and entrepreneurship the following hypotheses were developed.

H_{01}: Automation as a factor of AI does not have any impact on small business and large company entrepreneurial effectiveness.
H_{02}: Data Analysis as a factor of AI does not have any impact on small business and large company entrepreneurial effectiveness.
H_{03}: Customer Service as a factor of AI does not have any impact on small business and large company entrepreneurial effectiveness.
H_{04}: Predictive Analysis as a factor of AI does not have any impact on small business and large company entrepreneurial effectiveness.
H_{05}: Personalisation as a factor of AI does not have any impact on small business and large company entrepreneurial effectiveness.

STATISTICAL DATA ANALYSIS

The chapters present the analysis of the influence of various determinants of artificial intelligence on the entrepreneurial effectiveness related to both small business and large company entrepreneurs. The five determinants of artificial intelligence are automation, data analysis, customer service, predictive analysis, and personalization.

The influence of automation on entrepreneurial effectiveness is presented in Table 1. The analysis reveals that the majority of the respondents representing 35.3% (large company-21%; small business-14.3%) stated that automation activity is excellent in their company. The respondents representing 23.3% (large company-13.7%; small business-9.7%) revealed that the automation in entrepreneurial activity is good in their company. However, 18.3% (large company-11.3%; small business-7%) are satisfied with the automation of entrepreneurial activity, 12.7% (large company-2.7%; small business-10%) stated that the automation process is poor and 10.3% (large company-1.3%; small business-9%) revealed that the automation process is not

Table 1. Influence of automation on entrepreneurial effectiveness

Type of Business		Automation					Total
		Not in Force	**Poor**	**Satisfied**	**Good**	**Excellent**	
Small Business Entrepreneur	Count	27	30	21	29	43	150
	% of Total	9.0%	10.0%	7.0%	9.7%	14.3%	50.0%
Large Company Entrepreneur	Count	4	8	34	41	63	150
	% of Total	1.3%	2.7%	11.3%	13.7%	21.0%	50.0%
Total	Count	31	38	55	70	106	300
	% of Total	10.3%	12.7%	18.3%	23.3%	35.3%	100.0%

	Value	df	Asymptotic Significance (2-sided)
Pearson Chi-Square	38.705[a]	4	0.000
Likelihood Ratio	41.665	4	0.000
Linear by Linear Association	26.306	1	0.000
N of Valid Cases	300		

a. 0 cells (0.0%) have an expected count of less than 5. The minimum expected count is 15.50.

in force in their organizations. Thus, it can be inferred that the majority of small business and large company entrepreneurs are satisfied with the automation of entrepreneurial activity. The chi-square tests related to the influence of automation on entrepreneurial effectiveness. It can be observed that the Pearson chi-square value (38.705; $p=0.000<0.05$) reveals that there is a significant influence of automation on entrepreneurial effectiveness.

The influence of data analysis on entrepreneurial effectiveness is presented in Table 2. The analysis reveals that the majority of the respondents representing 48% (large company-25.3%; small business-22.7%) stated that data analysis is excellent in their organization. The respondents representing 20.3% (large company-12%; small business-8.3%) revealed that the data analysis in entrepreneurial activity is good in their organization. However, 19% (large company-8%; small business-11%) are satisfied with the data analysis in entrepreneurial activity, 5.3% (large company-2.3%; small business-3%) stated that the data activity process is poor and 7.3% (large company-2.3%; small business-5%) revealed that the data analysis process is not in force in their organizations. Thus, it can be inferred that the majority of small business and large company entrepreneurs are satisfied with the automation of entrepreneurial activity. The chi-square tests related to the influence of data analysis

Table 2. Influence of data analysis on entrepreneurial effectiveness

Type of Business		Data Analysis					Total
		Not in Force	Poor	Satisfied	Good	Excellent	
Small Business Entrepreneur	Count	15	9	33	25	68	150
	% of Total	5.0%	3.0%	11.0%	8.3%	22.7%	50.0%
Large Company Entrepreneur	Count	7	7	24	36	76	150
	% of Total	2.3%	2.3%	8.0%	12.0%	25.3%	50.0%
Total	Count	22	16	57	61	144	300
	% of Total	7.3%	5.3%	19.0%	20.3%	48.0%	100.0%

	Value	df	Asymptotic Significance (2-sided)
Pearson Chi-Square	7.008[a]	4	0.135
Likelihood Ratio	7.094	4	0.131
Linear-by-Linear Association	4.363	1	0.037
N of Valid Cases	300		

a. 0 cells (0.0%) have an expected count of less than 5. The minimum expected count is 8.00.

on entrepreneurial effectiveness. It can be observed that the Pearson chi-square value (7.008; p=0.135>0.05) reveals that there does not exist a significant influence of data analysis on entrepreneurial effectiveness.

The influence of customer service on entrepreneurial effectiveness is presented in Table 3. The analysis reveals that the majority of the respondents representing 48.3% (large company-27%; small business-21.3%) stated that customer service is excellent in their company. The respondents representing 20.7% (large company-12.3%; small business-8.3%) revealed that customer service is good in their enterprise. However, 20.3% (large company-8.7%; small business-11.7%) are satisfied with the customer service activity, 6% (large company-1%; small business-5%) stated that the customer service is poor and 4.7% (large company-1%; small business-3.7%) revealed that the customer activity is not in force in their organizations. Thus, it can be inferred that the majority of small business and large company entrepreneurs are satisfied with the automation of entrepreneurial activity. The chi-square tests related to the influence of customer service on entrepreneurial effectiveness. It can be observed that the Pearson chi-square value (18.215; p=0.001<0.05) reveals that there is a significant influence of customer service on entrepreneurial effectiveness.

The influence of predictive analysis on entrepreneurial effectiveness is presented in Table 4. The analysis reveals that the majority of the respondents representing 54.7% (large company-29.7%; small business-25%) stated that predictive analysis is

Table 3. Influence of customer service on entrepreneurial effectiveness

Type of Business		Customer Service					Total
		Not in Force	Poor	Satisfied	Good	Excellent	
Small Business Entrepreneur	Count	11	15	35	25	64	150
	% of Total	3.7%	5.0%	11.7%	8.3%	21.3%	50.0%
Large Company Entrepreneur	Count	3	3	26	37	81	150
	% of Total	1.0%	1.0%	8.7%	12.3%	27.0%	50.0%
Total	Count	14	18	61	62	145	300
	% of Total	4.7%	6.0%	20.3%	20.7%	48.3%	100.0%

	Value	df	Asymptotic Significance (2-sided)
Pearson Chi-Square	18.215[a]	4	0.001
Likelihood Ratio	19.261	4	0.001
Linear-by-Linear Association	13.513	1	0.000
N of Valid Cases	300		

a. 0 cells (0.0%) have an expected count of less than 5. The minimum expected count is 7.00.

Table 4. Influence of predictive analysis on entrepreneurial effectiveness

Type of Business		Predictive Analysis					Total
		Not in Force	Poor	Satisfied	Good	Excellent	
Small Business Entrepreneur	Count	8	25	15	27	75	150
	% of Total	2.7%	8.3%	5.0%	9.0%	25.0%	50.0%
Large Company Entrepreneur	Count	2	8	15	36	89	150
	% of Total	0.7%	2.7%	5.0%	12.0%	29.7%	50.0%
Total	Count	10	33	30	63	164	300
	% of Total	3.3%	11.0%	10.0%	21.0%	54.7%	100.0%

	Value	df	Asymptotic Significance (2-sided)
Pearson Chi-Square	14.838[a]	4	0.005
Likelihood Ratio	15.535	4	0.004
Linear-by-Linear Association	10.558	1	0.001
N of Valid Cases	300		

a. 0 cells (0.0%) have an expected count of less than 5. The minimum expected count is 5.00.

Table 5. Influence of personalization on entrepreneurial effectiveness

Type of Business		Personalization					Total
		Not in Force	Poor	Satisfied	Good	Excellent	
Small Business Entrepreneur	Count	19	12	35	29	55	150
	% of Total	6.3%	4.0%	11.7%	9.7%	18.3%	50.0%
Large Company Entrepreneur	Count	1	9	25	36	79	150
	% of Total	0.3%	3.0%	8.3%	12.0%	26.3%	50.0%
Total	Count	20	21	60	65	134	300
	% of Total	6.7%	7.0%	20.0%	21.7%	44.7%	100.0%

	Value	df	Asymptotic Significance (2-sided)
Pearson Chi-Square	23.348[a]	4	0.000
Likelihood Ratio	26.967	4	0.000
Linear-by-Linear Association	19.339	1	0.000
N of Valid Cases	300		

a. 0 cells (0.0%) have an expected count of less than 5. The minimum expected count is 10.00.

excellent in their company. The respondents representing 21% (large company-12%; small business-9%) revealed that predictive analysis in entrepreneurial activity is good in their company. However, 10% (large company-5%; small business-5%) are satisfied with the predictive analysis of entrepreneurial activity, 11% (large company-2.7%; small business-8.3%) stated that the predictive analysis is poor and 3.3% (large company-0.7%; small business-2.7%) revealed that the predictive analysis is not in force in their organizations. Thus, it can be inferred that the majority of small business and large company entrepreneurs are satisfied with the automation of entrepreneurial activity. The chi-square tests related to the influence of predictive analysis on entrepreneurial effectiveness. It can be observed that the Pearson chi-square value (14.838; $p=0.005<0.05$) reveals that there is a significant influence of predictive analysis on entrepreneurial effectiveness.

The influence of personalization on entrepreneurial effectiveness is presented in Table 5. The analysis reveals that the majority of the respondents representing 44.7% (large company-26.3%; small business-18.3%) stated that personalization is excellent in their company. The respondents representing 21.7% (large company-12%; small business-9.7%) revealed that the personalization in entrepreneurial activity is good in their company. However, 20% (large company-8.3%; small business-11.7%) are satisfied with the personalization in entrepreneurial activity, 7% (large company-3%; small business-4%) stated that the personalization process is poor and 6.7%

(large company-0.3%; small business-6.3%) revealed that the personalization in entrepreneurial activity is not in force in their organizations. Thus, it can be inferred that the majority of small business and large company entrepreneurs are satisfied with the automation of entrepreneurial activity. The chi-square tests related to the influence of personalization on entrepreneurial effectiveness. It can be observed that the Pearson chi-square value (23.348; $p=0.000<0.05$) reveals that there is a significant influence of personalization on entrepreneurial effectiveness.

KEY STRATEGIES FOR SUCCESSFUL DIGITAL TRANSFORMATION

The key strategies recommended by PwC (2023) for successful digital transformation of workplace, people, process and technology are:

1. **Digital Strategy**: Digital strategy is a platform for optimising the business benefits of technology-focused initiatives. A successful digital strategy calls for an interdisciplinary and cross-functional team with executive leadership and success-oriented team members to deliver an effective customer experience.
2. **IT Architecture Design**: Architectural infrastructure is the main component which can be defined as a series of principles or guidelines used by an enterprise to reach and capture the optimum functional deliverables. The IT architecture further includes the flowchart covering software and hardware design, system integration design, leveraging technology and benchmarking technology standards with global practices.
3. **Vendor Strategy**: digital transformation always seeks an effective vendor management strategy that will control vendor sourcing and researching, obtaining quotes, turnover times, contracts, relationship management, performance evaluation and many other functions which helps in streamlining diverse functions for maximum efficiency with parties involved (Hsu et al., 2022).
4. **Agile Systems and Process Development**: Agile software methodology is an iterative and incremental strategy that emphasizes the importance of delivering a working product quickly and frequently. It builds software incrementally in a systematic manner.
5. **Implementations and Rollout**: Once a technology has been sufficiently defined, designed and documented, built and tested, the final step is implementation and rollout. Implementation refers to the process of putting a strategy into action, this may include all the above steps in a sequential process i.e. executing all strategies successfully. Rollout refers to the process of launching the technology

Figure 2. Benefits of AI on entrepreneurship

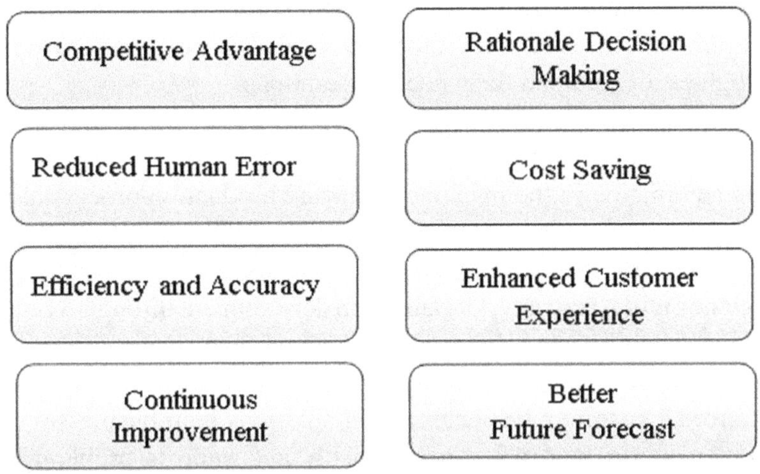

or the system to a larger audience or to the organisation to be operated upon for significant and better results.

6. **Organisation People and Change**: For a successful digital transformation strategy organisation should consider all options train people according to their roles and put efforts to fit them into the change brought through digital transformation.

BENEFITS OF AI ON ENTREPRENEURSHIP

The emergence of artificial intelligence has been a benefit for effective entrepreneurial activities. An entrepreneur can operate various business activities with ease and reach the customer in the market with more confidence. Figure 2 presents the various benefits of artificial intelligence on entrepreneurship.

1. **Competitive Advantage:** AI as an underlying theme in every entrepreneur's startup provides a significant competitive advantage in terms of quick and fast processing of information and generating reports necessary for business decisions to be taken.
2. **Rationale Decision Making**: AI is known for making smarter decisions. Smarter decisions are envisaged through future forecasting, analysing trends, developing models and quantifying uncertainties to make a rational decision imitating human intelligence.

3. **Reduced Human Error**: Automation tools can automate interactions, where the scope for human error is reduced and a lot of time is saved for better time management. This is important for businesses that cannot afford to make even the slightest of errors in their line of operations.
4. **Cost Saving**: Time saved is money saved is what organisations believe and automation leads to doing tasks less than half of the time when done manually. Using automation in the manufacturing and production process also leads to reduced wastage, labour cost and optimum utilisation of resources, which reduces the cost of the overall process.
5. **Efficiency and Accuracy**: Organisation development through AI ensures 24/7 service availability and the same level of performance throughout the day. Tasks and operations undertaken via the AI platform ensure 100% efficiency.
6. **Enhanced Customer Experience**: AI solutions help businesses respond to customer queries and grievances quickly and address problem statements efficiently. The further use of chatbox coupled with other apps can provide customised solutions to customer problems.
7. **Continuous Improvement**: AI is a self-evolving technology and this always leads to better experience. Software update or technical advancement to the existing machine or technology renders it sustainable in the long run.
8. **Better Future Forecasts**: Time is important everywhere and with AI tools, managers can use past year data to build and mimic efficient models for future forecasts. Many organisations are already working on these models and reaping good dividends.

CHALLENGES OF AI ON ENTREPRENEURSHIP

There are certain risks related to AI that entrepreneurs would come across while establishing the business and while operating the business activities. Figure 3 presents the different challenges and risks of artificial intelligence on entrepreneurship (eCommerce Fastlane, 2023):

1. **Initial Investment:** The contemplation of AI in business structure will call for a significant amount of investment to be made in technology. This particular factor is something which is a challenge for many entrepreneurs. In addition to that most of the traditional investors being risk averse contemplate AI-based investment leading to an initial struggle to obtain investments in AI-based ventures.
2. **Ethical Consideration:** AI is the future, no discussions on that but with the pace with which AI is moving forward, a lot of researchers have raised their

Figure 3. Challenges of AI on entrepreneurship

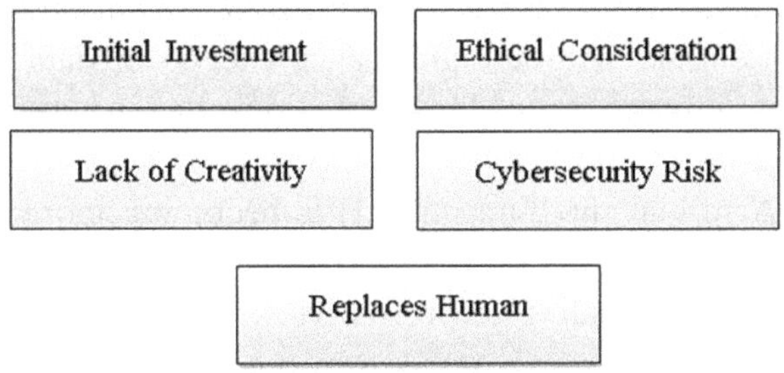

concerns about the lack of internal controls and standards in place to direct the decisions that the system makes. AI is often run based on information fed to it and most of the time, even a small error or bias in the data will lead to unfair or biased decisions that may reinforce stereotypes, lead to violation of rules and create human rights concerns.

3. **Lack of Creativity:** AI is built on the various combinations and recombinations of existing ideas which may always make a decision only based on known variables from the information fed to the system over time. But the challenge comes when a sudden new unforeseen element is introduced. AI though progressive still can't replicate human creativity and dynamism leading to obsolete solutions.
4. **Cybersecurity Risk:** as AI keeps taking big leaps it cannot overrun the reality of cybersecurity risk, which is the evident probability of loss or risk resulting from cyber-attack or data breach in the organisation. Cybersecurity risk, time and again relates to loss of confidentiality and integrity towards organisations leading to catastrophic consequences.
5. **Replace Human:** In a country like India especially there is thought among many individuals that AI integration would lead to unemployment and poverty among developing economies. This particular thought affects efficient AI integration and will lead to societal unrest. AI further doesn't have that personalisation service with efficiency that a human touch can provide. Though this argument is very much limited, economies have their inhibitions towards complete AI integrations within organizations.

CONCLUSION AND MANAGERIAL IMPLICATIONS

The present study further reinvigorates the fact that determinants of AI are indeed very important for small business entrepreneurs and large company entrepreneurs.

In the present study readers can observe that the impact of automation, customer service, predictive analysis and personalisation as a part of AI being highly significant in contributing to entrepreneurial significance except for data analysis which is indicates need for improvement in AI in terms of developing better strategic patterns (Holzinger et al., 2019).

Nevertheless Artificial Intelligence (AI) is becoming more and more widely used, and many businesses are already using AI technology to create some kind of impact and obviously leading to profits. However, substantial financial gains are hard to come by and are hardly realised by most organisations. Building an AI foundation based on the correct data, technology, and personnel is a challenge for many organisations. Alternatively, they may have established this basis, leverage it to produce successive AI solutions, and yet question why the financial gains are only marginal. Large financial gains are probably only possible when businesses provide a variety of efficient methods for people and AI to collaborate and learn from one another. These triumphs, while uncommon, aren't exclusive to any one sector, nor are they exclusive to big businesses or digital natives. Rather, the things that set these most prosperous companies apart are their hard work and dedication to using AI for learning. They become adept at adapting human and machine roles dynamically as circumstances change, not only at using machines. They promote interpersonal learning rather than machine learning.

REFERENCES

Azuma, R., Baillot, Y., Behringer, R., Feiner, S., Julier, S., & MacIntyre, B. (2001). Recent advances in augmented reality. *IEEE Computer Graphics and Applications*, *21*(6), 34–47. doi:10.1109/38.963459

Balasubramanian, N., Ye, Y., & Xu, M. (2022). Substituting human decision-making with machine learning: Implications for organizational learning. *Academy of Management Review*, *47*(3), 448–465. doi:10.5465/amr.2019.0470

Berger, E. S. C., von Briel, F., Davidsson, P., & Kuckertz, A. (2021). Digital or not – The future of entrepreneurship and innovation. *Journal of Business Research*, *125*, 436–442. doi:10.1016/j.jbusres.2019.12.020

Carr, S. (2010). *Personalisation: A rough guide* (rev. ed). Social Care Institute for Excellence.

Chalmers, D., MacKenzie, N. G., & Carter, S. (2021). AI and entrepreneurship: Implications for venture creation in the fourth Industrial Revolution. *Entrepreneurship Theory and Practice*, *45*(5), 1028–1053. doi:10.1177/1042258720934581

Dinh, T. N., & Thai, M. T. (2018). AI and blockchain: A disruptive integration. *Computer, 51*(9), 48–53. doi:10.1109/MC.2018.3620971

E-commerce Fastlane. (2023). *The impact of AI on business opportunities and challenges for entrepreneurs*. Retrieved from https://ecommercefastlane.com/the-impact-of-ai-on-business-o pportunities-and-challenges-for-entrepreneurs/

Elia, G., Margherita, A., & Passiante, G. (2020). Digital entrepreneurship ecosystem: How digital technologies and collective intelligence are reshaping the entrepreneurial process. *Technological Forecasting and Social Change, 150*, 119791. Advance online publication. doi:10.1016/j.techfore.2019.119791

Giuggioli, G., & Pellegrini, M. M. (2023). Artificial intelligence as an enabler for entrepreneurs: A systematic literature review and an agenda for future research. *International Journal of Entrepreneurial Behaviour & Research, 29*(4), 816–837. doi:10.1108/IJEBR-05-2021-0426

Holzinger, A., Haibe-Kains, B., & Jurisica, I. (2019). Why imaging data alone is not enough: AI-based integration of imaging, omics, and clinical data. *European Journal of Nuclear Medicine and Molecular Imaging, 46*(13), 2722–2730. doi:10.1007/s00259-019-04382-9 PMID:31203421

Hsu, C., Lee, J. N., Fang, Y., Straub, D. W., Su, N., & Ryu, H. S. (2022). The role of vendor legitimacy in IT outsourcing performance: Theory and evidence. *Information Systems Research, 33*(1), 337–361. doi:10.1287/isre.2021.1059

Iansiti, M., & Lakhani, K. (2020). *Competing in the age of AI: Strategy and leadership when algorithms and networks run the world*. Harvard Business Review Press.

Jussupow, E., Spohrer, K., Heinzl, A., & Gawlitza, J. (2021). Augmenting medical diagnosis decisions? An investigation into physicians' decision-making process with artificial intelligence. *Information Systems Research, 32*(3), 713–735. doi:10.1287/isre.2020.0980

Kraus, S., Clauss, T., Breier, M., Gast, J., Zardini, A., & Tiberius, V. (2020). The economics of COVID-19: Initial empirical evidence on how family firms in five European countries cope with the corona crisis. *International Journal of Entrepreneurial Behaviour & Research, 26*(5), 1067–1092. doi:10.1108/IJEBR-04-2020-0214

Kumar, V., & Garg, M. L. (2018). Predictive analytics: A review of trends and techniques. *International Journal of Computer Applications, 182*(1), 31–37. doi:10.5120/ijca2018917434

Lévesque, M., Obschonka, M., & Nambisan, S. (2022). Pursuing impactful entrepreneurship research using artificial intelligence. *Entrepreneurship Theory and Practice*, *46*(4), 803–832. doi:10.1177/1042258720927369

Lindebaum, D., Vesa, M., & Den Hond, F. (2020). Insights from "The Machine Stops" to Better Understand Rational Assumptions in Algorithmic Decision Making and Its Implications for Organizations. *Academy of Management Review*, *45*(1), 247–263. doi:10.5465/amr.2018.0181

Meissner, P., & Keding, C. (2021). The human factor in AI-based decision-making. *MIT Sloan Management Review*, *63*(1), 1–5.

Oztemel, E., & Gursev, S. (2020). Literature review of Industry 4.0 and related technologies. *Journal of Intelligent Manufacturing*, *31*(1), 127–182. doi:10.1007/s10845-018-1433-8

PwC. (2023). 54 of the companies have implemented AI for business PwC India Survey. Retrieved from https://www.pwc.in/press-releases/2023/54-of-the-companies-have-implemented-ai-for-business-pwc-india-survey.html

Raisch, S., & Krakowski, S. (2021). Artificial intelligence and management: The automation- augmentation paradox. *Academy of Management Review*, *46*(1), 192–210. doi:10.5465/amr.2018.0072

Ransbotham, S., Khodabandeh, S., Kiron, D., Candelon, F., Chu, M., & LaFountain, B. (2020). *Expanding AI's impact with organizational learning*. MIT Sloan Management Review and Boston Consulting Group. Retrieved from http://dln.jaipuria.ac.in:8080/jspui/bitstream/123456789/10852/1/MITSMR-BCG-Report-2020-Expanding%20AI%20impact%20with.pdf

Rojas, A., & Tuomi, A. (2022). Reimagining the sustainable social development of AI for the service sector: The role of startups. *Journal of Ethics in Entrepreneurship and Technology*, *2*(1), 39–54. doi:10.1108/JEET-03-2022-0005

Roundy, P. T. (2022). Artificial intelligence and entrepreneurial ecosystems: Understanding the implications of algorithmic decision-making for startup communities. *Journal of Ethics in Entrepreneurship and Technology*, *2*(1), 23–38. doi:10.1108/JEET-07-2022-0011

Schlick, J., Stephan, P., Loskyll, M., & Lappe, D. (2014). Industrie 4.0 in der praktischen Anwendung. Industrie 4.0 in Produktion, Und Logistik, A. Anwendung·Technologien·Migration (pp. 57–84).

Townsend, D. M. D. M., & Hunt, R. A. (2019). Entrepreneurial action, creativity, and judgment in the age of artificial intelligence. *Journal of Business Venturing Insights*, *11*, e00126. doi:10.1016/j.jbvi.2019.e00126

Treiblmaier, H. (2018). The impact of the blockchain on the supply chain: A theory-based research framework and a call for action. *Supply Chain Management*, *23*(6), 545–559. doi:10.1108/SCM-01-2018-0029

UghuluD. J. (2022). The role of Artificial intelligence (AI) in Starting, automating and scaling businesses for Entrepreneurs. *ScienceOpen* preprints.

KEY TERMS AND DEFINITIONS

Agile System: Agile System is a design services provider offering cutting-edge image processing technologies. They offer system-level software, firmware, and electrical engineering services.

Artificial Intelligence: The term artificial intelligence (AI) describes the way robots may simulate or approximate human intellect. Artificial intelligence aims to improve perception cognition, and learning using computer power.

Cross-functional Team: A cross-functional team is an assemblage of individuals with diverse areas of competence who collaborate to accomplish a shared objective. Employees from every level of an organisation are usually included.

Cybersecurity: Cybersecurity is the discipline of defending programmes: networks, and systems from online threats. Typically, the goals of these assaults are to disrupt regular corporate operations, obtain, alter, or delete sensitive data, or employ ransomware to demand money from customers.

Entrepreneur: An entrepreneur is a person who launches or runs a business: frequently via risk-taking. They may also be characterised as those who invest in and/or start enterprises, assuming the majority of the risks and benefits.

Entrepreneurship: The development or extraction of economic value using methods that often involve more risk than what a standard firm would accept and may involve values other than just financial ones is known as entrepreneurship.

Industrialization: The process of industrialization starts when a nation starts utilising machines to carry out jobs that were previously completed by people. An agrarian civilization becomes an industrial one through a social and economic revolution.

Machine Learning: A subfield of artificial intelligence (AI) called machine learning (ML) gives computers the ability to learn from data and get better over time. Algorithms for machine learning can identify patterns in data and use that knowledge to forecast future events.

Chapter 4
AI-Enabled Industrial Applications

Khaja Baseer Kamalapuram
https://orcid.org/0000-0002-4524-2922
Mohan Babu University, India

Maria Joseph B. Joseph
https://orcid.org/0009-0003-6232-3892
Jawaharlal Nehru Technological University, India

Abhishek
Mohan Babu University, India

Jahir Pasha Jahir
G. Pullaiah College of Engineering and Technology, India

ABSTRACT

The project's objective is to provide an explanation of AI-enabled industrial applications and how they can benefit businesses. One of the primary factors that contribute to a movement closer to the fourth industrial revolution is AI. Automation has the potential to enhance economic growth worldwide by streamlining tasks and improving human performance. Additionally, it can aid in decision-making and facilitate interconnected supply chains by providing real-time data from various sources, allowing for total optimization and transparency that might not be possible with the most effective methods currently in use. On a larger scale, AI may completely replace human workers. Artificial intelligence can be used to link the real and virtual worlds in a loop. In this project overview, the authors talk about how AI and human workers can work together to automate a wide range of tasks and the challenges we'll face while developing and investing in these solutions.

DOI: 10.4018/979-8-3693-0790-8.ch004

INTRODUCTION

Artificial intelligence (AI) is the term used to characterise computer systems that can carry out tasks that ordinarily need human intellectual capacity, such as learning, decision-making, natural language processing, perception, and reasoning. The main goal of AI is to build intelligent machines that can think and learn like humans.

AI is broadly classified into two types: narrow or weak AI, which is meant for a particular task such as voice recognition or board games, and common or well-built AI, which is intended to execute any complex tasks that a human can perform.

There are several subfields of AI, including:

1. Machine learning: A type of artificial intelligence known as machine learning enables machines to steadily improve their performance on a job by learning from experience.
2. An area of artificial intelligence called "natural language processing" focuses on teaching machines to understand, analyse, and produce human dialect.
3. The field of computer vision is concerned with giving machines the ability to comprehend visual data from the outside world, such as pictures and films.
4. Robotics: Designing robots that can interact with the physical world and carry out tasks that are traditionally performed by humans is the field of robotics, a subfield of artificial intelligence.

AI is used in various applications, including speech recognition, computer vision, natural language processing, autonomous vehicles, medical diagnosis, and financial trading. However, the development of AI also raises concerns about its potential impact on employment, privacy, and safety, which need to be carefully addressed by policymakers and society as a whole.

INTRODUCTION TO THE CONCEPTS

The concept of using technology to replicate human intelligence is not new. In fact, the term "artificial intelligence" was coined in the year 1955 at a conference held at Dartmouth University (Guszcza et al., 2017). However, because technological evolution takes time, especially for a sophisticated technology like artificial intelligence, the concept only recently been created to the point where it can finally be widely used. This technology, in all of its incarnations, has the potential to fundamentally alter how firms operate in the modern economy. According to Coteleer and Sniderman

Figure 1. AI-Technology landscape

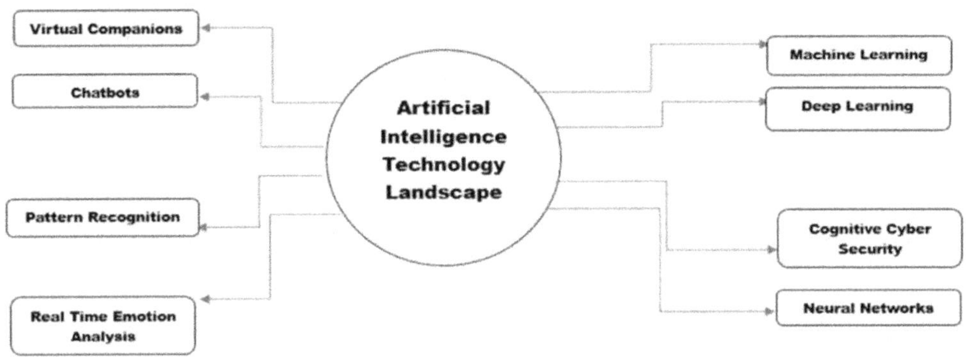

(2017), it is widely regarded as one of the key drivers of advancement in the Fourth Industrial Revolution, often known as Industry 4.0

This project's objective is to provide an explanation of AI-enabled industrial applications and how they can benefit businesses. One of the primary factors that contribute to a movement closer to the fourth industrial revolution is AI. By automating work and improving human performance, for instance, This technology has the potential to enhance economic growth worldwide by streamlining tasks and improving decision-making processes. Additionally, it can aid in creating interconnected supply chains by providing real-time data from multiple sources, allowing for total optimization and transparency that might not be possible with the most effective methods currently in use. On a larger scale, AI may completely replace human workers. Artificial intelligence can be used to link the real and virtual worlds in a loop. In this project overview, we talk about how AI and human workers can work together to automate a wide range of tasks and the challenges we'll face while developing and investing in these solutions.

There are two major chapters in this project review. The initial section discusses AI-Enabled Industrial Applications by incorporating some of the most important advanced artificial intelligence technologies and comparing current technological development to human capabilities. The following section discusses the potential for automation that can be realized using today's emerging technology, as well as how current technology can be used to improve people's work. The challenges associated with the operational implementation of AI-based solutions are also discussed.

Applications of Artificial Intelligence in Industry

The primary goal of Artificial Intelligence (AI) is to enhance the value of products by improving their features for end-users. This has resulted in the development of new automated products like robotic vacuum cleaners and virtual personal assistants (Schatsky et al., 2015). Other examples of automated products include self-driving cars and trucks, chatbots, drones and robotic automation (Manyika et al., 2017). AI's processing power is especially beneficial for analysing large datasets, as cognitive technologies can analyse the data, draw conclusions, and make accurate predictions. Many businesses are utilizing AI to generate insights that can reduce costs, improve efficiency, and increase revenue. Process apps, which are discussed in detail in the following sections, are designed to replace, atomize, and automate human labour while also providing support and reinforcement (Schatsky and Schwartz, 2015), or improve customer service (Schatsky et al., 2015). The two main themes of the rest of this article are process automation and the use of artificial intelligence's potential in information processing.

AI and Human Workforce Integration

AI has the capability to work alongside humans, either replacing, atomizing, automating, facilitating, or augmenting human work. Substitution involves AI completely replacing human work, such as an interactive voice response system replacing call centre workers. AI can break down work into smaller tasks, automating as many tasks as possible, while leaving the non-automated tasks to the human. For instance, AI can translate text, and the human can check and correct any errors. AI can also be utilised to undertake less important duties, freeing up skilled workers to focus on more rewarding aspects of their jobs. Journalists can concentrate on in-depth reporting by using AI, for instance, to create routine income reports. Utilising cognitive technologies to improve employees' capacities and increase their productivity at work is a complimentary strategy. For instance, Verdande Technology created a case-based reasoning system to assist oil and gas drilling engineers in their work. This system automatically identifies similar scenarios that have happened in other wells to help diagnose the issue and offer remedies.

Artificial Intelligence Creates Loop Between the Physical and Digital Realms

Artificial intelligence creates a feedback loop between the physical and digital realms by using sensors and other technologies to gather data from the physical world, then using that data to make decisions and take actions in the digital world, which

Figure 2. AI creating loop between physical and digital worlds

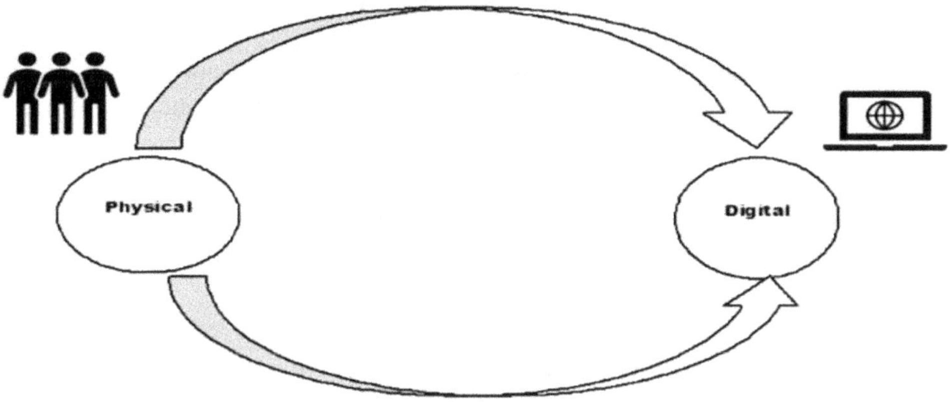

in turn can affect the physical world. This loop can be described as a A feedback loop is a system in which the output is recirculated into the input, resulting in a continuous cycle.

For example, consider a self-driving car. The car's sensors gather data about its physical surroundings, such as the position of other vehicles on the road, the location of traffic lights and signs, and the condition of the road surface. This data is processed by AI algorithms, which make decisions about how to navigate the car safely and efficiently.

The car then takes action in the physical world by accelerating, braking, turning, and so on, based on the decisions made by the AI. If the car encounters unexpected obstacles or changes in the environment, it may gather more data through its sensors and use that data to adjust its behaviour.

This loop between the physical and digital worlds can also be seen in other applications of AI, such as smart homes, where sensors and other devices gather data about the physical environment and AI algorithms make decisions about how to control heating, lighting, and other systems to optimize comfort and efficiency. Overall, the loop between the physical and digital worlds is a fundamental aspect of many AI systems and allows them to operate effectively in the real world.

Artificial Intelligence in the Field of Production

Artificial intelligence (AI) is increasingly being used in production processes to improve efficiency, quality, and safety. Here are some ways that AI is being used in production:

1. Predictive maintenance can monitor equipment in real-time to spot future failures and plan maintenance before they happen, minimising downtime and maintenance costs.
2. Quality manage: Artificial Intelligence can analyse images and video to identify defects and anomalies in products, reducing the need for manual inspections.
3. Inventory management: AI algorithms can optimize inventory levels by predicting demand and supply, reducing stockouts and excess inventory.
4. Production scheduling: AI can optimize production schedules based on demand, available resources, and other factors, improving efficiency and reducing lead times.
5. Robotic automation: AI can control robots to perform repetitive tasks such as assembly, packaging, and material handling, reducing the need for human labour.
6. Energy management: AI algorithms can monitor and optimize energy usage in production processes, reducing energy consumption and costs.
7. Supply chain optimization: Data from clients, logistics companies, and suppliers can be analysed by AI to optimise supply chain operations, increasing productivity and lowering costs.
8. Worker safety: AI can monitor worker behaviour and environmental conditions to identify potential safety hazards and prevent accidents.
9. Predictive analytics: Artificial intelligence (AI) can evaluate production data to find patterns and trends and then provide insights that can be used to improve product quality and streamline production procedures.

In general, artificial intelligence (AI) has the ability to alter manufacturing processes, making them more effective, sustainable, and secure..

Industrial AI

Industrial AI refers to the use of artificial intelligence (AI) in industrial settings such as manufacturing, energy, and transportation. Industrial AI is different from other applications of AI because it must be able to handle large-scale, complex, and dynamic processes that are typically found in industrial environments. Here are some ways that industrial AI is different:

1. Data volume and complexity: Industrial processes generate vast amounts of data that must be collected, processed, and analysed in real-time. The data is often complex and diverse, including sensor readings, images, videos, and text.

Figure 3. Bar graph showing factors of AI in production

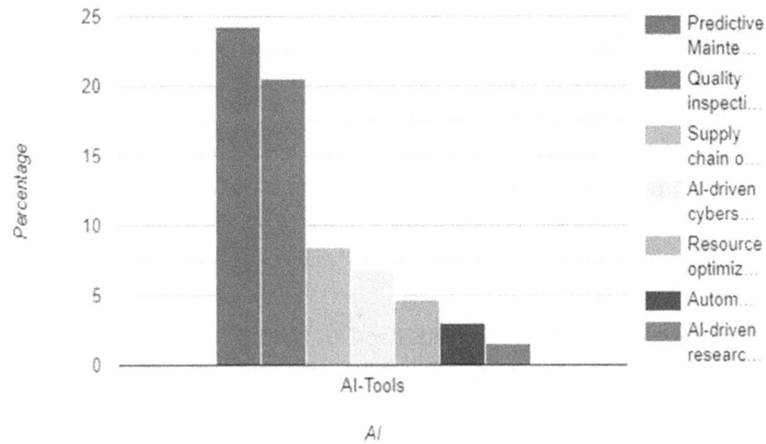

2. Real-time requirements: Industrial processes require real-time monitoring, control, and decision-making to ensure safety, quality, and efficiency. Industrial AI must be able to process data and make decisions in real-time, often with strict latency requirements.
3. Integration with existing systems: Industrial AI must be integrated with existing industrial systems, such as control systems, supervisory systems, and enterprise resource planning systems. This requires specialized skills and expertise.
4. Safety and reliability: Industrial AI must be safe and reliable, with fail-safe mechanisms to prevent accidents and minimize downtime. This requires robust testing, validation, and verification procedures.
5. Heterogeneous environments: Industrial environments are often heterogeneous, with a mix of old and new equipment, different communication protocols, and diverse data sources. Industrial AI must be able to work with different equipment and data sources.
6. Regulatory compliance: Industrial AI must comply with various regulations and standards, such as safety standards, cybersecurity standards, and environmental regulations. This requires specialized expertise and knowledge.

In summary, industrial AI is different from other applications of AI because of the unique requirements and challenges of industrial settings. Industrial AI requires specialized skills, expertise, and tools to address these challenges and deliver safe, reliable, and efficient solutions.

Artificial Intelligence in the Field of Manufacturing

- Energy Management
- Product Development
- Industrial and Collaborative Robotics
- Predictive Maintenance
- Supply Chain Optimization

Let us look into it in detail

- Energy Management: AI is being used in manufacturing to optimize energy usage and reduce costsIt can be applied to real-time energy monitoring, anomaly detection, and energy consumption pattern optimisation. AI can also be used to predict energy demand and help manufacturers plan energy usage accordingly. This can lead to significant cost savings and reduced carbon emissions.
- Product Development: AI is being used to advance the product development process by automating design, simulation, and testing. AI can be used to generate and evaluate design options, simulate product behaviour under different conditions, and identify design flaws early in the development process. This can help manufacturers diminish marketing, progress product excellence, and lessen price.
- Industrial and Collaborative Robotics: AI is being used to improve the performance and safety of industrial and collaborative robots. AI can be used to optimize robot motions, plan robot trajectories, and detect and avoid collisions with humans and other objects. AI can also be used to monitor robot performance, predict maintenance needs, and reduce downtime.
- Predictive Maintenance: AI is being used to improve the maintenance of manufacturing equipment by predicting equipment failures before they occur. AI helps in analyse equipment performance data, detect anomalies, and predict when equipment is likely to fail. This can help manufacturers schedule maintenance more effectively, reduce downtime, and extend equipment life.
- Supply Chain Optimization: AI is being used to optimize supply chains by forecasting demand, optimizing accounts levels, and improving logistics. AI can be used to analyse customer data, predict demand for products, and optimize inventory levels. AI can also be used to optimize logistics by identifying the most efficient transportation routes and modes.

the use of AI in manufacturing is fetching increasingly important for improving efficiency, reducing costs, and improving quality and safety. By leveraging AI in

Figure 4. AI in manufacturing

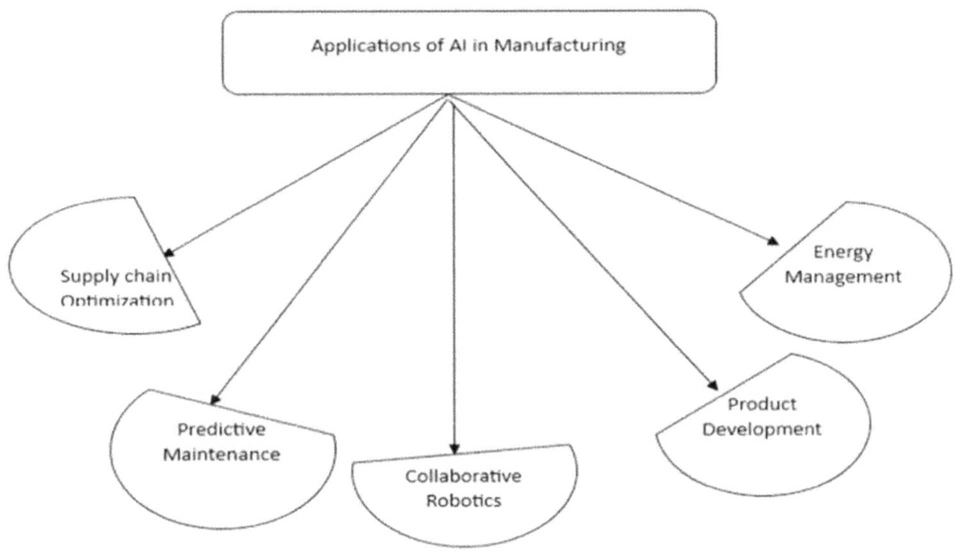

these different areas, manufacturers can gain a competitive advantage and improve their bottom line.

Enhancement of the Supply Chain and AI

The use of AI in force chain operation has the implicit to revise the way businesses operate. AI also helps to optimize and computerize numerous features of force chain operation, including requirement soothsaying, force operation, logistics and transportation, and supplier operation. By doing so, businesses can ameliorate their functional effectiveness, reduce costs, and ameliorate client satisfaction.

One crucial area where AI can be used in force chain operation is demand soothsaying. Directly vaticinating demand is pivotal for businesses to insure they've the right quantum of force at the right time. AI can be used to dissect literal deals data, external factors similar as rainfall patterns and profitable pointers, and indeed social media trends to prognosticate unborn demand. This can help businesses to make informed opinions about force situations, product schedules, and pricing strategies.

Another area where AI can be used in force chain operation is force operation. AI can help businesses to optimize their force situations, icing that they've enough stock to meet client demand while avoiding overstocking. This can be done by assaying data on deals trends, supereminent times, and product schedules to prognosticate when force situations are likely to be depleted. AI can also be used to automate the

Figure 5. AI and supply chain

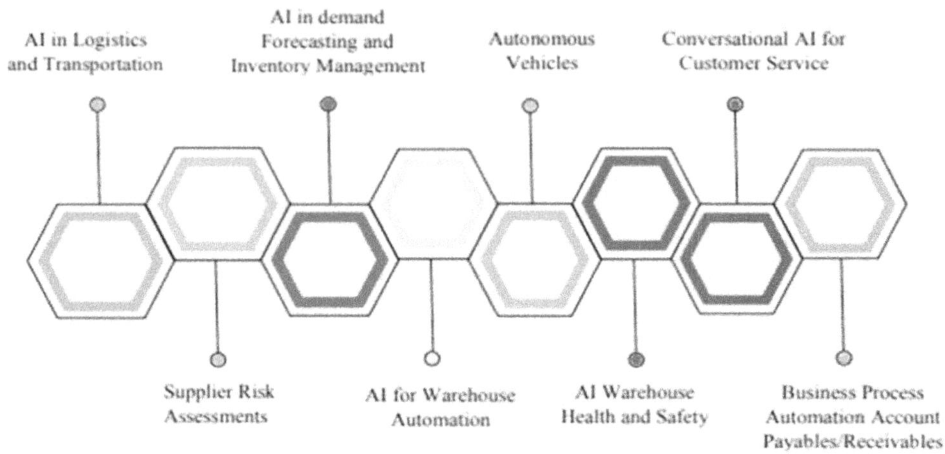

ordering process, generating purchase orders automatically when force situations reach a certain threshold.

Logistics and transportation are also areas where AI can be used to ameliorate force chain operation. AI can be used to optimize transportation routes and schedules, taking into account factors similar as business patterns, rainfall conditions, and motorist vacuity. This can help to reduce transportation costs and ameliorate delivery times. AI also helps in to cover shipments in real scenarios, furnishing businesses with lesser visibility into the status of their shipments and enabling them to take action if problems arise.

Eventually, AI can be used to ameliorate supplier operation. By assaying data on supplier performance, businesses can identify which suppliers are most dependable and offer the stylish prices. AI can also be used to automate the supplier selection process, generating a shortlist of suppliers grounded on specific criteria similar as price, lead time, and quality.

While the use of AI in force chain operation offers numerous benefits, there are also some challenges that need to be addressed. One of the biggest challenges is data quality. To be effective, AI algorithms bear high- quality data, and numerous businesses struggle with data quality issues. Another challenge is the need for professed labor force to develop and apply AI results. Eventually, there are also enterprises around the implicit impact of AI on jobs, with some experts advising that AI could lead to job losses in certain areas of force chain operation.

In conclusion, the use of AI in force chain operation offers numerous benefits, including bettered effectiveness, reduced costs, and bettered client satisfaction. still, businesses need to be apprehensive of the challenges and implicit pitfalls associated with AI, and take way to address these issues. With the right approach, AI has the implicit to transfigure the way businesses operate, enabling them to operate more efficiently and effectively in an decreasingly complex and competitive global business.

Applications of AI

Artificial intelligence (AI) has numerous applications that span across various industries and domains. These include

- Recognition of images
- Processing and recognition of speech
- Generation of natural language
- Processing of natural language
- Sentiment analysis
- Predictive maintenance
- Fraud detection
- Chatbots
- Recommendation systems
- Autonomous vehicles
- Virtual assistants
- Cybersecurity
- Medical diagnosis
- Robot-assisted surgery
- Object detection
- Face recognition
- Emotion recognition
- words-to-speech conversion
- Speech-to-words conversion
- Optical character recognition
- Music recommendation
- Video recommendation
- Automated trading
- Credit scoring
- Risk assessment
- Sales forecasting
- Inventory management
- Demand forecasting
- Supply chain optimization
- Customer segmentation
- Price optimization

- Personalized marketing
- Personalized advertising
- Language translation
- Content moderation
- Content recommendation
- Fraud prevention
- Content analysis
- Search engine optimization
- Augmented reality
- Virtual reality
- Image manipulation
- Image generation
- Text generation
- Customer service automation
- Email filtering
- Event prediction
- Sentiment classification
- Facial expression analysis
- Autonomous drones

These are very few applications of AI. It has a wide range of applications

AI in the Field Healthcare

AI has the capacity to transform the medicalcare industry by enabling precise and efficient diagnoses, customized treatments, and better patient outcomes. The ability of AI-powered systems to analyse enormous amounts of patient data, including electronic health records and medical imaging, to find patterns and insights that may not be immediately apparent to human doctors, is one of their main advantages. This enables medical personnel to make better-informed choices regarding patient management, treatment regimens, and diagnosis.

Medical imaging is one of the primary areas where AI can have a significant impact. AI algorithms can be trained to detect abnormalities and diagnose diseases in medical images, such as CT scans, MRIs, and X-rays. This helps radiologists and other healthcare professionals identify potential issues earlier and more accurately, leading to faster and more effective treatment options.

Personalised medicine is another field in which AI is having a significant impact. AI systems are able to forecast how patients will respond to various therapies by looking for patterns in massive volumes of patient data. This enables clinicians to customise treatment programmes for specific individuals, raising the possibility of positive results and lowering the danger of negative reactions.

AI can also be used to improve patient monitoring and management. By analysing data from wearable devices and other monitoring tools, AI algorithms can detect changes in patient health and alert doctors and caregivers to potential issues. This leads to earlier intervention and improved outcomes, particularly for patients with chronic conditions.

Despite the benefits, there are also challenges to implementing AI in healthcare. Protecting patient privacy and ensuring ethical use of data are crucial issues when implementing AI in healthcare. Furthermore, there are concerns about the potential for AI algorithms to perpetuate existing healthcare biases and disparities. It is essential to address these issues and work towards fair and equitable access to AI-powered healthcare for all patients.

Overall, AI has the ability to transform healthcare by providing more accurate diagnoses, personalised treatments, and better outcomes, patient outcomes. While there are challenges to implementing AI in healthcare, the benefits are clear, and continued research and development in this area will be critical for improving healthcare outcomes and advancing medical knowledge.

Artificial Intelligence is also being used to progress clinical supervisory by providing physicians with more accurate and personalized information about a patient's condition, treatment options, and potential outcomes. Healthcare professionals may make better decisions and customise therapies to the needs of specific patients by using machine learning algorithms to analyse vast volumes of medical data, discover trends, and make predictions. Additionally, AI is assisting in automating administrative activities like appointment scheduling and medical data management, freeing up healthcare professionals to concentrate on patient care. AI has the ability to revolutionise the healthcare sector and enhance patient outcomes on a global scale as it develops and gets better.

Artificial Intelligence (AI) is transforming the media and entertainment industry by providing advanced solutions for content creation, analysis, and personalization. AI algorithms are transforming the way content is produced, distributed, and consumed by audiences around the world.

One of the most significant applications of AI in the media and entertainment industry is content creation. AI-powered tools are being used to generate original content, from news articles to music and even movies. For example, AI can analyze patterns and trends in data, including social media conversations, to generate news stories automatically. AI can also be used to create personalized music playlists or recommend movies based on a user's viewing history.

AI is also being used to enhance the viewing experience for audiences. For example, AI algorithms can analyze audience behavior to personalize recommendations and

Figure 6. AI in the field of healthcare

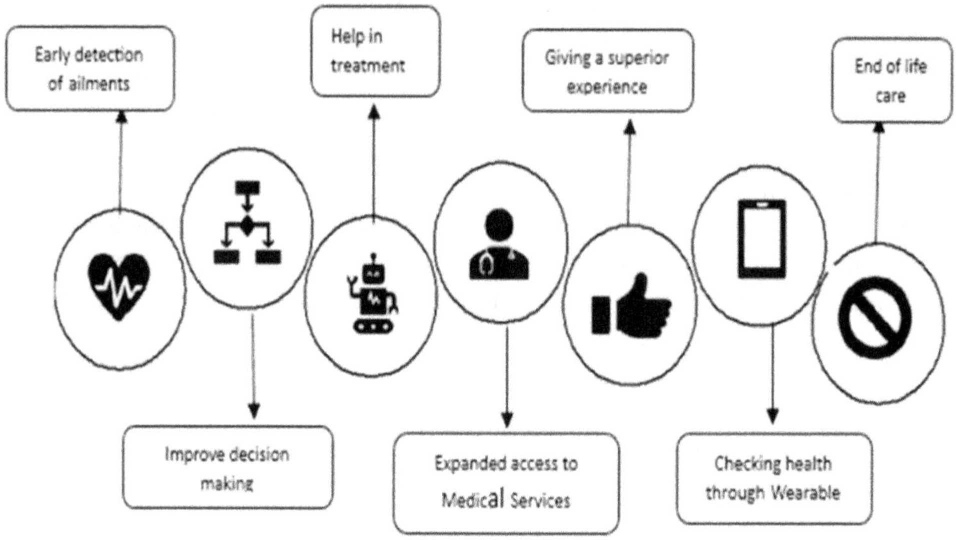

suggest new content. AI-powered chatbots can provide interactive experiences for viewers, such as answering questions about a show or providing additional information about a character.

In addition to content creation and personalization, AI is also transforming the way media and entertainment companies analyze and manage their data. With large amounts of data generated by user behavior, social media interactions, and content creation, AI algorithms can analyze and make sense of the data quickly and accurately. This enables companies to make better decisions regarding content creation and distribution, as well as to optimize their marketing and advertising efforts.

Another area where AI is making an impact in the media and entertainment industry is in production and post-production. AI-powered tools can analyze and identify patterns in large amounts of footage, making it easier for editors to find relevant content and create more compelling stories. AI can also be used to automate repetitive tasks, such as captioning, reducing the time and resources required for post-production.

Overall, AI is transforming the media and entertainment industry in many ways, from content creation and personalization to data analysis and production. As AI continues to evolve and progress, it has the potential to revolutionize the industry and provide audiences with more engaging and personalized experiences than ever before.

Figure 7. AI in field of media and entertainment

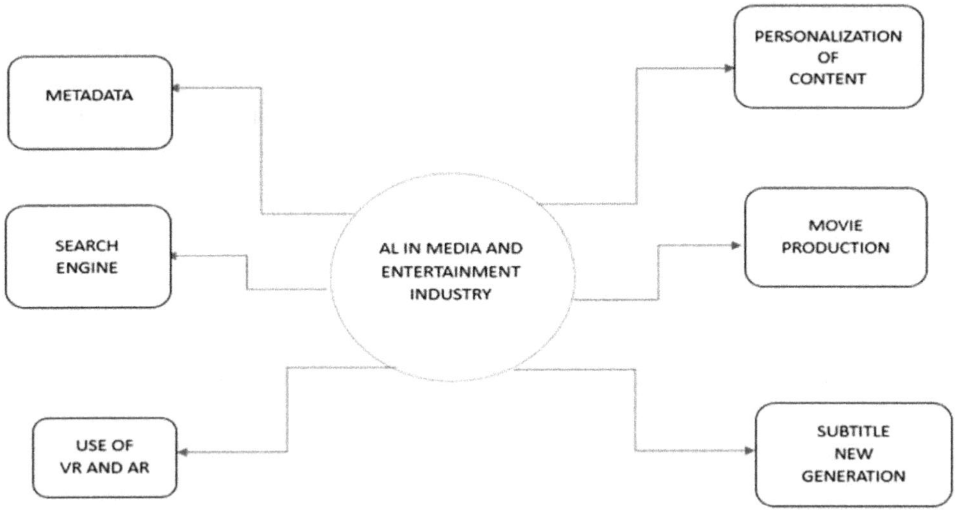

Challenges: AI Enabled Industrial Applications

AI has the potential to transform industrial applications in various ways, from enhancing product quality and increasing efficiency to improving safety and reducing costs. Therefore there are quite a lot of challenges that need to be solved before AI can be effectively implemented in industrial settings.

Data Availability and Quality: One of the key challenges for AI-enabled industrial applications is the availability and quality of data. Industrial environments generate a vast amount of data, but this data is often unstructured, incomplete, or of poor quality. Without high-quality data, it is difficult to train machine learning models to accurately predict outcomes or make informed decisions.

Interoperability and Integration: Industrial applications often rely on a variety of systems and technologies, which may not be designed to work together. This can make it difficult to integrate AI-enabled solutions into existing systems and workflows, and may require significant changes to be made to the infrastructure.

Security and Privacy: Industrial applications often involve sensitive data and processes that require a high level of security and privacy. AI systems must be designed to protect against cyber-attacks and unauthorized access, while also ensuring that data privacy regulations are adhered to.

Human Interaction and Trust: AI-enabled systems may be perceived as a threat to jobs and human decision-making, which can lead to resistance and lack of trust from workers. Therefore, it is important to involve workers in the design and implementation of AI systems to ensure that they are seen as a tool to enhance human capabilities rather than replace them.

Reliability and Safety: In industrial environments, even small errors or malfunctions can have significant consequences. AI-enabled systems must be designed to be reliable and safe, and must have fail-safe mechanisms in place to prevent catastrophic failures.

Regulatory Framework: AI-enabled industrial applications are subject to various regulations, and it can be challenging to navigate the complex regulatory landscape. Regulatory frameworks must be updated to account for the unique challenges posed by AI in industrial settings.

Another challenge for AI-enabled industrial applications is the lack of explainability and interpretability of the decision-making processes. Many machine learning algorithms operate as "black boxes", meaning that it can be difficult to understand how a particular decision was reached. This lack of transparency can make it challenging for human operators to trust the decisions made by AI systems, particularly in safety-critical applications. Therefore, it is important to develop methods for explainable AI that provide insights into the decision-making processes and enable humans to understand and verify the results. This can help to build trust and confidence in AI systems, and facilitate their adoption in industrial settings.

In conclusion, AI-enabled industrial applications have the potential to revolutionize various industries, but before they can be effectively applied, a number of issues must be resolved. Data accessibility and quality, integration and interoperability, security and privacy, human contact and trust, dependability and safety, and regulatory framework are some of these problems. To guarantee that AI is developed and implemented responsibly and sustainably, it will be necessary for industry, government, and academic institutions to work together to address these concerns.

CONCLUSION

Artificial Intelligence (AI) is transforming the industrial sector by enabling intelligent decision-making, reducing costs, improving productivity, and optimizing business processes. Industrial applications of AI have become increasingly popular due to the availability of large amounts of data and powerful computing resources. In this article, we will discuss the benefits of AI-enabled industrial applications and some of the most promising areas of development.

One of the primary benefits of AI-enabled industrial applications is improved operational efficiency. AI systems can analyze vast amounts of data from various sources, including sensors, machines, and production lines, to identify patterns and anomalies. This information can be used to optimize manufacturing processes, reduce downtime, and prevent equipment failures. Additionally, AI can be used to automate routine tasks, freeing up time for employees to focus on more complex and creative work.

Another benefit of AI-enabled industrial applications is improved quality control. AI algorithms can analyze product quality data in real-time, detect defects, and adjust the production process to improve quality. This can help reduce waste, improve customer satisfaction, and enhance brand reputation.

AI also has the potential to improve workplace safety. Industrial settings can be dangerous, and accidents can result in injury or even death. AI systems can monitor worker behavior, identify potential hazards, and take corrective action to prevent accidents. Additionally, AI can be used to optimize equipment maintenance, reducing the risk of equipment failure and preventing accidents.

There are several areas of development in AI-enabled industrial applications that show particular promise. Predictive maintenance is one of them. Utilising AI algorithms to analyse equipment data and forecast when maintenance is necessary is known as predictive maintenance. This can improve system performance, cut down on downtime, and increase equipment longevity.

Another area of development is intelligent supply chain management. AI can be used to optimize the supply chain, reduce costs, and improve delivery times. AI can analyze customer demand, predict future demand, and adjust production schedules to meet demand.

AI-enabled industrial applications also have the potential to revolutionize the field of robotics. AI algorithms can be used to create autonomous robots that can perform complex tasks without human intervention. This can help reduce costs, improve efficiency, and improve workplace safety.

In conclusion, AI-enabled industrial applications offer numerous benefits, including improved operational efficiency, quality control, workplace safety, and more. There are several areas of development in AI-enabled industrial applications that show particular promise, including predictive maintenance, intelligent supply chain management, and robotics. As the use of AI in industry continues to grow, it is clear that AI will play an increasingly important role in shaping the future of industrial production.

REFERENCES

Nayomi, B. (2023). *A Framework for Processing and Analysing Real-Time data in e-Commerce Applications*. 2023 8th International Conference on Communication and Electronics Systems (ICCES), Coimbatore, India. doi:10.1109/ICCES57224.2023.10192771

Arora, A., Bansal, S., & Singh, S. (2019). A review of industrial applications of artificial intelligence. *Journal of Advanced Research in Dynamical and Control Systems*, *11*(2), 872–881.

Baseer, K. K., Jaya Naga Varma, B., Harish, B., Sravani, E., Kumar, K. Y., & Varshitha, K. (2023). Design and Implementation of Electronic Health Records using Ethereum Blockchain. *2023 Second International Conference on Electronics and Renewable Systems (ICEARS)*, Tuticorin, India. 10.1109/ICEARS56392.2023.10085012

Baseer, K. (2020). Internet of Things:A Product Development Cycle for the Entrepreneurs. Helix, 10(2).

CGI. (1986). *Simulation Craft*. Carnegie Group Inc., Commerce Court at Station Square.

Pasha, M. (2022). IoT Technology Enabled Multi-Purpose Chair to Control the Home/Office Appliance. *Journal of Algebraic Statistics, 13*(1).

Hui, L., Wang, G., & Yu, S. (2019). AI-enabled intelligent manufacturing: A state-of-the-art survey. *Journal of Manufacturing Systems*, *50*, 59–68.

Joseph, B. M., & Baseer, K. K. (2023). IoT-Sensed Data for Data Integration Using Intelligent Decision-Making Algorithm Through Fog Computing. In H. Sharma, V. Shrivastava, K. K. Bharti, & L. Wang (Eds.), *Communication and Intelligent Systems. ICCIS 2022. Lecture Notes in Networks and Systems* (Vol. 689). Springer., doi:10.1007/978-981-99-2322-9_34

Liu, M., Chen, C., & Wei, H. (2021). *A systematic review of artificial intelligence applications*.

Marwala, T., & Hurwitz, E. (2019). *Artificial intelligence and the fourth industrial revolution*. Wiley.

Qian, Z., & Liao, W. (2021). Artificial intelligence for smart manufacturing: A review. *Robotics and Computer-integrated Manufacturing*, *68*, 101986.

Swetha, K., Shareef, C. I., Sreenivasulu, G., Baseer, K. K., & Pasha, M. J. (2023). *Study on Implementation of Electronic Health Records using Blockchain Technology*. 2023 4th International Conference on Electronics and Sustainable Communication Systems (ICESC), Coimbatore, India. 10.1109/ICESC57686.2023.10192992

Wang, K., Wan, J., Li, D., Zhang, C., & Zhang, H. (2021). Intelligent manufacturing in the era of artificial intelligence: A review. *Journal of Intelligent Manufacturing*, *32*(1), 153–174.

Wang, Y., & Wang, J. (2021). Research on the application of artificial intelligence technology in the field of intelligent manufacturing. In *2021 International Conference on Mechanical and Electrical Engineering, Automation and Information Engineering (MEAI)* (pp. 276-279). IEEE

Chapter 5
AI in Special Education:
Emerging Trends and Challenges

Suyesha Singh
Manipal University Jaipur, India

Paridhi Jain
https://orcid.org/0009-0002-8233-951X
Manipal University Jaipur, India

ABSTRACT

With recent technological breakthroughs, AI is developing as a revolution for mankind, and it has obvious potential advantages in a number of areas. The potential to improve the educational outcomes and experiences of children with exceptional needs by incorporating AI in special education is significant. The theoretical foundations of using AI in special education have been examined in this study and how AI technologies could enhance learning outcomes and promote inclusion. This study aims to further the understanding of how AI may successfully help students with special needs while simultaneously addressing the practical difficulties involved with its implementation. In conclusion, integrating AI into special education has enormous potential to enhance the educational results and experiences of kids with exceptional needs. The use of AI-driven technology may help special educators as well as persons with special needs by enabling real-time feedback and evaluation, individualized education and rehabilitation services, and training tailored to each individual's requirements.

DOI: 10.4018/979-8-3693-0790-8.ch005

INTRODUCTION

The use of digital technology has become an inevitable part of our lives. Digital technology has changed communication, information-seeking, and almost all areas of individual functioning. Relevant modifications have been made to the educational system as a result. Many countries have started incorporating digital technology in educational and special education settings.

After the advent of digital technology, the work environment altered as autonomous robotics, virtual assistants, IoT, virtual reality, and other technologies were introduced. People with special needs can benefit greatly from these technologies as well. People with special needs have a very difficult time joining the regular workforce because they find it difficult to adjust to change. Except in a few developing nations, integration of people with impairments into society at large can be difficult. The World Health Organization (WHO) estimates that 1.3 billion people, or 16% of the population of the globe, will have a disability by 2023. 93 million children are aged less than 14. They are denied equitable employment opportunities, suffer from social marginalization, prejudice, and stigma, and lack access to healthcare services (Garg & Sharma, 2020). People with disabilities are left behind in terms of education, employment opportunities, and independent living as a result of the absence of assistive technology. According to WHO (2023), there are around 2.5 billion people who require some sort of assistive technology or equipment.

These technologies can make life easier for people with or without disability. Recently, there has been a significant increase in public interest in the application of computerized learning in the classroom. Artificial intelligence in the field of education as well as special education could bring about a dramatic revolution in the educational system. AI can change how educators deliver, evaluate, and impart education in the field of special education. Special educators may enhance educational outcomes for students of all ages and educational backgrounds by tailoring learning experiences, providing targeted support, and implementing AI algorithms and intelligent systems.

For instance, as per Microsoft report, the commencement of artificial intelligence, machine learning, and chatbots can help children with Dyslexia to learn faster. The development of AI-based practices can help empower people with special needs to grow and develop.

As a result, the current study aims to examine the advantages and constraints of AI applications in the field of special education. Along with this, we have also discussed how AI practices may be used in special education. Understanding the current state and potential applications of AI in education, we may visualize a more adaptable, customized, and equitable learning environment that meets the diverse needs of special children.

Figure 1. Some common types of disabilities

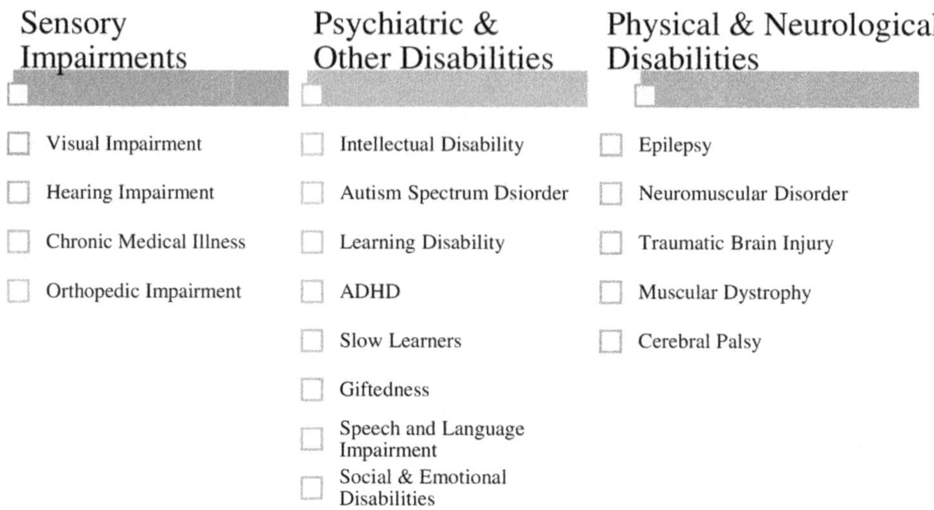

Special Education: The purpose of special education, often referred to as Special needs education is to help students who differ significantly from the general population in terms of their social, mental, or physical development. This type of specialized instruction is designed for kids who struggle with emotional, behavioral, or cognitive issues. Children who are bright and have superior academic skills are also included, as are those who have intellectual, hearing, visual, speech, or learning challenges. Additionally, children with orthopedic or neurological abnormalities are catered to in special education. Figure 1 illustrates some common types of disabilities.

According to UNESCO (2017), special education, also known as special needs education, refers to distinct courses, institutions, and programs of study created especially for children who are classified as having exceptional educational requirements. Or, to put it another way, special education is the type of instruction created to support the learning of students who, for various reasons, need extra assistance and flexible teaching techniques to engage with the curriculum and achieve their academic goals (UIS-UNESCO, n.d.).

According to the legislation, children with special needs are entitled to the same educational opportunities and extra support as children without disabilities. Wherever possible, the educational requirements of these children must be met where other peers go to school. If these kids struggle to study in the traditional educational system, only alternative classroom arrangements need to be made. The special classroom arrangements differ from regular classroom arrangements in that there are fewer pupils, more teachers, and an increased degree of assistance.

Figure 2. Characteristics of special classrooms

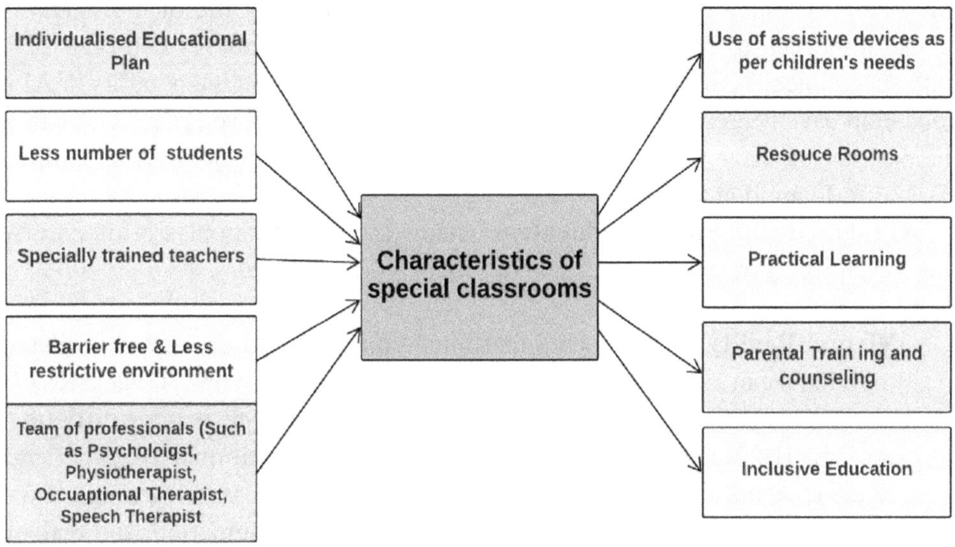

Gradually changing a regular classroom into a special classroom is crucial as these children take more time to adjust to a newer environment. Figure 2 illustrates the characteristics of special classrooms.

Elucidating Artificial Intelligence: The word "artificial intelligence" is an umbrella term that includes several different forms of technology, including neural networks, machine learning, and algorithms. A popular definition of AI is the following "Computers which execute cognitive functions often associated with human intellects, including the ability to learn and solve problems" (Baker & Smith, 2019). As per Chassignol et al. (2018), artificial intelligence is a study field as well theory. As a study field, it is a computer science study area, that majorly focuses on solving intelligence-related cognitive problems, such as solving the problem, learning, and recognition of patterns. On the other side, on theoretical ground, AI is directed and created towards the use of computer application that has human-like capabilities that can do everything just like human intelligence, that also can perform all the tasks such as recognition of speech, making decisions, translation of language, and visual perception. They pointed out the fact that artificial intelligence is a wide phase that encompasses a broad range of tools and approaches including algorithms, virtual reality, machine learning, and data mining rather than being one particular technology. By 2030, artificial intelligence will be worth $13 trillion. Additionally, it was predicted that automation brought on by AI will eliminate 800 million jobs (Hutson et al., 2022).

Integration of AI in Special Education: In the realm of special education, AI is helpful. Since the use of AI is increasing in the daily life of individuals it is also important to comprehend the usefulness of AI technology can be used in with special needs children (Morrison et al., 2017). Although the benefits of AI in education have been recognized by several researchers, however, researchers from the past decade have started focusing more on its advantages for special children (Drigas & Ioannidou, 2012).

AI methods for Special Education: Below are a few examples of modern AI methods utilized in teaching.

1. **Virtual Reality**: VR is a tridimensional computerized environment that an individual can experience. Through VR individuals can view 360 degrees of a scene. Children with special needs can encounter subjects that are difficult to see in real life with the aid of virtual reality. It provides an immersive experience to the teachers and students. In the UK virtual reality-based learning content is implemented. VR encourages creative thinking, imagination, and realistic travel experiences in the learners (Immersionvr, 2020).
2. **Chatbots**: A Chatbot is an automatic program that interacts with people. It will be used in special classroom settings in the upcoming years. It will be used in those classroom settings where students use laptops and iPads to study (Mohan, 2021). It will help in understanding concepts easily with an autogenerated setting in which students can learn things through audio, videos, slides, files, and images (Yellow.ai, 2022). It will help the student to learn things easily and it also reduces the task burden of teachers. It will also replace the emailing system (Khan, 2020).
3. **Educational Robotics**: The use of AI-based educational robotics has increased in the last few years. Educational robotics helps in improving children's STEM knowledge (Science, technology, engineering, mathematics), communication skills, social skills, and behavioral problems. Educational robotics is beneficial in many ways such as engaging students in a classroom setting, improving their understanding of programming and robotics, boosting their cognitive skills, and building proactive skills in children. Some popular educational robotics are Makeblock mBot, Robo Wunderkind, OWI 535, NAO, and LEGO Mindstorm EV3 (Iberdrola,2020).
4. **Learning Management System**: This system provides an online centralized platform to manage all the educational activities such as creating digital content, assigning coursework to learners, communicating with the students, their parents, and teachers, tracking the progress of students, feedback, and generating the grade cards of students. Some commonly used learning management systems

are Absorb LMS, Talent LMS, The Brainier LMS, Cornerstone Learning, Schoolx, and Talentcard (Brush, 2019).

5. **Intelligent tutoring system (ITS):** Learning from an ITS is similar to learning from humans (Luckin et al., 2016). In this approach, a professional training method is safely preserved in an expert model. After that, a student model is developed in which the student's abilities are evaluated using questions that are automatically produced, and then specific activities, pointers, and feedback are given to the student on their performance and level. In the fields of psychology, cognitive neuroscience, computer science, and machine learning, ITS systems are becoming more and more well-liked (Kulik & Fletcher, 2016).
6. **Pedagogical Agents (PA)**: A PA is a computer-generated figure that uses technology to enhance learning. It incorporates the motivational, social, and emotional components of technological education (Kim & Baylor, 2016) and engages learners through real people. In many PA activities, students can see virtual characters on their screens, such as "Siri" on Apple devices or "Clippy" in Microsoft Office, which is a virtual assistant that resembles a paper clip (Joshi et al., 2021). At the moment, even virtual people are made. In the future, every person will have a variety of PAs that will aid them in completing activities. These PAs interact with learners.
7. **Classcraft**: educators can boost student academic achievement and collaboration among students, parents, and instructors by using the interactive game Classcraft. In this, students must complete tasks or activities, and as a result, they are rewarded with points. It promotes good conduct and can assist the instructor in comprehending each student's learning on both an individual and a group level. By including learning objectives, teachers may design a range of assignments and contexts. These tasks are completed by students, who gain points. The inclusion of this exercise can promote feedback, teamwork, and creativity.
8. **3D Holograms**: It is an AI-supported holographic depiction in three dimensions. It includes producing holographic material that is interactive and lifelike. These holograms allow students to engage with them, control them, and view them from various perspectives, which can greatly increase their comprehension and memory of the material. By using 3D holograms, students may better comprehend challenging ideas in chemistry, neurobiology, and other subjects. These initiatives foster kids' intellectual curiosity, teamwork, and communication skills. The program encourages communication between educators and students, which fosters cooperation, inspiration, and feedback.

Current trends in the use of AI with children with special needs: Various AI-based software and applications are currently being utilized worldwide. The following is a description of some of the existing AI-based services utilized for people with disabilities:

1. **Specific Learning Disabilities (SLD) and Speech Impairment**: Reading, writing, and understanding are challenging for children with SLD. Early SLD diagnosis is crucial since it aids in the development and delivery of the most effective special education programs. Although there are several psychometric tests available to detect SLD in children, machine learning and AI-based algorithms make diagnosis easier and provide more accurate results (Lynch, 2023). Artificial intelligence-based devices help translate speech into text which helps people with speech and hearing impairment to communicate with others. Research done by 'The Center for Dyslexia, Diverse Learners, and Social Justice' at California University found that these digital devices can increase the reading and comprehension skills of Dyslexic children by up to 50%. These tools are also effective in reducing the distress and anxiety symptoms in SLD children (Innovative Minds, 2023).

For example, **'ROYBI Robots'** can assist in spotting speech difficulties in young children. Children with Speech difficulty, Down syndrome, and autism spectrum disorders can benefit from using this robot (ROYBI, 2022). **'Optical Character Recognition'** (OCR) is an artificial intelligence (AI)-driven technology. To recognize and extract text from photos and documents, It uses machine learning and AI approaches. Effective text recognition and translation into a machine-readable format requires AI-driven OCR systems to use a variety of algorithms to analyze the visual patterns and structures of letters in photographs (Stanberry & Raskind, 2022). For children with Dyslexia, various computer-based educational tools have been created. Another AI-driven program that assists students with dyslexia in reading and comprehending phonology is called '**Phonological Awareness Educational Software'**. It aids in distinguishing between sounds, picking out rhymes, and detecting phonemes (Drigas & Ioannidou, 2012). '**Proloquo2Go**' is an AI-based communication app that helps children with speech impairment and communication difficulty to interact with others.

A tool powered by AI designed for children with SLD is called the '**Expert System for Learning Difficulties**'. This tool assists in spotting patterns and trends and offers personalized care and action (Hernandez et al., 2009). The **'Perceptron-based Learning Disability Detector'** is built on an artificial neural network, which aids in recognizing different forms of SLD using various educational activities done by special educators (Jain et al., 2009). The **'mCLASS'** is an AI-based tool that helps in the early screening of Dyslexia in children till the age of 18. It also assesses the math-related difficulty and the child's literacy (Presence, 2023). Similarly, an

AI-based app known as '**Learning Ally**' converts the text into speech which helps children with SLD to listen to reading and learning materials. This app is beneficial for the comprehension and retention process. This AI-based tech tool popularly known as '**CENTURY Tech**' is beneficial in preparing individualized learning for normal as well as children with disabilities. This tool initially analyses the learning pattern of the child, then it will understand the strengths and weaknesses, after which it prepares the individualized learning content which can result in better learning outcomes (21K School, 2023). An AI-based tutoring system named as '**Brainly**' provides one-to-one tutoring classes for children with SLD. It also prepares individualized teaching plans.

A similar AI-driven program is the **'Word Prediction Program'**, which anticipates a user's intended term based on their usage patterns. It benefits children who struggle with spelling, word choice, and grammar. A voice recognition and translation program called '**Voiceitt**' is made to recognize and decipher distorted speech patterns. It recognizes and translates speech from people with speech-related problems or disabilities using AI-based techniques and machine learning (Jackblackwell, 2023). Similar to that, **'Speechify'** is another AI-powered smartphone app. By converting text to speech, this AI-based technology enables users to listen to papers, messages, articles, and novels in addition to reading them. **'Microsoft's Immersive Reader'** is another AI-based application helpful for dyslexic children. It reads the work in a louder voice, corrects the pronunciation, and improves the multidimensional learning experience.

2. **Autism Spectrum Disorder**: Language, communication, and social contact are difficult for children with autism spectrum conditions. They often exhibit repetitive and constrictive behavior. Virtual reality-based exercise is beneficial for children with ASD as it can create real-life social scenarios in which children can develop a better understanding of social cues, and can practices social skills. A project named '**Charisma**' was developed and run by 'The Center for Brain Health' at the University of Texas is a virtual reality-based program designed for high-functioning autistic adolescents and adults. It creates virtual social situations in which an autistic person can perform social interaction. This project gained massive success as the participants' recognition of emotion improved and their social anxiety was reduced (Inclusive Minds, 2023). Abdal Hameed et al. (2022) developed an Internet of Things (IoT) based system for children with ASD. In this IoT system, a sensor can assess the heartbeat of an ASD child and that can predict the current affective state of a child. Then this system will share the details with the parents, and details of the expected behavior through a mobile app. It also provides a virtual atmosphere for the

child to improve their social skills, especially eye contact. The system was tested on children aged 4 to 12 and satisfactory results were found.

'Fuzzy Logic' and **'Artificial Neural Networks'** help locate and diagnose ASD in children. children with ASD struggle with social skills, thus to aid them, robotics support programs are put in place. These **'Social Robots'** assist the children in better comprehending reciprocal emotions and social behavior. Humanoid robots have been used in British preschools to assist children with autism spectrum disorders in comprehending their own emotions as well as those of others. Similar to this, there is an AI-based game called **'LIFEisGame'** that was created especially for individuals with ASD. Children with ASD who play this game can identify facial emotions. Microsoft's artificial intelligence (AI) program '**Equadex'** enables kids with ASD to interact with others using pictograms and other visual cues (Pertus, 2017). Similar to this, an AI-based mobile app named '**Ostimo**' helps children with ASD to communicate effectively. It provides interactive speech therapy classes which is beneficial for ASD children to develop their conversation skills (21K School, 2023). An AI-based app known as '**Avaz**' helps children with ASD to express themselves through pictorial cues. Riedl et al. (2017) developed an AI-based platform to improve social skills and decrease their dependency on their parent, in high-functioning ASD cases.

3. **Attention Deficit Hyperactivity Disorder (ADHD)**: In early life, children who exhibit issues with impulsivity, hyperactivity, and inattention are said to have ADHD. AI use can aid in better identification and effective treatment planning of ADHD in children. Augmented reality-based programs (AR) convert real-world information in a digitalized way which makes the learning more innovative and different. It is useful for ADHD children who use visual learning as it can make learning easier. AR can help improve attention and concentration.

An AI-based technique called '**SVM Algorithms** helps in making a diagnosis of ADHD that is more precise. For the categorization of ADHD and other disorders, supervised learning approaches are used (Anuradha et al., 2010). Aguilar et al. created a **fuzzy instructional planner** in 2006 to help the Intelligent Tutorial System (ITS)'s instructional module. ITS is an educational platform that employs AI methods to give students with special needs individualized training, feedback, and assistance. These technologies support the use of interactive teaching tactics with ADHD youngsters, merging several teaching modalities and speeding up the learning process.

4. **Visual Impairment**: Children with visual impairments can attend regular schools, but it takes them a little longer to become used to the surroundings. Their transition to regular school requires a distinct set of aids. Microsoft created the AI-driven **'SeeingAI'** solution for those with vision impairment. The camera of a mobile device is used by this program to identify and characterize the user's surroundings. It analyses and interprets visual data taken in by the device's camera using algorithms for image recognition, computer vision, and natural language processing. This app has various features, including the ability to recognize and describe things, read text from papers or signs, identify colors, find and describe faces, offer audio location cues, and more. Similarly, An AI-based program called **'Lookout'** is designed for those with cognitive and visual impairments. It functions similarly to SeeingAI in that it guides users through their surroundings using a smartphone camera.
5. **Hearing Impairment**: Microsoft introduced the "**Microsoft Translator**," an assistive technology for the deaf. To provide more accurate and natural translations, it uses neural machine translation. These models understand patterns, language subtleties, and backgrounds. Additionally, Microsoft Translation offers **text-to-speech** and **speech-to-text** translation services that employ AI algorithms to translate spoken or written phrases into other languages (almost 60 distinct languages) and vice versa (Roach, 2018). **'AVA'** is an AI-based program that helps the deaf by using machine learning techniques. It instantly speaks words using speech recognition and transcription technology and also offers instant subtitles. Another program that offers real-time speech transcription is called 'OTTERAI' It is helpful for those with dysgraphia and hearing loss (Jackblackwell, 2023). An AI-based smartphone app called '**Rogervoice'** is utilized during conversations. With the aid of this app's speech recognition technology, which transforms spoken words into text, people with hearing impairments may better understand conversations. **'SymboTalk'** is a symbol-based artificial intelligence system that enables communication between users without the usage of words. For those with speech and hearing impairments, it facilitates communication. '**Voice Dream Reader'** is another app that is useful for children with hearing impairment, visual impairment, and autism spectrum disorder. This app changes text to speech which helps these children to interact with others.

Many contemporary hearing aids are made with the use of AI-based technologies. These innovations improve the functionality and quality of hearing aids. These hearing aids contain features including background noise reduction, speech augmentation, personalized sound and voice processing algorithms, and sound settings change based on user desire (Zeng, 2017).

6. **Physical Impairment**: For physical disabilities an AI-based application '**Kinems**' helps children with motor skill disabilities. It initially analyses children's movement in the present time, then it provides feedback and prepares individualized exercise plans.

Current Trends in India in the Application of AI-Based Practices With Special Needs Children

2 Indian school students named Vidhi & Lakshita developed an AI-based app 'Divyang Roshni' which helps in diagnosing Cerebral Palsy in children. This application has five distinct features first is to assess EMG through nerve stimulation, the second – is to identify symptoms, the third – is a suggestion to navigate CP, the fourth – recommend health care professionals and the last – suggest client questions to ask from the health care professionals (Raja, 2022). Not much data is available on its effectiveness.

Another initiative is taken by TCS. They developed an AI-based communication device. It is a social initiative by TCS. It identifies the communication problems faced by children with speech and communication problems. And neuro-muscular disabilities. It is developed by TCS Rapid Labs. It encompasses cognitive speech algorithms, which convert special children's gestures into speech. It is a cost-effective device as it costs less than 20 dollars. This AI-based communication device makes the lives of special children easier additionally it also benefits their caregivers. TCS survey revealed that it helps more than 3000 special children to communicate more effectively, it also saves around 65% of the time in communication (TCS, 2024).

In addition to this, in the year 2022, AIIMS and IIT Delhi collaboratively launched a website 'Readable.com' for children with Dyslexia. This AI-based website is useful in diagnosing Dyslexia, it also helps dyslexic children in reading, writing, and learning. This also helps in early diagnosing and early intervention. It is divided into 8 modules. Before launching this, AIIMS New Delhi conducted research on 44 children who underwent FMRI by using this. The findings indicate that the majority of these children improved in reading, writing, and learning languages (Ghosh, 2022).

In India, Anuradha et al. (2010), developed a Support Vector Machine (SVM) based algorithm to detect ADHD in children. It provides a more accurate diagnosis and is time-savvy. As per Anuradha et al. (2010), this is the first attempt to diagnose ADHD using the SVM algorithm. SVM is a machine learning-based algorithm that is used for regression and differentiation. This module encompasses a set of questionnaires, along with answers that help doctors diagnose disease. Subsequently, the data set was added and reinserted into the SVM module, which provides accurate diagnosis. It makes the diagnosis process easier. This system was tested on children aged 6 to 11 who participated during the formation of this module. The findings indicated that 88.67% succeeded in identifying ADHD.

Delavarian et al. (2010), created a decision support system for an accurate diagnosis of ADHD and to distinguish it from other similar physical and mental health issues such as depression and anxiety. It is important to differentiate between these disorders is difficult due to similar symptomatology. Initially, it was developed to help psychiatrists in helping in diagnosis, but later it was used in school as well to identify high-risk children. The data from 2 networks were compared i.e. radial basis function (RBF) and multilayer neural network (MLP). This process was tested over 294 students studying in twelve different schools in India. The accuracy of RBF was scored around 96.62% and MLP 95.5%. Along with this, a very small number of errors in diagnosis was found. That indicates that this is a reliable and valid instrument to diagnose and differentiate ADHD.

In the Indian setting, Jain et al. (2009) developed a model **'Perceptron-based Learning Disability Detector'** It is an AI-network neural model which helps in identifying dyslexia, dyscalculia, and dysgraphia by conducting curriculum tests by special educators. The data collection of this was done on 240 Indian children studying in various schools.

Advantages of Artificial Intelligence in Special Education: The Use of Artificial Intelligence is Beneficial for Children With Special Needs

The personalized learning experience that AI in special education offers is one of its main advantages. AI algorithms and machine learning **analyze the performance of children** with special needs, as well as their strengths and weaknesses, and then use this information to create individualized instructional materials. These specially created instructional materials span the disparity between the education of exceptional children and their integration into society (Frackiewicz, 2023).

Additionally, AI-based services aid in **early diagnosis and identification.** Both of these elements are helpful in special education since they provide the carers the ability to handle this problem skillfully before it worsens. AI-driven data can analyze a child's behavior patterns, and using this information may help special educators and carers design successful interventions.

AI in special education is advantageous in **keeping track of all the special children's progress**, activities, behavior, and performance. In that way, it is beneficial for special children, their caregivers, and special educators. For attendance, face recognition services can be used. Feedback can easily be provided.

AI is available around-the-clock, children with special needs and their parents may **access learning materials and resources** whenever they need them. These educational tools support independent learning without regard to time constraints. This method encourages self-directed learning.

AI-based services in special education help enhance **the language and communication** between children, parents, and teachers which aid in bridging the communication gap between all three.

AI system Learning Management Tool (LMS), is helpful in **pedagogical planning, and improving learning teaching experiences** (Dias et al., 2015). Similarly, Intelligent Tutors (IT) is advantageous as it helps in **providing timely feedback, guidance, and personalized study material**.

AI offers content that has been specially created to **meet the needs of both teachers and students**. The aids can assist youngsters with disabilities in overcoming obstacles and assimilating into society. It provides educators with chatbots, AI-based teaching assistants, and **automated grading systems** to minimize their labor. It also provides more accurate and efficient results as compared to traditional assessment methods. AI-based services also provide teachers with more innovating strategies to teach and train children in classroom settings and also provide them with more practical learning rather than sticking to only traditional classroom theoretical learning.

Other than this, AI in special education has several benefits, including **time efficiency, task automation, the ability to create adaptive learning groups for learners, support for special educators in focusing on individual student performance, and enhancements to students' learning, motivation, interest, self-esteem, and self-confidence** (Paranjape et al., 2019). AI in special education is free from cultural biases, prejudices, stigma, and diversity therefore anyone can take the benefits of these services.

Limitations of Artificial Intelligence in Special Education: Although AI technology offers numerous benefits, it also has certain downsides. One of the key disadvantages of employing AI in the field of special education is the **lack of privacy, abuse, biases, and data security** in some data and information. Due to this, anyone can access individuals' data which raises the question of privacy concerns. Transparent AI-driven services must be developed to solve this.

Similarly, there is **no regulatory authority** or association which can control AI-based services. There are various types of AI-driven software and applications currently functioning in the world for special populations. But there is the regulatory body to control these services additionally, the reliability and validity of these services also raise the question of effectiveness.

AI-based services are rapidly being used in diagnosing disabilities but no one can predict the **accuracy** of these services. Misdiagnosis can raise the risk for special children and for their caregivers as well. Artificial intelligence use in the field of special education is not governed by any established guidelines (Nebekar et al., 2017).

The **absence of human interaction** in the use of AI for special education requirements is another drawback. For children with special needs emotional and social support, an empathetic attitude, and individualized attention to learning things, AI-driven services lack all of these. It also hampers their communication style and social skills.

Another major limitation is the lack of teachers training in using AI-based technology in special education. Special educators need to be adequately trained to use this technology in classroom settings.

Children's creativity is impacted by both special education and AI in the classroom. Children quickly complete tasks at hand utilizing AI-based chatbots without even exerting any mental effort. Later, this has an impact on their cognitive abilities, creativity, and critical thinking. Additionally, it makes them more dependent on AI.

Services powered by AI are not very **adaptable**. These services were created using machine learning techniques and already available data. Since technology is always evolving, sometimes the information it gives is out of date. Additionally, it occasionally failed to comprehend people's needs and cognitive abilities. As a result, it presents skewed statistics at that point.

Due to **job loss and financial difficulties**, the use of AI in special education may be problematic for special educators.

Practical Implications: AI-based interactive strategies, such as AI-based robots and AI-based games, can be created to increase children's learning even if AI in special education technology is a little too advanced for kindergarten students (Zapata-Caceres & Martin-Barosso, 2021). Although social robots are employed with special needs children to help them develop their social skills, it has been discovered that they are not intended for use with any particular type of impairment (Papakostas et al., 2021). In the future, more detailed and comprehensive research can be done on the use of social robots for a person's disability.

Additionally, there are several misunderstandings regarding how AI in special education is used in the present day. Promoting AI literacy among the general population is crucial to eradicating this (Long & Magerko, 2020). Similarly, it is essential to pinpoint areas where AI in special education is transgressing boundaries between teachers and learners to lessen the detrimental effects of AI in special education on learners.

Theoretical Implications: The study emphasizes various uses for AI in special education that provide researchers, teachers, and children with special needs with theoretical ramifications. On a theoretical level, it's critical to develop standardized AI in education and special education use ethics. Since it can stop unethical behavior and unintentional injury (Loi et al., 2019). The cognitive process, which includes abstraction, problem-solving, and decision-making, was clarified by AI. It can support the creation of fresh educational concepts and theories. Additionally, AI-based services in special education have a wide scope. A comparative analysis of its usefulness in the special education field in the past, present, and future can provide relevant evidence of its effectiveness,

CONCLUSION

We may conclude the arguments above that technological innovation and improvement in special education improve and increase learning for both special children and society as a whole. Artificial intelligence is being used more and more in special education. The possibilities for future learning might be greater with AI. It can significantly transform the way that education is provided. AI is altering the state of education, but it won't replace teachers. Artificial intelligence was once utilized only in computer-based devices, but it is now also often used in web-based platforms, online platforms, and mobile technologies. Artificial intelligence in special education raises both the efficacy and quality of instruction. Additionally, because they may alter the learning materials to suit their requirements, it enhances pupils' learning. Overall, artificial intelligence has a big impact on both students' and teachers' lives.

As a result, it can be said that the employment of AI in the field of special education is effective. The ethical use of AI in the field of special education can raise the level of education and improve the standard of living for those with disabilities. In addition to helping with diagnosis, early intervention planning, and giving proper education to those with special needs, new technologies like AI-based robotics, chatbots, and IoT can lighten the strain on special educators and mental health experts. To employ AI to its full potential in the field of special education, a collaboration between several stakeholders is necessary, including special educators, mental health specialists, doctors, researchers, and other professionals (Ozdemir, 2019).

REFERENCES

Aguilar, R. M., Munoz, V., Noda, M., Bruno, A., & Moreno, L. (2010). Teacher Strategies Simulation by Using Fuzzy Systems. *Computer Applications in Engineering Education, 18*(1), 183–192. doi:10.1002/cae.20128

Anuradha, J., Tisha, Ramachandran, V., Arulalan, K.V., & Tripathy, B.K. (2010). Diagnosis of ADHD using SVM algorithm. In: *Proceedings of the Third Annual ACM Bangalore Conference*. ACM. 10.1145/1754288.1754317

Anuradha, J., Tisha, Ramachandran, V., Arulalan, K. V., & Tripathy, B. K. (2010). Diagnosis of ADHD using SVM algorithm. *Proceedings of the Third Annual ACM Bangalore Conference*. ACM. 10.1145/1754288.1754317

Baker, T., & Smith, L. (2019). *Educ-AI-tion rebooted? Exploring the future of artificial intelligence in schools and colleges*. Nesta Foundation. https://media.nesta.org.uk/documents/Future_of_AI_and_education_v5_WEB.pdf

Brush, K. (2019, December 30). *What is a learning management system (LMS) and what is it used for?* SearchCIO. https://www.techtarget.com/searchcio/definition/learning-management-system

Careerera. (2023, January). *What are the advantages and disadvantages of AI in education?* Careerera. https://www.careerera.com/blog/advantages-and-disadvantages-of-ai-in-education

Chassignol, M., Khoroshavin, A., Klimova, A., & Bilyatdinova, A. (2018). Artificial intelligence trends in education: A narrative overview. *Procedia Computer Science*, *136*, 16–24. doi:10.1016/j.procs.2018.08.233

Delavarian, M., Towhidkhah, F., Dibajnia, P., & Gharibzadeh, S. (2010). Designing a decision support system for distinguishing ADHD from similar children behavioral disorders. *Journal of Medical Systems*, *36*(3), 1335–1343. doi:10.1007/s10916-010-9594-9 PMID:20878211

Dias, S. B., Hadjileontiadou, S. J., Hadjileontiadis, L. J., & Diniz, J. A. (2015). Fuzzy cognitive mapping of LMS users' quality of interaction within higher education blended-learning environment. *Expert Systems with Applications*, *42*(21), 7399–7423. doi:10.1016/j.eswa.2015.05.048

Drigas, A. S., & Ioannidou, R.-E. (2012). Artificial intelligence in special education: A decade review. *International Journal of Engineering Education*, *28*(6), 1366–1372.

Frąckiewicz, M. (2023, May 3). *The potential of AI in special education*. TS2 SPACE. https://ts2.space/en/the-potential-of-ai-in-special-education/

Garg, S., & Sharma, S. (2020). Impact of artificial intelligence in Special need education to promote inclusive pedagogy. *International Journal of Information and Education Technology (IJIET)*, *10*(7), 523–527. doi:10.18178/ijiet.2020.10.7.1418

Ghosh, S. (2022, July 29). AIIMS' AI-based website for dyslexia offers fresh hope | Delhi news - Times of India. *The Times of India*. https://timesofindia.indiatimes.com/city/delhi/aiims-ai-based-website-for-dyslexia-offers-fresh-hope/articleshow/93196612.cms

Hernandez, J. (2009). Learning difficulties diagnosis for children's basic education using expert systems. *WSEAS Transactions on Information Science and Applications*, *6*(7), 1206–1215.

Hutson, J., Jeevanjee, T., Graaf, V. V., Lively, J., Weber, J., Weir, G., Arnone, K., Carnes, G., Vosevich, K., Plate, D., Leary, M., & Edele, S. (2022). Artificial intelligence and the disruption of higher education: Strategies for integrations across disciplines. *Creative Education*, *13*(12), 3953–3980. doi:10.4236/ce.2022.1312253

Iberdrola. (2020). Educational robotics: Definition, advantages, and examples. *Iberdrola*. https://www.iberdrola.com/innovation/educational-robots

Immersionvr. (2020, January 2). *VR for education*. Immersionvr. https://immersionvr.co.uk/about-360vr/vr-for-education/

Inclusive Minds. (2023, May 16). Unraveling the latest trends in special education technology. *Inclusive Minds*. https://inclusiveminds.org/unraveling-the-latest-trends-in-special-education-technology/

Jackblackwell. (2023, January 27). *10 best AI tools for people with disabilities (Free and paid). Pure Future AI - Unlock the Possibilities of Open-Source and Public API AI: Resources and Insight at Your Fingertips!* Pure Future. https://purefuture.net/2023/01/27/10-best-ai-tools-for-people-with-disabilities-free-and-paid/#google_vignette

Jain, K., Manghirmalani, P., Dongardive, J., & Abraham, S. (2009). Computational Diagnosis of Learning Disability. *International Journal of Recent Trends in Engineering*, *2*(3).

Jain, K., Manghirmalani, P., Dongardive, J., & Abraham, S. (2009). Computational Diagnosis of Learning Disability. *International Journal of Recent Trends in Engineering*, *2*(3).

Joshi, S., Rambola, R. K., & Churi, P. (2021). Evaluating artificial intelligence in education for the next generation. *Journal of Physics: Conference Series*, *1714*(1), 012039. doi:10.1088/1742-6596/1714/1/012039

Khan, A. (2020, February 18). 8 benefits of chatbots in the education industry. *Botsify*. https://botsify.com/blog/education-industry-chatbot/

Kim, Y., & Baylor, A. L. (2016). based design of pedagogical agent roles: A review, progress, and recommendations. *International Journal of Artificial Intelligence in Education*, *26*(1), 160–169. doi:10.1007/s40593-015-0055-y

Kulik, J. A., & Fletcher, J. D. (2016). Effectiveness of intelligent tutoring systems: A meta-analytic review. *Review of Educational Research, 86*(1), 42–78. doi:10.3102/0034654315581420

Loi, D., Wolf, C. T., Blomberg, J. L., Arar, R., & Brereton, M. (2019). *Co-designing AI futures. Companion Publication of the 2019 on Designing Interactive Systems Conference 2019 Companion*. doi:10.1145/3301019.3320000

Long, D., & Magerko, B. (2020). What is AI literacy? Competencies and design considerations. In *Proceedings of the 2020 CHI Conference on Human Factors in Computing Systems* (pp. 1–16). ACM. 10.1145/3313831.3376727

Luckin, R., Holmes, W., Griffiths, M., & Forcier, L. B. (2016). *Intelligence Unleashed: An argument for AI in education.* UCL. https://discovery.ucl.ac.uk/1475756/

Lynch, M. (2023, March 24). How artificial intelligence is improving assistive technology. *The Tech Edvocate.* https://www.thetechedvocate.org/how-artificial-intelligence-is-improving-assistive-technology/

Mohan, P. (2021, December 10). Artificial intelligence in education. *Times of India Blog.* https://timesofindia.indiatimes.com/readersblog/newtech/artificial-intelligence-in-education-39512/

Morrison, C., Cutrell, E., Dhareshwar, A., Doherty, K., Thieme, A., & Taylor, A. (2017). Imagining artificial intelligence applications with people with visual disabilities using tactile ideation. *Proceedings of the 19th International ACM SIGACCESS Conference on Computers and Accessibility.* ACM. 10.1145/3132525.3132530

Nebeker, C., Harlow, J., Espinoza Giacinto, R., Orozco-Linares, R., Bloss, C. S., & Weibel, N. (2017). Ethical and regulatory challenges of research using pervasive sensing and other emerging technologies: IRB perspectives. *AJOB Empirical Bioethics, 8*(4), 266–276. doi:10.1080/23294515.2017.1403980 PMID:29125425

Özdemir, V. (2019). Not all intelligence is artificial: Data science, automation, and AI meet HI. *OMICS: A Journal of Integrative Biology, 23*(2), 67–69. doi:10.1089/omi.2019.0003 PMID:30707659

Papakostas, G. A., Sidiropoulos, G. K., Papadopoulou, C. I., Vrochidou, E., Kaburlasos, V. G., Papadopoulou, M. T., Holeva, V., Nikopoulou, V., & Dalivigkas, N. (2021). Social robots in special education: A systematic review. *Electronics (Basel), 10*(2), 1398. doi:10.3390/electronics10121398

Paranjape, K., Schinkel, M., Nannan Panday, R., Car, J., & Nanayakkara, P. (2019). Introducing artificial intelligence training in medical education. *JMIR Medical Education, 5*(2), e16048. doi:10.2196/16048 PMID:31793895

Pertus, S. (2017, August 4). *How Equadex used cognitive services to help people with language disorders.* Microsoft Technical Case Studies. https://microsoft.github.io/techcasestudies/cognitive%20services/2017/08/04/equadexcognitives.html

Presence. (2023, March 1). 5 special education technology trends SPED directors must know about. *Presence.* https://presence.com/insights/special-ed-tech-trends-sped-directors-must-know/

Raja, A. K. (2022). *Girls from Delhi use AI for aiding children fighting cerebral palsy.* INDIAai. https://indiaai.gov.in/article/girls-from-delhi-use-ai-for-aiding-children-fighting-cerebral-palsy

Riedl, M., Arriaga, R., Boujarwah, F., Hong, H., Isbell, J., & Heflin, L. J. (2007). Graphical Social Scenarios: Toward Intervention and Authoring for Adolescents with High Functioning Autism. *Virtual Healthcare Interaction, Papers from the AAAI Fall Symposium.*

Roach, J. (2018, May 11). AI technology helps students who are deaf learn. *The AI Blog.* https://blogs.microsoft.com/ai/ai-powered-captioning/

ROYBI. (2022, May 20). *Artificial intelligence in special education.* ROYBI Robot. https://roybirobot.com/blogs/news/artificial-intelligence-in-special-education

21KSchool. (2023, September 28). Enhancing special education: AIs impact on teachers and schools. *World School For Georgia.* https://www.21kschool.world/ge/blog/ai-impact-on-teachers-and-schools/ doi:10.1155/2022/2247675

Stanberry, K., & Raskind, M. H. (2022, January 17). *Assistive technology for kids with learning disabilities: An overview.* Reading Rockets. https://www.readingrockets.org/article/assistive-technology-kids-learning-disabilities-overview

TCS. (2024). TCS' AI speech device helps kids who have cerebral palsy. *Tata Consultancy Services: Driving Innovation and Building on Belief.* https://www.tcs.com/what-we-do/pace-innovation/case-study/assistive-technology-celebral-palsy

UIS-UNESCO (UNESCO Institute for Statistics). (n.d.). *Special needs education.* In: Glossary. UIS-UNESCO. https://uis.unesco.org/en/glossary-term/special-needs-education

UNESCO. (2017). *A guide for ensuring inclusion and equity in education.* Paris: UNESCO. https://unesdoc.unesco.org/images/0024/002482/248254e.pdf

World Health Organization. (2023). *Assistive technology*. World Health Organization. https://www.who.int/news-room/fact-sheets/detail/assistive-technology

World Health Organization. (2023). *Disability and health*. WHO. https://www.who.int/news-room/fact-sheets/detail/disability-and-health#:~:text=Key%20facts,earlier%20than%20those%20without%20disabilities

Yellow.ai. (2022, September 9). 10 powerful use cases of educational chatbots in 2022. *Yellow.ai*. https://yellow.ai/chatbots/use-cases-of-chatbots-in-education-industry

Zapata-Caceres, M., & Martin-Barroso, E. (2021). Applying game learning analytics to a voluntary video game: Intrinsic motivation, persistence, and rewards in learning to program at an early age. *IEEE Access : Practical Innovations, Open Solutions*, *9*, 123588–123602. doi:10.1109/ACCESS.2021.3110475

Zeng, F. (2017). A new landscape for hearing aids. *The Hearing Journal*, *70*(12), 6. doi:10.1097/01.HJ.0000527871.60334.ad

Chapter 6
Sustainable Warriors Unleashed:
Unravelling the Triggers of Eco-Enthusiasm in a Developing Nation's SMME Community

Thembelihle Pita
https://orcid.org/0009-0003-5618-4814
University of KwaZulu-Natal, South Africa

Nigel Chiweshe
https://orcid.org/0000-0001-7757-211X
University of KwaZulu-Natal, South Africa

ABSTRACT

Several authors have researched and published articles clarifying sustainability and how large businesses participate in sustainability initiatives. On the other hand, there is a dearth of published research on the factors that motivate small and medium-sized enterprises (SMMEs) to engage in environmentally friendly business practices. To fill this void, this chapter presents the results from a study on the factors that influence SMMEs to engage in sustainable practices. Normative pressures have a greater influence when leading entrepreneurs to engage in sustainable practices. Interestingly isomorphic forces impact SMMEs in their pursuit of sustainability similarly to large corporations. From a managerial perspective, this chapter urges the micro, small, and medium-sized enterprise sector to place a greater emphasis on information exchange to accommodate the growing demand for businesses to become involved in sustainable development. In addition, entrepreneurs need to be more aggressive in encouraging internal innovation towards sustainable practices.

DOI: 10.4018/979-8-3693-0790-8.ch006

INTRODUCTION

The present-day society faces numerous pressing economic, social, and environmental challenges, resulting in instability, social unrest, and environmental risks (Chistov et al., 2021). These challenges are frequently denoted as the "grand challenges" or "planetary mega issues" in academic discourse. The authors Chistov et al. (2021) and Laasch et al. (2022) argue that these obstacles, which they refer to as "particular critical obstacles," play a crucial role in addressing significant societal and environmental challenges. The field of entrepreneurship has attracted considerable interest as a potential means of tackling prominent societal and environmental challenges, such as climate change and pervasive social inequalities (Gregori & Holzmann, 2020; Hahn et al., 2018; Ramlal & Chiweshe, 2022). Throughout history, the primary motivation driving entrepreneurial endeavours has largely been the desire to create economic value (Anand et al., 2021; Gregori & Holzmann, 2020). However, an increasing acknowledgement of worldwide social and environmental issues has led to a shift in the entrepreneurial sphere, where social and environmental goals are now incorporated alongside core business activities (Anand et al., 2021; Gregori & Holzmann, 2020; Hahn et al., 2018). There is a growing acknowledgment of the efforts made by present-day entrepreneurs in minimising the negative impacts they have on the environment. Furthermore, the authors Anand et al. (2021) and Hahn et al. (2018) emphasise the efforts made by organisations to incorporate pro-socio-environmental principles into their core business activities.

Numerous influential factors, such as the environment, laws, consumers, and social groups, often drive companies to adopt responsible behaviour and participate in sustainable practices (Bajdor et al., 2021; Pham et al., 2020). There are well-supported arguments concerning companies' significant role in environmental sustainability (Fernando et al., 2019; Knoppen & Knight, 2022). The empirical evidence of a growing recognition of environmental concerns and the importance of sustainability is demonstrated by the increasing allocation of resources towards Corporate Social Responsibility (CSR) initiatives, advertising, sustainability reporting, mitigation measures, carbon reduction, and other related endeavours (Malarvizhi & Yadav, 2008; Poddar et al., 2019). Prominent multinational enterprises, including Mahindra & Mahindra, Tata, and Godrej, have garnered recognition for their dedication to sustainable practices within their respective industries, as evidenced by their demonstrated environmental responsibility (Ghosh & Das, 2022; Sarangi, 2021).

Scholars have engaged in frequent discourse regarding the sustainability policies implemented by major corporations (Ramlal & Chiweshe, 2022). The prominence of these corporations in society and the observable impact of their policies contribute to this phenomenon. Cantele et al. (2020) argue that while the environmental consequences of a single small and medium-sized enterprise (SME) may appear negligible in comparison to those of a solitary large corporation, the combined impact of numerous SMEs is considerable in terms of resource utilisation, air and water contamination, and waste production. There is a prevailing consensus that they play a substantial role, encompassing a range of 60% to 70%, in the occurrence of industrial pollution within the European context. There is, however, limited knowledge from a developing world perspective, more so on the African continent.

The first step in encouraging businesses to embrace sustainability practices entails improving the receptiveness and comprehensiveness of their understanding of sustainability. The noteworthy presence of small, medium, and micro enterprises (SMMEs) within the business environment underscores their capacity to make substantial contributions towards the efficient allocation of resources, ultimately benefiting future generations (Crossley et al., 2021).

As previously stated, the academic discussion pertaining to sustainability practices is presently in its nascent phase, with a scarcity of studies focused on investigating the participation of small, medium, and micro enterprises (SMMEs) in sustainable practices (Cantele et al., 2020; Nhemachena, 2017; Ramlal & Chiweshe, 2022). The existing literature on the impact of small, medium, and micro enterprises (SMMEs) at the local level on the natural environment and their engagement with sustainable practices is limited in scope. Furthermore, there is a distinct requirement for additional scholarly literature focusing on the factors that motivate small, medium, and micro enterprises (SMMEs) to embrace sustainable practices within the unique framework of South Africa. The lack of research in this area can be primarily attributed to the prevailing emphasis of existing studies on various aspects of small, medium, and micro enterprises (SMMEs) in this particular region.

The primary objective of this chapter is to address the current gap in research by investigating the diverse determinants that impact the implementation of environmentally sustainable practices within small, medium, and micro enterprises (SMMEs) located in Pietermaritzburg, a city within the KwaZulu-Natal province of South Africa. The main aim of this chapter was to assess the impact of coercive pressure, normative pressure, mimetic pressure, and entrepreneurial values on the adoption of sustainability practices among small, medium, and micro enterprises (SMMEs). Furthermore, this chapter investigates the consequences and ramifications of implementing sustainability practices for entrepreneurs. The collection of primary data for this chapter was accomplished through the distribution of online questionnaires to a sample of 235 individuals who identified themselves as entrepreneurs. Subsequently, the gathered data underwent analysis employing descriptive and inferential statistical techniques. The empirical findings indicate that the adoption of sustainable practices by entrepreneurs is primarily driven by normative pressures, specifically the influence of consumers. The results of this chapter highlight the existence of similar patterns that resemble those observed in large corporations, emphasising the significance of knowledge sharing within the small, medium, and micro enterprise (SMME) sectors. Furthermore, it is advisable for entrepreneurs to proactively foster internal innovation in order to attain sustainability while simultaneously maintaining a practical perspective on the attainability of their goals. It is crucial to recognise that the findings of this chapter provide a unique perspective on the factors that influence entrepreneurs' adoption of sustainable practices in their businesses.

BACKGROUND

As previously mentioned, the current state of academic research on sustainability practices is in its early stages, with limited focus on the specific engagement of small, medium, and micro enterprises (SMMEs) in sustainable practices (Johnson, 2017). Simultaneously, the implementation of corporate responsibility and the adoption of sustainable programmes within the business sector represent only a partial strategy for operationalising a sustainable approach (Annan-Diab & Molinari, 2017).

The integration of sustainability has emerged as a pivotal component within the realm of contemporary business operations in the 21st century. Organisations of various sizes and across diverse industries are increasingly under pressure to ensure that they effectively address the social and environmental challenges of the world, aligning with the principles outlined in the Sustainable Development Goals (Annan-Diab & Molinari, 2017).

The initial step towards motivating businesses to adopt sustainable practices involves enhancing the responsiveness and comprehensiveness of sustainability perceptions. It is widely acknowledged that small, medium, and micro enterprises (SMMEs) represent a substantial portion of the business landscape. Consequently, it is imperative that these entities assume a pivotal role in ensuring efficient resource allocation for the benefit of future generations(Chiliya, 2016).

Africa continues to face challenges in achieving significant progress towards sustainable development. In 2012, the Economic Commission for Africa (ECA) provided an overview of the significant issues that impacted the 2002 World Summit on Sustainable Development (WSSD) (Economic commission for, 2012).

According to a study conducted by Tikly et al. (2018), a notable challenge encountered in the context of sustainable development in Africa is the fragmented approach employed. Therefore, in order to address this vulnerability, this chapter contributes valuable insights to the limited existing knowledge on the subject, particularly in the context of South Africa.

Issues, Controversies, Problems

Brammer et al. (2012) assert that small enterprises face significant challenges in achieving environmental sustainability. Their research findings indicate that these enterprises exhibit lower levels of concern regarding environmental issues compared to their larger counterparts. Simultaneously, prior research has infrequently delved into the participation of Small, Medium, and Micro Enterprises (SMMEs) in a comprehensive array of activities related to environmental preservation (Masarira, 2014).. This study aims to investigate the factors that drive small, medium, and micro enterprises (SMMEs) to adopt sustainable practices. According to Masarira (2014), a range of environmental issues, including climate change, resource depletion, biodiversity loss, and ecosystem integrity, are anticipated to present significant and challenging management obstacles in the twenty-first century.

Given the present significance of environmental management, a substantial amount of scholarly inquiry has been dedicated to examining the actions of corporations in addressing environmental issues. The majority of existing research in this area has focused on large corporations (Hoejmose & Adrien-Kirby, 2012). The lack of attention given to environmental management research in small, medium, and micro enterprises (SMMEs) is concerning, especially considering their significant presence in various sectors of the economy. Although there is considerable interest in environmental management among large corporations, particularly those operating in environmentally friendly sectors, the limited focus on SMMEs in existing research is noteworthy (Leonidou et al., 2015). For example, in the United Kingdom (UK) and other highly developed economies, small, medium, and micro enterprises (SMMEs) constitute over 90% of all business establishments and employ nearly 60% of the workforce in the private sector. Small, Medium, and Micro Enterprises (SMMEs) play a crucial role in the majority of economies, serving as the fundamental building blocks of the industrial system and constituting an essential component of a robust and prosperous market economy (Worthington & Patton, 2005).

The imperative for promoting sustainable practices, sustainable environmental protection, and biodiversity conservation has been recognised as a top priority by leaders on a global scale (Wyness et al., 2015) . Numerous factors, including global warming, emissions, climate change, deforestation, and the rapid decline of biodiversity, have led to increased awareness among both upstream and downstream participants in the manufacturing industry. This recognition has facilitated the adoption of sustainable production practices and environmentally sound management by companies (Beddington et al., 2012). Consequently, there is an ongoing increase in consumer demand for goods derived from natural or organic sources, such as herbal medicinal products, as opposed to solely chemical-based alternatives. The matter of sustainability imposes significant demands on small business proprietors, compelling them to transition towards environmentally-friendly practices and fulfil the increasing market demand for organically produced goods within a sustainable framework. Nevertheless, it should be noted that the existing body of literature pertaining to sustainable practices within the African context remains in its nascent stages (Uhlenbrock et al., 2018).

According to Kolk (2016), numerous companies have pursued sustainable development in the past decade. Numerous multinational corporations have implemented advanced sustainable development strategies that demonstrate a heightened level of environmental consciousness(Kolk, 2016). Although there is a growing awareness in society and among governments, small, micro, and medium enterprises continue to face a lack of support. The compact nature of these entities effectively hinders noticeability, while their limited proportion poses a significant enforcement obstacle for the authorities (Hillary, 2017).

According to a study conducted in the United Kingdom, there is evidence to suggest that a growing number of enterprises, including small, medium, and micro-sized enterprises (SMMEs), have begun to implement ecological management programmes (Viviers, 2009). Nevertheless, the extent to which small, micro, and medium enterprises in South Africa actively participate in sustainable practices, as well as their willingness and capacity to adopt and implement such practices, remains unclear (Maziriri, 2018). There exists a scarcity of scholarly investigations pertaining to the influence exerted by local Small, Medium, and Micro Enterprises (SMMEs) on the natural environment, as well as their involvement in sustainable practices. Moreover, there is a scarcity of scholarly literature concerning the determinants that impact the involvement of small, medium, and micro enterprises (SMMEs) in adopting sustainable practices within the specific context of South Africa. This dearth of research is evident as the majority of existing studies on this topic are limited in scope.

The concept of notion has been extensively explored in developed nations, with less emphasis on developing countries (Yadav et al., 2018). Hence, this chapter aims to address the existing gap in knowledge.

SOLUTIONS AND RECOMMENDATIONS

The majority of entrepreneurs (71%) indicated that their engagement in sustainable practices is driven by their awareness of environmental laws, which in turn influence their decision to adopt such practices. Additionally, 60% of the participants reported that they engage in sustainable practices due to the pressure exerted on them by the government. These findings demonstrate that small, medium, and micro enterprises (SMMEs) possess knowledge regarding environmental laws and regulations. This indicates that the South African government actively contributes to promoting sustainable practices among various businesses by implementing and enforcing relevant legislation.

59% of the respondents, actively participate in sustainable practices. Their engagement in such practices is primarily driven by their periodic evaluation of their products, ensuring compliance with environmental laws and regulations. This demonstrates that small, medium, and micro enterprise (SMME) owners engage in regular product inspections to ensure compliance with environmental laws and regulations.

A small proportion of entrepreneurs, specifically (35.32% of the sample), indicated their involvement in sustainable practices. This limited engagement can be attributed to the absence of government incentives encouraging entrepreneurs to adopt sustainable practices. The findings of this study indicate a limited allocation of government funding towards supporting small, medium, and micro enterprises (SMMEs) in their adoption of sustainable practices.

Moreover, the data reveals that only a small number of participants reported receiving incentives from the government, and these incentives were primarily granted to SMMEs with a longer operational history. During the course of this study, it was observed that the COVID-19 pandemic had a significant impact on the business landscape, leading to widespread closures and substantial job losses. Consequently, a considerable number of individuals turned to entrepreneurship. This indicates a substantial proportion of entrepreneurs who are relatively inexperienced in the business domain. In response to the adverse impact of the COVID-19 pandemic on South Africa's economy and businesses, the government of South Africa implemented a debt relief finance scheme aimed at providing assistance to small, medium, and micro enterprises (SMMEs) that have been significantly affected, either directly or indirectly, by the pandemic. The aforementioned facility is a financial assistance programme that offers soft loans to small, medium, and micro enterprises (SMMEs) with the objective of providing them with necessary support to sustain their operations amidst the challenges posed by the Covid-19 pandemic. The programme is specifically designed to cover a duration of six months, commencing from April 2020, (Khan, 2021)The lack of government incentives reported by the majority of participants can be attributed to their non-receipt of such incentives.

From an economic standpoint, South Africa is currently facing significant challenges. The government has implemented a system of incentives primarily in the form of loans, which are subject to specific eligibility criteria. Consequently, individuals or entities failing to meet these criteria are unable to secure the funding. Out of the total number of entrepreneurs surveyed, a minority of 83 individuals (35.32%) reported receiving incentives from the government. These entrepreneurs are characterised by their extensive experience in the business sector, which renders them eligible for a significant portion of the government funding opportunities available. According to Puppim de Oliveira and Jabbour (2017) SMME owners tend to reject the sustainability business case and instead adopt a more pragmatic perspective. They believe that environmental sustainability initiatives result in increased business costs, which they perceive as lacking sufficient motivation to voluntarily implement sustainability measures.

The findings of the study revealed that a majority of the entrepreneurs, actively participated in sustainable practices. This can be attributed to their recognition of the fact that implementing socially responsible activities can lead to a competitive edge for their respective companies. Additionally, 91% of the sample reported engaging in sustainable practices as they perceive it to be a significant source of competitive advantage. The findings indicate that the primary motivation behind businesses engaging in socially responsible activities is profit driven. These businesses aim to maximise their profits and perceive the adoption of sustainable practices as a means to gain a competitive advantage. This finding aligns with existing scholarly literature. Furthermore, a majority of the firms surveyed express a strong inclination towards engaging in discussions pertaining to sustainability, with over fifty per cent emphasising the importance of this topic. Additionally, a significant proportion, approximately twenty-five per cent, intend to disclose information regarding their sustainability efforts actively.

This study reveals that small, medium, and micro enterprises (SMMEs) exhibit a strong willingness to allocate necessary resources towards the adoption of sustainable practices. 48% of the respondents, indicated possessing all the necessary resources for implementing sustainable practices. This relatively low proportion of entrepreneurs reporting adequate resources underscores the limited availability of resources and financial means among small, medium, and micro enterprises (SMMEs).

The survey results revealed that 34% reported a low response rate, suggesting a lack of knowledge on how to adopt sustainable practices effectively. This dearth of information poses challenges for SMMEs in implementing such practices.

79.15% of the respondents, expressed their commitment to adopting sustainable practices. These entrepreneurs cited their firm's belief that such practices would effectively mitigate pollution as the primary motivation behind their decision. A mere 46.81% of the respondents, indicated that their organisations integrate sustainable practices within their business plans.

77% of the sample, expressed the significance of sustainability practices. This commitment is evident through the adoption of eco-saving operational practices, as well as the undertaking of various social and economic responsibilities and initiatives. The findings presented here challenge the prevailing notion that small, medium, and micro enterprises (SMMEs) exhibit a reluctance to embrace sustainable practices and demonstrate a lack of involvement in addressing sustainability issues. The findings of this study demonstrate that small, medium, and micro enterprises (SMMEs) not only contribute significantly to economic growth but also fulfil a crucial function in safeguarding the environment.

Entrepreneurs ought to contemplate the adoption of data-driven methodologies for sustainable endeavours, wherein they provide consumers with pertinent information to enable them to make well-informed choices. One approach to achieve this objective is through the classification of products into three categories: A, B, and C, denoting varying degrees of environmental friendliness. Category A represents products that are highly environmentally friendly, while category B encompasses products that possess a lesser degree of environmental friendliness. Finally, category C comprises products that exhibit the lowest level of environmental friendliness. Through the implementation of this strategy, it is anticipated that consumers will predominantly select products categorised as A, followed by those categorised as B or C. The potential for the government to adopt and establish a universal ABC rating system holds the promise of empowering consumers to make environmentally conscious purchasing choices. It is imperative for entrepreneurs to consistently prioritise customer feedback.

Entrepreneurs are required to provide training to their employees as sustainability cannot be attained solely through a single idea. Instead, the cultivation of novel and innovative ideas is imperative, and the acquisition of knowledge and skills becomes invaluable in this pursuit. Entrepreneurs should seek opportunities to collaborate with fellow entrepreneurs who have already embraced sustainable practices, in order to acquire knowledge and strategies for effectively addressing sustainability challenges. The government can contribute to the promotion of employment by providing financial assistance in the form of grants to entrepreneurs who engage in the recruitment and skill development of individuals.

Develop strategic initiatives that will facilitate the cultivation of a culture of sustainability among all employees within their respective organisations. It is imperative that all staff training sessions encompass the dissemination of knowledge and the provision of practical solutions pertaining to the implementation of sustainable practices. Additionally, these sessions should include detailed information regarding the immediate and enduring advantages associated with the adoption of sustainable practices.

Encourage the small, medium, and micro enterprise (SMME) sectors to prioritise and enhance their efforts in knowledge exchange. It is imperative for business owners to adopt a more proactive approach in fostering internal innovation aimed at promoting sustainable practices, while simultaneously maintaining a pragmatic perspective on the attainability of such goals.

It is recommended that the government acknowledge and provide incentives to enterprises that perceive sustainability as a means to gain a competitive edge. It is imperative for both the government and investors to allocate resources towards these businesses, as doing so would demonstrate the inherent value of sustainability in enhancing not only present circumstances, but also future prospects. Although there are government programmes aimed at fostering sustainability and promoting green economic activity within the small, medium, and micro enterprise (SMME) sector, the communication aspect continues to be intricate and limited. It is imperative for the government to adopt a more proactive stance in disseminating information to the small, medium, and micro enterprise (SMME) sector. This information should not only emphasise the significance of holistic sustainable practices as a sound business strategy, but also provide a comprehensive understanding of the implementation process. The inquiry that should be posed by the government is whether sustainability is being effectively promoted as a superior choice, both in terms of policy implementation and educational initiatives. The topic of education

The implementation of sustainable practices or the concept of sustainability in its entirety must be customised and aligned to correspond with the diverse stages within business operations. Many companies are currently prioritising sustainability as a means to reduce long-term costs. Although not intended as a critique, it is important to emphasise that small, medium, and micro enterprises (SMMEs) face the need for a significant investment of time and effort in employee training and fostering a sense of commitment in order to achieve comprehensive corporate sustainability. The ability to identify the content to be conveyed, determine the appropriate manner of presentation, and select the appropriate organisational level within the company to facilitate communication are essential factors in achieving organisational objectives.

FUTURE RESEARCH DIRECTIONS

Further research is required to gain a deeper understanding of the motivations behind the adoption of sustainable practices in South Africa. Insufficient data is available for reference and educational purposes. The existing body of knowledge acknowledges the presence of CO2 measures and other factors within extensive statistical data. However, further investigation is required to delve deeper into the practical implementation of sustainability, enabling us to comprehend its daily and moment-to-moment impact on our lives. Further research is required in South Africa to ensure an adequate supply of matrix and data. Without such research, the measurement of sustainability will continue to be elusive, leaving us with aspirations but lacking a clear path towards achieving them. Future research should also prioritise a comprehensive investigation into the sustainability practices of small, medium, and micro enterprises (SMMEs). This research should aim to identify and analyse the specific opportunities and challenges encountered by SMMEs in the implementation of their sustainability initiatives.

CONCLUSION

Numerous enterprises are diligently endeavouring to integrate sustainability principles into their routine business practices. Entrepreneurs have been observed to exhibit a higher propensity for engaging in sustainable practices due to their heightened awareness and comprehensive understanding of the environmental regulations and policies that necessitate compliance. Chi-square tests were performed to assess the statistical significance of the observed pressure. The resulting P-value coefficient was determined to be $p = .001$, indicating that it is smaller than the predetermined alpha value of .05. Therefore, it can be inferred that the adoption of sustainable practices is linked to the exertion of coercive influences.

Normative pressures exert a substantial and favourable impact on the adoption and execution of sustainable practices. According to the findings of this study, it has been observed that customer expectations have a significant impact on the extent to which organisations adopt sustainable practices. The coefficient for the p-value associated with the pressure variable was found to be $p = .001$, indicating statistical significance at a significance level of $\alpha = .05$. Therefore, it can be inferred that the adoption of sustainable practices is linked to normative influences.

Entrepreneurs who perceive the adoption of socially responsible practices as conferring a competitive edge to their organisation are more inclined to actively pursue sustainable practices. The coefficient for the P-value associated with this pressure measurement was found to be $p = .001$, indicating statistical significance at a significance level of $\alpha = .05$. Hence, it can be inferred that the adoption of sustainable practices is influenced by mimetic pressures.

Entrepreneurs whose organisations prioritise business social responsibility by addressing the needs of consumers, employees, and communities are more inclined to adopt sustainable practices. Based on the results of this study, it can be inferred that when companies or entrepreneurs view business operations through the lens of social responsibility, they are more inclined to actively participate in sustainable practices. The coefficient for the P-value of this pressure measurement was found to be $p = .001$, indicating statistical significance at a significance level of $\alpha = .05$. Therefore, it can be inferred that the adoption of sustainable practices is correlated with the embodiment of entrepreneurial principles.

REFERENCES

Anand, A., Argade, P., Barkemeyer, R., & Salignac, F. (2021). Trends and patterns in sustainable entrepreneurship research: A bibliometric review and research agenda. *Journal of Business Venturing*, *36*(3), 106092. doi:10.1016/j.jbusvent.2021.106092

Annan-Diab, F., & Molinari, C. (2017). Interdisciplinarity: Practical approach to advancing education for sustainability and for the Sustainable Development Goals. *International Journal of Management Education*, *15*(2), 73–83. doi:10.1016/j.ijme.2017.03.006

Bajdor, P., Pawełoszek, I., & Fidlerova, H. (2021). Analysis and Assessment of Sustainable Entrepreneurship Practices in Polish Small and Medium Enterprises. *Sustainability (Basel)*, *13*(7), 3595. doi:10.3390/su13073595

Beddington, J. R., Asaduzzaman, M., Bremauntz, F. A., Clark, M. E., Guillou, M., Jahn, M. M., Erda, L., Mamo, T., Van Bo, N., & Nobre, C. A. (2012). *Achieving food security in the face of climate change: Final report from the Commission on Sustainable Agriculture and Climate Change.*

Brammer, S., Hoejmose, S., & Marchant, K. (2012). Environmental management in SME s in the UK: Practices, pressures and perceived benefits. *Business Strategy and the Environment*, *21*(7), 423–434. doi:10.1002/bse.717

Cantele, S., Vernizzi, S., & Campedelli, B. (2020). Untangling the Origins of Sustainable Commitment: New Insights on the Small vs. Large Firms' Debate. *Sustainability (Basel)*, *12*(2), 671. doi:10.3390/su12020671

Chiliya, N. (2016). *Towards Sustainable Development in Small, Micro and Medium Adventure Tourism Enterprises*. University of Johannesburg.

Chistov, V., Tanwar, S., & Yadav, C. (2021). Sustainable Entrepreneurship and Innovation. *Addressing the Grand Challenges through Radical Change and Open Innovation*.

Crossley, R. M., Elmagrhi, M. H., & Ntim, C. G. (2021). Sustainability and legitimacy theory: The case of sustainable social and environmental practices of small and medium-sized enterprises. *Business Strategy and the Environment*, *30*(8), 3740–3762. doi:10.1002/bse.2837

Economic commission for, A. (2012). Economic Report on Africa 2012: Unleashing Africa's Potential as a Pole of Global Growth. *Economic commission for Africa.*

Fernando, Y., Chiappetta Jabbour, C. J., & Wah, W.-X. (2019). Pursuing green growth in technology firms through the connections between environmental innovation and sustainable business performance: Does service capability matter? *Resources, Conservation and Recycling*, *141*, 8–20. doi:10.1016/j.resconrec.2018.09.031

Ghosh, S., & Das, N. (2022). Corporate Social Responsibility in the Time of Pandemic: An Indian Overview. In COVID-19, the Global South and the Pandemic's Development Impact (pp. 77-92). Bristol University Press.

Gregori, P., & Holzmann, P. (2020). Digital sustainable entrepreneurship: A business model perspective on embedding digital technologies for social and environmental value creation. *Journal of Cleaner Production*, *272*, 122817. doi:10.1016/j.jclepro.2020.122817

Hahn, R., Spieth, P., & Ince, I. (2018). Business model design in sustainable entrepreneurship: Illuminating the commercial logic of hybrid businesses. *Journal of Cleaner Production*, *176*, 439–451. doi:10.1016/j.jclepro.2017.12.167

Hoejmose, S. U., & Adrien-Kirby, A. J. (2012). Socially and environmentally responsible procurement: A literature review and future research agenda of a managerial issue in the 21st century. *Journal of Purchasing and Supply Management*, *18*(4), 232–242. doi:10.1016/j.pursup.2012.06.002

Johnson, M. P. (2017). Knowledge acquisition and development in sustainability-oriented small and medium-sized enterprises: Exploring the practices, capabilities and cooperation. *Journal of Cleaner Production*, *142*, 3769–3781. doi:10.1016/j.jclepro.2016.10.087

Khan, H. (2021). *COVID-19 in South Africa: An Intersectional Perspective based on Socio-economic Modeling and Indigenous Knowledge Base.*

Knoppen, D., & Knight, L. (2022). Pursuing sustainability advantage: The dynamic capabilities of born sustainable firms. *Business Strategy and the Environment*, *31*(4), 1789–1813. doi:10.1002/bse.2984

Kolk, A. (2016). The social responsibility of international business: From ethics and the environment to CSR and sustainable development. *Journal of World Business*, *51*(1), 23–34. doi:10.1016/j.jwb.2015.08.010

Laasch, O., Ryazanova, O., & Wright, A. L. (2022). Lingering covid and looming grand crises: Envisioning business schools' business model transformations. *Academy of Management Learning & Education*, *21*(1), 1–6. doi:10.5465/amle.2022.0035

Leonidou, L. C., Fotiadis, T. A., Christodoulides, P., Spyropoulou, S., & Katsikeas, C. S. (2015). Environmentally friendly export business strategy: Its determinants and effects on competitive advantage and performance. *International Business Review*, *24*(5), 798–811. doi:10.1016/j.ibusrev.2015.02.001

Malarvizhi, P., & Yadav, S. (2008). Corporate environmental disclosures on the internet: An empirical analysis of Indian companies. *Issues in Social & Environmental Accounting*, *2*(2), 211–232. doi:10.22164/isea.v2i2.33

Masarira, S. K. (2014). *An analysis of small business social responsibility practices in South Africa*. University of South Africa.

Nhemachena, C. (2017). *Motivations of sustainable entrepreneurship in Gauteng province*.

Pham, N. T., Chiappetta Jabbour, C. J., Vo-Thanh, T., Huynh, T. L. D., & Santos, C. (2020). Greening hotels: Does motivating hotel employees promote in-role green performance? The role of culture. *Journal of Sustainable Tourism*, 1–20.

Poddar, A., Narula, S. A., & Zutshi, A. (2019). A study of corporate social responsibility practices of the top Bombay Stock Exchange 500 companies in India and their alignment with the Sustainable Development Goal s. *Corporate Social Responsibility and Environmental Management*, *26*(6), 1184–1205. doi:10.1002/csr.1741

Puppim de Oliveira, J. A., & Jabbour, C. J. C. (2017). Environmental management, climate change, CSR, and governance in clusters of small firms in developing countries: Toward an integrated analytical framework. *Business & Society*, *56*(1), 130–151. doi:10.1177/0007650315575470

Ramlal, N., & Chiweshe, N. (2022). An Interrogation of Entrepreneur Perspectives on the Nexus of Sustainability and Entrepreneurship: Sustainable Entrepreneurship. In Institutions, Resilience, and Dynamic Capabilities of Entrepreneurial Ecosystems in Emerging Economies (pp. 139-157). IGI Global.

Sarangi, G. K. (2021). *Resurgence of ESG investments in India: Toward a sustainable economy*.

Tikly, L., Joubert, M., Barrett, A. M., Bainton, D., Cameron, L., & Doyle, H. (2018). *Supporting secondary school STEM education for sustainable development in Africa*. University of Bristol, Bristol Working Papers in Education Series.

Uhlenbrock, L., Sixt, M., Tegtmeier, M., Schulz, H., Hagels, H., Ditz, R., & Strube, J. (2018). Natural Products Extraction of the Future—Sustainable Manufacturing Solutions for Societal Needs. *Processes (Basel, Switzerland)*, *6*(10), 177–177. doi:10.3390/pr6100177

Viviers, S. (2009). Going green: An SMME perspective. *The Southern African Journal of Entrepreneurship and Small Business Management*, *2*(1), 30–49. doi:10.4102/sajesbm.v2i1.18

Worthington, I., & Patton, D. (2005). Strategic intent in the management of the green environment within SMEs: An analysis of the UK screen-printing sector. *Long Range Planning*, *38*(2), 197–212. doi:10.1016/j.lrp.2005.01.001

Wyness, L., Jones, P., & Klapper, R. (2015). Sustainability: What the entrepreneurship educators think. *Education + Training*, *57*(8/9), 834–852. doi:10.1108/ET-03-2015-0019

Yadav, N., Gupta, K., Rani, L., & Rawat, D. (2018). Drivers of sustainability practices and SMEs: A systematic literature review. *European Journal of Sustainable Development*, *7*(4), 531–531. doi:10.14207/ejsd.2018.v7n4p531

ADDITIONAL READING

Binder, J. K., & Belz, F. M. (2015). Sustainable entrepreneurship: what it is. Handbook of entrepreneurship and sustainable development research, 1, 30-71.

Chen, Y., Xin, Y., Luo, Z., & Han, M. (2021). The impact of stable customer relationships on enterprises' technological innovation based on the mediating effect of the competitive advantage of enterprises. *Sustainability (Basel)*, *13*(7), 3610. doi:10.3390/su13073610

Dean, T. J., & McMullen, J. S. (2007). Toward a theory of sustainable entrepreneurship: Reducing environmental degradation through entrepreneurial action. *Journal of Business Venturing*, *22*(1), 50–76. doi:10.1016/j.jbusvent.2005.09.003

Muñoz, P., & Cohen, B. (2018). Sustainable entrepreneurship research: Taking stock and looking ahead. *Business Strategy and the Environment*, *27*(3), 300–322. doi:10.1002/bse.2000

Ramlal, N., & Chiweshe, N. (2022). An Interrogation of Entrepreneur Perspectives on the Nexus of Sustainability and Entrepreneurship: Sustainable Entrepreneurship. In Institutions, Resilience, and Dynamic Capabilities of Entrepreneurial Ecosystems in Emerging Economies (pp. 139-157). IGI Global.

Rodgers, C. (2010). Sustainable entrepreneurship in SMEs: A case study analysis. *Corporate Social Responsibility and Environmental Management*, *17*(3), 125–132. doi:10.1002/csr.223

Sadiq, M., Nonthapot, S., Mohamad, S., Chee Keong, O., Ehsanullah, S., & Iqbal, N. (2022). Does green finance matter for sustainable entrepreneurship and environmental corporate social responsibility during COVID-19? *China Finance Review International*, *12*(2), 317–333. doi:10.1108/CFRI-02-2021-0038

Schaefer, K., Corner, P. D., & Kearins, K. (2015). Social, environmental and sustainable entrepreneurship research: What is needed for sustainability-as-flourishing? *Organization & Environment*, *28*(4), 394–413. doi:10.1177/1086026615621111

Schaltegger, S., & Wagner, M. (2011). Sustainable entrepreneurship and sustainability innovation: Categories and interactions. *Business Strategy and the Environment*, *20*(4), 222–237. doi:10.1002/bse.682

Stubbs, W. (2017). Sustainable entrepreneurship and B corps. *Business Strategy and the Environment*, *26*(3), 331–344. doi:10.1002/bse.1920

KEY TERMS AND DEFINITIONS

Coercive Pressure: Relates to the impact that manifests when enterprises perceive a dependence on their peripheral environments to acquire resources that enhance their ability to survive.

Economic Sustainability: Refers to the strategic management approach aimed at minimising operational costs through systematic management, enhancing labour productivity, allocating more resources towards research and development, and investing in training and other forms of human capital.

Entrepreneurial Values: Considered essential prerequisites for the manifestation of entrepreneurial behaviour. Entrepreneurial values necessitate the possession of certain attributes, namely creativity, risk-taking propensity, inventiveness, the ability to achieve in a multi-dimensional manner, ambition, and independence.

Environmental Sustainability: Refers to the practise of safeguarding natural resources by closely monitoring the impact of human activities, commonly referred to as the human footprint, on the natural environment. The concept involves the proper utilisation of both renewable and non-renewable resources, along with the controlled release of emissions and the effective management of waste absorption.

Institutional Theory: Elucidates the processes through which consensus is established regarding sustainability, as well as the development and dissemination of sustainability concepts and practices within organisations.

Normative Pressure: Pertains to the exertion of influence by customers, wherein their demand for environmentally friendly products serves as a significant factor motivating businesses to adopt further sustainable approaches and practices within their operations.

Social Sustainability: A focal point that places emphasis on the advancement and progress of society in terms of growth and development.

Sustainability: Refers to the potential for achieving conditions that ensure the long-term well-being of a collective of individuals and their future generations within a specific ecological system.

Sustainable Entrepreneurship: Can be defined as the deliberate emphasis on preserving the environment, ensuring the well-being of ecosystems, and fostering community development while actively seeking opportunities to create new products, processes, and services for the purpose of generating gains. These gains encompass both economic and non-economic benefits that contribute to the welfare of individuals, the economy, and society at large.

Chapter 7
Technology and Communication:
Technically Leading Towards Fictional Connections

Parul Mishra
Amity University, India

ABSTRACT

The present chapter is an attempt to revive the ancient communication skills and techniques and its influence on the relationships; it is by no means a suggestion that technology is less significant. The long hours given to mobiles have put a negative impact on the human relationships. The use of AI techniques has now become an everyday thing which certainly shall, at a point of time, be dangerous for the critical and mental growth of humans. Excessive use of technology has a negative impact.

COMMUNICATION: AN INTEGRAL PART OF THE SOCIETY

If early communication methods are been discussed it shall include a disorganized collection of making sounds, drawing in stones, imperial communication, pigeon post, etc. (Gascoigne, 2019). However, humans reached a new milestone in communication after the invention of the first practical telephone by Alexander Graham Bell in 1876 (Biography, 2018). Without communication it becomes impossible to do any kind of work in the society. After a few years, mobiles took the place of telegrams and telephones and got developed in the 1940s by engineers of AT&T (Switch, 2020). The mobile technologies are experiencing everyday changes leading to

DOI: 10.4018/979-8-3693-0790-8.ch007

progress. The development is comprehensive of all kinds of technical and virtual transportations. In addition to this, front-runners of mobile technologies like mobile device companies and the related app makers try to attract the gradually growing massive sect of mobile consumers to realize their conditions. A smartphone is smart enough to make calls, send e-mails, watch and share photos and videos, play video games and music, keep track of appointments and contacts, surf the Internet, use voice search, check news and weather, use chat applications for voice calls and texting like WhatsApp and interact on various social networks like Facebook, Instagram etc. The initiation of cyberspace was one of the most important spaces given in the phase of development of communication technologies. Moreover, the internet played a critical part in dropping the cost of communication and promoting efficiency within various communication channels. Before the advent of internet, it was hard to communicate which was a drawback in the growth of the nation. Communication before internet was costly and time consuming especially when the people were located on geographical locations. There are many other factors which were affected by the lack of smooth and uninterrupted communication. Due to the high cost of communication, it was very difficult to maintain meaningful relations between people so in short, the implementation of internet technologies brought the world closer and together (Steinfeld, Ellison, and Lampe, 2008). Now people could communicate at low costs despite of the physical distance between them. The internet and internet-based communication channels have improved the quality of human interactions and also of relationships.

Smartphones vs. Smart Users

Nowadays, the smartphones have engulfed all the strata of the society. The use of smartphones is no more known as unusual . However, these smartphones can do more than just communicate in a short span of time. Talking about the work done in the modern era, there is hardly anything that cannot be done by smartphones. However, all the features come with a cost; their impact on social behaviour and human affairs are striking. In the contemporary era, public is so much dedicated towards mobile technology that a massive downfall in the intensity of relationships has been observed. The traditional human interaction is purely at stake because of this smooth communication. Due to the innovative techniques features such as Instant messages and phone calls have become so available that humans have lost interest in face-to-face communication. A survey done on 120 senior students of Al-Azhar University revealed that mobile technology has dramatically reduced the face-to-face communication of subjects with their close people (Elsobeihi & Naser, 2017). The reason behind this is that these students have become more reliant on mobile technology as it offers communication with many more diverse people with different backgrounds (Elsobeihi & Naser, 2017). It is a matter of debate that individuals are using this technology more for surfing social media sites of entertainment than for their academic/work purpose. Around 87% of people use their phones from 2 to 8 hours daily and a possible reason for this addiction was the era of the COVID-19 pandemic. During the pandemic people started using phones for their work, However, it is noted that more than 8 hours use of these sites and online work is harmful for mental health of an individual. It is noticeable that individuals are giving more importance to their reel life compared to their real life. Nonetheless, it has been observed that the online time of an individual has increased significantly with the development of mobile technology and around 98% of the world in the age group 11 to 30 are more addicted to this technology. It is a signal to the coming generations that the consequences of the growing mobile technology on social behaviour and human relationships tends to be adverse. Regular usage of mobile phones is showing several serious effects on the mental health of people and one among them is Nomophobia, a kind of fear that an individual feels during the absence of mobile phones and results in a disturbance of his psychological conditions. The kind of inclination society has today for smooth communication, in the name of growth, will undoubtedly result into many disorders; fewer people will be inclined to communicate with a person in the traditional method. The rapid advancement of electronic media and technology with various features such as messaging, calls and other documentation work has been made quick and easier. The growth, no doubt, is helping the industry and the academia to grow however, with the growth of mental diseases among the users. It is squeezing out the real essence of what is called human, the man made machines are controlling the God made Man.

Consequence of Telecommunications on Relationships

Telecommunication has led humans to a newer world of talking without talking. Since mobile technology is rapidly evolving, and it is expected that this will continue for the unforeseeable future, it is therefore certain that these adverse effects will become much more severe in the future times. The allure of face-to-face communication does not exist anymore, the time spent with family is also very short compared to online social life, the letters have taken place of mails and fax. Therefore, when it comes to talk about human relationships mobile technology has an insignificant contribution to the connectivity maintenance of human relationships. Overall, mobile technology is harmful to certain extent. One has to have a balanced aptitude to handle both, the technology and the men. The current society is swift in adopting every change offered to it by the communication technology.

Technology: Boon or Bane

Mobile phones are boon to this century. The use of the same has become a significant part of the society. Keeping mobile is no more luxury on the contrary, it has become necessity in the COVID times. It is not only limited to be known as communication ruse but also a necessary social accessory. In comparison to fixed telephones the number of mobile phones has increased as it is portable and easy to carry unlike the traditional heavy boxes. Therefore, it cannot be wrong to say that the mobile phones nowadays have become no less important than their own life. In fact, for a successful life, it is an essential ownership. Recent research quote that around 4.5 billion people are using smartphones across the world. A large number of surveys have been conducted on the youth worldwide which shows that for young generation cell phones are more important than food for them. With several features such as texting, calling, listening to music, playing phone games and much more, the phone has become an integral part of their lifestyles, and without it they may face several symptoms related to paranoia. The Telecom Regulatory Authority of India shared the update that there are around 929.37 million mobile phone users in India, making the nation world's second-largest cell phone using developing country. Mobile phones such as Motorola, Nokia, Samsung, Sony Ericsson etc. are the popular brands which have their hold in Indian market by introducing latest mobile phones at regular intervals. There has been quite an enormous amount of popularity of cellular phones in younger generation within a short span of time (Hakoama & Hakoyama, 2011). Youth is more inclined towards using mobile phones for activities other than communication than the older generation (Mackay & Weidlich, 2007) because in adolescence stage, people are more susceptible to changing fashion trends and style, building them more tech savvy which creates certain behavioral disorders. On the contrary, administrators and teachers frequently consider the use of cell phones by students at schools, restraining them from their education and this arises as hurdles in their education (Johnson & Kritsonis, 2007). Moreover, mobile phones have aided in smoothening the progress of social release of youngsters from parental authority (Ling, 2004). Due to more use of mobile phones on constant basis it results in various physiological health hazards such as headaches, fatigue, and other health-related symptoms. The usage of mobile phones is causing many defects in the society. It is one of the causes that is responsible for accidents; during driving it is one of the major causes of accident, and some controversy still exists in the usage of mobile phone whether it is capable of producing tumours or not. People who use mobile phones more than 8 hours on a daily basis show several symptoms which affect their psychological level. They do not show any strange corporeal and mental indications because of which their ailment goes unobserved by others. Current research shows that usage of online communication platforms will expand up to 50-60% over the upcoming four to five years. This expansion will be important in ensuring that people will communicate more efficiently and enjoy the benefits of the platform of internet communication. However, the major problem is of internet addiction and breakdown in interpersonal communications which result to higher levels of loneliness in societies (Parasuraman, Sheridan and Wickens,2010).

Expansion of Technology and its Role in Communication

There are wide and huge advantages of technology at human workplace. For instance, people can use various communication tools to interact or exchange information at work. A large number of people are using various business technologies to change the way their employees communicate and interact in the workplace. The advancement of technology is leading the world to a total new era of digits. An era where number game would actually be a part and parcel of everybody's life. By number game is meant the coding strategies. People from all over the world are using various communication tools such as text messages or video conferencing on Skype, WhatsApp, Telegram, Zoom, Google meet, Webex, to name a few to share and exchange information with each other. These virtual communication tools are helpful in sharing screens as well which help in project making and group decision-making. Besides all communication technologies can be used in every field. In short communication technologies helps to improve communication. People can also use internet technologies to innovate ways of promoting anything online. It enables improved communication. people can use different business technologies to create business innovative ideas for growth and expansion. A wide range of technological challenges were created, and people were rewarded who came up with inventive concepts using technology. Moreover, people can use internet technology to develop new ways of promoting anything online whether it's industry or academics. Various platforms can be used by people of one organization to socialize and creative with other people of different organization. this later results in brainstorming and in short it encourages innovation and creativity. Due to the use of technology various works can be done with greater efficiency and leading increase in production in a short span of time. The use of computers has less chance of errors. Due to the use of internal networks at the workplace, people don't have to move to different departments which saves a lot of time. The large use of the internet and computers has saved time and space as now people from any location can work from anywhere. Technological tools like virtual meetings save time as they don't need to be present physically and data will be shared online. Despite the advantages, there are also some disadvantages of technology in the human workplace such as distraction. The advanced use of social networking sites at the work place when not required, perhaps causes distraction and hence can affect the productivity of the employees. For ceasing this habit many organizations have blocked access to specific websites such as Facebook, Twitter, and YouTube so that there remains no space for distractions. Other technologies which cause distraction in the workplace are smartphones, computers, etc. The technology involves a high cost to buy and also to maintain. Many organizations cannot afford full-time specialists, so they hire monthly contractors for work done. If technology tools in the organization do not maintain properly such as computers, then it will result in decreased production, and buying them new results in high costs. Most of the work in organizations is performed by technology and as a result, people become lazy at work.

A Curse for Critical Thinking

Technology is killing critical thinking. It has made learner a puppet. Simple tasks related to daily life such as calculations are done by calculators, hence the brain is at rest it remains unused. People in the organization communicate via phone, text messages, or Gmail, which results in the elimination of face-to-face communication which is important for building workplace relationships. Despite the advantages that come with technology it sometimes appears to be risky especially in the case of data security as all people in the organization have access to private information so which can be a big threat. The people in the organization mostly come with flash drives so there is a risk that they can transfer data from the computer and can take benefit from their personal gains. There are a large number of resolutions to reinstate humanity and to launch a stability between social usage of technology and the existing interaction that one needs to have with each other such as it is important to focus on what happened to our traditional social interaction as technology emerged, developed, and grew; it is perceptible that people used to spend more time together and human relations were strong before the involvement of technology. A trial should be given to attend, conduct and inspire gathering such as meetings, conversations, and dinners where people meet and reach one another to share experiences, resources, and ideas. These intellectual and entertaining gatherings can help moulding the youth of today accordingly. Irrespective of the technology based industry and academics one should not avoid friendly facial expressions, understanding, politeness, and respect among human beings regardless of their age, nationality, colour, the language they speak, religious beliefs, or points of view. Efforts should be made to organise presentations about amity, conversations and social interactions among human beings. Writing articles and booklets on these subjects can also prove to be an intellectual effort by the people. These articles can be for publications in newspapers and magazines anywhere in the world. This shall help the people understand the value of traditional communication. Moreover, it would help disseminating relevant information such as brochures and maps in neighbourhoods, universities, etc or in the city to reassure individuals to get the idea of their environment and contribute to interesting and exciting events.

The Art of Artificial Intelligence

Artificial Intelligence yet another clutch gripping the whole humanity and human relationships. The Meta Verse, Scikit Learn, TensorFlow, PyTorch, CNTK, Caffe, Apache MXNet, Keras, OpenNN. Artificial Intelligence (AI) is going through something of a "hot topic" moment, as applications such as ChatGPT show the world just how powerful and capable it is growing. The emergence of this new breed of "generative" AI tools has made it clear in recent months that it is no longer something that is only important in the realm of academic research or Silicon Valley tech giants. And far from simply being the latest "viral sensation," AI has truly become a technology that any business or individual can leverage to revolutionize the way they work or go about any number of day-to-day activities. In reality, when we use the term AI today, we are usually referring to a technology known as "machine learning." Rather than simulating every aspect of natural intelligence like robots in movies, this simply refers to software algorithms that are able to learn – becoming better and better at carrying out one specific task as they are exposed to more data. Machine learning powers a large number of revolutionary tools that have changed the way we live -from searching for information online with Google, to shopping with Amazon, watching movies on Netflix, or hailing a ride with Uber. Now the latest breed of AI applications offers us the chance to use it for just about any task we can think of. Applications like **Chat GPT**, a conversational interface; **Dall-E 2**, takes text prompts and transforms them into computer graphics (images, photos, drawings, paintings, etc.); Stable **Diffusion 2**, another text-to-image generative; **Lumen5**, video creation tool; Automated music generator; **Looka** helps in business branding by creating unique business logos; Podcastle, An audio recording and editing platform; **Gen1,** Cloud-based text-to-video platform that creates new videos; **Lalal. ai,** This tool uses a neural network system called Phoenix to automate audio source separation; **Deep Nostalgia**, innovative tool lets you animate the faces in family photos so you can see them smile, blink, and laugh, just as if you had recorded a video of them back in the day; **Murf**, a text-to-speech engine that makes it simple to create natural-sounding synthetic vocal recordings in 15 languages from a choice of over 100 voices and dialects; **Legal Robot**, tool is designed to automatically translate complex and confusing "legalese" into straightforward language that can be understood by anyone; **Cleanup.Pictures**, lets you retouch images by removing unwanted objects, defects, or even people; **Fireflies**, plugs into popular video conferencing tools like Zoom, Teams, or Webex and automates the process of taking notes and creating transcriptions; **Krisp** is another conference calling operation.

This shows how much reality lies in the Artificial intelligence. This intelligence sector should no more be famous as 'artificial', because it is portraying what actually humans and human mind expects, more than that indeed.

Summing Up

Technology no doubt is a boon to the century however, in the long run it has end. Hence it can be summed up that mobile technology has both negative and positive effect on social behaviour and social dealings. The impression is typically traced in the adolescent to adult age range, and the rapid progression of mobile technology has instigated a huge increase in its convention. As a consequence, people prefer giving more importance to their online social life than real social life. It is commonly known to all that frequent use of mobile phone suffers Nomophobia without knowing the slightest idea about it, as a result their emotional intelligence suffers and face severe deteriorations related to body and mind . In addition to all this, people seem to believe that mobile phones help them preserve their relationships. On the contrary, indeed, it is observed that mobile phones may help to keep close-range connectivity. Additionally, it does help for long distance relationships. However, a healthy recommendation is to reduce the extent of these adverse effects. The routine recommended will consist of assigned hours for different activities, and the activity with the most urgency will be on priority of the number of hours. The pace which technology has taken to leap indicates a signal of tech-future. The problems persisting will no longer exist in the future. Hence, people should be updated and upgraded carefully with the use of technology in their social lives. It is accepted by the society and its people that people will be avoiding connecting face to face with each other rather they will prefer to connect via technology. It is partly because they spend more time on their mobile and internet and therefore have little time and interest for interaction with their friends and family, perhaps because the internet offers them the platform for personal interactions with many people of diverse backgrounds around the world. The current analysis of the research in the related field claims that more than 78% of students observed a dereliction in the quality of their conversation with others when technology is present or applied. This indicated strongly that face–to–face communication is at the verge of extinction. If necessary, measures will not be taken and executed twenty first century is definitely going to be witness of an end of convention.

REFERENCES

Ellison, N., Steinfield, C., & Lampe, C. (2008). The benefits of Facebook "friends:" Social capital and college students' use of online social network sites. *Journal of Computer-Mediated Communication*, *12*(4), 1143–1168. doi:10.1111/j.1083-6101.2007.00367.x

Elsobeihi, M., & Naser, S. (2017). Effects of Mobile Technology on Human Relationships. *International Journal of Engineering and Information Systems*, *1*(5), 110–125. https://www.researchgate.net/publication/319212701_Effects_of_Mobile_Technology_on_Human_Relationship

Gascoigne, B. (2019). *History of communication*. History World. http://www.historyworld.net/wrldhis/PlainTextHistories.asp?historyid=aa93

Hakoama, M., & Hakoyama, S. (2011). The Impact of Cell Phone Use on Social Networking and Development among College Students. *The AABSS Journal*, *15*, 1–20.

USwitch. (2020). *History of mobile phones: What was the first mobile phone?* U Switch. https://www.uswitch.com/mobiles/guides/history-of-mobilephones/#:~:text=Mobile%20phones%20were%20invented%20as. • https://www.forbes.com/sites/bernardmarr/2023/02/28/beyond-chatgpt-14-mind-blowing-ai-tools-everyone-should-be-trying-out-now/?sh=21831bdd7a1b

Johnson, C. (2007). *National School Debate: Banning Cell Phones on Public School Campuses in America*. Semantic Scholar.

Ling, R. (2004). *The Mobile Connection: The Cell Phone's Impact on Society*. Elsevier., doi:10.1145/1029383.1029381

Mackay, M. M & Weidlich O. (2007). Australian Mobile Phone Lifestyle Index (3rd ed.). Special Topic: Advertising on the Mobile Phone. Australian Interactive Media Industry Association.

Parasuraman, R., Sheridan, T., Wickens, C. (2000). A model for types and levels of human interaction with automation. *IEEE transactions on systems, man, and cybernetics*. IEEE. DOI:. doi:10.1109/3468.844354

Toppr. (2019). *Uses of Mobile Phones Essay for Students*. Toppr. https://www.toppr.com/guides/essays/uses-of-mobile-phones-essay/

Chapter 8
Urdu Cursive Word Recognition Using an Advanced Intelligent Model of Optimized Deep Learning

V. Asha
New Horizon College of Engineering, India

N. Uma
New Horizon College of Engineering, India

Balasubramanian Prabhu Kavin
https://orcid.org/0000-0001-6939-4683
SRM Institute of Science and Technology, India

Gan Hong Seng
XJTLU Entrepreneur College, Xi'an Jiaotong-Liverpool University, China

ABSTRACT

Many historically significant documents are only accessible in paper record form, making text recognition a crucial problem in the arena of digital image processing. Text recognition techniques primarily aim to convert paper documents into digital files that can be easily managed in a database or other server-based entity. Size, colour, font, orientation, backdrop complexity, occlusion, illumination, and lighting all make text identification more difficult in photos from real-world settings. Variations in writing style, several forms of the same letter, linked text, ligature diagonal, and condensed text make Urdu text identification more difficult than with non-cursive scripts. To separate the spatial correlation and appearance correlation (DSSAC) of the mapped convolutional channel, the suggested intelligent model employs the deep separable convolutional layers in place of the conventional design in the U-Net. To achieve cursive region, capture, the research offers a model called DSSAC-RSC.

DOI: 10.4018/979-8-3693-0790-8.ch008

INTRODUCTION

The modern world has digitised to save time and increase productivity thanks to the rise of automation and computerization. Optical Character Recognition (OCR) is a crucial step in the process of digitising manuscript writings (Narwani et al., 2022), and the digitization process as a whole is an important milestone in the development of technology. Optical Character Recognition (OCR) is the process of creating editable text from scanned copies of a written document. As the need arises, OCRs are tailored to a certain language and even specific fonts. The research vision (Nasir et al., 2021) has been mostly focused on text extraction from natural pictures. Assisting the visually handicapped, autonomous recognition, scene interpretation, robot navigation, and licence plate detection are some possible real-world uses (Umair et al., 2022). Text extraction from documents is a well-studied topic, and there are several commercial systems on the market with a recognition accuracy of over 99% based on the cited text (Kashif 2021). Scene graphics have a complicated structure that makes it difficult to recognise text. Scene photos provide a distinct set of difficulties than scanned documents, such as sensor noise, blur, variable objects, unexpected layouts, unpredictable lighting conditions, random angles and obscured or distorted lettering (Aarif & Sivakumar 2022). Many books and government papers written in Urdu may benefit from being digitised, and here is where optical character recognition (OCR) comes in (Chandio et al., 2022).

Urdu is widely spoken in South Asia. The mainstream of the Indian population speaks it, and it is also the official language of Pakistan. It is a widely spoken language, with about 170 million native speakers (Rashid & Kumar Gondhi 2022). Due to its letters' intricate structure and ligature-based nature, where fonts are connected to construct words and sentences, Urdu script makes text recognition more difficult than extracting Latin text (Shafi & Zia, 2021). In contrast to English, Urdu is written from right to left and features two distinct script types, known as Nastaleeq and Naskh. Nastaleeq is a hanging, ornate script based on Perso-Arabic (Thirumalraj et al., 2023). Since Urdu script is cursive, it is more difficult to recognise Urdu writing in natural imagery than it is to recognise text in other languages like English (Arafat et al., 2022). Due to the need for a sufficient dataset, however, researchers and businesses have paid scant attention to Urdu scene text. The Urdu alphabets' cursive nature allows for a wide variety of writing styles (ul Sehr Zia et al., 2022). Both when used alone and in conjunction with other alphabets, these forms exhibit some degree of variation. In Section 1.1, a more detailed explanation is provided.

Figure 1. Diverse styles of an Urdu appeal used in cursive words

Position	Final	Middle	Initial	Isolated
Glyph	ـس	ـسـ	سـ	س
Word	بس	تیسرا	سبزی	لباس
Roman Urdu	Bs	Teesra	sabzi	Libas
English Translation	Bus	Third	Vegetable	Dress

Urdu Script

Urdu script is word is connected with additional and can have four various styles depending on its location. Figure 1 displays the four characters that make up the Urdu alphabet.,

Isolated.
Primary.
Central.
Final.

Figure 1 displays the style of a single letter at the location it appears in the Roman Urdu and English translations of the respective words. Urdu is written in a chaotic fashion, and the connection between individual letters to make words is known as a ligature.

Digital document conversion makes it simple to make changes to text as needed (Butt et al., 2022). Therefore, the document may be simply updated. Therefore, there are numerous demands for Urdu OCR that must be met before text recognition technologies can be implemented. The primary challenge of digitising Urdu documentation is resolving this issue (Rehman et al., 2021). Several options exist, but they all have drawbacks that prevent them from being the best option. Urdu script is cursive and quite distinct from Latin script, and it has various typefaces and font styles. Fewer data sets are available since little study has been done on Urdu (Khan et al., 2021). Recognising text in images is difficult since it first requires localising the words or phrases. Images being processed for text recognition may have backgrounds of varying colours or styles depending on the original content's origin (Ahmed et al., 2022). As a result, it's important to first determine the precise location of the text in the image before attempting to identify it. The lack of a data set is also a major factor in the poor accuracy of previous studies (Zahid et al., 2022). There must be a data set suitable for the specific requirements of each investigation (Riaz et al., 2022). Urdu's unique writing conventions make automatic text identification and recognition difficult. The most important results of this study are as follows:

In light of these issues, we present a DSSAC-RSC network-based approach to natural scene picture segmentation for the Urdu language. We feed the network photos from a binary array, have it determine if the pixels' values represent the foreground or background, have it anticipate segmentation outcomes, and then have it output chunks of the image in Urdu.

MOTIVATION

1. To address the issue of computation efficiency in networks, we suggest a DSSAC-RSC network built on the U-Net architecture by inserting a deep into the model in place of the conventional convolution layer.
2. Second, we include a Dense Residual block into a DSSAC-RSC network, using a full-scale jump connection strategy to achieve versatile feature fusion and quicken the convergence time of the deep network.
3. Thirdly, we enhance the DSSAC-RSC's segmentation precision by including an active contour model that guarantees a perfect match between an object's interior and exterior boundaries.

The remaining sections of the paper are as shadows: In Section 2, we define the relevant literature, and in Section 3, we provide a brief summary of the suggested model. Experiment results and comments are presented in Section 4. Lastly, Section 5 discusses what comes next in terms of research.

RELATED WORKS

In order to demonstrate the efficacy of RNN models for character recognition, (Misgar et al., 2023) have proposed a methodology to automate process, The 250 writers' responses were recorded on a single A4-sized piece of paper. There are 132 Urdu letter forms and 10 numeric shapes on each sheet. This is the first time such a huge dataset has been offered, and it includes all the different forms of Urdu character numbers, to the best of the authors' knowledge. To build the groundwork for a comparison of the classification skills of RNN and LSTM models, experiments have been conducted independently for the number, whole characters, and for the entire data set. Despite the inherent difficulties of the Urdu script, the RNN and

LSTM models performed better in terms of accuracy. Maximum accuracy for RNN is 96.96% for numeric data, 85.22% for whole characters, and 73.62% for the entire dataset, whereas LSTM excels at these tasks with maximum accuracy of 97.80% for numeric data, 97.43% for full characters, and 91.30% for the entire dataset. The suggested dataset also provides a fresh avenue for study, demonstrating the enormous potential not just for the Urdu language but also for other languages using comparable character sets, such as Arabic, Persian, etc.

Resolution-free cursive text detection and identification are proposed by (Zubair et al., 2023). Before using the Visual Geometry Group (VGG-16), text is detected using a CNN. Second, we employ the Long model on the retrieved features from CNN and VGG-16 independently for text recognition. Both the CNN + LSTM and the VGG-16 + LSTM hybrid models suggested here exceed the state-of-the-art approaches, with 91% and 96% accuracy, respectively.

Using a CNN for the feature extraction phase, a bi-directional Gated Recurrent Unit network (BiGRU) as the encoder, and a decoder, (Zia et al., 2023) offer an encoder-decoder based hybrid deep learning technique. The encoder (BiGRU) and decoder (GRU) of the method employ the Urdu ligature characteristics obtained from the CNN layer to provide accurate sentence recognition by identifying individual letters and joiners. According to our experiments, our projected CNN-BiGRU-GRU a 6 percentage point increase in Character Recognition Accuracy (86.95 and a 10 percentage

(FAHAD et al., 2023) suggest a large-scale study of the handwriting of native Urdu speakers from a variety of backgrounds. The dataset is made more thorough by include both the standalone characters and the ligatures. For the sake of a more complete corpus, we also encourage participation from people with physical disabilities. We also discuss the state of the art in Urdu recognition data sets and provide a contrast of the suggested set to the state of the art.

Using high-resolution, extraction, (Rahman et al., 2023) have industrialized a novel approach to fixing the problems with recognition. Our suggested UTRNet construction, a hybrid CNN-RNN model, displays state-of-the-art presentation on benchmark datasets. We improve the ground truth of the current IIITH dataset by introducing the UTRSet-Real, a large-scale annotated dataset with over 11,000 lines, and synthetic dataset with 20,000 lines closely approximating real-world. Due to the Urdu script's complexity and the dearth of annotated real-world data, previous efforts have had difficulty generalizing to the language. Also included is the Urdu text line detection benchmark dataset UrduDoc, which was created by us. We have also developed a web-based program that combines UTRNet with a text detection model to do full-stack Urdu OCR on paper documents. Our efforts not only improve upon existing methods of Urdu optical character recognition (OCR), but also open the door for more investigation into and development of OCR for the Urdu language.

In (Bhatti et al., 2023) demonstrate the use of CNN and their modifications for the classification of a new Urdu number dataset. To extract features for use by the Softmax classifier, we propose a bespoke CNN model. We evaluate its performance with that of GoogLeNet and the residual network (ResNet). With the Softmax classifier, our suggested CNN achieves an accuracy of 98.41%, while the SVM classifier achieves an accuracy of 99.0%. We are able to get an accuracy of 95.61% on GoogLeNet and 96.4% on ResNet. To further include real-world issues, we also create datasets for handwritten Urdu numerals and Pakistani money digits. When compared to other OCR models in the literature, ours has the highest accuracy rates.

For the purpose of pattern recognition in a set of isolated handwritten Urdu letters, (Zargar et al., 2023) provide the development and comparison of two popular machine learning models. Both models are based on networks, the first on Support Machines and the second on convolutional networks. Compared to the publicly available Urdu dataset UHaT, the SVM method did not offer impressive results; nevertheless, the CNN-based implementation accomplished an accuracy of 99.34% on the test set. The resource and time usages of the implementations are taken into consideration when comparing the metrics of the outcomes, in addition to the most crucial aspect: accuracy. In order to produce the broadest possible output, the methods have not been adjusted to each individual piece of data.

Urdu, a widely spoken language, employs a distinctive script that includes cursive writing styles. Cursive writing poses challenges for automated recognition systems due to the varying shapes and connections between characters. Developing an accurate and efficient Urdu Cursive Word Recognition system is crucial for applications such as document processing, handwriting analysis, and text-to-speech conversion.

PROPOSED SYSTEM

Figure 2 depicts the process by which the study was conducted, and the next subsection offers an explanation of the suggested model.

Dataset

In order to train the suggested models, to captured around 2500 photos of natural scenes and created a new dataset of 14100 cropped images of Urdu words (Chandio et al., 2022). All the word graphics had to be manually segmented due to overlapping, and then scaled to 100 by 64 pixels. Figure 3 depicts several examples of segmented word pictures from natural scene photographs in Urdu.

Huge numbers of picture files representing different textual permutations for Urdu words make up the collection. Images of handwritten Urdu writing on walls and signs

Figure 2. Workflow of the proposed model

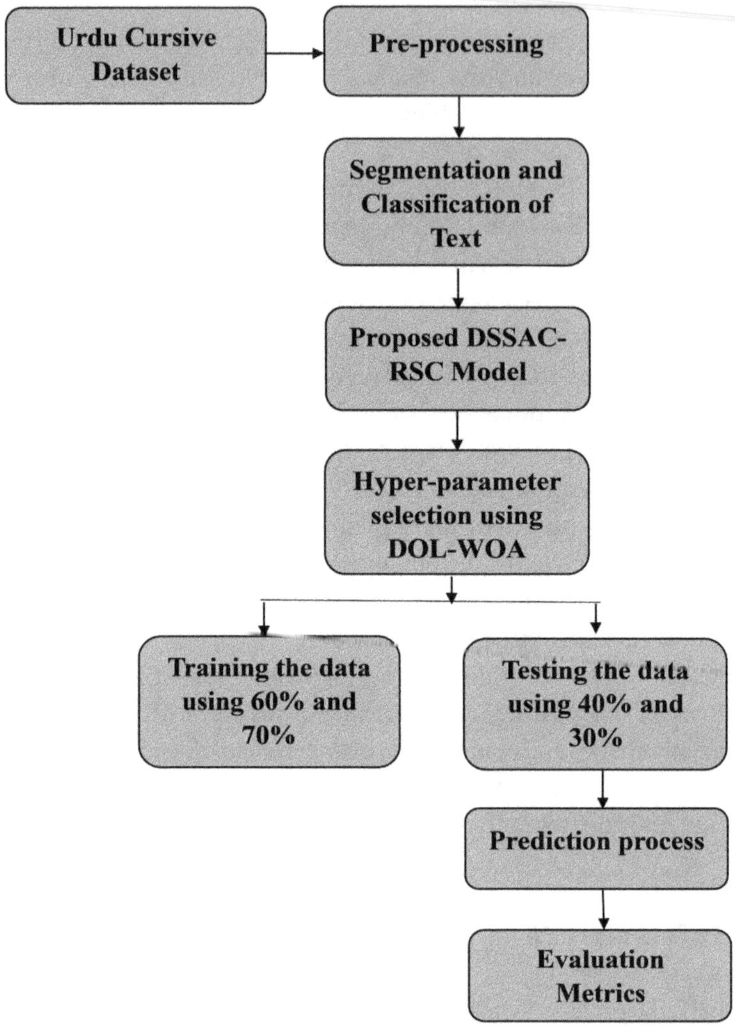

are also included in the dataset. Several instances of intra-ligature, inter-ligature, and diagonal text stretching were found in cropped word pictures. Recognising handwritten writing that is stretched, overlapped, or diagonal, when present in natural scene photos, is more difficult than recognising simple and typewritten (superimposed) text. This dataset can serve as a standard because it comprises the first substantial number of cropped photos of natural scenes with Urdu words. Additionally, additional cursive languages, like Arabic, Persian, and Sindhi, can leverage the dataset for natural scene text identification. There were 12600 samples used for training and 1500 used for testing. The input features values to speed up the

Figure 3. Sample segmented images

training and convergence of the network. In order to improve the accuracy of deep networks, to adopt a data augmentation strategy to rotate the pictures at random angles (no more than 10 degrees) to expand the size of the dataset. The data-augmented cropped photographs of Urdu words were solely employed in the training set.5.

Text Transcription

Due to the interwoven text and overlapping characters in cursive scripts like Arabic and Urdu, it is more challenging to separate each character of the ground truth text in a picture. ligatures. For instance, if an image text it is essential to stipulate where the character starts and. The other characters in the truth text go through the same procedure. This becomes more multifaceted when an image as.

Proposed Segmentation: DSSAC-RSC NETWORK

U-Net is a network in which the encoder and decoder are mirror images of one another (Cho et al., 2014). To extract visual characteristics, the encoder executes four sets of convolutions and down sampling, while the matching decoder does four sets of convolutions and up sampling to obtain accurate placement.

In propose an advanced version of U-Net's RSC network using DSSAC nodes. The essential components of a DSSAC-RSC network are a feature extractor, a pixel labelling train, an active contour predictor, and an image outputter. The network's fundamental characteristic is its architecture, which takes segmentation into account with active contour limitations. The encoder's convolutional layers, batch normalisation (BN) layers, and pooling layers all work together to execute the encoder's primary function: feature extraction. The convolutional layer's goal is to provide "local perception." To avoid gradient explosion or dispersion (Glorot et al., 2011), the BN layer monitors the deep network's output as it spreads. By placing the BN layer after the convolution layer, to can ensure that the loss function is convex and free of any unexpected gradient values. Nearing saturation, activation functions like sigmoid are less effective in a deep network. Overfitting may be prevented with ReLU because of its ability to lessen parameter dependencies.

The decoder's job is to take the feature map that the encoder (Tian et al., 2019) produces and assign pixel labels to them. The decoder's structure is broadly analogous to that of the encoder. It has the same amount of channels and spatial scales, as well as layers, and ReLU layers. The transposed convolution in Unet is replaced by the Bilinear function in DSSAC-RSC. The bilinear function is faster than the bicubic interpolation in resizing images (Huang & Cao 2020). The horizontal and vertical four-point pixel values that surround the spot to be interpolated define its interpolated grey value. By filtering out the noise in the adjacent may be minimised and picture distortion is prevented. To progress the performance of the encoder-decoder network, add overlaid layers. The active contour model in DSSAC-RSC is located in the superimposed layers. The former is where we'll save all the coarse characteristics to picked up from the neural network. The contour is constrained and the segmentation results are refined.

Depthwise Separable Convolution

The conventional convolution kernel operates on all of the image's channels concurrently. The feature maps are represented by the convolution kernels. As can be seen in Figure 4, the relationship between spatial convolution is concurrently learnt.

For a kernel of $W_{width} \times W_{height}$ (W_{width} and W_{height} respectively matching the size of the convolution kernel in both width and height.The dimensions of the output feature map are (W; H; B) if the dimensions of the input feature map are (W; H; A) (W; H correspond to the width and height of the picture, W D H, Convolution X_1 is often calculated as follows.:

$$X_1 = W_{width} \times W_{height} \times A \times B \times W^2 \tag{1}$$

DSSAC-RSC, on the other hand, uses convolution, which includes both depthwise convolution [28] and the former is in charge of filtering inputs, the latter is in charge of mapping output characteristics. Each of the four input channels in a 2-D plane is convoluted using a unique convolution kernel in depth-wise convolution. The computation of a convolutional operation in depth is $W_{width} \times W_{height} \times W^2$.

Figure 4. The dispensation of depthwise divisible convolution

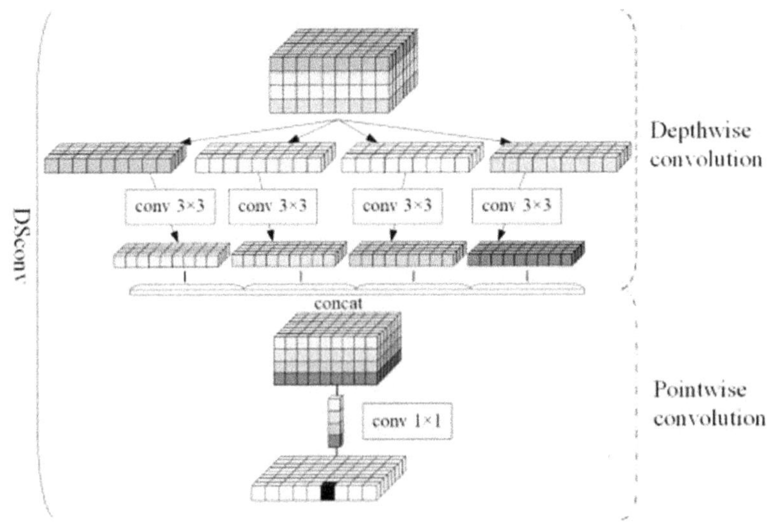

One issue with depthwise convolution processing is that it does not make use of important spatial location data. Pointwise convolution can be used to mix the feature maps that are generated as an output. One-to-one convolution conducts convolution operations on numerous convolution layers in less time than both 3x3 and 5x5 convolution. Therefore, to set 1 × 1 convolution to extract essential characteristics of the input tensor, which may balance the depth of the picture while minimising the dimensionality. Point-by-point convolution is computed as ABW2. Combining the results of depth convolution and point convolution yields the total depthwise separable convolution X2.:

$$X_2 = W_{width} \times W_{height} \times A \times W^2 + A \times B \times W^2 \tag{2}$$

The result of depthwise separable convolution is inferior to that of regular convolution if only a single attribute is retrieved. However, the depthwise divisible convolution can save more computation time as the network depth and sum of extracted rise. Here is the breakdown of how much more work depthwise separable convolution takes compared to regular convolution:

$$\frac{X_2}{X_1} = \frac{W_{width} \times W_{height} \times A \times W^2 + A \times B \times W^2}{W_{width} \times W_{height} \times A \times B \times W^2} = \frac{1}{B} + \frac{1}{W_{width} \times W_{height}} \tag{3}$$

Based on previous work, the standard size for the convolution kernel is 33. In this piece, the number of output channels B is set to 4 to account for the 4 modalities. The benefits to computer performance become more pronounced as the number of channels grows.

Residual Skip Connection

DSSAC-RSC employs residual dense connection in the encoder- to address the problem of a finite number of data streams. Because the fundamental building component of networks, each successive layer is a product of the layers that came before it along the channel. It can improve the feature propagation capacity, which in turn leads to better picture reproduction. The network's blocks are interconnected densely on a global scale (Zhang et al., 2020).

All of the current block's valid information is relayed to the next convolutional layer, which is the job of the connection (Zhang et al., 2018). The number of picture characteristics grows proportionally with the depth of the network. In this study, to perform local feature fusion before to up-sampling to extract and fuse useful features in each basic unit, as too numerous convolutional layers would lead to information redundancy. The U-Net framework requires upsampling by a factor of 4, therefore if there are too many characteristics shared throughout the network's four nodes, the training process will take too long. The concept of a residual network (Lin et al., 2017) is used in this article. To incorporate global characteristics and convey the context info from the front of the residual dense block to the back. In this way, DSSAC-RSC is able to glean the hierarchical structure's deep characteristics.

The extraction of shallow features is made possible by having convolutional layers that are depth-separable. Shallow feature learning, and global feature fusion make up the bulk of the residual dense block's network architecture. The efficient feature information of each component is learned by adaptive local feature fusion. Dimensionality reduction achieved by learning shallow local features in conjunction with global feature fusion. To improve the network's generalization ability and lessen its degradation during development of the DSSAC-RSC network module, a full-scale skipping connection is implemented. In order to more accurately represent the influence of results, the U-Net network's long skipping connection is paired with the short skipping connection of the residual network among cascading processes.

Active Contour Model

When segmenting noisy photos, the processing will result in a variety of contour lines, not all of which will be accurate. Because of the irregular pixel distribution, it will be difficult to detect the object's edges. DSSAC-RSC incorporates area segmentation with boundary line segmentation to forecast both the inside and outside of a boundary, hence solving the aforementioned issues. The active contour model (Chen et al., 2019) employs partial differential minimize an energy function based on the picture gradient, which is used to determine the segmentation edge line. Accordingly, the contour line will steadily head in the direction of edge.

The DSSAC-RSC network model identifies an out-of-the-ordinary region, and establish an initial curve there. The DSSAC-RSC model's final ReLU layer serves as the backdrop for this section. Until the energy functional is reduced, the curve will continue to approach the goal contour. The shape of the distortion curve, v(s), is

$$v(s)=\left[x(s),y(s)\right],s\in[0,1] \tag{4}$$

the coordinates of the contour point in the picture, x(s) and y(s), respectively. The Fourier transform of the independent boundary variable s. The contour's link to the energy function is given by:

$$E=\int_0^1 \frac{1}{2}\left[a(s)\left|\frac{dv}{ds}\right|^2+\beta(s)\left|\frac{d^2v}{ds^2}\right|^2\right]ds+\int_0^1 -|\nabla G_\sigma * I(x,y)^2\, ds \tag{5}$$

a(*s*) is the elastic contour. $\left|\frac{dv}{ds}\right|$ is to speed at which the distortion curve. *β*(s) is the strength coefficient that bounds the speed of the distortion curve to contour. $\left|\frac{d^2v}{ds^2}\right|$ is to switch the degree of curve contour.

The first term in (5) stands for internal energy and places limits on the smoothness and curvature of the contour. Last but not least, have "external energy," which stands for the coincidental alignment of the contour constraint curve with the image's neighborhood details..

$$E_{out}\left(v(s)\right)=-\left|\nabla G_\sigma * I(x,y)\right|^2 \tag{6}$$

where G_σ is the primary purpose of the ReLU, for example, is a function with a standard deviation of, and equation is employed for the aforementioned energy useful as:

$$-av''(s)+\beta v''+\nabla E_{out}(x,y)=0 \tag{7}$$

By solving the local least of functional E, as shown in Equation (7), and iteratively refining the edge contour, the optimal boundary can be found (Yang &X. Jiang, 2020).

Hyper-Parameter Tuning Using the Presented EWOA

The enhancement of WOA is the primary topic of this section. First, to present a revolutionary dynamic learning technique based improvement (IDOL). The adapted search strategy and the DOL policy make up its exploration-exploitation modes, and adaptive mode switching rules are used to strike a healthy balance between the two. IDOL is carried out in EWOA's two phases, which involve population initialization prior to evolution and generation jumping. After the encircling prey phase of EWOA, the AIW is added to improve exploration and prevent being stuck in a local optimum. IDOLWOA and AIWWOA are two variations on a theme that each enhance standard WOA in their own ways.

IDOL Strategy

The mechanism of DOL reveals that the search space decreases with time as the population converges iteratively. To address this issue, DOL includes a fixed weight w_d as described in Eq. (8) to ensure that it not only improves exploration capabilities but also preserves the original convergence of OBL. Increasing w_d leads to a greater disparity between XDO and X, which in turn enhances population diversity. However, if w_d is allowed to grow, convergence speed and exploitation capabilities will suffer.

$$X^{DO}=X+r^2 w_d\left(X^{RO}-X\right) \tag{8}$$

IDOL differs from DOL in that rather than adopting a pre-set weight w_d, IDOL may adaptively transition between the two modes to tackle the aforementioned issues. Mode one is used to increase IDOL's exploitation, while mode two is employed to increase exploration. IDOL's exploration- is reached by the use of a flexible switching rule that adapts to the organism's fitness level at any given time.

Mode-one: DOL

By increasing the group's search space when the weight of DOL is 1, IDOL enhanced the exploitation potential of WOA based on DOL. Hence, X^{IDOL} is distinct as Eq. (9).

$$X^{IDOL} = X + r^3\left(r^4 X^O - X\right) \tag{9}$$

where XO is found using Eq. (9), and r3, r4 are uniformly distributed between [0,1].

Second Method: Adapted Search Technique

This mode is based on the WOA's hunting for prey phase, which involves expending the search area through the exchange of information between unrelated people. The Lévy flight operative has also been incorporated into this mode to further improve its mutation capabilities. Since the Lévy distribution random number occasionally exhibits a long-step mutation, it is frequently employed to enhance MAs. In (10), to see a straightforward power-law interpretation of Lévy flight.

$$L(s) \sim |s|^{-1-\beta}, 0 \leq \beta \leq 2 \tag{10}$$

where = 1.5 and s is a random phase magnitude derived approximating the Lévy distribution via Mantegna's approach, as shown in Eq. (11). Both $\mu = N\left(0, \sigma_\mu^2\right)$ and $v = N\left(0, \sigma_v^2\right)$ obey deliveries, where the charge of σ_u and σ_v can be intended as Eq. (12).

$$s = \frac{\mu}{|v|^{1/\beta}} \tag{11}$$

$$\sigma_\mu = \left[\frac{\text{“}(1+\beta) \times sin(\pi \times \beta / 2)}{\text{“}(1+\beta / 2) \times \beta \times 2^{(\beta-1)/2}}\right]^{1/\beta}$$
$$\sigma_v = 1 \tag{12}$$

Equation (13) is derived by exchanging the original operative A with the Lévy flight operative s, which has better mutation performance.

$$X^{IDOL} = X^{r} - r^{5} s\left(X^{rand} - X\right) \tag{13}$$

where r^5 is a random sum mid (0,1).

Adaptive IDOL Manner Switching Rules

As the algorithm reaches a dead end after a certain number of iterations, switching modes to boost search performance is required. The mode switching threshold T make up the IDOL mode switching rule, which is crucial. Both J and T start out at 0, and as the iteration progresses, J is accumulated whenever a solution is not obtained after a round of repetition according to the formula J = J + 1; when fitness is obtained, the iteration reset to 0. In addition, the algorithm's convergence speed degrades as the number of iterations rises. To avoid frequent switching after the iteration reaches its latter stage, the mode-switching threshold should be raised so that more time may be spent in the present mode. As a result, T = T + T during mode transitions. Using both theory and experiment, to settle on a value of 5 for T. IDOL-based WOA may achieve higher performance using these settings.

AIW-Based Adaptive Encircling Prey Stage

Standard WOAs with a prey stage encircle all agents at a random distance depending on the A derived by the initial equation, and this value falls linearly each iteration. But at this point, the agent's exploration performance would suffer since the step size is being decreased gradually. This study incorporates the AIW into the encircling phase to broaden the group's perspectives and prevent individuals from becoming too invested in any one solution. Adjust the AIW rendering to agents, then multiply it by the target prey of the present agent to obtain a new target. Eq. (14) describes the enhanced surrounding prey stage.:

$$X_i\left(t+1\right) = w_i\left(t\right).X^{*}\left(t\right) - A.\left|C.X^{*}\left(t\right) - X_i\left(t\right)\right| \tag{14}$$

Among them, the AIW operator $w_i(t)$, $w_i(t) \in [0,1]$ This may be modified dynamically in response to the location of the agent. The AIW is kept or raised when the agent's location in the solution space is optimal. Specifically, the weight agent is set to the extreme value so that it may converge on the present prey as quickly as feasible when its fitness is greater than the mean populace. When the current agent's fitness is lower than average, a lower value is given to w_i (t). The weaker the performance, the less of an influence the prey has on the position update for this set. The search agent has a better probability of escaping from the local optimum if the present target has been identified as such. As a result, the AIW technique improves the team's search capabilities and allows them to avoid early convergence. The present agent's fitness is used in conjunction with a mapping function to establish the precise AIW solution. The gap between fitness and AIW may be bridged using a modified Versoria function. It has a nonlinear curve and less processing cost than sigmoid functions and other nonlinear mapping functions with comparable shapes. Adaptive particle swarm optimization (AWPSO) is one area where it has been put to good use. To express w(t) using the tweaked Versoria mapping function, we get Eq. (15).

$$w_i(t) = \begin{cases} 1 - \dfrac{1}{\left(\varphi.\left(a_i(t) - \dfrac{1}{2}\right)^2 + 2\right)} \; if a_i(t) \leq 0.5 \\ \dfrac{1}{\left(\varphi.\left(a_i(t) - 1/2\right)^2 + 2\right)} \; otherwise \end{cases} \tag{15}$$

where $a_i(t), a_i(t) \in [0,1]$ characterizes the all agents among the regular fitness, which is labelled as Eq. (16), and ϕ is a regulation constant set to 300 in following trials.

$$f_{ave}(t) = \sum_{i=1}^{N_p} f_i(t) / N_p$$

$$f_{min}(t) = min\{f_1(t), f_2(t), \ldots, f_{Np}(t)\}$$

$$a_i(t) = \left(f_i(t) - f_{min}(t)\right) / \left(f_{ave}(t) - f_{min}(t)\right) \tag{16}$$

where $f_i(t)$ means the t repetition; $f_{ave}(t)$ and $f_{min}(t)$ signify the regular value and least worth of all N_p size populaces' fitness.

The Formation of EWOA

To create EWOA, to include the IDOL tactic into AIWWOA. The EWOA IDOL is crucial to the operations of population seeding and generation skipping. The best group may be chosen using the greedy rule by comparing the IDOL-generated group's fitness to that of the original group.

IDOL Initialization

The starting population is formed in a completely arbitrary manner. After the accidental loading of X_(i,j) as specified by Eq. (17), the IDOL mode-one is used to create a better initial population to union degree; this DOL's asymmetric reconstruction space..

$$X_{i,j}^{IDOL} = X_{i,j} + r_i^3 \left(r_i^4 X_{i,j}^O - X_{i,j} \right) \tag{17}$$

where i=1,2,…,N_p is the populace size, j=1,2,…,D is the breadth of agents, r_1 and r_2 are random statistics in (0,1), and $X_{i,j}^O$ is site of $X_{i,j}$ inside space. If the updated agent goes outside the interval after the IDOL initialization procedure, a random location inside the interval must be generated for them.

$$X_{i,j}^{IDOL} = rand\left(a_j, b_j\right), ifX_{i,j}^{IDOL} \left\langle a_j \right\| X_{i,j}^{IDOL} \rangle b_j \tag{18}$$

where a_j and b_j are limits of search space. Afterward the random loading and IDOL loading, N_p fittest go-betweens are designated from $X \cup X^{IDOL}$.

Improvement by AIW

The WOA is enhanced by the AIW, which uses Eq. (14) to inform the sites of go-betweens in phase. This equation comprises the key factor: $w_i(t)$, presented in Eq. (15).

IDOL Generation Jumping

The ideal solution's updating situation is taken into account when switching to the appropriate IDOL mode during the creation of the WOA algorithm. In order for the algorithm to discover a better solution, this extra group operation may result in more precise junction or selection mutation to further boost population variety.

IDOL allows for the population to be refreshed at each cycle. Which IDOL mode is really carried out is decided by the convergence state parameter (J). In order to create the hopping process in an optimal manner, as specified by Eq. (19), the IDOL is used.

$$X_{i,j}^{IDOL} = \begin{cases} X_{i,j} + r_i^3\left(r_i^4\left(a_j + b_j - X_{i,j}\right) - X_{i,j}\right) if mode > 0 \\ X_{i,j}^{rand} - r_i^5 s_i\left(X_{i,j}^{rand} - X_{i,j}\right) otherwise \end{cases} \quad (19)$$

where $X_{i,j}^{rand}$ is a randomly designated discrete at the present cohort (i=1,2,…,N_p, j=1,2,…,D), $[a_j, b_j]$ is space of jth dimension, r_i^3, r_i^4, r_i^5 symbolize random statistics among (0,1), and s_i is a chance vector produced by Eq. (11). Arbitrarily choice a mode at the commencement Eq. (20) initially, mode = −mode if $J>T$ when spreads the threshold.

mode= sign(rant(0,1) – 0.5) (20)

After IDOL, the limits of the search space are adjusted using Eq. (21) to boost IDOL's performance.

$$a_j = min\left\{X_{i,j}, X_{2,j}, \ldots, X_{Np,j}\right\}$$

$$b_j = max\left\{X_{i,j}, X_{2,j}, \ldots, X_{Np,j}\right\} \quad (21)$$

Finally, N_p better those will be selected from $X \cup X^{IDOL}$. After using the projected model, the weight deterioration is set to 1×10–4. The early set to 3×10–4. The default batch size is 20. There will be 350 epochs. To prevent the model from being over-fit, we implement an early halting mechanism. After 18 iterations, training is terminated routinely if the minimal loss difference has stabilized.

RESULTS AND DISCUSSION

Experiments were performed on a reduced dataset of Urdu natural scenes with the goal of demonstrating the efficacy of the suggested approaches for text recognition. The studies used the free and open-source TensorFlow framework written in the Python programming language, and were run on an NVIDIA GeForce GTX memory.

Evaluation Metrics

Scene text recognition systems have traditionally been evaluated using two metrics: a character-level metric, measured a rate. The latter measure is more stringent since it only marks a prediction as true if it properly identifies each label. When evaluating CRR, however, the truth text is used as the evaluation metric, with the smallest distance being the best. Given that the suggested techniques for cropped Urdu text credit need no segmentation, the CRR was used to evaluate how well cropped word recognition performed.

$$CRR = \frac{N_{char} - \sum ED(P_T, G_T)}{N_{char}} \times 100\% \tag{22}$$

where N_{char} is the sum of typescripts, ED distance, P_T and G_T are the foretold text tags and the ground truth text tags, correspondingly.

The presentation of word gratitude was assessed in WRR as

$$WRR = \frac{N_{cword}}{N_{word}} \times 100\% \tag{23}$$

where N_{cword} is the total sum of test set, whereas the sum of successfully identified words is. It was shown that the WRR does not conduct a fair assessment of the suggested technique, because it considers a huge sum of recognized words erroneous if a single properly. Therefore, in this research, examined using a different statistic to assess WRR.

$$WRR_{1F} = \frac{N_{cword} + N_{1F}}{N_{word}} \times 100\% \tag{24}$$

where N1F is the total number of false-character-free words that were recognized. The assessment metric treats the term as correct even if it misidentifies a single character. If it detects more than one erroneous character, the whole word is rejected. Tables 1 and 2 show the average results obtained after applying our dataset to established methods like LSTM [17,18], RNN [17,18, 21], and CNN [23,22,21,19].

In above Table 1 signifies that the Text recognition accuracy comparison for 80%-20%. In the analysis of CNN model reached the CRR (%) as 91.35 and the WRR (%) rate as 73.40 and also finally the WRR1F (%) asc85.39 respectively. Then the RNN model reached the CRR (%) as 93.61 and the WRR (%) rate as 84.26 and also

Table 1. Text recognition accuracy comparison for 80%-20%

Models	CRR (%)	WRR (%)	WRR_{IF} (%)
CNN	91.35	73.40	85.39
RNN	93.61	84.26	90.82
LSTM	93.83	86.05	92.41
DSSAC-RSC	95.63	89.47	94.30

finally the WRR1F (%) as 90.82 respectively. Then the LSTM model reached the CRR (%) as 93.83cand the WRR (%) rate as 86.05cand also finally the WRR1F (%) as 92.41 respectively. Then the DSSAC-RSC model reached the CRR (%) asc95.63 and the WRR (%) rate as 89.47 and also finally the WRR1F (%) as 94.30 respectively.

Results of Deep Learning Models with DOL-WOA are shown in Table 2 above. The CNN perfect attained an accuracy as 86.23, an F-measure rate of 83.50, a sensitivity range of 86.20, and finally a precision range of 82.80 in the analysis of a 70% Train- 30% Test ratio. The RNN model then achieved accuracy of 84.74, F-measure rate of 84.20, F-measure rate of 84.40, and finally precision range of 83.90, respectively. Following that, the LSTM model achieved an accuracy of 92.06, an F-measure rate of 90, an F-measure rate of 92.10, and finally a precision range of 89.60. The DSSAC-RSC model then achieved an accuracy of 96.49, an F-measure

Figure 5. Analysis of Projected Perfect with Existing Procedures

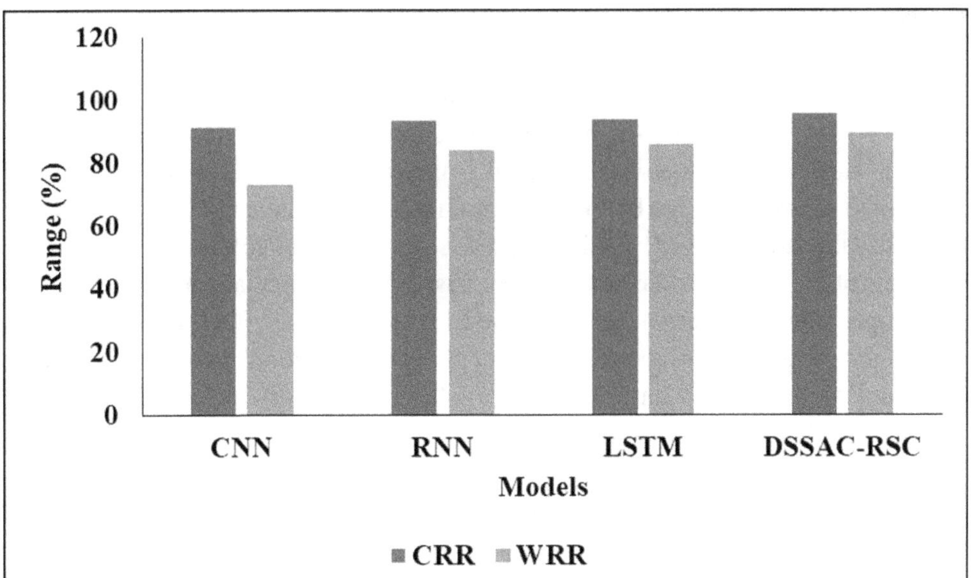

Table 2. Results of deep learning models with DOL-WOA

	Model	AC (%)	F-M (%)	S (%)	P (%)
70% Train- 30% Test	CNN	86.23	83.50	86.20	82.80
	RNN	84.74	84.20	84.40	83.90
	LSTM	92.06	90.80	92.10	89.60
	DSSAC-RSC	**96.49**	**96.50**	**96.50**	**96.50**
60% Train-40%Test	CNN	86.89	84.30	86.90	83.70
	RNN	84.93	84.50	84.90	84.20
	LSTM	92.12	90.90	92.10	89.70
	DSSAC-RSC	**95.86**	**95.80**	**95.90**	**95.80**

rate of 96.50, an F-measure degree of 96.50, and lastly a precision range of 96.50, all in the respective ranges. The CNN model then achieved an accuracy of 86.89, an F-measure rate of 84.30, 86.90, and finally a precision range of 83.70 using a 60% Train-40% Test ratio. The RNN model then achieved an accuracy of 84.93, a precision range of 84.20, an F-measure rate of 84.90, and so forth. The LSTM model then achieved accuracy of 92.12, F-measure rate of 90.90, F-measure rate of 92.10, and precision range of 89.70, respectively. The DSSAC-RSC model then achieved an accuracy of 95.86, an F-measure rate of 95.80 and 95.90, and a precision range of 95.80, respectively.

CONCLUSION

Text recognition techniques were offered in this research for cropped images of Urdu words. To solve the issue of manually segmenting each letter in a word picture, a segmentation-free technique was presented. In this study, propose using a DSSAC-RSC network to segment cursive Urdu handwritten images. Reduced training parameters and loss value are achieved by using depthwise divisible convolution to separate the channels of the mapped convolution layer based on their spatial correlation against their appearance correlation. In order to reduce the negative effects of poor contrast and uneven brightness, introduce the concept of dense residual blocks into DSSAC-RSC and use full-scale skip influences to stabilize the loss in the deep network. DSSAC-RSC makes use of the active perfect to reduce the effects of picture noise and edge slits, to bring about distortion tracking, to lecture the issue of edge blur, and to ultimately enhance the precision of the segmentation process. A fresh dataset of clipped Urdu scene text was created for the purpose of evaluating the offered approaches. This dataset was created to recognize Urdu text in real-world settings

Figure 6. Validation analysis of proposed model with existing techniques

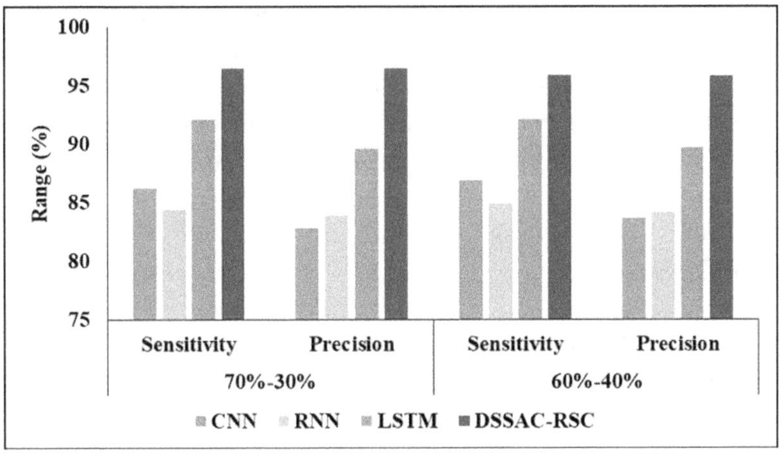

for the first time. All potential text variants, handwritten writing, are included in the collection of 14100 Urdu word pictures. The suggested technique with shortcut connections outdone all previous models, with a 95% CRR, 89.47% WRR, and 94.30% WRR1F. The offered solutions still have significant flaws due to the intricacy of the languages represented by cursive scripts. Using a language model with

Figure 7. Graphical analysis of various DL models

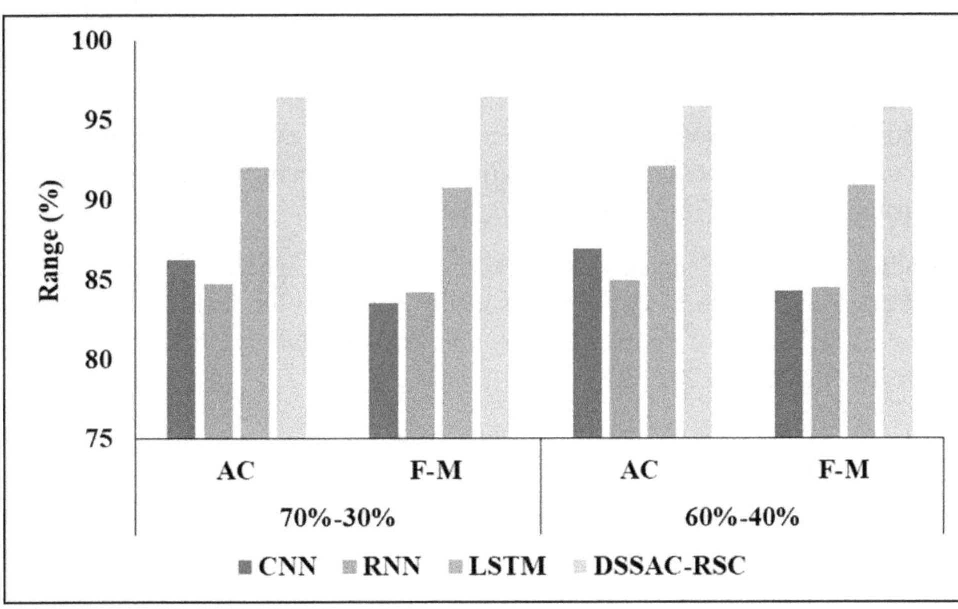

linguistic information can help reduce these recognition problems. Improved Urdu text recognition in the future depends on the application of attention and transformer approaches. Moreover, will create a model for simultaneous recognition of Urdu text in natural acts. Explore the use of pre-trained models on large handwriting datasets or general text recognition datasets. Fine-tune these models on the specific task of Urdu Cursive Word Recognition to leverage transfer learning.

REFERENCES

Aarif, K. O., & Sivakumar, P. (2022). Multi-Domain Deep Convolutional Neural Network for Ancient Urdu Text Recognition System. *Intelligent Automation & Soft Computing*, *33*(1).

Ahmed, G., Alyas, T., Iqbal, M. W., Ashraf, M. U., Alghamdi, A. M., Bahaddad, A. A., & Almarhabi, K. A. (2022). Recognition of Urdu Handwritten Alphabet Using Convolutional Neural Network (CNN). *Computers, Materials & Continua*, *73*(2), 2967–2984. doi:10.32604/cmc.2022.029314

Arafat, S. Y., Ashraf, N., Iqbal, M. J., Ahmad, I., Khan, S., & Rodrigues, J. J. (2022). Urdu signboard detection and recognition using deep learning. *Multimedia Tools and Applications*, *81*(9), 1–23. doi:10.1007/s11042-020-10175-2

Bhatti, A., Arif, A., Khalid, W., Khan, B., Ali, A., Khalid, S., & Rehman, A. U. (2023). Recognition and classification of handwritten urdu numerals using deep learning techniques. *Applied Sciences (Basel, Switzerland)*, *13*(3), 1624. doi:10.3390/app13031624

Butt, M. A., Ul-Hasan, A., & Shafait, F. 2022, May. Traffsign: Multilingual traffic signboard text detection and recognition for urdu and english. In *International Workshop on Document Analysis Systems* (pp. 741-755). Cham: Springer International Publishing. 10.1007/978-3-031-06555-2_50

Chandio, A. A., Asikuzzaman, M. D., Pickering, M. R., & Leghari, M. (2022). Cursive text recognition in natural scene images using deep convolutional recurrent neural network. *IEEE Access : Practical Innovations, Open Solutions*, *10*, 10062–10078. doi:10.1109/ACCESS.2022.3144844

Chen, X., Williams, B. M., Vallabhaneni, S. R., Czanner, G., Williams, R., & Zheng, Y. (2019). Learning active contour models for medical image segmentation. *Proc. IEEE/CVF Conf. Comput. Vis. Pattern Recognit. (CVPR)*. IEEE. 10.1109/CVPR.2019.01190

ChoK.van MerrienboerB.GulcehreC.BahdanauD.BougaresF.SchwenkH.BengioY. (2014). *Learning phrase representations using RNN encoder-decoder for statistical machine translation*. arXiv:1406.1078. http://arxiv.org/abs/1406.1078 doi:10.3115/v1/D14-1179

Chollet, F. (2017). Xception: Deep learning with depthwise separable convolutions. *Proc. IEEE Conf. Comput. Vis. Pattern Recognit. (CVPR)*. IEEE. 10.1109/CVPR.2017.195

Glorot, X., Bordes, A., & Bengio, Y. (2011). Deep sparse rectifier neural networks. *Proc. 14th Int. Conf. Artif. Intell. Statist.*

Huang, Z., & Cao, L. (2020). Bicubic interpolation and extrapolation iteration method for high resolution digital holographic reconstruction. *Optics and Lasers in Engineering*, *130*(Jul), 106090. doi:10.1016/j.optlaseng.2020.106090

Kashif, M. (2021). *Urdu Handwritten Text Recognition Using ResNet18*. arXiv preprint arXiv:2103.05105.

Khan, H. R., Hasan, M. A., Kazmi, M., Fayyaz, N., Khalid, H., & Qazi, S. A. (2021). A holistic approach to Urdu language word recognition using deep neural networks. Engineering, Technology &. *Applied Scientific Research*, *11*(3), 7140–7145.

Lin, T.-Y., Dollar, P., Girshick, R., He, K., Hariharan, B., & Belongie, S. (2017). Feature pyramid networks for object detection. *Proc. IEEE Conf. Comput. Vis. Pattern Recognit. (CVPR)*. IEEE. 10.1109/CVPR.2017.106

Misgar, M. M., Mushtaq, F., Khurana, S. S., & Kumar, M. (2023). Recognition of offline handwritten Urdu characters using RNN and LSTM models. *Multimedia Tools and Applications*, *82*(2), 2053–2076. doi:10.1007/s11042-022-13320-1

Narwani, K., Lin, H., Pirbhulal, S., & Hassan, M. (2022). Towards AI-enabled approach for urdu text recognition: A legacy for urdu image apprehension. *IEEE Access : Practical Innovations, Open Solutions*.

Nasir, T., Malik, M. K., & Shahzad, K. (2021). MMU-OCR-21: Towards end-to-end Urdu text recognition using deep learning. *IEEE Access : Practical Innovations, Open Solutions*, *9*, 124945–124962. doi:10.1109/ACCESS.2021.3110787

Rahman, A., Ghosh, A., & Arora, C. (2023). UTRNet: High-Resolution Urdu Text Recognition In Printed Documents. arXiv preprint arXiv:2306.15782. doi:10.1007/978-3-031-41734-4_19

Rashid, D., & Kumar Gondhi, N. (2022). Scrutinization of Urdu handwritten text recognition with machine learning approach. In *International Conference on Emerging Technologies in Computer Engineering* (pp. 383-394). Cham: Springer International Publishing. 10.1007/978-3-031-07012-9_33

Rehman, A., Ul-Hasan, A., & Shafait, F. (2021). High performance Urdu and Arabic video text recognition using convolutional recurrent neural networks. In *Document Analysis and Recognition–ICDAR 2021 Workshops: Lausanne, Switzerland*. Springer International Publishing.

Riaz, N., Arbab, H., Maqsood, A., Nasir, K., Ul-Hasan, A., & Shafait, F. (2022). Conv-transformer architecture for unconstrained off-line Urdu handwriting recognition. [IJDAR]. *International Journal on Document Analysis and Recognition*, *25*(4), 373–384. doi:10.1007/s10032-022-00416-5

Shafi, M., & Zia, K. (2021). Urdu character recognition: A systematic literature review. *International Journal of Applied Pattern Recognition*, *6*(4), 283–307. doi:10.1504/IJAPR.2021.118914

Thirumalraj, A., Asha, V., & Kavin, B. P. (2023). An Improved Hunter-Prey Optimizer-Based DenseNet Model for Classification of Hyper-Spectral Images. In AI and IoT-Based Technologies for Precision Medicine (pp. 76-96). IGI Global. doi:10.4018/979-8-3693-0876-9.ch005

Tian, Z., He, T., Shen, C., & Yan, Y. (2019). Decoders matter for semantic segmentation: Data-dependent decoding enables flexible feature aggregation. *Proc. IEEE/CVF Conf. Comput. Vis. Pattern Recognit. (CVPR)*. IEEE. 10.1109/CVPR.2019.00324

Umair, M., Zubair, M., Dawood, F., Ashfaq, S., Bhatti, M. S., Hijji, M., & Sohail, A. (2022). A Multi-Layer Holistic Approach for Cursive Text Recognition. *Applied Sciences (Basel, Switzerland)*, *12*(24), 12652. doi:10.3390/app122412652

Yang, X., & Jiang, X. (2020, January). A hybrid active contour model based on new edgestop functions for image segmentation. *International Journal of Ambient Computing and Intelligence*, *11*(1), 87–98. doi:10.4018/IJACI.2020010105

Zahid, H., Rashid, M., Hussain, S., Azim, F., Syed, S. A., & Saad, A. (2022). Recognition of Urdu sign language: A systematic review of the machine learning classification. *PeerJ. Computer Science*, *8*, e883. doi:10.7717/peerj-cs.883 PMID:35494799

ZargarH.KóczyL. T. (2023). Handwritten Urdu Character Recognition and Comparative Analysis with Popular Machine Learning Algorithms. Available at SSRN 4461891. doi:10.2139/ssrn.4461891

Zhang, Y., Tian, Y., Kong, Y., Zhong, B., & Fu, Y. (2018). Residual dense network for image super-resolution. *Proc. IEEE/CVF Conf. Comput. Vis. Pattern Recognit.* IEEE. 10.1109/CVPR.2018.00262

Zhang, Z., Wu, C., Coleman, S., & Kerr, D. (2020). DENSE-INception U-net for medical image segmentation. *Computer Methods and Programs in Biomedicine*, *192*(Aug), 105395. doi:10.1016/j.cmpb.2020.105395 PMID:32163817

Zia, S., Azhar, M., Lee, B., Tahir, A., Ferzund, J., Murtaza, F., & Ali, M. (2023). Recognition of printed Urdu script in Nastaleeq font by using CNN-BiGRU-GRU Based Encoder-Decoder Framework. *Intelligent Systems with Applications*, *18*, 200194. doi:10.1016/j.iswa.2023.200194

Zubair, M., Umair, M., Alhussein, M., Hussain, H. A., Aurangzeb, K., & Asghar, M. N. (2023). *Scene Character Recognition from Cursive Text Using Deep Learning Models.*

Chapter 9
Shattering the Glass Ceiling of Women Entrepreneurship in the Digital Retail Landscape

Pallavi Mishra
https://orcid.org/0000-0002-8315-8473
Amity University, India

Tanushri Mukherjee
Amity University, India

ABSTRACT

With its unprecedented ability to harness collective intelligence Web 2.0 has ushered possibilities in digital entrepreneurship. Digital entrepreneurship has occupied an indispensable place in the business industry as it has a dynamic approach to engross customers on online platforms and to promote their products and services. Over the years, access to digital technology has played a major role in empowering women to do business.The famous women entrepreneurs of Nykaa, Zivame, Limeroad and Sugar Cosmetics have paved a way for entrepreneurial development that features each kind of new digital business, and an analysis of how those traits determine the success factors of women entrepreneurship. In the panorama of entrepreneurship, the function of women has been evolving step by step over the years. One place wherein their effect has been specifically noteworthy is virtual media entrepreneurship. This chapter delves into the arena of girls' entrepreneurs within the virtual media area, brands like Nykaa, Zivame, Limeroad and SUGAR Cosmetics.

DOI: 10.4018/979-8-3693-0790-8.ch009

INTRODUCTION

Web 2.0 has opened new business opportunities due to its unmatched capacity to leverage collective knowledge. The government and non-profit organizations are currently implementing performance management systems based on internationally recognized monitoring and evaluation (M&E) frameworks. The transformations are driven by technology and are inextricably linked to a firm that is navigating digital entrepreneurship. Digital entrepreneurship is the creation of a new enterprise using unique digital technology or the novel use of such technologies. It is a convergence of technology and business in which firms want to have a massive global effect; technology uses digitalization and artificial intelligence to improve the quality of choices and spread their business as well as customer operations. The introduction of Web 2.0 cleared the door for holistic and integrative digital entrepreneurship; it emphasizes a digital ecosystem from various angles, developing a conceptual model of a social network, digital capital, and institutional framework. Social media and new digital technologies are frequently utilized in the digital arena to connect people all over the world with their fresh inventive ideas. For example, Mark Zuckerberg is a digital entrepreneur who generates digital wealth through the Facebook platform. By dissolving boundaries, social media has developed as a business for entrepreneurs to connect internationally and make income. Technology is used by digital businesses to innovate business models, customer experiences, and internal capabilities that support essential functions. The term refers to both digital-only players and traditional players who use digital technologies to conduct business. Through a multidimensional communication paradigm, social media provides a forum for entrepreneurs to share their ideas and get feedback. Traditional entrepreneurship is also establishing a presence on Internet platforms to increase the intensity of the business. Because of the viability of digital platforms, new approaches and technologies are being developed. The primary distinction between digital and conventional entrepreneurship is both tangible and intangible. If a new company delivers a digital product, it may see certain differences in client responses. (M. Rezvani, 2018). The rise of female entrepreneurs symbolizes the dawn of a new age. If we look back at the history of female entrepreneurs, it was not what it is now. In many nations before the twentieth century, women were not regarded as members of the commercial industry or as sources of augmenting income.

The emergence of women entrepreneurs marks a transitional period, reflecting a significant shift in historical norms. In the landscape of women working in business was very different, especially before the twentieth century. The social consciousness of the time often relegated women to non-commercial roles, and their potential to contribute significantly to economic development was often overlooked.

The business industry has witnessed a drastic transformation that has moved on, and women are increasingly recognized as awesome contributors to the world of activism. Not only are these changes a sign of progress, but they also signal the breaking down of barriers that once kept women from having limited influence.

In contemporary society, professional women play an important role in creating businesses, innovating and challenging traditional ideas. Empowering women in business is not just about financial success; It is a testament to the resilience, creativity and leadership skills women bring to the table.

As we celebrate the rise of women entrepreneurs, we acknowledge their achievements in creating an inclusive and diverse work environment. These changes are not only reshaping jobs but contributing to a more equitable and vibrant global economy The beginning of this new era signals not only economic growth but a major social shift in realizing and harnessing the potential of all individuals functionally, regardless of gender.

In terms of the economy and trade, women were mostly in charge of running the home, and their work as housewives was inefficient. Similar to how the term "entrepreneur" was previously only used to refer to men, women have gradually made their way up the occupational ladder from domestic work to the highest positions with the developments in technology, growing industrialization, globalisation, and social norms. Women have successfully broken down all barriers and advanced in all facets of life at home and at work in recent years, proving that they are also equal in the business world. Recent surveys have shown that women use social media more frequently than males, with 71% of women using it compared to 62% of men. On the other hand, technology was once thought to be a male-dominated field, but times have changed, and women are now active on the same level as men. There are hundreds of examples from successful women, including Sheryl Sandberg, the CEO of Facebook, and Marissa Maya, the president and SEO of Yahoo (Entrepreneur, 2016). E-commerce has enabled numerous Indian entrepreneurs to launch their firms.

In the panorama of entrepreneurship, the function of women has been evolving step by step over the years. One place wherein their effect has been specifically noteworthy is virtual media entrepreneurship. This chapter delves into the arena of girls' entrepreneurs within the virtual media area, brands like Nykaa, Zivame, Limeroad and SUGAR Cosmetics. These organizations have not only disrupted traditional industries but additionally inspired limitless girls to challenge the virtual landscape.

Women entrepreneurs are sometimes referred to as "survivalists," as they dominate low-skill, low-capital-intensive, and frequently informal micro businesses. Women are more likely to concentrate on businesses that are a logical outgrowth of their domestic pursuits, like the service sector. The potential for growth of women-owned enterprises is outlined below, and it is driven less by lofty goals and more by the need to survive. Women make up 74% of people working in the microenterprise sector. More than 65 percent of the women working in cottage handicraft enterprises (micro-businesses) processed food and drinks. Women account for about half of the world's population. As a result, increasing women's socioeconomic engagement at the global, regional, national, and local levels entails successfully using enormous potential resources (Kumar, 2016).

THE PERSONIFICATION OF WOMEN ENTREPRENEURS IN INDIA

Women dominate the microenterprise industry of India, including both rural and urban regions. According to the official statistics office, women manage about 70% of all micro and small businesses in India. Women play a variety of roles in society, especially when participating in constructive activities like agriculture, trade, and industry; they are responsible for caring for the family, including food preparation, health care, and education; however, their contribution to small, medium, and large businesses is declining. Women make up a bigger proportion of India's informal sector operators, as well as those running micro and small businesses (Brush, Henry, & J. Gatewood, 2010). The increasing number of female company owners is a contemporary global trend, particularly in emerging nations. Women hold more than 25% of all businesses in sophisticated market economies. Despite widespread belief that women are "pushed" into business ownership rather than "drawn" to it, recent research indicates that many women, particularly younger women, actively prefer to work for themselves. However, there is little in the way of statistical or analytical data to have a deeper understanding of women's experience as business owners, their contribution to economic development, or the challenges they face in starting, running, and expanding their business. As a result, this contribution is not fully acknowledged or understood. Women make up 74% of people working in the microenterprise sector. More than 65 percent of the women working in cottage handicraft enterprises (micro-businesses) processed food and drinks (Chakraborti, Dasgupta, & Jana, 2002).

CONCEPTUAL FRAMEWORK OF WOMEN ENTREPRENEURS IN DIGITAL AGE

The conceptual framework reflects the evolution of women in entrepreneurship, starting from traditional roles and barriers to the opportunities presented by the digital age. It highlights various factors influencing women's entrepreneurial journey,

Table 1. Traditional age challenges and digital age opportunities for women

Traditional Age challenges for Women Entrepreneurs	Digital Age opportunities for Women Entrepreneurs
Gender Bias & Discrimination	Access to Digital Imfrastructure and Skills Development
Entrepreneurial Challenges	Digital Marketing and Branding strategies
Supportive Policies	Networking & Collaboration
Empowerment	Impact & Success

including gender bias, access to digital infrastructure and skills, entrepreneurial challenges, supportive policies, empowerment, and the impact and success achieved by women entrepreneurs. Each aspect interacts with and influences the others, shaping the overall landscape of women entrepreneurship. These encompass patterns of gender bias, the availability of digital resources and abilities, hurdles faced in entrepreneurship, helpful policies, empowerment.

CHALLENGES AND TRIUMPHS OF WOMEN ENTREPRENEURS

Women entrepreneurs often face difficulties in accessing capital to start and scale their digital retail businesses as the digital retail landscape is highly competitive, with numerous established players. Breaking into the market and differentiating a new business can be tough for women entrepreneurs but women entrepreneurs often bring fresh and innovative perspectives to the digital retail industry, leading to the development of unique business models and products that resonate with consumers. Women in digital retail have established strong communities and networks to support one another. These networks provide valuable resources, mentorship, and partnerships. Some women entrepreneurs have excelled by targeting specific niches or underserved markets, allowing them to establish a strong presence and loyal customer base. Women-led businesses have successfully expanded their reach globally through online platforms, reaching customers beyond their local markets. Therefore, women entrepreneurs in the digital retail industry face a range of challenges, but their resilience, innovation, and collaborative efforts have enabled them to overcome these obstacles and achieve remarkable successes. Their contributions to the industry continue to grow, fostering a more diverse and inclusive digital retail landscape (Dhameja, 2002).

RISE OF WOMEN IN DIGITAL MEDIA ENTREPRENEURSHIP

Women marketers have traditionally faced various boundaries, from unequal get entry to investment to societal expectations. However, the virtual generation has supplied them with unparalleled possibilities for business ownership and innovation. Nykaa and Zivame exemplify this shift, as they were based with the aid of Falguni Nayar and Richa Kar, respectively, two girls who saw ability in the e-commerce and splendour sectors.

As time passed, several definitions of the topic emerged as a result of new advances and technology introduced into modern life. Like other areas, entrepreneurship has become a vast topic, with some institutions teaching the issue in four semesters to students of various grades for them to become self-sufficient and generate more employment, as well as learn how to be a good leader among groups. We will focus on the most recent and up-to-date information because there are numerous definitions for the terms themselves. The term was taken from the French verb “Entrenprendre”, which refers “to undertake” and Richart Cantillon was the first to use it in his 1970 manuscript. A significant portion of entrepreneurship research has concentrated on the economic importance and risk of entrepreneurship. Women’s entrepreneurial potential may be fully realised, resulting in increased innovation, economic growth, and job creation. This brief has detailed the current scenario in India and outlined the factors that contribute to the country’s female entrepreneurship rate. Overcoming these hurdles requires individual women’s tenacity and desire, as well as addressing structural elements in the external environment over which they have little influence. Firstly, the low rates of female entrepreneurship are part of a larger gender gap in economic involvement and opportunity therefore policies targeted at increasing the number of women in senior and leadership roles are required. These policies will assist women in obtaining experience and expertise, allowing them to establish their own enterprises. Second, it is necessary to increase awareness about unconscious prejudices and how they harm women entrepreneurs. Women entrepreneurs must cope with unfavourable perceptions since changing mindsets takes time. Sharing their success stories on social and conventional media gives younger female entrepreneurs hope and proof that business can be a woman’s world as well, boosting their confidence. Third, women entrepreneurs in India require improved access to capital and networks. NITI Aayog’s Women Entrepreneurship Platform plays a role of Catalyst for Women Entrepreneurship, and Zone Start-ups, India’s accelerator for women in technology, are just a few of the groups that promote women entrepreneurs. Fourth, to assist in retaining skilled women, more inclusive, non-discriminatory, and safe work environments are required, particularly in the technology sector. Measures to increase the safety of public areas are required so that women can move between their homes and offices without the emotional burden of always worrying about their safety. Fifth, to follow their entrepreneurial aspirations, women entrepreneurs require additional support from their families and social networks. Household and care giving responsibilities should not be viewed as only the duty of women. Achieving wider development goals, such as growth with equity, depends on the entrepreneurship development of women. Especially contrasted with its male colleagues, research shows that many women entrepreneurs labour in tough settings. Many cultures believe that the job of women is to establish and maintain the house, such as fetching water, cooking, and raising children. Women's standing in India has been evolving since turn of the century as a result of increasing industry, globalisation, and social regulation. Indeed, women entrepreneurs will contribute to economic advancement. Women are currently working in a variety of occupations, including those related to trade, industry, and engineering. Women are likewise eager to start businesses and participate to the progress of the country. Their importance is being acknowledged, and initiatives are being done to encourage female entrepreneurship (Rai, 2019). The epidemic has been difficult for small companies, particularly those owned by women." At the same time, data from our applications revealed that women had shown exceptional resilience, leadership, and positivity throughout these trying times. In 2020, women launched twice as many fundraisers on Facebook as men and received twice as many donations, accounting for 64% of all funds raised. "Women have also led the way in building communities and mobilising resources, forming 2.7x more COVID-19-related groups than males and having four times the number of members." Most significantly, despite obstacles and uncertainty, women continued to launch businesses. 20% of Instagram Business accounts created since November 2020 include the phrase "female/women owned," (Balakrishnan, 2021). Both urban and rural areas have experienced an increase in job losses and unemployment as a result of COVID-19 second wave, with semi-urban and rural areas seeing much more severe pandemic aftereffects than urban areas. According to Bain and Company research, COVID-19 had a negative impact on over 73% of women-owned businesses in India, while revenue for nearly 20% of women entrepreneurs plummeted to zero. Customer demand has been muted, supply lines have been disrupted, and a lack of financial resources has resulted in the closure of an increasing number of women-led businesses. In fact, according to our latest Udyam Stree campaign study, 57% of women entrepreneurs have seen a decline in their business since April 2020, resulting in a loss of revenue streams. Furthermore, firms that rely on offline forms of manufacturing and distribution have suffered considerably higher losses than those that use digital channels (Nagma, 2021). The cosmetics industry has attracted numerous businesses due to its rapid growth. A well-known business in the cosmetics industry is Nykaa. It offers a range of products from many businesses on the same platform. In 2012, Falguni Nayar started it. She

Table 2. E-Commerce sites for women entrepreneurs

E-Commerce sites Women Entrepreneurs dealing women products	
Zivame	**Diverse Lingerie Products**
Nykaa	**Extensive Beauty Products**
Limeroad	**Fashion Clothing**
Sugar Cosmetics	**Wide Cosmetic Products**

identified an important future potential for online trading and developed a broad vision around that prospect (Wagman-Geller, 2018).

The chapter underlines four major E-commerce sites Zivame, Nykaa, Limeroad, and Sugar Cosmetics as women entrepreneurs are playing a vital role in selling women-oriented products.

Business Model of Nykaa

Nykaa operates as a multi-brand online beauty store in India, offering a wide range of cosmetics, skin care, hair care, fitness products. The company business model encapsulates e-commerce platform, where customers can browse and purchase beauty and wellness products. They offer a wide range of products from different brands that cater to different customer preferences. Nykaa offers beauty services through its Nykaa Luxe store and Nykaa on trend kiosks. These services include makeup, skincare consultations, and more. Revenue is generated through service fees and sales of beauty products used in these businesses (Gupta, 2018).

Nykaa Network is a content-driven platform of beauty tutorials, product reviews and news. While the platform doesn't generate direct revenue, it does help build brands, drive customer engagement and e-commerce sales.

Nykaa, India's leading beauty and wellness e-commerce platform, has employed several effective marketing strategies to establish its strong presence in the market. Nykaa has a user-friendly and visually appealing website and mobile app, providing customers with an easy and convenient shopping experience. Nykaa has introduced its own private-label products, which are marketed as high-quality and competitively priced alternatives to popular brands. These products help improve margins and promote brand loyalty. The Nykaa Network is a content-rich platform featuring beauty tutorials, product reviews, and articles. This content not only educates and engages customers but also enhances Nykaa's brand image as a beauty expert. Nykaa's marketing strategies blend these elements to create a dynamic and adaptable approach that resonates with its target audience, fosters brand loyalty, and positions the company

Figure 1. NYKAA marketing strategies

as a leader in the beauty and wellness industry in India. This customer-centric and digitally savvy approach has played a pivotal role in Nykaa's remarkable success.

Nykaa's success is attributed in part to its effective omnichannel marketing strategy, which seamlessly integrates various marketing channels to enhance the customer experience.

Social Media Engagement: Nykaa maintains a strong presence on social media platforms like Instagram, Facebook, and YouTube. Here's how Nykaa effectively utilizes social media platforms like Instagram, Facebook, and YouTube. Nykaa frequently showcases its products through eye-catching visuals and videos on Instagram, Facebook, and YouTube. They leverage these platforms to announce new product launches, seasonal promotions, and limited time offers. engages with its audience by posting content that encourages interaction. This includes asking questions, running polls, and hosting giveaways. They respond promptly to comments and messages, fostering a sense of community and customer loyalty.

Influencer Partnerships: Nykaa collaborates with beauty influencers and makeup artists on Instagram and YouTube. These influencers create content, tutorials, and reviews featuring Nykaa products, which helps reach a wider and more targeted audience. Nykaa, has strategically used influencer partnerships to strengthen its presence in the digital landscape by working with social media influencers, beauticians and makeup artists, Nykaa has leveraged the power of online marketing and engagement has been successfully implemented. These connections allow Nykaa to reach a broad and diverse audience, while also benefiting from the credibility and authenticity that influencers bring to the table by partnering with influencers and their target demographics so over the years, it has successfully built a buzz around their products, providing users with the content and sense of community they adored and not as this approach gave them brand recognition. Nykaa's groundbreaking partnership exemplifies the constant evolution of digital marketing in the beauty industry, where authenticity and communication play a key role in attracting and retaining customers.

Interactive Stories: Nykaa has embraced interactive content as a creative and engaging way to connect with its customers. Through this interactive content, Nykaa provides users with an immersive experience that blends entertainment with aesthetic education. Users can explore a variety of beauty-related topics, from skincare routines to medical advice, all while interacting with the content in an engaging and informative way. This interactive content is not only a valuable resource for beauty enthusiasts but also allows Nykaa to showcase its wide range of products in a contextual manner. By promoting a dynamic and interactive online environment, Nykaa engages its audience, promotes user engagement and strengthens its position as a digital leader in the beauty industry.

Content Marketing Strategies: Nykaa has excelled in the realm of content marketing, setting a high standard in the beauty and cosmetics industry. Through its well-curated blog posts, videos, social media content, and expert articles, Nykaa consistently delivers valuable and informative content to its audience. This content isn't solely focused on product promotion but extends to beauty tips, tutorials, and trends, catering to the diverse needs and interests of its customer base. Nykaa's content marketing strategy not only establishes the brand as a trusted authority in the beauty space but also nurtures a loyal community of beauty enthusiasts. By consistently providing relevant and engaging content, Nykaa enhances its brand visibility, fosters customer loyalty, and ultimately drives sales, showcasing how effective content marketing can be when executed with precision and authenticity.

Affiliate Marketing: Nykaa has successfully leveraged the power of affiliate marketing to extend its reach and increase sales in the competitive cosmetics industry through its affiliate program. Nykaa partners with bloggers, influencers, and content creators who wear Nykaa's products promote through their online platforms are collaborative. These affiliates earn revenue for each sale generated through their unique referral network, creating a mutually beneficial partnership. Nykaa's affiliate marketing strategy not only leverages the reach and credibility of these influencers but also enables the brand to tap into niche audiences and effectively target demographics. This approach has proven to be a win-win, as affiliates gain revenue opportunities and Nykaa expands its market, increasing conversion and revenue The Nykaa affiliate marketing program demonstrates the potential brands can make their online jump with greater sales by influencing and leveraging digital products.

Table 3. Components of Nykaa's business model

Component	Description
E-commerce Retail	Main revenue source, selling beauty and wellness products from various brands.
Private Label	Offering own-brand products, providing higher margins.
Nykaa Network	Content-driven platform for brand building and customer engagement.
Nykaa Pro	Exclusive platform for beauty professionals, earning revenue through membership fees and product sales.
Nykaa Fashion	Expansion into the fashion segment, adding a new revenue stream.
Affiliate Marketing	Partnering with influencers for commissions on referrals.
Nykaa Pro	Exclusive platform for beauty professionals, earning revenue through membership fees and product sales.
Affiliate Marketing	Partnering with influencers for commissions on referrals.
Advertising and Promos	Selling ad space on the platform for product promotions.

Season Sale: Nykaa's seasonal sales are highly anticipated events for beauty enthusiasts across India. These sales typically occur during key festive and holiday periods, offering customers an excellent opportunity to indulge in their favourite beauty and cosmetic products at discounted prices. Nykaa's Seasonal Sale extravaganza often includes a wide range of products, from makeup essentials to skincare staples, haircare products, fragrances, and more. With enticing discounts and exclusive offers, customers can revamp their beauty routines, explore new trends, or stock up on their beloved brands without breaking the bank. Nykaa's Seasonal Sales are not only a shopping delight but also a chance to explore the latest beauty innovations, making them a much-anticipated event on every beauty enthusiast's calendar.

Zivame, founded by Richa Kar in 2011, stands as a prominent example of women entrepreneurship in India's e-commerce landscape. Richa Kar's vision and determination led to the creation of a platform that revolutionized the lingerie shopping experience for women in the country. Zivame provided a discreet and convenient way for women to shop for intimate apparel, challenging societal taboos and stigmas surrounding lingerie. Under her leadership, the brand not only disrupted the traditional brick-and-mortar lingerie retail model but also paved the way for open conversations about body positivity and self-confidence. Richa Kar's entrepreneurial journey with Zivame is a testament to the potential of women-led businesses in breaking barriers and reshaping industries while empowering women to embrace their individuality and choices.

Buying bras in India may be agonising, what with male salespeople hanging around, ignorant salesgirls, and an air of humiliation surrounding the process. Richa Kar, the creator of online lingerie boutique Zivame, set out during 2011, the disrupt all of that. (The name "zivame" is derived from the Hebrew word "ziva," which means "radiant.") Kar's website has 5,000 designs, 50 brands, and 100 sizes, but more importantly, it provides shoppers with privacy and dignity when purchasing.

Zivame Instagram is quite visual and creative, showcasing videos from across the world with user-generated material. Whether it is a regular video or an IGTV, Zivame has managed to captivate its audience with their content. Zivame provide a range of lingerie's along with night wear for women with customised size option availability. Zivame has a very good online reach as it provides full confidential and ease to their customer while buying such stuff. Zivame has a wider and amazing content for branding and for promoting its product on Instagram. On Instagram they have videos, pictures which promote their product which attracts the customer and help in getting the idea whether the stuff suited on them or not.

E-commerce Retail: Zivame primarily functions as an online lingerie and intimate apparel retailer wherein customers can browse and purchase a wide range of lingerie products, including bras, panties, nightwear, shapewear, activewear, and more through the Zivame website and mobile app. It is primarily operating through its user-friendly website and mobile app that offers an extensive and diverse range of lingerie products to cater to varying preferences and body types. By embracing e-commerce, Zivame has not only transformed the lingerie shopping experience but has also empowered women to explore and express their individual style and comfort. Their success in the e-commerce retail space underscores the significance of convenience and variety in today's digital shopping landscape.

Product Sourcing: Zivame's product sourcing strategy is a key element of its business model. Zivame curates a diverse collection of products by sourcing from a wide range of brands, both domestic and international. This approach allows them to offer customers an extensive selection, ensuring that they can find products that suit their specific tastes and preferences. Zivame collaborate with various brands, Zivame can provide lingerie options that cater to various styles, sizes, and price points. Additionally, Zivame has also introduced its private label lingerie and apparel lines, giving them greater control over the design, quality, and pricing of select products. This dual approach to product sourcing, through both partnerships and private labels, enables Zivame to maintain a competitive edge in the market and meet the diverse needs of its customers.

Influencer's Collaborations: Zivame's influencer collaborations have played a pivotal role in enhancing the brand's visibility and resonance in the world of lingerie and intimate apparel. By partnering with influencers, especially those with a strong presence in the fashion and lifestyle sectors, Zivame has been able to reach a broader and more engaged audience. These collaborations often involve influencers creating content, such as blog posts, videos, or social media posts, where they showcase and endorse Zivame's products. Beyond just promoting products, these influencers often

Table 4. Aspects of Zivame business model

Aspect	Description
Customer Segments	1. Women seeking lingerie and intimate wear.
	2. Men looking to purchase lingerie as gifts.
	3. B2B segment: Providing lingerie solutions for corporates.
Value Proposition	1. Wide range of lingerie and intimate wear products.
	2. Discreet shopping experience for sensitive items.
	3. Expert sizing guidance and fit solutions.
	4. Accessible pricing and frequent discounts.
Channels	1. E-commerce website and mobile app.
	2. Exclusive brand stores.
	3. Online marketplaces.
Customer Relationships	1. Online customer support and chat.
	2. Email support for inquiries and issues.
	3. Social media engagement and feedback.
	4. Loyalty programs and rewards.
Revenue Streams	1. Sales of lingerie and intimate wear products.
	2. Subscription models for recurring revenue.
	3. Corporate sales for B2B solutions.
	4. Licensing and franchising opportunities.
Key Resources	1. E-commerce platform and technology.
	2. Inventory and supply chain management.
	3. Trained staff for customer support and fitting.
Key Activities	1. Product sourcing, design, and manufacturing.
	2. Digital marketing and advertising campaigns.
	3. Inventory management and order fulfilment.
	4. Customer education and fitting solutions.
Key Partnerships	1. Lingerie brands for product collaborations.
	2. Logistics and delivery partners.
	3. Payment gateways and financial institutions.
	4. Corporates seeking B2B lingerie solutions.
Cost Structure	1. Product procurement and manufacturing costs.
	2. Marketing and advertising expenses.
	3. Employee salaries and operational costs.
	4. Technology and e-commerce platform maintenance.

promote body positivity, self-confidence, and empowerment, aligning with Zivame's mission to celebrate and cater to women of all shapes and sizes. Such partnerships not only boost brand awareness but also create a sense of trust and relatability, as customers can see real individuals endorsing and using Zivame products. Zivame's influencer collaborations exemplify the synergy between e-commerce and social media, proving the effectiveness of influencer marketing in the world of fashion and intimate wear.

Seasonal sales: Zivame's seasonal sales are eagerly anticipated events for lingerie and intimate apparel shoppers in India. During these sales, Zivame typically offers attractive discounts, special promotions, and exclusive deals on a wide range of their products. These sales often coincide with major shopping seasons, festivals, or special occasions, providing customers with an excellent opportunity to revamp their lingerie collection, explore new styles, or simply stock up on essentials at more budget-friendly prices. Zivame's commitment to offering quality products at affordable rates becomes even more pronounced during these seasonal sales, making it a win-win for both the brand and its loyal customers. These sales events not only contribute to heightened customer engagement but also reinforce Zivame's position as a go-to destination for lingerie shopping in the digital realm, emphasizing affordability, variety, and convenience.

Technology and Platform: Zivame's technology and platform serve as the backbone of its success in the e-commerce lingerie industry. With a keen focus on providing an exceptional user experience, Zivame has developed a user-friendly and intuitive website and mobile app. These platforms enable customers to effortlessly browse, select, and purchase a wide range of lingerie products. One of Zivame's standout technological features is its virtual fitting room, which employs augmented reality (AR) to help customers visualize how lingerie items would fit them, enhancing confidence in their choices. Additionally, Zivame offers size calculators and fit consultants to ensure customers find the perfect fit. The platform also prioritizes security through encrypted payment processing and discreet packaging. Furthermore, Zivame leverages data analytics and AI to offer personalized product recommendations, making the shopping experience more tailored and enjoyable. Overall, Zivame's technology and platform embody its commitment to customer satisfaction and convenience in the world of online lingerie shopping (Mitra, 2008).

BUSINESS MODEL OF LIMEROAD

Limeroad, co-founded by Suchi Mukherjee, is a testament to the pioneering spirit of women entrepreneurs in the e-commerce sector. Suchi Mukherjee's vision and leadership have been instrumental in shaping Limeroad into a unique social commerce platform that combines fashion, community, and e-commerce. Her entrepreneurial journey showcases the determination and innovation that women bring to the technology and retail space. By fostering a vibrant online community of fashion enthusiasts and leveraging user-generated content, Limeroad has not only disrupted traditional e-commerce models but has also provided a platform for women to express their creativity and style. Suchi Mukherjee's success with Limeroad serves as an inspiring example of women's entrepreneurship, highlighting the transformative potential of female-led businesses in the digital age.

Limeroad is an innovative and distinctive player in the e-commerce space, known for its social commerce platform. At the heart of Limeroad's approach is the encouragement of user-generated content, where individuals become "scrapbookers" by creating and sharing their fashion and lifestyle inspirations. This unique concept fosters a vibrant community of fashion enthusiasts who not only shop for clothing, accessories, and home decor but also engage in social interactions, follow their favorite scrapbookers, and discover new trends and styles. Limeroad seamlessly integrates e-commerce into this social platform, enabling users to purchase products directly from the collections they discover. With a focus on personalization, content-driven marketing, and a mobile app that empowers users on the go, Limeroad redefines online shopping as an interactive and community-driven experience, making it a standout player in the world of e-commerce.

BUSINESS MODEL OF LIMEROAD

User-generated content: User-generated content (UGC) lies at the heart of Limeroad's innovative business model. The platform empowers users to become content creators and curators, allowing them to express their unique fashion and lifestyle tastes. Users, known as "scrapbookers," create collections, style looks, and share their inspirations with the Limeroad community. These scrapbooks serve as a source of inspiration for other users, who can discover new fashion trends and products through them. UGC fosters a sense of belonging and community among users, who can engage with one another through comments, likes, and follows. This dynamic social interaction not only enhances user engagement but also drives sales as users are encouraged to shop directly from the collections they admire. Limeroad's reliance on UGC sets it apart in the e-commerce landscape, turning shopping into a collaborative and community-driven experience.

"Love, Create, Share, and Shop" is a slogan or tagline that encapsulates the essence of LimeRoad, an e-commerce platform focused on fashion and lifestyle products. It is a concise representation of LimeRoad's mission, which is to offer a personalized, creative, and socially engaging shopping experience to its customers.

Table 5. Aspects of Limeroad business model

Aspect	Description
Customer Segments	1. Fashion-conscious individuals, predominantly women.
	2. Sellers and small businesses looking to showcase their products.
Value Proposition	1. Vast selection of fashion and lifestyle products.
	2. User-generated content for inspiration and trends.
	3. Social shopping experience with scrapbooking.
	4. Opportunities for sellers to reach a wider audience.
Channels	1. E-commerce website and mobile app.
	2. Social media platforms for community engagement.
Revenue Streams	1. User-generated content and peer recommendations.
	2. Customer support and assistance.
	3. Loyalty programs and rewards.
	4. Interactive features like scrapbooking.
Key Resources	1. Sales of fashion and lifestyle products.
	2. Commission from seller transactions.
	3. Advertising and sponsored content.
Key Activities	1. E-commerce platform and technology.
	2. Seller network and product catalog.
	3. User-generated content and community.
Key Partnerships	1. Product listing, curation, and merchandising.
	2. Digital marketing and social media engagement.
	3. Seller onboarding and support.
	4. Content creation and community management.
Cost Structure	1. Sellers and brands for product listings.
	2. Payment gateways and financial institutions.
	3. Social media platforms for marketing.

It highlights the brand's commitment to fashion, individual expression, community, and convenience.

Community and social interaction: Community and social interaction are fundamental elements of Limeroad's unique approach to e-commerce. The platform fosters a vibrant online community of fashion enthusiasts who come together to share, discover, and engage with each other. Users can follow their favorite scrapbookers, comment on collections, and interact with fellow members who share similar fashion interests. These interactions create a sense of connection and belonging, turning the

Figure 2. LimeRoad personalised slogan

act of shopping into a social experience. The social networking features on Limeroad not only facilitate discussions about fashion and lifestyle but also encourage users to explore new styles and trends, thereby increasing the platform's stickiness and user retention. This emphasis on community and social interaction sets Limeroad apart from traditional e-commerce platforms, making it a destination not just for shopping but also for fashion discovery and meaningful connections within the online fashion community (Ries, 2011).

Merchandising and e-commerce: Limeroad seamlessly integrates merchandising and e-commerce within its social commerce platform. Users can explore a vast catalog of fashion, accessories, and home decor products curated by various sellers and brands. What sets Limeroad apart is that users can shop directly from the collections and looks they discover on the platform. This integration of e-commerce allows for a convenient and immediate shopping experience, aligning user inspiration with action. The platform connects users with an extensive network of sellers and brands, ensuring a diverse and ever-evolving product catalog. By combining the art of merchandising with e-commerce in a social context, Limeroad offers a dynamic and engaging online shopping experience that leverages user-generated content and community interactions to drive sales and fashion discovery.

SUGAR COSMETICS

SUGAR Cosmetics, founded by Vineeta Singh and Kaushik Mukherjee, stands as a shining example of women entrepreneurship in the beauty and cosmetics industry. Vineeta Singh, in particular, has been instrumental in shaping the brand's identity and success. Under her leadership, SUGAR Cosmetics has become known for its commitment to offering high-quality and cruelty-free makeup products that celebrate diversity in beauty. Vineeta's entrepreneurial journey reflects the power of women in challenging traditional norms and establishing thriving businesses in traditionally male-dominated sectors. SUGAR Cosmetics has not only disrupted the Indian cosmetics market but has also inspired countless aspiring women entrepreneurs by showcasing the potential for innovation and empowerment within the beauty industry.

Cruelty Free & Vegan beauty products: SUGAR Cosmetics has gained acclaim for its strong commitment to cruelty-free and vegan beauty products. This means that their makeup formulations and ingredients are not tested on animals, and they do not use animal-derived ingredients in their products. This ethical stance aligns with the growing consumer demand for more sustainable and animal-friendly beauty options. SUGAR Cosmetics' dedication to cruelty-free and vegan products reflects a broader industry trend toward greater transparency and responsibility in cosmetics manufacturing. It resonates with environmentally conscious and socially aware consumers who seek makeup that is not only high-quality and stylish but also in line with their values of ethical and sustainable living. SUGAR Cosmetics' cruelty-free and vegan stance is a pivotal aspect of its brand identity, appealing to a diverse and conscientious customer base.

Brand Ambassadors and Influencer marketing: Sugar Cosmetics has effectively leveraged brand ambassadors and influencer marketing as key components of its marketing strategy. The brand collaborates with popular beauty influencers, makeup artists, and social media personalities who have a strong following and influence in the beauty and fashion industry. These influencers endorse and promote Sugar Cosmetics' products through various digital channels, including social media platforms, YouTube, and blogs. These partnerships not only increase brand visibility but also lend credibility and authenticity to the products. By featuring relatable and trusted individuals who showcase the makeup's application and results, Sugar Cosmetics connects with its target audience on a personal level, fostering a sense of trust and loyalty. This influencer-driven approach has been pivotal in driving brand engagement and reaching a wider customer base in the competitive cosmetics market (Chakraborti, Dasgupta, & Jana, 2002).

Promotional Campaigns: The campaign encourages people to express themselves freely through makeup and cosmetics. It celebrates the idea that makeup is a form of self-expression, allowing individuals to showcase their creativity and unique

Table 6. Aspects and descriptions of SUGAR Cosmetics

Aspect	Description
Customer Segments	1. Young and trendy individuals interested in cosmetics.
	2. Beauty enthusiasts seeking cruelty-free products.
	3. Online shoppers looking for accessible beauty solutions.
Value Proposition	1. Affordable, high-quality cosmetics and beauty products.
	2. Commitment to cruelty-free and vegan product offerings.
	3. Diverse range of makeup and beauty products.
	4. Trend-driven and fashion-forward product collections.
Channels	1. E-commerce website and mobile app.
	2. Exclusive brand stores and kiosks.
	3. Presence on popular online marketplaces.
Customer Relationships	1. Online customer support and assistance.
	2. Social media engagement and feedback.
	3. Loyalty programs, rewards, and special offers.
Revenue Streams	1. Sales of cosmetics and beauty products.
	2. Subscription models and beauty boxes.
	3. Collaborations and limited-edition collections.
	4. Licensing opportunities and brand extensions.
Key Resources	1. Product development and design teams.
	2. Manufacturing and supply chain infrastructure.
	3. E-commerce platform and technology.
Key Activities	1. Product research, development, and innovation.
	2. Marketing and advertising campaigns.
	3. Inventory management and order fulfilment.
	4. Customer education on makeup application and trends.
Key Partnerships	1. Suppliers and manufacturers for cosmetics.
	2. Retail and distribution partners.
	3. Beauty influencers and makeup artists for promotion.
Cost Structure	1. Product manufacturing and procurement costs.
	2. Marketing and advertising expenses.
	3. Employee salaries and operational costs.
	4. Technology and e-commerce platform maintenance.

style. The campaign celebrates diversity and individuality. It sends the message that beauty is not one-size-fits-all, and everyone should embrace their unique features

Figure 3. Sugar Cosmetics campaign

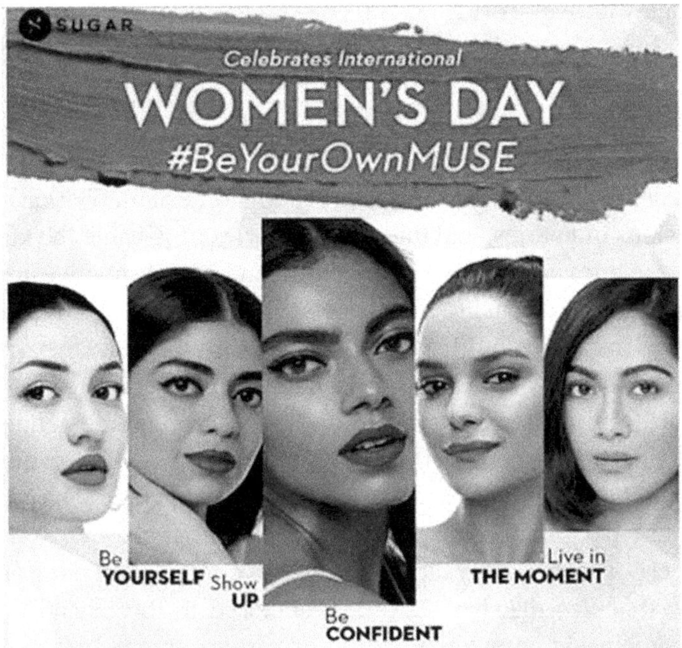

and quirks. The campaign highlights the creative aspect of makeup application. It encourages people to experiment with different looks, colors, and styles, fostering a sense of fun and playfulness in the world of cosmetics. For instance, the "Be Your Own Muse" campaign by Sugar Cosmetics; an empowering and inspirational initiative that encourages individuals to embrace and celebrate their unique beauty and self-expression. This campaign is a testament to the brand's commitment to promoting self-confidence and self-love. "Be Your Own Muse" underscores the importance of self-confidence and self-acceptance. It emphasizes that true beauty comes from within, and that makeup should enhance one's natural beauty rather than masking it.

Subscription Services: Sugar Cosmetics has ventured into the realm of subscription services, offering beauty enthusiasts the opportunity to enjoy a curated selection of makeup products regularly. These subscription services often take the form of beauty boxes or kits, where customers can sign up for a monthly or quarterly subscription. Subscribers receive a surprise assortment of Sugar Cosmetics' latest and most popular makeup products, allowing them to discover new shades and formulations regularly. This subscription model not only adds an element of excitement to the beauty routine but also fosters brand loyalty and customer engagement. It's an innovative way for Sugar Cosmetics to keep its audience engaged and eager to explore the brand's ever-evolving product offerings while enjoying the convenience of regular beauty deliveries (Mitra, 2008).

CONCLUSION

Women entrepreneurship has emerged as a driving force of innovation and economic growth in various industries, and the success stories of Zivame, Nykaa, Limeroad, and Sugar Cosmetics exemplify the dynamic and transformative impact women entrepreneurs can have on business landscapes. These brands have not only redefined their respective industries but have also broken through gender barriers, proving that leadership and innovation know no gender boundaries.

The business model of Zivame reflects its e-commerce retail model, has revolutionized the way women shop for intimate wear in India. Its focus on convenience, diversity of product offerings, and technology-driven features has made lingerie shopping a more personalized and empowering experience.

The business of model of Nykaa, underlines its content marketing and influencer partnerships strategies that has set a new standard in the beauty and cosmetics industry. It combines e-commerce with informative content, offering customers a one-stop destination for beauty products and expert advice. Whereas Limeroad's unique social commerce model integrates community and e-commerce seamlessly. By encouraging user-generated content and social interactions, Limeroad has created a fashion discovery platform that not only connects users with products but also fosters a sense of belonging within the online fashion community.

Sugar Cosmetics, with its cruelty-free and vegan products, has demonstrated that ethical and sustainable beauty can be both trendy and successful. It caters to a socially conscious audience seeking cosmetics that align with their values.

These women entrepreneurs have demonstrated that innovation, inclusivity, and a deep understanding of customer needs are key ingredients for success. They have not only disrupted traditional business models but have also paved the way for more conscious and community-driven industries. These brands continue to inspire women entrepreneurs worldwide, showing that with determination and vision, they can achieve remarkable success in the business world.

In conclusion, women entrepreneurs like the founders of these brands have not only disrupted traditional business models but have also paved the way for more inclusive and diverse industries. Their innovative approaches, coupled with a commitment to quality and customer-centricity, have made them leaders in their respective domains, inspiring future generations of women entrepreneurs to dream big and break new ground in the world of business.

REFERENCES

Balakrishnan, R. (2021). *Women Entrepreneurs*. YourStory. https://yourstory.com/herstory/2021/09/women-entrepreneurs-leveraged-facebook-instagram-whatsapp-covid19/amp

Brush, C. G., Henry, C., & Gatewood, J. E. (2010). Women Entrepreneurs and the Global Environment for Growth. Edward Elgar.

Chakraborti, J., Dasgupta, M., & Jana, B. (2002). *How Women Entrepreneurs are Reshaping the Beauty and Wellness Business in India*. Emerald Publishing Limited.

Davidsson, P. (2016). What Is Entrepreneurship? *International Studies in Entrepreneurship, 33*, 1–19. doi:10.1007/978-3-319-26692-3_1

Dhameja, S. (2002). *Women Entrepreneurs Opportunities, Performance and Problems*. Deep & Deep Publications.

EE-HUB. (2017, APRIL). *Policy Recommendation*. The European Entrepreneurship Education Network. http://ee-hub.eu/component/attachments/?task=download&id=492:EE-HUB-Policy-Recommendations-web

Gupta, U. (2018). *Story of the beauty entrepreneur Falguni Nayar*. Kindle Edition.

Korreck, S. (2019, September 25). *ORF.* ORF Online. https://www.orfonline.org/research/women-entrepreneurs-in-india-what-is-holding-them-back-55852/

Kumar, P. (2016). *Indian Women as Entrepreneurs: An Exploration of Self-Identity*. Palgrave Macmillan. doi:10.1057/978-1-137-60259-6

Mitra, S. (2008). *Entrepreneur Journeys*. Createspace Independent Pub.

Nagma, M. (2021, July 26). Tales of Grit and Courage. *ETNOWNEWS*. https://www.timesnownews.com/business-economy/economy/article/tales-of-grit-and-courage-the-journey-of-women-entrepreneurs-in-india-during-covid/780697

Pai, S. &. (2021, December). NYKAA: A Comprehensive Analysis of a Leading Indian E- Commerce Cosmetic Agency. *International Journal of Case Studies in Business, IT and Education, 5*(2).

Rai, R. (2019). The Contribution of Women Entrepreneirs in the Economic Development of India. *Journal of Global Values,* (10).

M.Rezvani, M. L. (2018). organisational entrepreneurial alaertness framework in opportunity discovery. *academy of entrepreneurship journal.*

Ries, E. (2011). *The Lean Startup: How Today's Entrepreneurs Use Continuous Innovation to Create Radically Successful Businesses.* USA: Crown Currency; Illustrated edition.

Wagman-Geller, M. (2018). *Women Who Launch: The Women Who Shattered Glass Ceilings*. Mango.

Chapter 10
A Wikipedia Narration of the GameStop Short Squeeze

Evangelos Vasileiou
https://orcid.org/0000-0002-4543-4828
University of the Aegean, Greece

Elroi Hadad
https://orcid.org/0000-0001-5808-7098
Shamoon College of Engineering, Israel

Aikaterini Chalkiadaki
University of the Aegean, Greece

ABSTRACT

This paper examines the usefulness of Wikipedia pageviews as indicator of the performance of stock prices. We examine the GameStop (GME) case, which drew the investors' and scholars' attention in 2021 due to the Short Squeeze (SSQ), and its skyrocketing price increase since 2021. We use the daily number of pageviews of Wikipedia pages for COVID-19, GME, and SSQ as explanatory variables for the period 31/12/2018-30/3/2022. The results show strong statistical evidence that increased number of Wikipedia pageviews for COVID-19, which represents the fear of the pandemic, has a negative impact on the GME performance. Moreover, the findings show that the increased interest in information regarding the short squeeze, as expressed by the increased number of pageviews of the relative Wikipedia page, is positively linked with the GME price. This approach holds the potential to yield benefits not only for entrepreneurs within the finance sector but also across various other fields. It serves as a valuable proxy for gauging the demand for goods, services, and/or overall interest in a market.

DOI: 10.4018/979-8-3693-0790-8.ch010

INTRODUCTION

Since 2020, the major issue that has puzzled humanity throughout the whole world is the COVID-19 pandemic. Up to May 2022, more than 510 million COVID-19 cases and more than 6 million deaths have been reported[1]. An indication for the increased worldwide interest regarding the COVID-19 pandemic in the years 2020 and 2021 is that in both years COVID-19 related searches were amongst the top searches[2].

Scholars in several fields of study, e.g. medicine, sociology, phycology etc., included the impact of COVID-19 in their research[3]. Scholars examined the impact of COVID-19 in economics and finance: Agosto and Giudici (2020), Wójcik and Ioannou (2020), Vasileiou, Samitas, Karagiannaki, and Dandu (2021).

During the pandemic period, lockdowns were imposed worldwide in order to limit the spread of the virus, and this was an additional reason why news consumption from online news media and social networks has increased in the last years (Van Aelst et al (2021)). However, when a user searches for information on the internet, they do not only gain information, but they also give information regarding the issues which draw their attention (Ripberger (2011)).

Internet searches and social media platforms have been beneficial for financial modeling in the last decades: Bollen and Mao (2011), Vosen and Schmidt (2011), Preis, Moat, and Stanley (2013), Kristoufek (2015), Huang, Rojas, and Convery (2020).

A notable number of studies use Wikipedia as a sentiment indicator[4] of the performance of financial markets: Kristoufek (2013), Xu and Zhang (2013), Behrendt, Peter, and Zimmermann (2020), Gómez-Martínez, Orden-Cruz, and Martínez-Navalón (2022). Similarly, during the time of the pandemic, internet searches conducted through platforms like Google Trends, Twitter, and Wikipedia have played a significant role as an explanatory variable at least in two main aspects: (a) influencing the performance of various assets during this period, as indicated by Vasileiou (2021a) and Chatterjee and French (2022), and (b) contributing to the understanding of the outbreak of the pandemic, as investigated by O'Leary and Storey (2020).

The objective of this paper is to examine memes stocks using the volume of the pageviews in Wikipedia. Meme stocks were one of the financial issues that drew the attention of investors in 2021 according to the Google Trends yearly review[5]. Meme stocks are stocks that presented a skyrocketing price increase in 2021 due to increased popularity especially amongst non-experienced retail investors through social media. The term meme stock is derived from the internet memes that were shared among traders. The first widely known meme stock was Gamestop (GME); AMC, BlackBerry, Bed, Bath & Beyond are some of the companies that also belong to this group.

A brief but necessary overview of the facts of the GME case follows. The GME corporation is a US video game and consumer electronics retail company with over 5,000 stores worldwide[6]. However, GME suffered significant losses during the last years because digital distribution services were able to offer the same good, e.g. a video game, at lower prices; brick-and-mortar retailers such as GameStop have additional costs, i.e. rent, wages etc, that drive their prices up. These negative conditions motivated many investors to apply a short sale strategy, but the increased short-sales interest made GME the most shorted share in 2020[7]. Given the extreme short selling of GME (GameStop), a collective of small investors, primarily organized through the subreddit r/Wallstreetbets, strategically coordinated the purchase of GME stocks by capitalizing on the active option market. When the hedge funds that had short strategies to the GME stock had to buy the shares back, this group of investors refused to sell the GME shares and this led to the skyrocketing increase in the stock price.

In this paper, we examine the GME performance for the period 31/12/2018-30/3/2022, using as explanatory variables only the number of the pageviews for terms that quantitatively represent several aspects of this case. We employ an asymmetry Exponential GARCH model which better fits to our dataset in order to analyse the relationship between these variables.

The rest of the paper is structured as follows: Section 2 describes the theoretical background and the preliminary data, Section 3 presents the econometric model, and Section 4 concludes the study.

THEORETICAL BACKGROUND, EXPLANATORY VARIABLES, AND PRELIMINARY DATA

Internet searches are a very useful tool in finance, especially in the last decades. How could the internet searches contribute to financial modeling? As the health risk increases, so does risk aversion (Decker and Schmitz (2016)) and this leads to a decline in stock prices. However, measuring fear is not an easy task. During the COVID-19 pandemic, many studies incorporated internet-based indices as variables in studies that examined the impact of the pandemic on financial markets. The indices which are based on Google Trends were used as a quantitative indication of health risk (Baig, Butt, Haroon, and Rizvi (2021), Vasileiou (2021b)).

In our study, our indices are based on Wikipedia pageviews. In particular, the number of pageviews for COVID-19 issues that are included in Wikipedia is used as proxy. An increased number of pageviews of the Wikipedia pages: "Coronavirus", "COVID-19", "COVID-19 pandemic", "COVID-19 Omicron", and "COVID-19

Delta", are linked with increased health risk fear[8]. Figure 1 shows the outcome of this process.

In addition to Covid related words, we also included several other terms that are linked with the GameStop case: the number of Wikipedia pageviews for "GameStop" (GME) and "Short Squeeze" (SSQ), represent the interest in the GME Corporation and the term Short Squeeze. Figure 2 shows the number of pageviews of the aforementioned explanatory variables throughout this period. We expect increased fear of COVID-19 to have a negative impact on GME performance, and the increased interest in the GME Corporation and the Short Squeeze to have positive co-movement with the GME stock price. This is because increased interest in the GME case, as retail investors turned to Internet sources to gather information about GME, is linked to the skyrocketing increase in the GME price.

The performance of the GME stock, which is the dependent variable in this paper, is presented in Figure 3. The first part shows that from the beginning of the sample period up to the 3rd quarter of 2020 the GME stock declines, but after this period the GME rises and in 2021 the stock price presents a skyrocketing performance. Daily returns show that the volatility is not constant, and it increases considerably beginning 2021. These characteristics show that there is volatility clustering, which is a common stylized fact in financial time series, but the positive relationship between price and volatility is an indication of anti-leverage effect, which is the opposite of the leverage effect that is the commonly expected stylized fact (Black (1976).

However, as far as the memes stocks, Vasileiou (2021c) examines the GME case under the efficient market hypothesis, without using any explanatory variable in the mean or in the conditional variance equation, and provides empirical evidence for an anti-leverage effect, which is considered an indication of abnormality because the leverage effect it is in contrast to the expected stylized fact (leverage effect).

The second part of Figure 3 shows that the time series is leptokurtic and does not follow the normal distribution, while the third part confirms that there is volatility clustering, as the autocorrelation plot of the absolute returns shows. Thus, Figure 3 indicates that a model that captures the volatility clustering and the asymmetry impact of returns could be more appropriate for our study than a linear one.

The GME returns (Figure 3a) do not present stationarity, but figure 2 shows the indices of the explanatory variables are not stationary. Therefore, to address stationarity issues, we employ the first differences of the independent variables. Table 1 provides the descriptive statistics of all variables used in our study. As anticipated, the variables do not adhere to a normal distribution; however, they are stationary, allowing us to utilize them without additional modifications.

Figure 1. The process of downloading the number of pageviews per Wikipedia page: An example of the COVID-19 variable

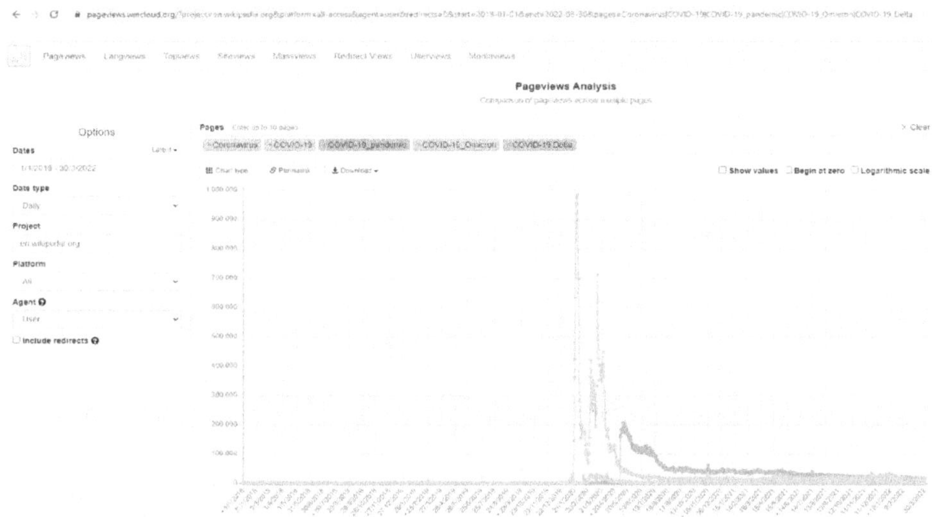

(a) **Performance plot:** the GME prices and daily returns plot demonstrates non-constant volatility, indicating the presence of volatility clustering, and an anti-leverage effect, where increased stock prices correspond to higher volatility.

(b) **Histogram:** the histogram of GME returns shows that the time series is leptokurtic and does not follow the normal distribution (black line).

(c) **Autocorrelation function of the absolute returns:** the autocorrelation plot of the absolute values of GME returns shows that there is volatility clustering because high (low) price changes tend to be followed by high (low) price changes.

ECONOMETRIC MODEL

In our analysis, we explored various econometric models to identify the most suitable one that best fits our dataset. The presence of volatility clustering in the data renders Ordinary Least Squares (OLS) models inappropriate for our sample, thus, we tested

Figure 2. Graphical representation of the daily number of pageviews for the COVID-19, GameStop, and Short-Squeeze

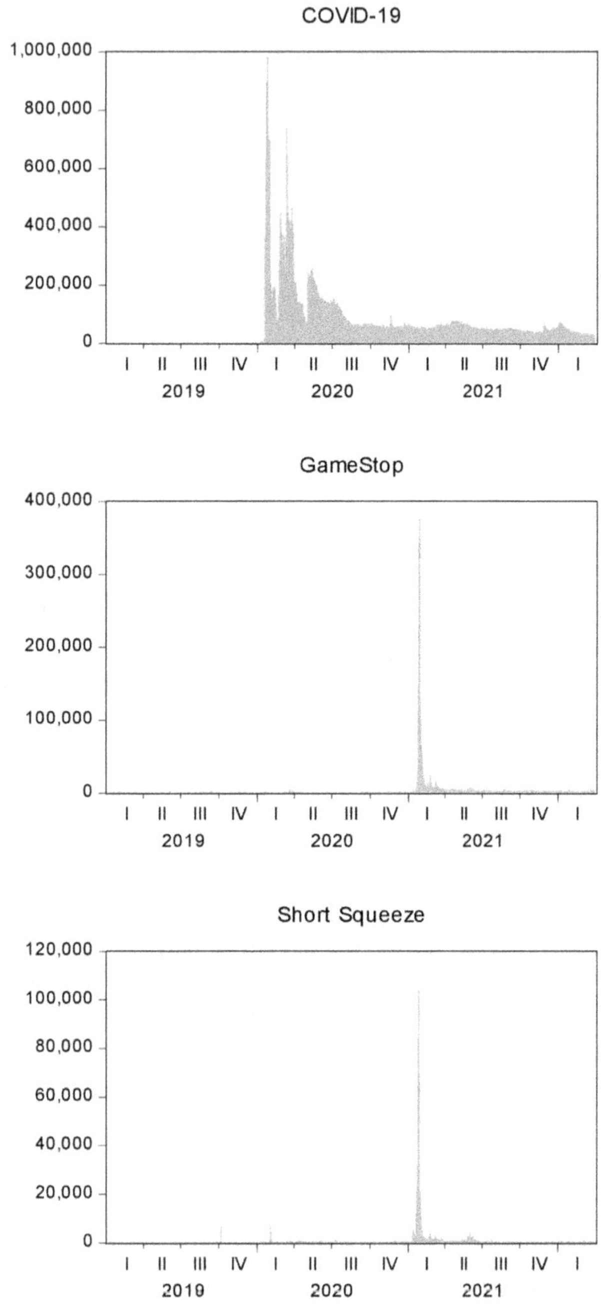

Figure 3. Plots of the GME time series

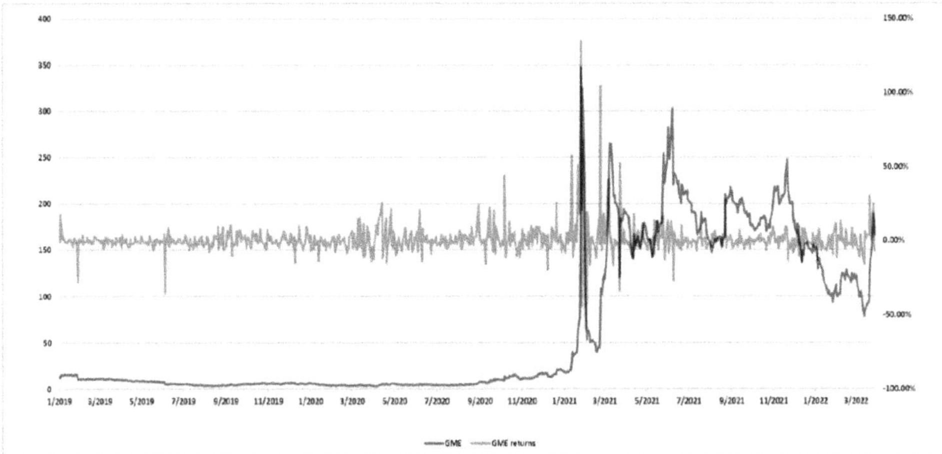

GARCH family models that capture stylized facts such as volatility clustering, and volatility asymmetries. The most appropriate models were the asymmetry GARCH models. E-GARCH was the most appropriate according to the Akaike and Schwarz criteria (AIC and SIC, respectively), and the T-GARCH model follows. We apply both models, in order to test the robustness of the results. The mean equation of our model is

Figure 4. Plots of the GME time series

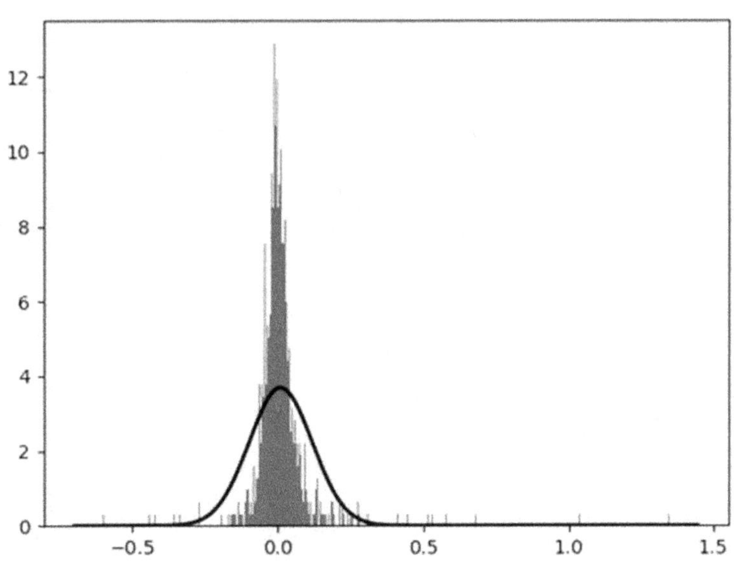

Figure 5. Plots of the GME time series

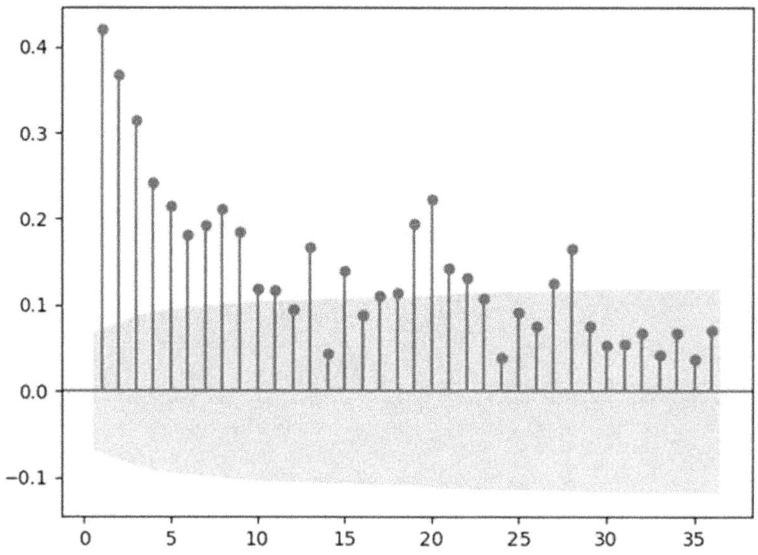

$$GME\ returns_t = a_0 + d\_covid_t + d\_GME_t + d\_SSQ_t + \varepsilon_t \quad (1)$$

Table 1. Descriptive statistics: This table presents the descriptive statistics of the variables that are used in this analysis

	GME returns	d_Covid	d_GME	d_SSQ
Mean	0.008	35.196	3.9266	0.313
Median	-0.002	-22.000	-12.000	-2.000
Maximum	1.348	390,923.000	205,301.0	51,033.000
Minimum	-0.600	-452,760.000	-24,3480.0	-47,567.000
Std. Dev.	0.108	32,371.180	12,086.52	2,964.726
Skewness	4.610	0.822	-2.972	-0.398
Kurtosis	52.683	101.332	314.8482	218.332
Jarque-Bera	87,027.280*	329,248.800*	3,311,732.000*	1,578,458.000*
ADF	-14.109***	-11.164***	-16.972***	-15.775***
Observations	817	817	817	817

Notes: *** indicates statistical significance at the 1% confidence level. The table shows that the time series do not follow the normal distribution (Skewness≠0, Kurtosis>0 (leptokurtic), and Jarque-Bera tests statistically significant) and that they are stationary (ADF tests statistically significant).

where GME $returns_t$ are the daily arithmetic returns of GME, d_covid_t, d_GME_t, and d_SSQ_t are the time series of the first difference of the number of pageviews of COVID-19, Gamestop, and Short Squeeze Wikipedia pages for the respective searches. ε_t is the error term that follows the Generalised Error Distribution (GED).

As far as the conditional variance, the equation for the EGARCH(1,1,1) model is

$$\log(\sigma_t^2) = c_0 + ARCH_{EGARCH} \times \left|\frac{\varepsilon_{t-1}}{\sigma_{t-1}}\right| + GARCH_{EGARCH} \times \log\left(\sigma_{t-1}^2\right) + \gamma_{EGARCH} \times \frac{\varepsilon_{t-1}}{\sigma_{t-1}} \quad (2)$$

where the modeling of the variance equation with the log guarantees the non-negativity of the σ_t^2 even when the parameters are negative. c_0 is the constant term of the conditional variance equation, $ARCH_{EGARCH}$ and $GARCH_{EGARCH}$ are the coefficients of the respective terms, and γ_{EGARCH} is the leverage effect term. If $\gamma_{EGARCH}<0$ and statistically significant, this is evidence for the leverage effect (and vice versa).

Additionally, using the same mean equation, equation (1), we employ the GJR(1,1,1) (GJR or TGARCH, hereafter[9]) which has the following conditional variance

$$\sigma_t^2 = d_0 + ARCH_{GJR} \times \varepsilon_{t-1}^2 + GARCH_{GJR}\sigma_{t-1}^2 + \gamma_{GJR} \times \varepsilon_{t-1}^2 I_{t-1} \quad (3)$$

where $ARCH_{GJR}$ and $GARCH_{GJR}$ are the coefficients of the respective terms for the GJR model, and d_0 is the constant term. The I_{t-1} is a binary term for the asymmetry, and when $\varepsilon_{t-1}<0$ I_{t-1} equals to 1 and zero otherwise. If γG_{JR} is positive and statistically significant, this is an indication of the leverage effect (and vice versa).

The empirical results are presented in Table 2. Part (a) reports the EGARCH findings and part (b) reports the TGARCH model. The empirical evidence leads to the same conclusions in both cases. Fear of the pandemic as this expressed by the number of Wikipedia pageviews has a negative and statistically significant impact on the performance of the GME, which is consistent with what the theory suggests. The searches for GME have positive impact, as expected, but they do not have a statistically significant influence on the GME returns. The increased number of Short Squeeze searches present statistically significant and positive linkage with the GME performance and confirm the theoretical background we presented.

Regarding the variance equation, all the ARCH, GARCH and the asymmetry terms present statistical significance. Moreover, the asymmetry terms, either we use the EGARCH or the TGARCH model, quantitatively confirm our assumptions for anti-leverage effect[10]. These results are in contrast to the conventional theory, because they suggest when prices increase, the volatility increases also (and vice versa). Our results, offer further proof that the anti-leverage effect could be assumed as an indication of abnormal performance, corroborating previous observations by scholars (Vasileiou (2021c)).

The Q-statistics and the LM tests confirm the econometric validity of our models. The non-negativity constrain of the EGARCH model is secured by the fact that it is estimated in logarithmic values, and for the TGARCH model the non-negativity constrain is admissible because the constant $ARCH_{GJR}$, and $GARCH_{GJR}$ coefficients are positive numbers and the sum of ARCH_{GJR} and γ_{GJR} coefficients is higher than zero (ARCH_GJR+ γGJR ≥0).

These results quantitatively explain the GME story: the GME stock had a negative trend and COVID-19 further contributed to this because on-site sales declined due to the pandemic; this led to negative expectations for the GME case. When the health risk reduced, this contributed to better expectations for the GME. The number of Wikipedia pageview for GME related terms does not have a statistically significant impact on GME performance, but the coefficient was positive as expected. The increased number of SSQ searches are linked with GME price increases because the skyrocketing price rise of GME led not only to increased interest in the GME, but also to increased interest in what SSQ means. As far as the anti-leverage effect is concerned, our findings suggest that an anti-leverage effect emerges when periods of skyrocketing stock profits emerge, and the assumption is that this is an indication of abnormality because nothing has fundamentally changed to justify these GME price changes since 2021.

The mean equation of our model is

$$\text{GME returns}_t = a_0 + \text{d\_covid}_t + \text{d\_GME}_t + \text{d\_SSQ}_t + \varepsilon_t \qquad (1)$$

where GME returns_t are the daily arithmetic returns of GME, d_covid_t, d_GME_t, and d_SSQ_t are the time series of the first difference of the number of pageviews of COVID-19, Gamestop, and Short Squeeze Wikipedia pages for the respective searches. ε_t is the error term that follows the Generalised Error Distribution (GED).

As far as the conditional variance, the equation for the EGARCH(1,1,1) e EGARCH(1,1,1) model is

$$\log(\sigma_t^2)c_0 + ARCH_{EGARCH} \times \left|\frac{\varepsilon_{t-1}}{\sigma_{t-1}}\right| + GARCH_{EGARCH} \times \log(\sigma_{t-1}^2) + \gamma_{EGARCH} \times \frac{\varepsilon_{t-1}}{\sigma_{t-1}} \qquad (2)$$

where the modeling of the variance equation with the log guarantees the non-negativity of the σ_t^2 even when the parameters are negative, $ARCH_{EGARCH}$ and $GARCH_{EGARCH}$ are the coefficients of the respective terms, and γ_{EGARCH} is the leverage effect term. If $\gamma_{EGARCH}<0$ and statistically significant, this is evidence for the leverage effect (and vice versa).

Additionally, using the same mean equation, equation (1), we employ the GJR(1,1,1) (GJR or TGARCH, hereafter) which has the following conditional variance

$$\sigma_t^2 = d_0 + ARCH_{GJR} \times \varepsilon_{t-1}^2 + GARCH_{GJR}\sigma_{t-1}^2 + \gamma_{GJR} \times \varepsilon_{t-1}^2 I_{t-1} \tag{3}$$

where $ARCH_{GJR}$ and $GARCH_{GJR}$ are the coefficients of the respective terms for the GJR model, and if $\varepsilon_{t-1}<0$ the binary term I_{t-1} equals to 1 and zero otherwise. If γG_{JR} is positive and statistically significant, this is an indication of the leverage effect (and vice versa).

The results show with increased statistical significance that COVID-19 had a negative impact on GME returns and that the interest in Short Squeeze had a positive impact on the stock market performance. The interest in GME as this is expressed by the Wikipedia searches is positive, but it is not statistically strong. Finally, both GARCH asymmetry models provide strong evidence for anti-leverage effect.

CONCLUSION

Our findings suggest that Wikipedia searches can be a useful indicator of the performance of stock prices. In the GME case, the COVID-19 pandemic had a negative and statistically significant impact on the GME price, which is logical because health risk increases risk aversion and has a negative impact on stock prices (Decker and Schmitz (2016)). This impact is strong especially on prices of companies that are based on on-site sales, such as GME.

The searches for GME do not have a statistically significant impact on GME returns during the examined period, and several assumptions can be made as to why: (i) investors were not informed about GME via Wikipedia, but from other websites, (ii) when the interest in GME increased, the stock price had already gained a significant part of its abnormal returns, (iii) for a period of time GME had negative perspective, thus, GME searches had negative sentiment, but when the Short Squeeze emerged the sentiment changed without completely removing the impact of the first period. Sentiment analysis can also be used to examine this issue in future research, and in particular, researchers can utilize wavelet coherence methodology which has gained

Table 2. Econometric modeling and empirical findings: (a) EGARCH model; (b) TGARCH model

(a) EGARCH (1,1) estimation			**(b) TGARCH (1,1) estimation**	
		Mean Equation		
c	-0.003109*** (0.001086)		c	-0.003121*** (0.001113)
d_Covid	-6.27E-08** (2.84E-08)		**d_Covid**	-7.71E-08*** (2.94E-08)
d_GME	2.63E-07 (5.85E-07)		**d_GME**	3.06E-07 (7.08E-07)
d_SSQ	5.06E-06*** (1.67E-06)		**d_SSQ**	4.85E-06*** (1.75E-06)
Variance Equation				
c_0	-0.305603*** (0.046290)		d_0	0.000221*** (4.91E-05)
ARCH	0.205013*** (0.048476)		**ARCH**	0.166256*** (0.043192)
γE_{GARCH}	0.072862** (0.035271)		γG_{JR}	-0.152704*** (0.050146)
GARCH	0.970471*** (0.006316)		**GARCH**	0.849033*** (1.75E-06)
		Q-statistics and ARCH LM Tests		
Q_1	0.025		Q_1	0.140
Q_2	2.148		Q_2	1.796
Q_3	2.766		Q_3	2.529
Q_4	4.187		Q_4	3.496
Q_5	4.329		Q_5	3.612
LM_1	0.027		LM_1	0.055
LM_2	0.050		LM_2	0.077
LM_3	0.078		LM_3	0.137
LM_4	0.127		LM_4	0.168
LM_5	0.168		LM_5	0.217

Notes: *** and ** indicate statistical significance at the 1% and 5% confidence level, respectively. For the the LM test we report the F-statistic.

popularity in the financial literature in recent years (Umar, Gubareva, Yousaf, and Ali (2021), Rubbaniy, G., Khalid, A. A., Syriopoulos, K., & Samitas, A. (2021)).

The number of Wikipedia Short Squeeze pageviews has a positive and statistically significant impact on GME returns. This is consistent with what we would expect because many inexperienced retail investors wanted to learn (more) about the term short squeeze when the GME short squeeze case emerged and led to abnormal growth.

With regard to volatility, our findings show that during the examined period there is an anti-leverage asymmetry meaning that there is a positive co-movement between stock prices and volatility which is not consistent with the popular-normal stylized fact of the leverage effect (Black (1976)). This conclusion confirms the findings of previous studies (Vasileiou (20221c)) that an anti-leverage effect could be linked with abnormal skyrocketing price increases.

Indeed, the approach of analyzing GME returns, along with the first differences of pageviews for COVID-19, Gamestop, and Short Squeeze Wikipedia pages, presents numerous advantages. While originally applied in the finance sector, this methodology extends its benefits to a wide range of fields.

Entrepreneurs in finance can leverage this approach to gain valuable insights into the dynamics of stock market volatility and investor sentiment. However, its applicability extends beyond finance. The analysis serves as a valuable proxy for gauging the demand for goods and services in diverse markets. By understanding the level of interest and engagement with relevant Wikipedia pages, businesses can assess consumer sentiment and anticipate market trends.

Moreover, researchers can utilize this approach to conduct sentiment analysis, measure public interest in specific topics, or evaluate the impact of events on various domains. Policymakers can also benefit by using such data to assess public awareness of critical issues like COVID-19, allowing them to devise more informed and targeted policies.

Ultimately, this versatile methodology opens doors for cross-disciplinary applications, empowering decision-makers and stakeholders across industries to make well-informed choices based on a deeper understanding of underlying dynamics and trends.

REFERENCES

Agosto, A., & Giudici, P. (2020). COVID-19 contagion and digital finance. *Digital Finance*, *2*(1), 159–167. doi:10.1007/s42521-020-00021-3 PMID:33179008

AngelJ. (2021). Gamestonk: What Happened and What to Do about It. Available at SSRN 3782195. doi:10.2139/ssrn.3782195

Baig, A. S., Butt, H. A., Haroon, O., & Rizvi, S. A. R. (2021). Deaths, panic, lockdowns and US equity markets: The case of COVID-19 pandemic. *Finance Research Letters*, *38*, 101701. doi:10.1016/j.frl.2020.101701 PMID:32837381

Behrendt, S., Peter, F. J., & Zimmermann, D. J. (2020). An encyclopedia for stock markets? Wikipedia searches and stock returns. *International Review of Financial Analysis*, *72*, 101563. doi:10.1016/j.irfa.2020.101563

Black, F. (1976) Studies in stock price volatility changes. In: *Proceedings of the 1976 Meeting of the Business and Economic Statistics Section*. American Statistical Association.

Bollen, J., & Mao, H. (2011). Twitter mood as a stock market predictor. *Computer*, *44*(10), 91–94. doi:10.1109/MC.2011.323

Chatterjee, U., & French, J. J. (2022). A note on tweeting and equity markets before and during the Covid-19 pandemic. *Finance Research Letters*, *46*, 102224. doi:10.1016/j.frl.2021.102224 PMID:35431675

Decker, S., & Schmitz, H. (2016). Health shocks and risk aversion. *Journal of Health Economics*, *50*, 156–170. doi:10.1016/j.jhealeco.2016.09.006 PMID:27792902

Glosten, L. R., Jagannathan, R., & Runkle, D. E. (1993). On the relation between the expected value and the volatility of the nominal excess return on stocks. *The Journal of Finance*, *48*(5), 1779–1801. doi:10.1111/j.1540-6261.1993.tb05128.x

Gómez-Martínez, R., Orden-Cruz, C., & Martínez-Navalón, J. G. (2022). Wikipedia pageviews as investors' attention indicator for Nasdaq. *International Journal of Intelligent Systems in Accounting Finance & Management*, *29*(1), 41–49. doi:10.1002/isaf.1508

Huang, M. Y., Rojas, R. R., & Convery, P. D. (2020). Forecasting stock market movements using Google Trend searches. *Empirical Economics*, *59*(6), 2821–2839. doi:10.1007/s00181-019-01725-1

Kristoufek, L. (2013). BitCoin meets Google Trends and Wikipedia: Quantifying the relationship between phenomena of the Internet era. *Scientific Reports*, *3*(1), 1–7. doi:10.1038/srep03415 PMID:24301322

Kristoufek, L. (2015). Power-law correlations in finance-related Google searches, and their cross-correlations with volatility and traded volume: Evidence from the Dow Jones Industrial components. *Physica A*, *428*, 194–205. doi:10.1016/j.physa.2015.02.057

Liu, B. (2020). *Sentiment analysis: Mining opinions, sentiments, and emotions*. Cambridge university press. doi:10.1017/9781108639286

O'Leary, D. E., & Storey, V. C. (2020). A Google–Wikipedia–Twitter model as a leading indicator of the numbers of coronavirus deaths. *International Journal of Intelligent Systems in Accounting Finance & Management, 27*(3), 151–158. doi:10.1002/isaf.1482

Preis, T., Moat, H. S., & Stanley, H. E. (2013). Quantifying trading behavior in financial markets using Google Trends. *Scientific Reports, 3*(1), 1–6. doi:10.1038/srep01684 PMID:23619126

Ripberger, J. T. (2011). Capturing curiosity: Using internet search trends to measure public attentiveness. *Policy Studies Journal: the Journal of the Policy Studies Organization, 39*(2), 239–259. doi:10.1111/j.1541-0072.2011.00406.x

Rubbaniy, G., Khalid, A. A., Syriopoulos, K., & Samitas, A. (2021). Safe-haven properties of soft commodities during times of COVID-19. *Journal of Commodity Markets, 100223.*

Tetlock, P. C. (2015). The role of media in finance. Handbook of media Economics, 1, 701-721. doi:10.1016/B978-0-444-63685-0.00018-8

Umar, Z., Gubareva, M., Yousaf, I., & Ali, S. (2021). A tale of company fundamentals vs sentiment driven pricing: The case of GameStop. *Journal of Behavioral and Experimental Finance, 30*, 100501. doi:10.1016/j.jbef.2021.100501

Van Aelst, P., Toth, F., Castro, L., Štětka, V., Vreese, C. D., Aalberg, T., Cardenal, A. S., Corbu, N., Esser, F., Hopmann, D. N., Koc-Michalska, K., Matthes, J., Schemer, C., Sheafer, T., Splendore, S., Stanyer, J., Stępińska, A., Strömbäck, J., & Theocharis, Y. (2021). Does a crisis change news habits? A comparative study of the effects of COVID-19 on news media use in 17 European countries. *Digital Journalism (Abingdon, England), 9*(9), 1208–1238. doi:10.1080/21670811.2021.1943481

Vasileiou, E. (2021a). Behavioral finance and market efficiency in the time of the COVID-19 pandemic: Does fear drive the market? *International Review of Applied Economics, 35*(2), 224–241. doi:10.1080/02692171.2020.1864301

Vasileiou, E. (2021b). Explaining stock markets' performance during the COVID-19 crisis: Could Google searches be a significant behavioral indicator? *International Journal of Intelligent Systems in Accounting Finance & Management, 28*(3), 173–181. doi:10.1002/isaf.1499

Vasileiou, E. (2021c). Does the short squeeze lead to market abnormality and antileverage effect? Evidence from the Gamestop case. *Journal of Economic Studies (Glasgow, Scotland).*

Vasileiou, E., Samitas, A., Karagiannaki, M., & Dandu, J. (2021). Health risk and the efficient market hypothesis in the time of COVID-19. *International Review of Applied Economics*, *35*(2), 210–223. doi:10.1080/02692171.2020.1864299

Vosen, S., & Schmidt, T. (2011). Forecasting private consumption: Survey-based indicators vs. Google trends. *Journal of Forecasting*, *30*(6), 565–578. doi:10.1002/for.1213

Wójcik, D., & Ioannou, S. (2020). COVID-19 and finance: Market developments so far and potential impacts on the financial sector and centres. *Tijdschrift voor Economische en Sociale Geografie*, *111*(3), 387–400. doi:10.1111/tesg.12434 PMID:32836484

Xu, S. X., & Zhang, X. (2013). Impact of Wikipedia on market information environment: Evidence on management disclosure and investor reaction. *Management Information Systems Quarterly*, *37*(4), 1043–1068. doi:10.25300/MISQ/2013/37.4.03

Zhang, L., Wang, S., & Liu, B. (2018). Deep learning for sentiment analysis: A survey. *Wiley Interdisciplinary Reviews. Data Mining and Knowledge Discovery*, *8*(4), e1253. doi:10.1002/widm.1253

ENDNOTES

1 https://www.worldometers.info/coronavirus/

2 See https://trends.google.com/trends/yis/2020/GLOBAL/ and https://trends.google.com/trends/yis/2021/GLOBAL/, respectively.

3 In May 2022, more than 5 million studies are related to COVID-19. (https://scholar.google.com/scholar?hl=el&as_sdt=0%2C5&q=covid+19+pandemic&btnG=&oq=COVID-19).

4 Sentiment analysis can be described as the computational study of peoples' opinions, sentiments, and emotions towards specific events or products (Zhang, Wang, and Liu (2018), Liu (2020)). Internet users do not only get information when they use it, but they also give information on what draws their attention, i.e. increased internet searches for COVID-19 mean increased health risk-fear, and increased searches for a stock (or company) means that something happened that drew the users' interest-attention.

5 Top searches in 2021 according to Google Trends https://trends.google.com/trends/yis/2021/GLOBAL/ .

6 https://www.sec.gov/Archives/edgar/data/1326380/000132638016000320/a10k-fy15q4.htm

7 Angel (2021) shows that the average short positions are around 5% of the outstanding shares, but the GME had a significantly higher ratio of short positions.

8 These terms were selected based on a Python code for the most appropriate Wikipedia pages for COVID-19.

9 GJR is the acronym of the names of Glosten, Jagannathan, and Runkle (1993) who initially introduced the model.

10 Both models show that there is an anti-leverage effect because $\gamma_{EGARCH}>0$ and $\gamma_{GJR}<0$ and both are statistically significant.

Chapter 11
Potential of Business Intelligence and Analytics on the Performance of Tourism and Hospitality Companies

Mahsa Amiri
https://orcid.org/0009-0007-3867-5299
Faculty of Economics, Universidade do Algarve, Portugal

Célia M. Q. Ramos
https://orcid.org/0000-0002-3413-4897
School for Management, Hospitality and Tourism (ESGHT), Research Center for Tourism, Sustainability, and Well-Being (CinTurs), Universidade do Algarve, Portugal

ABSTRACT

Nowadays, making the right business decisions is crucial for companies. With the enhancements in connectivity, data accessibility has been expanding rapidly. Information is meaningful, data and business intelligence (BI) turn data into information to support the decisions of persons or companies with the purpose of efficiency and effectiveness increasing. However, selecting the right BI system which can be adopted perfectly by a business is an important issue which still needs further studies. The given study comprises the literature review which focuses on BI and analytics, and it continues to study the structure of a BI system and the effects such systems may cause. The findings contribute to a better comprehension of BI and more efficient feedback from BI systems by choosing the right ones. The future collaboration between BI and artificial intelligence (AI), also BI and sustainability goals, are further given topics in this study

DOI: 10.4018/979-8-3693-0790-8.ch011

INTRODUCTION

In recent years the ability to transform data into useful information is becoming a crucial competitive and success factor for the companies. The huge amount of collected data needs to be converted to information in a timely manner before the data gets old and useless (Hočevar & Jaklič, 2010).

By daily accomplishments in the technology, most of the customer's requests, including tourism related services, are done online through websites or applications. Consequently, there would be an enormous amount of data related to the customers, which can be stored as costumer behavior and their perception (Fuchs *et al.*, 2015). Using this data is a golden advantage for businesses to improve their performance. The market area is a place to compete and using the users' experiences which is a great help for the companies to increase their abilities in this competition. As Rostami (2014) says, recently, the competition in the market is not only for profit and loss, but also it would be for survival or bankruptcy.

The data which is gathered through the online gates, is not informative and it needs to be processed and transformed to sensible information. Business Intelligence (BI) try to analyze and process this data and make it useful for the clients (Fuchs *et al.*, 2015).

Business Intelligence can be considered as extracting and analyzing the data to improve decision-making as Bustamante *et al.* (2020) mentioned in their research. The concept of Business Intelligence (BI) includes connected processes such as: gathering and organizing information, analyzing, and controlling data to provide reports, and support for management activities (Lapa *et al.*, 2014).

Business intelligence enables users to realize complex information quickly and consequently take faster and more efficient decisions (Hočevar & Jaklič, 2010). Techniques, technologies, systems, methodologies, and applications through BI science are applied inside organization systems which help them to receive acknowledgement of the work while getting better perception for decision making and increasing profits (Vajirakachorn & Chongwatpol, 2017). In a study by Pearson (2018) it is mentioned that every dollar spent on analytics and business intelligence solutions would deliver $13.01 in average. In conclusion, a BI implementation in the business can aid in the creation, improvement, or redefinition of marketing and trade products, services, and/or procedures. As a result, the companies would have lower costs and increased revenue in the end. In this approach, BI implementation can assist any organization or firm, regardless of size, business area, or position in domestic and international markets (Lapa *et al.*, 2014). Unprecedented insight into consumer sentiment, client demands, and the identification of new business prospects are some of the results (Vajirakachorn & Chongwatpol, 2017) which lead to operational work optimization, better relations between customers and suppliers, increased profit, more supportive decisions, and competitive advantages in the market (Bustamante *et al.*, 2020).

The benefits of BI adoption in businesses encourage scholars to study and research on this topic. In this study the goal is to understand the process of business intelligence and to comprehend how it would assist the companies to improve and act more efficiently. To clarify the path of the research three principal questions are stated and the goal of the study would be finding proper answers for them.

1) What is the definition for business intelligence?
2) What are the important steps to implement BI in a business?
3) What do we mean by the effects of BI?

In the way to find answers to these questions, the knowledge and experiences from various scholars will be reviewed and compared.

BACKGROUND

The origin of BI can be found within the activities of military intelligence done by a vast variety of secret services of all times. Intelligence has been a significant factor in military success for thousands of years where soldiers would scout, monitor, and analyze data about the activities of their rivals (Nickolas, 2000; Prescott, 1995). This is also supported by Albescu *et al.* (2008) speaking about a war-like approach to the business relationship with competitors.

This methodological transmission of intelligence activities, typically used within the military branch to business activities was first described by Millar Devens in 1865. The author refers to the concept of business intelligence by explaining the methods of a banker, gaining profit by receiving and acting upon information about his environment, prior to his competitors (Bentley, 2017).

Although the early definition was mentioned by Devens (Bentley, 2017), there was no scientific definition of BI until Luhn, whom in his article called: "A Business Intelligence system", gave a generalized description of BI (Luhn, 1958).

For Luhn (1958) a business is defined as collection of activities carried on for whatever purposes, be it science, technology, commerce, industry, law, government, defense, and so on. The author defines intelligence, following Webster Dictionary, as "the ability to apprehend the interrelationships of presented facts in such a way as to guide actions towards a desired goal" (Luhn, 1958, p. 314). As he describes a business intelligence system as a system to disseminate information to the various sections of any industrial, scientific, or government organization. This intelligence system uses data-processing machines for auto-abstracting and auto-encoding of documents and also for creating interest profiles for any "action points" in an organization.

Nevertheless, the term BI was not used extensively until 1990s when Howard Dresner adopted the phrase in his research and consequently, BI was used in Gartner group projects and became common among scientific areas (Negash & Gray, 2008).

From there on, many definitions of business intelligence have been presented in the literature during the last 40 years. Partly they are contradicting each other, however some complementing.

In order to have a better understanding of a BI process, it is worthful to review the basic components of it. Through the studies, various items are considered as BI essential components.

BI implementation can be defined as the process of putting business intelligence inside a business. Implementation of BI inside a business is costly, also it can take a long time (up to one year) (Horakova & Skalska, 2013). In addition, it may face various challenges that can cause failure in the result (Yeoh & Koronios, 2010).

It is also important to have a brief review on the background of the most common components of BI in the literature. Olszak and Ziemba (2007) explain that the structure of a BI system consists of a set of tools, technologies, and software namely as: ETL (Extract, Transform, and Load) tools, data warehouses, OLAP (On-Line Analytical Processing), data mining tools, reporting tools, and applications for presentation.

Negash and Gray (2008) explain that different components are connected via software and make a BI system. These components are as follows: OLAP, data mining, database mining, visualization, marketing, executive information systems, knowledge management, and geographic information systems.

Horakova and Skalska (2013) propose that there are various tools and components relating to BI which are data sources, connection tools, data transformation tools (commonly named ETL), visualization tools, BI front-end tools, measurement tools for business impacts and feedback, BI development plan, etc.

Nyanga *et al.* (2019) name ETL tools, data warehouse, OLAP techniques, and data mining as the common components among BI systems.

Consecutively, this study follows the explanation of Höpken and Fuchs (2021) regarding BI components which are: (i) data collection, (ii) ETL, (iii) data warehouse, and (iv) OLAP, data mining and reporting. In the following these elements are described briefly.

ETL components receive and extract data, transform it, and make data ready to be loaded on data warehouses (Nyanga *et al.,* 2019). It is important to mention that data warehouse is not complete without ETL tools (Nyanga *et al.,* 2019).

Collected data needs to be stored in a place like data warehouse (Nyanga *et al.,* 2019; Negash & Gray, 2008). Since a data warehouse save a large amount of data and information, and not all these information is useful for BI purposes, therefore the most useful data which should be reached routinely for analyzing are gathered in a new place called data mart (Negash & Gray, 2008). Data warehouses not only contribute to store data but also support analytics strategies (Inamdar & Gursoy, 2019).

Facts and dimensions are two elements of a data warehouse (Nanda *et al.*, 2019). Fact is described as the given values and fact tables include measurements or metrics for a business procedure (Nanda *et al.*, 2019). Dimensions are considered as information which empower clients to direct into business issues (Nanda *et al.*, 2019) and presents the description of the facts.

The on-line analytical processing is defined as multidimensional databases for data discovery and analytical processes (Nanda *et al.*, 2019). OLAP and data mining are considered techniques for searching among huge data and analyze them from various aspects (Nyanga *et al.*, 2019). Slice-and-dice, drill down, ad-hoc queries, real-time analysis, and forecasting are some of the common analytic methods in this part (Negash & Gray, 2008). OLAP servers are responsible for applying multi-operations on data (Nanda *et al.*, 2019). The last phase, in addition to the OLAP and data mining, provides reporting functionalities to enable access to the data and generate interactive data visualization and descriptive data analyses (Höpken & Fuchs, 2021).

MAIN FOCUS OF THE CHAPTER

This part of chapter explains some important challenges regarding the BI studies mentioned by other authors. BI definition, implementation, effects, and the measurement of the effects are the topics which are explained deeply. The main challenges regarding these four subjects are discussed and in the next section, the effort would be to find a solution for them.

Definition

Duo to the complexity of the problem of finding a definition for BI, efforts have been made in the literature to categorize the main aspects under which the existing definition have been developed.

In according to Atre (Shaw, 2004), BI is business success realized through rapid and easy access to actionable information through timely and accurate insight into business conditions about customers, finances and market conditions.

For some researchers, BI encompasses data warehousing, business analytics tools, and content/knowledge management (Moss & Hoberman, 2004).

Olszak and Ziemba (2007), define BI as "asset of concepts" which include process and methods not only with the purpose of decision-making development but also for supporting the fair's strategy.

Furthermore, there are authors combining both technical and managerial aspects in their attempts for describing the definition. They believe that, by passing time, definition of BI has developed from one-dimensional to a multi-dimensional definition (Shollo & Kautz, 2010).

Dresner defines BI as an "umbrella term" which includes systems, methods, and theories with the purpose of decision-making improvements (Negash & Gray, 2008). Similarly, Muntean (2018) describes BI as an umbrella term for Information systems, technologies, and strategies which are used by businesses to extract useful information from big data which support the business in decision-making process.

Chee *et al.* (2009) through a survey on BI definitions over decades, group the definitions into three categories: BI definitions under a management aspect, under a technological aspect, and under a product aspect. Under a product aspect, the same as Chee *et al.* (2009), some authors see business intelligence as a product of in-depth analysis of detailed business data as well as analysis practices using BI tools.

Skyrius (2021), in a more general approach, proposes even four different aspects of how BI can be understood. The first is the view of business intelligence under the aspect of an information system which is intended to cover a variety of information sources, including internal and external ones. The second feature shows BI as a cyclical process in which BI needs to be seen as an iterative loop which covers the intelligence process in several steps from initial definition of information requirements to utilization of results and feedback on possible improvements. As third feature BI is explained as a technology platform including a mixture of variant technologies which are located in three layers called data layer, action layer, and delivery layer. Finally, the fourth feature indicates that BI must be seen as a chain of information activities that start with simple issues and continues to the most complicated needs.

Following explanations described above regarding finding a perfect definition for business intelligence, some authors doubt whether generating a perfect definition of BI is probable at all and will be most likely the subject of discussion for the foreseeable future (Skyrius, 2021).

In conclusion, choosing a united explanation which can be acceptable through all the definitions stated in different studies would be difficult.

The difficulty to find an all-encompassing definition is owed mainly to two facts: Firstly, the fast technological development in IT (Information Technology), accompanying with the ever-growing and changing requirements of the companies make it hard to develop precise definitions. Secondly, the characteristics of definitions depend on the question, under which aspect one looks at business intelligence.

Implementation

In the last section, the most common components of BI through the eyes of various scholars were introduced. Regarding the implementation of BI, there are two important topics which are discussed in the research and generally speaking, they need to be studied before taking any action.

The first subject is the stages that the business wants to go through in order to have a BI. The steps which the companies can take may be varied related to different scholars. Regarding the second issue, there is an overwhelming accordance in literature that implementation should be controlled and measured by critical success factors (CSF) (Mungree *et al.*, 2013; Ravasan & Savoji, 2014; Yeoh & Koronios, 2010). The CSFs are the few key areas of activity in which favorable results are required to reach certain goals (Bullen & Rockart, 1981). They are used to qualify success, to understand what the business needs to achieve its objectives such as to make business operations more efficient. In continue, these two topics will be explained in detail.

Stages

The number of stages varies from one study to another study since some authors have a more general approach toward stage definition meanwhile others have more specific ones.

Olszak and Ziemba (2007) introduce only two general steps for building BI. The study explains that the creation of BI is the first stage of the implementation process. This level includes preparing data sources, choosing BI tools, designing and employing BI. The second step called consumption of BI consists of analyses, monitoring, division and making differences.

Other authors (Nyanga *et al.* 2019; Shollo & Kautz, 2010) describe four stages of implementation. The first stage is about data collection. This is the level at which companies need to make targets and select priorities. In the second stage, the firm analyzes collected data and looks for necessary relations and signs. The results of analyzed data create knowledge and information in the third stage. The last stage is taking action and making decisions.

CSFs

As it is mentioned before, the CSFs can be considered as a support for a successful accomplishment of the BI implementation (Mungree *et al.*, 2013). Concerning the CSFs while implementing BI systems, decreases potential risks and optimize resource and efforts usage toward a BI success (Magaireah *et al.*, 2019).

On the other hand, businesses may notice that success in factor's execution not necessarily guarantee a successful implementation, but it accelerates the path for sure (Femenia-Serra *et al.*, 2022).

Yeoh and Koronios (2010), adopted a case study approach and identify three different dimensions for CSFs framework as organizational, process, and technological dimensions.

In another research by Ravasan and Savoji (2014), the process level is divided into two different parts, human resources, and project management. Therefore, the study suggests four dimensions for BI implementation's CSFs which are named as organizational, human resources, project management, and technical.

Zafary (2020) in a recent study, demonstrates structural factors, behavioral factors, environmental factors, processes, output, consequences, and the effect of subcomponents as seven influential issues on BI implementation success.

Some of the important CSFs among the studies related to BI will be explained shortly in the following.

Management Support

Committed management support is known as the most important success factor among the studies (El-Adaileh & Foster, 2019; Nasab *et al.*, 2015; Mungree *et al.*, 2013; Yeoh & Koronios, 2010). A powerful management can provide sufficient resources allocation as well as getting over the internal resistance politics (Nasab *et al.*, 2015; Mungree *et al.*, 2013).

Resources

The next key factor for BI success is providing influential resources. Resources can be divided into three groups which are: Data source system, organization resources, and IT infrastructure (El-Adaileh & Foster, 2019). Data source refers to the quality of collected data and the place where it was collected. Furthermore, it may be defined as the location where data is stored. The study demonstrates that this factor has a strong effect on implementation success.

The term organizational resource is related to technical, financial, and human resources inside a firm (El-Adaileh & Foster, 2019). Nasab *et al.* (2015) illustrate organizational resources as the second crucial factor upon BI success and believe this requirement needs to be set early in the process.

Implementation of a BI system requires a skilled team regarding knowledge, experience, and technical issues (El-Adaileh & Foster, 2019; Nasab *et al.*, 2015; Mungree *et al.*, 2013). Nasab *et al.*, (2015) indicate that technical skills are crucial for employees to meet their responsibilities and a team with insufficient skills may cause failure in the project. The project team must include members from diverse departments with different visions and ideas (El-Adaileh & Foster, 2019) also distinct interpersonal and technical skills (Mungree *et al.*, 2013). Bringing together a team with a varied range of views and competencies can assist the production of a greater number of solutions for complicated challenges (El-Adaileh & Foster, 2019). Also, the study of Yeoh and Koronios (2010) illustrates the benefits of a strong team which includes personnel from both technical and business parts with cross-functional abilities. This kind of skilled team assists in adaptive maintenance, and responding to challenges, also it is a support not only for the installation process but also for further operational stages (Magaireah *et al.*, 2019).

IT infrastructure is also a crucial resource for BI implementation which is mentioned in various studies (El-Adaileh & Foster, 2019; Mungree *et al.*, 2013; Yeoh & Koronios, 2010). Yeoh and Koronios (2010) claim that a scalable and flexible technical framework is a key factor in technical issues. The study argues that BI applications and systems tend to grow as a matter of size, and mostly they become larger than expected. Therefore, a BI system should be flexible and scalable enough to responds adequately also be capable of building long-term solutions. Similarly, El Adaileh and Foster (2019) explain the direct impact of an accurate and confidential IT infrastructure on BI success over longer periods.

Clear Vision

A sharp vision is another necessary element which should be considered while implementing BI since it has significant impacts on the success rate (El-Adaileh & Foster, 2019; Ravasan & Savoji, 2014; Mungree *et al.*, 2013; Yeoh & Koronios, 2010). Visions help organizations to plan their projects. Moreover, the BI system needs to be attached to the company's vision (El-Adaileh & Foster, 2019) since it directs the implementation process (Nasab *et al.*, 2015). According to Yeoh and Koronios (2010), if BI is not tied closely to the business vision, it cannot fulfil the company's objectives. Hence, the BI system would not meet the demands of the business, nor customers and this can be the most common reason for failure during implementation. El-Adaileh and Foster (2019) emphasize that it is essential a vision covers the long-term objectives of a business. These objectives lead the strategic plans of the company and maximize the BI system benefits (Magaireah *et al.*, 2019).

User Integration

Studies show that user participation in both implementation and further stages plays an important role in BI success (El-Adaileh & Foster, 2019; Magaireah *et al.*, 2019; Nasab *et al.*, 2015; Mungree *et al.* 2013).

As Yeoh and Koronios (2010) explain, users are aware of their needs better than a designer or developer who doesn't have direct experience with products. This fact suggests that good user participation during the process creates better communication with the system and develops the quality of the system by receiving feedback from customers (Magaireah *et al.*, 2019). In the end, customers meet their expectations thus the satisfaction level would be enhanced (Magaireah *et al.*, 2019).

All the mentioned stages and success factors regarding the BI implementation are considered from the view of the company which wants to implement BI itself. However, it is worthful to mention in recent years there has been a notable desire among businesses to hire a second party as a consultant which take the responsibility to apply all or some of the stages inside an organization. It is crucial to integrate the consultant's effect into this context since a high number of businesses prefer to hire a consultant for the implementation or projects which are not quite successful. For instance, in the UK between the years 2000 and 2015 unfinished or unsuccessful consultants of any kind, have incurred around 4 billion USD in wasted efforts to the British government (Guild, 2015).

It is also interesting to note that general CSFs regarding the relationship between consultants and their clients have been developed for a long time. However, they never found their way in the literature concerning BI implementation.

Effects

Implementation of business intelligence systems inside a business is a big step which brings various effects with it. There are several studies talking about how business intelligence implementation affects positively on businesses. There are scholars who try to concentrate on a few positive aspects and measure them in detail while some other studies explain the overall influence of BI with wider aspects. Some categorizations of possible effects coming from BI are described in the following.

Watson and Wixom (2007), sort BI benefits as follows: cost saving due to better data structure, saving time for both suppliers and users, providing better-qualified information and enhancement in decision-making as a result, optimization in business operations, and better support for approaching business goals.

Hočevar and Jaklič (2010), explain that BI can bring many positive effects on different aspects such as revenue management, profit enhancement, timesaving, better customer satisfaction, competitiveness, cost reduction, increase in market share, and faster decision-making. In continuing, the authors describe some advantages in detail. As the authors claim, the ability to analyze more data increases the functionality of companies in terms of comparing and planning. In addition, BI with the goal of relationship optimization, develop customer's satisfaction and increase customer loyalty. Moreover, the authors believe that making faster and more efficient decisions is a potential benefit which is approached by BI technology. They call BI as an information technology whose efficiency in decision-making is its goal.

Wieder *et al.* (2012) through a case study, introduce a model and confirm that using BI inside business directly affects positively the overall performance of a company.

Horakova and Skalska (2013) in their study refer to the positive effects of BI on both managerial and employee aspects. They explain that expensiveness, which is the profit earned from products and services, can be developed in time through extra information provided by BI and it results in successful enterprise management. On the other hand, BI tools are assumed to be a support for staff to solve strategic, tactical, and operative problems.

Accordingly, Daneshvar Kakhki and Palvia (2016) in their study on American companies, measured the effects of the BI system on overall business performances. The authors propose a model which indicates that BI implementation has positive effects on ROI (return of investment), ROE (return on equity), and ROS. As a result, the performance of the company improves through the enhancement of these factors by BI implementation.

Another study by Rouhani *et al.* (2016) indicates three main benefits of decision support systems such as BI which are more qualified knowledge processing, and reduction in time and cost of making a decision. The study goes further and identifies beneficial opportunities gained from BI systems as effective decisions, increasing competitive advantages, and stakeholders' satisfaction.

In another study, Yiu *et al.* (2021) explain BI implementation has positive impacts on profitability and it reduces business risks regarding profits. The study argues that using BI systems enhances sales forecasting, operation planning, and production objectives. These elements result in better sale and efficiency development (Yiu *et al.*, 2021). On the other hand, BI implementation inside businesses provides informative reports regarding economic conditions which reduces the number of decisions made based on human intuitions, thus it optimizes the final decision's results, improves the quality of the decision, and decreases the related risks to the company (Yiu *et al.*, 2021).

Another possibility of the BI system is registering all significant activities done by staff. Therefore, there can be a control system for the performance of all employees and their share of the total turnover. This allows to lay off staff with bad performances or to motivate beneficial employees with motivation plans such as a bonus system.

BI provides precise information (Madyatmadja *et al.*, 2021) which increases the functionality of businesses in terms of making decisions and planning (Hočevar & Jaklič, 2010).

Through the collected data, managers receive practical information regarding clients, products, and services. They can observe who are the regular consumers of their services in the concept of future loyalty plans. Also, they would be informed about the qualified products and services to continue or to reform the poor ones. The results not only assist the business in the current decision-making but also support the plans and predictions in the long term.

In the same way, there are advantages to using BI in travel agencies. Recently, customers mostly prefer to customize their trips directly on the internet. Benefits gained from BI can assist travel agencies to rise the positive points and compete in the market to interest more customers.

A study of the customers' behavior results in a better understanding of their actual and future desires. BI analytics enable travel agents to predict trends and changes in customer demands and also to find new travel destinations or any other tourism offers.

This effect of BI can be especially advantageous in the pot-corona time to understand whether the client's behavior has been influenced by the pandemic rules. The same thing can be applied to the impact of climate change or the current global political conflicts on customer decisions for travelling. For instance, BI dashboards can visualize if the regular clients book their trips earlier, whether they choose travel destinations with different climates if they try to avoid long distances or the influence of the above-mentioned factors on the budget.

Sales Optimization

The study by Turktarhan *et al.* (2021) confirms that BI can have notable effects on the user's sale optimization.

An important factor in optimizing sales is successful marketing. Correct marketing secures regular customers, enlarges the company's market share, and targets potential customers.

BI services, provide a rich analytical report for the marketing department, to customize targeting advertisements based on customer preferences. By studying the previous booking time, BI can propose the optimal time to start advertising. For example, whether the clients prefer to purchase products in the last-minute offers, or prefer early bookings, or how long is the time between booking and the beginning of the journey in general. In the same way, BI can control if the selling of the allotments is happening according to the plan, or if it is necessary to add extra marketing support by targeting interested groups. In addition, marketing measures, by observing the market continuously, may lead the business to recently opened markets caused by customer behavior changes. This can be counted as a competitive advantage for tour operators since they can enter the new market early and receive a bigger share of that market.

Measurement of Effects

While there are different discussions on the business performance concept, there is no generally accepted term as definition for BI performance and how to measure it (Daneshvar Kakhki & Palvia, 2016).

Measurement of the BI performance can be achieved through the measurement of a BI process. One method regarding performance measurement is to measure the outcome effects of the process. In this regard, various opinions related to the effects and the way to measure them, are explained by different authors.

To understand how BI can influence on a company, it is necessary to know what kind of effects are being generated during this process. Based on the type of effects presented by each study, diverse measurement method is being proposed by different authors.

Lönnqvist and Pirttimäki (2006) say since the output of a BI is intelligence, many effects generated from BI are non-financial or even intangible benefits however, the non-financial benefits would lead to financial outcomes but there would be a time lag to receive these outcomes.

In the same way, Pirttimäki *et al.* (2006) in their study explain the effects of BI, if they occur, are intangible by nature like improved decision-making.

Pirttimäki *et al.* (2006) name various methods regarding effects measurement. The authors explain calculating methods such as Return on Investment (ROI) or Competitive Intelligence Measurement Model (CIMM) cannot be reliable since the output of the BI is intelligence and it is not clear how to measure it precisely. The study reviews that one of the methods for measuring the effects could be comparison between the results and the project targets set. Furthermore, an approach to measure the effects is called subjective measurement of effectiveness which is based on customer's perceive (like satisfaction). In this method, users would provide questions regarding the products and the results would illustrate how effective the users consider the intelligence products. The authors conclude that there are two main challenges regarding the measurement of BI effects. The first difficulty in measuring effects is the intangible nature of them which makes it difficult to quantify the result of the effect. The second challenge is distinguishing between the benefits received by BI and the achievements from ordinary decision-making or other factors. For example, it may be complicated to determine which cost saving or new revenues result from BI, and which result from other managerial actions. Therefore, measurement of BI effects would be desirable, but it could be problematic at the same time.

In a study by Watson and Wixom (2007), the authors explain there are two general impacts generated from BI which are local and global impacts. The study demonstrates that local benefits are easy to measure such as cost saving on IT infrastructure or time saving for data suppliers. On the other hand, through moving from local impacts to global ones, effects become more complicated to be measured.

In another study by the same authors, Wixom and Watson (2010), they even go further and call benefits tangible and intangible. They believe benefits such as a reduction in headcount by replacing the manual reporting process or cost savings are tangible since they can be tracked and captured in spreadsheets. Therefore, tangible effects are easier to measure and usually, they will happen typically at the department level. However, benefits like process improvements or competitiveness creation are called intangible which are more difficult to be quantified. These kinds of effects would have impacts across the organization.

In the same way, Hočevar and Jaklič (2010), in their research argue that advantages reached from BI could be directly visible or less obvious to determine whether they are the result of BI or other indicators. For instance, the ability of users to access data, create various reports, and having better perspective of data are considered as visible benefits. While, regarding the income increasement in a period, it is hard to measure the contribution of BI precisely. Due to this fact, the advantages could be even greater than what was expected.

The authors categorize the BI benefits into four groups. First, measurable or quantifiable benefits are clear to measure such as an increase in revenue and profit, or reduction in time needed to operate certain tasks. The second group is indirectly quantifiable benefits. This group is mostly related to customer satisfaction. For example, higher satisfaction may lead to customer loyalty and this influences sales volume. Non-measurable benefits are considered the third group of BI effects. The examples of this type could be the better motivation of employees, the influence of IT on communication quality within the organization and so on. The last group of benefits are unpredictable ones which can be new opportunities or creative ideas for a firm. As the study explains, many benefits received from BI are non-financial or even intangible therefore measuring them is problematic.

The authors believe the calculating measurement methods such as ROI, cost-benefit calculating, and the Net Present Value (NVP) are insufficient or unfeasible in BI systems. The study explains qualitative methods such as case studies and user satisfaction analyses with the help of quantitative methods to provide a wider perception of the situation. For instance, indirect quantifiable benefits (customer satisfaction) can be measured through surveys, monitoring the sale volume, or the re-order ratios.

However, some authors believe that considering quantitative values as such is sufficient to measure the effect of BI. Daneshvar Kakhki and Palvia, (2016) say that there are quantitative items that have a direct relation with the business performance such as sale growth, Return on Sale (ROS), ROI, customer satisfaction, market share, profitability, etc. and measuring these values calculate the effectiveness of BI.

In the same way, Yiu *et al.* (2021) believe profitability and firm risk reduction as the effects of business intelligence systems, and they measure these effects with quantitative methods such as ROI.

As can be seen through diverse explanations, one of the challenges regarding effects would be that there are different opinions about the type of effect. In the literature, there is no unified explanation of tangible and intangible, or easy and difficult-to-measure effects. An effect which is considered as a tangible effect in a study may be named as intangible in another one. In the same way, an effect that can be measured easily for a researcher is difficult to measure for another one.

As an example, in the study by Hočevar and Jaklič (2010) increasing in revenue is explained as a quantifiable factor which is easy to measure. On the other hand, Pirttimäki *et al.* (2006) believe it is difficult to measure recent revenue caused by BI since there is no assurance if this revenue results from BI or any other actions.

In conclusion, it is difficult to measure the benefits when it is difficulty to determine the effects themselves (Hočevar & Jaklič, 2010).

SOLUTIONS AND RECOMMENDATIONS

What is BI?

One of the first challenges regarding BI is presenting a comprehensive definition. Finding an appropriate definition for the term of BI which is universally acceptable is one of the goals of this study. For this purpose, the first step is to examine what a definition is and what constitutes a useful scientific definition.

In this study, a definition is considered practical when it follows two main conditions. Firstly, it must describe the nature and the most significant elements of something and secondly, the explanation and the elements should be independent of time as well as technology developments.

These factors can also be seen through the dictionaries and official definitions. As an example, we can consider the definition of cars. According to the Cambridge Online Dictionary, a car is defined as a vehicle with an engine, four wheels, and seats for a small number of people. The definition looks interesting under two mentioned aspects: First, it describes a device consisting of about 30,000 parts with only 19 words in an understandable way. Second, with this definition it is possible to describe Henry Ford's first car, the Quadricycle made in 1896, in the same way the newest Ferrari model Purosangue 2022 can be described. Although there are 126 years of technical developments in the car industry between the two car examples.

This leads the study to the point that BI needs to be described more generally as it has been done in the literature, to approach an ultimate definition also making space for technical development and structural changes.

Therefore, the next step would be finding the essential nature of BI and the indispensable parts of it. BI is offering data-based support for making business decisions. The data must be gathered, processed, and presented. This process is undoubtedly indispensable for describing BI. Based on this viewpoint, data collection, data processing, and results are the most essential components of BI.

This explanation also covers the latest BI as it covers the earliest one. Back to the literature, the earliest submitted function of BI was in a bank where the manager tried to make better decisions and compete with other bankers, by collecting data from the environment and processing these data (Bentley, 2017). At the time of this example, there were no computers or technologies to support the act of business intelligence. However, business intelligence became possible due to its process aspect.

Therefore, considering several recent components in BI definition, such as technologies, data warehouses, software, etc. may not be the correct approach to describe BI. However, using the most recent IT tools and technologies is a huge support for running BI in industries at the current time.

After studying the main facts of a definition, it seems that the BI explanation from a process aspect would be the optimal choice since the importance of BI is what it does and not how or with which elements it does it. In this study, business intelligence is considered as a process including data collection, data processing, and results which support the act of decision making. This view includes the basic nature and the most essential parts also it can be used practically for the past, present and even future.

How BI Can Be Implemented

When we accept BI as a process, the next step would be the implementation of this process within the businesses and companies. As it was mentioned in the last section, there are various phases and factors which are studied to improve the path of BI implementation. However, there are some other crucial elements which need to be considered and decided as the first step of implementing BI. as it was explained, one of these distinctions is whether BI is implemented by a company itself or there would be a second party involved. In this study, there are two general issues, which are assumed as crucial points for making a BI implementation and they are explained in the following.

Distinction Regarding the Implementor

The primary fact regarding how BI can be implemented inside a business, is that who is implementing BI. This can be a challenging matter for companies that should be decided at first since it will affect all further steps. There are different options related to the implementors:

a. **In-house implementation:** For this type of implementation, the company decides to adopt the BI system and take all the stages itself. This method could be costly for businesses since they need to include a full-time IT department and specialists for developing and working with the system (Bestaieva, 2022). Also, software and tools implemented inside the company need to be updated continuously. On the other hand, the company can hold the technology with no limitations. That means the managers can use it time regardless, based on their needs as they apprehend the requirements of their company better than others.

b. **Outsourcing implementation:** This method is divided into two different models. First, it is related to companies who outsource BI implementation. Therefore, a second party will take responsibility for installing a suitable BI system for that business and train the employees to work with the system (Bestaieva, 2022). The second model is for companies who decide to outsource a whole project to another party. In this type of implementation, the main company explains the requirements of a project to a BI consultant company, and the consultant company is responsible for finding results for that specific problem.

Distinction Regarding CSFs

After discussion regarding the different views of an implementor, it is also required to apply this distinction to CSFs.

In the same way, CSFs explained in the studies such as management support, clear vision, skilled team, and resources are focused on the company's capabilities itself. In other words, the mentioned factors are functional when the case of implementation is in-house type that the business desires to implement BI itself without the help of other parties.

When there is a second party such as a BI consultant company, the existing CSFs are not applicable anymore. This fact is explained through two examples.

Regarding a clear vision, it is discussed that the factor should be determined by the company and management. Imagine the company is giving the responsibility of a project to a consultant company. In this case, the required vision can only arise by the consultant part through understanding the company's general requirements and resources. Therefore, adjusting the right vision for a specific project would crucially depend on the consultant's high-quality and experienced activities.

As an extra example, the quality of resources is being considered. In the case that a consultant company is implementing BI inside a business, this factor depends on the implementor and not on the main company. Therefore, the consultant company must select the finest equipment and tools by studying the main company's history and requirements.

Due to the explained reasons, the author acknowledges the disregard of the other participant's activities in the implementation process as a significant gap regarding the CSF concept. Taking this point into consideration can improve the success rate of an implementation.

As a result, this study attempts to form a separate category of CSFs which is required to be considered in the case of outsourcing implementation. The proposed CSFs are described as follows:

a. **Consultant's capability and experience:** it is crucial that the consultant company has long-term expertise in planning and implementing BI. It is also critical that the analysts and consultants are skilled and experienced not only in BI implementation but also in the client's business context. When consultant specialists have a background in the business theme, they can offer practical solutions regarding projects and implementation.
b. **Understanding and explaining: The** consultant company should be efficient enough to understand the client company's internal structure, available staff, and resources to maximize the benefits for the company.

The consultants must develop a clear plan for the BI implementation program that could be understandable even for non-IT specialists such as management or the economy department so they can receive a clear vision of the whole project, costs, and supports that they need to provide.

c. **Training and involvement of staff:** It is also important that the consultant company has the ability to teach clients the correct use of BI systems and involve the staff in all levels of the process.

A summary of CSFs from the aspect of in-house implementation (collected from other authors) and out-source implementation (presented in this chapter) are shown in Table 1.

Table 1. Summary of CSFs from the Aspect of In-House Implementation and Out-Source Implementation

	In-house implementation (Most mentioned in the articles)	Out-source implementation
CSF	• Management support • Clear vision • Skilled team • User integration • Resources: - Data resources - Organization resources - IT infrastructure	• Consultant's capability and related experiences • Understanding and explaining the abilities of the consultant • Training and involvement of staff

How to Measure the Effects of BI

As discussed in the last section, it is difficult to determine the effects of a BI process as well as measure the benefits (Hočevar & Jaklič, 2010). There are various opinions regarding the definition of the effects which front each other when it comes to different authors.

One of the less-mentioned issues in this regard is the dependency of BI's effects on its users. BI cannot be considered as a fully automatic system like AI-controlled products, which delivers the desired results on its own, once it is initialized. BI can be considered as a process whose result empowers the action of decision-making by the user. Due to this fact, when BI is implemented, it has no effects nor any benefits on its own. Such an effect or benefit develops when the user is using BI.

Accordingly, an effect which needs to be measured is not the result of a BI system, but only the result of an interaction between the user and the system. This fact can be seen through the example of a poorly implemented BI system which can have the same negative impacts on final effects as a well-implemented BI that is used poorly or incorrectly by the user. For instance, Hočevar and Jaklič (2010) mention in the case of report creation, based on the company target the value of the task could be different whether the manager follows the work itself or leaves it to another person and saves time for other tasks. Therefore, the value of the task could vary based on the users.

This leads the study to the following definition. The effect that BI has on a company is the result of the interaction between the BI system and the users.

With the assumption that there is an interaction between the user and BI and the effect has been generated, the second challenge would be the influence of external indicators on the results of that effect. To be clearer, when there is an effect from a BI process, there would be several factors from outside the process atmosphere, which may have impacts on the results of the company's decisions.

Therefore, it becomes difficult to determine how much of the measured effect is related to BI and how much is related to other indicators (Pirttimäki *et al.*, 2006). The following indicators are considered as the important factors in this study which influence on final benefits.

Interpretation Ability

In the context of BI measuring quantitative results alone would be worthless. It is also important to be able to interpret the result.

For example, in a questionnaire regarding the creation of new destinations for a tourism company, the company may receive several new destinations. However, it is crucial to know who filled out the questionnaires and to collect some personal information to interpret the result. In other words, the final decision regarding the new destination depends on the target group of that company. Therefore, the detailed information of the people who fill the questionary is important.

Similarly, the result obtained from BI would not be useful if it is not interpretable. Hence, it is decisive to know that what are the sources of the collected data as well as the circumstances of the measurement.

Macroeconomic Environment

Every business is exposed to external factors such as economic, political, or even technological factors which affect the business's operation and performance. Some practical examples of these factors could be the economic situation of the traveler's, or legal restrictions.

As the external effects also influence the results provided by BI, they should be always considered while measuring the effects which are coming from BI. In other words, the measured effects must be adjusted for external influences in order to reach the actual BI effect.

For example, think of a case in which there is a 30% decrease in the number of travellers to a certain destination based on the economic situation. As the result, there would be a 10% decrease in the number of guests for a hotel which is equipped with a BI system. Although there is a reduction in the number of clients for that hotel, if you want to compare the 10% reduction rate of the hotel to the general reduction rate of 30%, there would be a +20% benefit for that hotel gained from strategic plans made by the BI process.

Reference Values

The results of an effect measurement always remain relative as long as there are no reference values developed to compare the measurement results with. When there is no reference value described for a company, it is not possible to realize exactly whether the effects of BI are positive and if it is so, to what extent. It is important to mention that the formation of such reference values depends entirely on the corporate strategy.

For instance, for a start-up company which in the first few years puts its focus on gaining a certain amount of the market share and not making a profit, a weak effect of BI regarding profit enhancement is not seen as a negative effect. Therefore, in some circumstances, the measured effect size could be zero compared to the reference value.

Time Difference Between Action and Result

One of the problems of BI is that there are differences between the time that a decision is made and the time that a result occurs (Lönnqvist & Pirttimäki, 2006). This time lag varies from one decision to another. Because of these time difference periods, sometimes it is not clear to identify which gained benefit is related to which decision. As an example, imagine that a company, based on the results received from BI, include a new service for the clients but it takes a long time for the company to see the results of this decision. After a few months, due to the other analyses, the company decided to invest in advertising which can have a faster influence. In the end, when the company gain benefits, it may be hard to relate the final benefits to a certain decision.

Based on the explained challenges, it can be concluded that the precise measurement of the BI effects would be difficult to achieve. However, the proposed considerations would make the measurement more reliable. It is suggested that in order to measure the effect two phases need to be considered. The first phase is to understand the role of the user in the quality of the created effect. An effect is not directly a result of BI but is a result of the interaction of BI and the user. As it is discussed in previous parts, BI is a process to support the decisions. However, the decisions as such are made by the user, not the BI system. Therefore, BI cannot have an effect alone, but when the user makes a decision based on the BI results, the effects of that decision can be seen. It is also notable to mention if the user takes the action based on personal perceptions not based on the BI results, the advantages or disadvantages of the action cannot be called BI effects since they are not related to the BI process outcomes.

The second phase would be when the effect has been created. In this phase, the influences of external indicators on the effect should be mentioned. Interpretation

Figure 1. Two phases regarding the phase measurement
Source: Authors

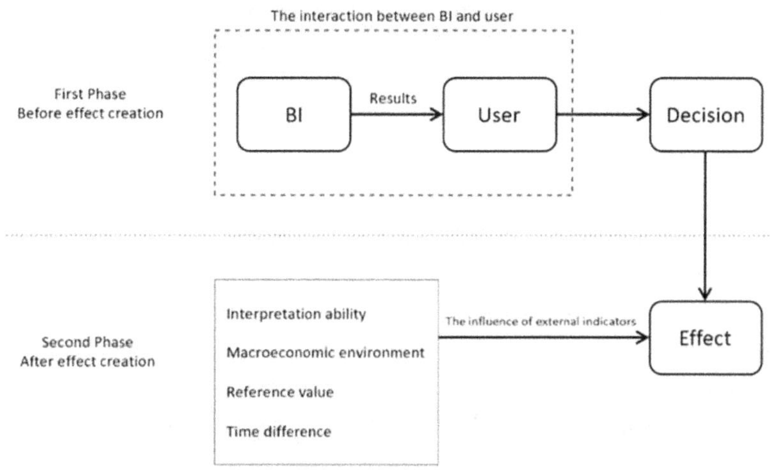

conditions, the macroeconomic environment, the firm's reference values, and the time lag between making a decision and having a result are the most important indicators which affect the final impacts.

Considering these two phases in the process of effect measurement may result in a more precise answer. These two phases are shown in Figure 1.

FUTURE RESEARCH DIRECTIONS

In this study, there is an effort to explain some new points of view regarding BI which could benefit from further research.

Recently, the interest of the business to employ a BI consultant instead of taking all the implementation stages is increasing more and more. Therefore, research about all the aspects of BI implementation, when the second party is involved, is crucial. In this study, the different issues regarding the CSFs were explained. However, these factors can be extended through various opinions in the future. Furthermore, the generation of steps towards selecting the right consultant based on the business's needs could be studied.

It is also mentioned that the outcome of the BI process is highly dependent on the role of the user. However, there were limitations in providing further research on the effective factors related to the BI user, which may optimize the outcome of this process. As an example, in future studies, a user evaluation system could be applied to the effects measurement methods.

In addition, it is important to consider the influence of external indicators on the results of a BI process. A limited number of these indicators are explained in this study. Nevertheless, further research is required to complete the list of these indicators in order to have a more precise comprehension of the BI effects and influences.

CONCLUSION

Regarding the BI definition, it is explained that there are still uncertainly for its comprehension among studies. As it is discussed, the best definitions are the ones which include the basic nature of the subject with crucial elements and have a long-lasting impression. Due to this fact, data collection, data processing, and results are considered as the most important elements of BI. considering technologies and digital components as parts of BI cannot be a right approach since BI can be still meaningful even without these elements. Therefore, in this study BI is defined as a data driven process providing supports for making decisions.

There are some influential points which should be considered before the implementation of BI in a business. First, it is necessary to decide who is implementing BI. If the company prefers to take all the stages itself, the implementation would be in-house type. The advantage of this method is that the new decision support process can be time-independent for the business, and they can benefit from it in any case. Also, the company can use BI based on their specific requirements which can be more effective. On the other hand, this approach is costly, and it needs an IT department to look after the system and upgrade the components when it is required. Outsourcing implementation is another method of BI implementation for companies who would rather hire a second party for this purpose. There are two approaches to this option. The company may ask a consulting firm to install the whole process inside the business and train the internal employees to work with it. The other option is when a company collaborate with a BI consultant firm only on certain projects.

The other essential key point of BI implementation is related to CSFs which are considered as control factors to determine implementation effectiveness. In the same way, there is a distinction between internal and external implementors, there should be contrasting views of CSF based on the type of implementor. However, in the reviewed studies, most of the CSFs explained are functional when the implementation is in-house type. This matter is considered as a significant gap regarding CSF research. As a result, the study suggests a second CSFs group in the case of outsourcing implementation which includes: the consultant's qualifications in capability and experience, understanding and explaining, and efficient staff training.

Regarding the effects measurement methods, two main challenges are explained in this study. Firstly, the effects cannot be directly related to BI as such. They are created from an interaction between BI and the user. BI provides correct information to support the user in decision making and after that user decides, the effect would be generated. Secondly, there are other factors which have an influence on the results. Interpretation ability, macroeconomics environment, reference values, and the time difference between a decision and the generated effect are the major elements which can be applied to the previous measurement methods for a more reliable measurement outcome. Notably, due to the discussed challenges, it can be concluded that a precise and accurate measurement of BI contribution on the effects is hardly achievable. However, adopting the mentioned filters inside the measurement methods enhances the efficiency of this measurement estimation.

ACKNOWLEGMENT

This paper is financed by National Funds provided by FCT- Foundation for Science and Technology through project UIDB/04020/2020.

REFERENCES

Albescu, F., Pugna, I., & Paraschiv, D. (2008). Business intelligence & knowledge management–Technological support for strategic management in the knowledge based economy. *Revista Informatica Economică*, *4*(48), 5–12.

Bentley, D. (2017). *Business Intelligence and Analytics*. PDF Drive. https://www.pdfdrive.com/business-intelligence-and-analytics-e56416503.html.

Bestaieva, D. (2022). *The full Guide on Business Intelligence Implementation in 2022*. Clever Road.

Bullen, C. V., & Rockart, J. F. (1981). *A primer on critical success factors*. MIT Press. https://dspace.mit.edu/bitstream/handle/1721.1/1988/SWP-1220-08368993-CISR-069.pdf?sequen.

Bustamante, A., Sebastia, L., & Onaindia, E. (2020). BITOUR: A Business Intelligence Platform for Tourism Analysis. *ISPRS International Journal of Geo-Information*, *9*(11), 671. doi:10.3390/ijgi9110671

Chee, T., Chan, L. K., Chuah, M. H., Tan, C. S., Wong, S. F., & Yeoh, W. (2009). Business intelligence systems: state-of-the-art review and contemporary applications. *In Symposium on progress in information and communication technology*. IEEE.

Daneshvar Kakhki, M. & Palvia, P. (2016). Effect of business intelligence and analytics on business performance. *AIS Electronic Library* (AISeL), 1-10.

El-Adaileh, N. A., & Foster, S. (2019). Successful business intelligence implementation: A systematic literature review. *Journal of Work-Applied Management, 11*(2), 121–132. doi:10.1108/JWAM-09-2019-0027

Femenia-Serra, F., Alzua-Sorzabal, A., & Pousa-Unanue, A. (2022). Business intelligence and the public management of destinations: The view of DMOs. In *Information and Communication Technologies in Tourism 2022: Proceedings of the ENTER 2022 eTourism Conference*, (pp. 417-422). Springer International Publishing.

Fuchs, M., Höpken, W., & Lexhagen, M. (2014). Applying business intelligence for knowledge generation in tourism destinations–A case study from Sweden. In *Tourism and leisure: Current issues and perspectives of development* (pp. 161–174). Springer Fachmedien Wiesbaden.

Guild. (2015). *Why Do Consulting Engagements Fail?* Guild. https://blog.guild.im/why-do-consulting-engagements-fail-dab
33a471b29

Hočevar, B., & Jaklič, J. (2010). Assessing benefits of business intelligence systems–a case study. *Management, 15*(1), 87–119.

Höpken, W., & Fuchs, M. (2022). Business Intelligence in Tourism. In *Handbook of e-Tourism* (pp. 497–527). Springer International Publishing. doi:10.1007/978-3-030-48652-5_3

Horakova, M. & Skalska, H. (2013). Business Intelligence and Implementation in a Small Enterprise. *Journal of Systems Integration* (1804-2724), *4*(2), 50-61.

Inamdar, S. R., & Gursoy, K. (2019). *Cloud hosted business-data driven BI platforms.* Availabe at: https://scholarship.libraries.rutgers.edu/discovery/delivery/01RUT_INST:ResearchRepository/12643384890004646?l#136435357
70004646

Lapa, J., Bernardino, J., & Figueiredo, A. (2014). A comparative analysis of open source business intelligence platforms. *In Proceedings of the International Conference on Information Systems and Design of Communication*, (pp. 86-92). ACM. 10.1145/2618168.2618182

Lönnqvist, A., & Pirttimäki, V. (2006). The measurement of business intelligence. *Information Systems Management, 23*(1), 32–40. doi:10.1201/1078.10580530/45769.23.1.20061201/91770.4

Luhn, H. P. (1958). A business intelligence system. *IBM Journal of Research and Development, 2*(4), 314–319. doi:10.1147/rd.24.0314

Madyatmadja, E. D., Adiba, C. N. A., Sembiring, D. J. M., Pristinella, D., & Putra, A. M. (2021). The Positive Impact of Implementation Business Intelligence and Big Data in Hospitality and Tourism Sector. *International Journal of Emerging Technology and Advanced Engineering, 11*(6), 59–71. doi:10.46338/ijetae0621_07

Magaireah, A. I., Sulaiman, H., & Ali, N. (2019). Identifying the most critical factors to business intelligence implementation success in the public sector organizations. *The Journal of Social Sciences Research, 5*(2), 450–462. doi:10.32861/jssr.52.450.462

Moss, L., & Hoberman, S. (2004). *The importance of data modeling as a foundation for business insight.* Design.

Mungree, D., Rudra, A., & Morien, D. (2013). *A framework for understanding the critical success factors of enterprise business intelligence implementation. Proceedings of the Nineteenth Americas Conference on Information Systems,* Chicago, Illinois.

Muntean, M. (2018). Business intelligence issues for sustainability projects. *Sustainability (Basel), 10*(2), 335. doi:10.3390/su10020335

Nanda, A., Gupta, S., & Vijrania, M. (2019). A comprehensive survey of OLAP: recent trends. *In 2019 3rd International Conference on Electronics, Communication and Aerospace Technology (ICECA), IEEE,* (pp. 425-430). IEEE.

Nasab, S. S., Selamat, H., & Masrom, M. (2015). A delphi study of the important factors for BI system implementation in the public sector organizations. *Jurnal Teknologi, 77*(19), 113–120. doi:10.11113/jt.v77.6539

Negash, S., & Gray, P. (2008). Business intelligence. In *Handbook on decision support systems 2* (pp. 72–80). Springer. doi:10.1007/978-3-540-48716-6_9

Nickolas, J. D. (2000). *Flattening the Military Force Structure.* Army Command and General Staff Coll Fort Leavenworth Ks School of Advanced Military Studies.

Nyanga, C., Pansiri, J., & Chatibura, D. (2019). Enhancing competitiveness in the tourism industry through the use of business intelligence: A literature review. *Journal of Tourism Futures, 6*(2), 139–151. doi:10.1108/JTF-11-2018-0069

Olszak, C. M., & Ziemba, E. (2007). Approach to building and implementing business intelligence systems. *Interdisciplinary Journal of Information, Knowledge, and Management, 2*(1), 135–148. doi:10.28945/105

Pearson, A. W. (2018). *The predictive airliner*. Intelligencia Publishing.

Pirttimäki, V., Lönnqvist, A., & Karjaluoto, A. (2006). Measurement of Business Intelligence in a Finnish Telecom-munications Company. *Electronic Journal of Knowledge Management*, *4*(1), 83–90.

Prescott, J. E. (1995). The evolution of competitive intelligence. *International review of strategic management, 6,* 71-90.

Ravasan, A. Z., & Savoji, S. R. (2014). An investigation of BI implementation critical success factors in Iranian context. [IJBIR]. *International Journal of Business Intelligence Research*, *5*(3), 41–57. doi:10.4018/ijbir.2014070104

Rostami, N. A. (2014). Integration of Business Intelligence and Knowledge Management–A literature review. *Journal of Intelligence Studies in Business*, *4*(2), 30–40. doi:10.37380/jisib.v4i2.95

Rouhani, S., Ashrafi, A., Ravasan, A. Z., & Afshari, S. (2016). The impact model of business intelligence on decision support and organizational benefits. *Journal of Enterprise Information Management*, *29*(1), 19–50. doi:10.1108/JEIM-12-2014-0126

Shaw, T. (2004). *Shaku Atre Interview: What is Business Intelligence?* DSS Resources. http://dssresources.com/interviews/atre/atre07092004.html

Shollo, A., & Kautz, K. (2010). Towards an understanding of business intelligence. *ACIS 2010 Proceedings, 86*. https://aisel.aisnet.org/acis2010/86

Skyrius, R. (2021). *Business Intelligence*. Springer International Publishing. doi:10.1007/978-3-030-67032-0

Turktarhan, G., Gopalan, R. & Ozkul, E. (2021). Big Data and Business Intelligence in Hospitality and Tourism. *University of South Florida M3 Center Publishing, 17*(9781732127593), 5.

Vajirakachorn, T., & Chongwatpol, J. (2017). Application of business intelligence in the tourism industry: A case study of a local food festival in Thailand. *Tourism Management Perspectives*, *23*, 75–86. doi:10.1016/j.tmp.2017.05.003

Watson, H. J., & Wixom, B. H. (2007). The current state of business intelligence. *Computer*, *40*(9), 96–99. doi:10.1109/MC.2007.331

Wieder, B., Ossimitz, M., & Chamoni, P. (2012). The impact of business intelligence tools on performance: A user satisfaction paradox? *International Journal of Economic Sciences and Applied Research*, *5*(3), 7–32.

Wixom, B., & Watson, H. (2010). The BI-based organization. [IJBIR]. *International Journal of Business Intelligence Research*, *1*(1), 13–28. doi:10.4018/jbir.2010071702

Yeoh, W., & Koronios, A. (2010). Critical success factors for business intelligence systems. *Journal of Computer Information Systems*, *50*(3), 23–32.

Yiu, L. D., Yeung, A. C., & Cheng, T. E. (2021). The impact of business intelligence systems on profitability and risks of firms. *International Journal of Production Research*, *59*(13), 3951–3974. doi:10.1080/00207543.2020.1756506

Zafary, F. (2020). Implementation of business intelligence considering the role of information systems integration and enterprise resource planning. *Journal of intelligence studies in business, 10*(1), 59-74.

KEY TERMS AND DEFINITIONS

Artificial Intelligence: The simulation of human intelligence processes, especially by computer systems. It presents many business potentialities, such as sales forecasting, customer segmentation, fraud detection, and quality control.

Business Intelligence: This results from information systems that combine data with analytical tools to provide information relevant to decision-making while seeking to improve the quality and availability of this information to decision-makers.

Decision-Making: The process of making choices. After detecting a problem involves gathering information and assessing alternative resolutions, the chosen alternative is implemented, which will be identified as the chosen decision.

Sustainability: It considers three dimensions: environmental, social and economic, interlinked to meet the needs of the present without compromising those of future generations and where the technology can support the three dimensions.

Tourism Industry: One of the largest industries in the world. It emerged to satisfy the human need to travel to and see different places as part of the service sector, including hospitality (e.g., accommodation, restaurants), transportation (e.g., airlines, car rental), travel facilitation and information (e.g., tour operators, tourist information centres), and attractions and entertainment (e.g., heritage sites and traditional and cultural events).

Chapter 12
AI Unleashed:
Transforming Event Experiences and Engagement

Tanushri Mukherjee
https://orcid.org/0000-0001-5120-7982
Amity University, India

Pallavi Mishra
Amity University, India

ABSTRACT

This chapter will delve into the dynamic landscape of event management and how artificial intelligence (AI) is revolutionizing the overall event experience. AI technologies have left no area untouched, and, similarly, event planners and event entrepreneurs have also integrated AI in every phase of seamless event execution. Through a comprehensive exploration of AI-driven tools and technologies in the realm of event management, the chapter aims to shed light on how AI is reshaping the entire process of event design, delivering a personalised touch to its attendees thus influencing the nature of engagement strategies. The chapter aims to provide the readers with a holistic understanding of the transformative potential and responsible use of AI in creating unforgettable event experiences. The researcher also employs qualitative research method and seeks the perception of seasoned event professionals related to the topic to further add to its relevance and significance.

INTRODUCTION

"According to a recent 2018 survey, 88% of event professionals said they would be

DOI: 10.4018/979-8-3693-0790-8.ch012

relying on AI, up 107% from 2017 (42%). Event Planners have realized the significant benefits of integrating AI into their event planning checklist." (cleproductions.com)

Times have changed and the advent of the digital era with its plethora of tools and engaging platforms have remarkably transformed the business models of every organization making them more innovation driven, sustainable and inclusive. With the dawn of a new era of innovative communication approaches influencing the mindset of the populace, the fact cannot be denied that content which is relatable, interactive, engaging and customer-oriented draws the attention of the masses. In the parlance of successful business operation and cut-throat competition, customer satisfaction and value co-creation has assumed the centerstage. In midst of the prevailing business scenario and every organization looking out for that "**One second of magical attention of the potential customers or audiences**", the challenge lies in how to grab that one second of precious attention in a manner which would be beneficial for the organization. Customer data and its analysis has become the strongest weapon for the digital marketers to create an edge in the potential market and secure a robust place for their brands. In such a scenario, Artificial Intelligence with its ever invasive and highly appealing tools and applications have made a successful inroad into every business sector. It would not be incorrect to state that the present times is of "Personalization" an one can see its influence on every aspect of business operation, whether it be organizing an event, disseminating a message, or mapping the mindset of the stakeholders or reaching out to the stakeholders in the most influential manner resulting in noteworthy stakeholder satisfaction and engagement. With the application of advanced Artificial Intelligence (AI) tools, businesses can now map individual behavior and attitudes in an impeccable manner and gain a deeper understanding of the driving factors and preferences behind consumer purchase decision and consumer motivation thus helping in the adoption of a design thinking approach and framing accurate consumer personas. AI Tools have ushered in an innovative technology driven revolution which every organization needs to integrate in its business model. It has given a new direction to marketing and customer relationship strategies and patterns as brands are presently more focused on niche segmented target appeal instead of wild mass notifications. The key factor behind the widespread application of AI in every business area is its immense ability to execute tasks which would otherwise require human intervention and a lot more time (IBM).

Event Industry, being called Sunrise Industry, has been making progress in leaps and bounds with a double-digit growth and generating noticeable revenue in almost every category. According to FICCI-EY Report, 23 "The live events segment is expected to grow at a CAGR of 22% over the next three years to reach INR134 billion by 2025". The report further states that "The core difference between the pre- and post-COVID-19 events segment is the increase in share of ticketed event revenues vis-à-vis sponsorship". In contemporary times where social media has influenced our lives in various ways, it cannot be denied that it has also casted a significant impact on how we celebrate and capture the smallest of moments of joy which are priceless for us.

Today Artificial Intelligence has achieved progress across multiple industries with the potential to perform even better in future. The use of AI is significantly influencing the quality of experiences of event attendees as per their needs and expectations thus making a significant contribution in the generation of value and excellent return on investment. AI has emerged as a major catalyst of change in every sector of business as a vital independent resource, ushering in a new level of human-non-human interaction. AI is a multifaceted non-human actor with a wide range of capabilities. AI is helping the event professionals in many ways to deliver an event seamlessly with remarkable outcome and with more significant impact.

Despite artificial intelligence's tremendous potential, some pertinent questions remain like- How will AI evolvein the coming years? Will AI surpass and replace human intelligence, and in which industries can it be applied more effectively with optimum potential? In contributing to critical discourse revolving around the widespread application of AI, researchers have questioned whether these latest technological advancements can add real value or if it is overhyped.

INNOVATIVE AND EXPERIENTIAL WORLD OF EVENTS

Events have always been the most impactful marketing strategy remembered for providing a mix of tangible and intangible experiences to the attendees. The touch and feel advantage and greater scope of interactions a client gets in an event has proved to be the strongest reason behind it being called a powerful experiential marketing tool. Event management has in the last decades evolved into a basket of memorable experiences and occurrences ranging from personal to corporate to artistic and cultural all encompassed in the categories of IP Based Events or Managed Events or Digitally activated events thus being more than just about organizing weddings. Today, it is amongst the most highly contributing sectors of GDP. According to Indian Events and Activations industry expected to cross Rs 10,000 crore by 2020-21: EY Report. (2017), the market of events is expanding each new day with its exponential growth and due to the major factors of digital activation, sports leagues, rural expansion and government initiatives followed by IPs, personal events, product launches, expansion of mini-metros and BTL spends. The growing need for interactive and engaging marketing communication and image building strategies for organizations and the growing inclination towards celebrating every moment has greatly stimulated the need and significance of events multi folds. With the growing craze of the clients to organize events as one of the highly engaging branding strategies, it has also emerged as a highly demanding career option for the present generation who are showing active interest in the industry.

With increased standard of living of the people, growth in disposable income, growing impact of globalization and urbanization and economic reasons like executing hospitality, tourism, business, festive and entertainment events, the industry has assumed new proportions of significance. Every event is a unique magical moment to captivate the hearts of participants with their innovative concepts and event design and the application of the latest technology.

Today, with the pandemic having wreaked havoc throughout the globe, adversely affecting businesses and industries regarding the whole, the necessity for good event management solutions and practices is even more crucial than ever before. The need to come out even more knowledgeable and eventually successful, at the same time, is much more challenging as post pandemic the industry is at its lowest, both financially and when it comes to sustaining the industry and facing the challenges as customer choices and preferences and the priorities of people have undergone sea change. However, in spite of odds, the pandemic showed a new path for the event planners to let the industry keep functioning with changed models. The times witnessed the influx of virtual events along using the new hybrid model of event management and the event planners doing their best to readily adopt the new technology and create unique experiences for their customers by capitalizing on the technological along with other resources available.

IMMERSIVE INFLUENCE OF ARTIFICIAL INTELLIGENCE IN THE TECHNOLOGY DRIVEN ERA

We find AI influencing almost every area of organizational operation and it's a revolution which cannot be ignored. Business leaders irrespective of the size of organizations have realized the immense utility of the technology in the field of creating a competitive edge in the market, whether it be by simplifying the manner of functions of organizations or establishing closer ties with the stakeholders by developing a complete knowledge about their thoughts and opinions or whether it be collecting and analyzing valuable consumer data and knowing the changing graph of stakeholder attitudes and opinion. Artificial Intelligence may be a broad field of computing concerned with creating intelligent computers capable of doing activities that normally require human intelligence. Computer Science, as against natural intelligence, is intelligence displayed by robots and has gained tremendous popularity in today's globe. According to Schroer, A. (2023), AI by its excellent analysis quality enables business organisation to take major decisions in very less time based on valuable data analysis. Advanced online search engines, recommendation systems, chat bots, data analytics, virtual reality, interpreting human speech, self-driving automobiles and automatic decision-making are all samples of AI applications which have enabled smooth and effective functioning of organizations. Risq, F. (2021) also expresses that AI will continue to develop and evolve more and more to analyse huge gigabytes of data very quickly and with more accuracy and gathering data and then analysing it properly drawing valuable interpretations is something which organisations are looking out for in today's times.

The entire graph of event management comprising of all the phases right from research, to creating the event design and concept to event planning, preparations, and execution- all are nowadays handled by the event professionals with more efficiency and least pain because of the unimaginable benefits offered by varied AI Tools. The technology is being utilized in the events sector to handle massive volumes of event attendee data that would otherwise be illegible or require a professional to distill, taking several months. According to SpeedNetworking.com, an event technology site, AI has simplified the otherwise very complex task of getting a knowledge about attendee data and their likes, interests and preferences and then conceptualizing an event based on like-minded attendees. It is also used to evaluate venue possibilities depending on the audience size, amenities, and event type. The advantages of AI in this sector can range from reading the client's event needs and choose the best providers for them to helping in drafting innovative and most liked content, to providing valuable insights regarding event scheduling to several highly creative event apps and chatbots. Having data readily available for the organization to decide means speedier decision- making and less wasted time and having a more targeted niche approach. Wilson, C. (2019) points out that AI has been immensely useful for the event marketing team as it enables them to get the pulse of event attendee persona and then execute a tested marketing campaign or social media promotion plan based on fruitful analysis of big data. The author discusses about the various available AI enabled event apps which guide event planners to decipher individual preferences and guides the attendees too in the right direction based on the information provided by them.

CONCEPTUAL FRAMEWORK RELATING AI WITH EVENTS

The chapter is based on a very popular Media Research Theory named Uses and Gratifications Theory and New Media of Jay Blumler and Elihu Katz. There is no doubt in the fact that AI enabled tools to have made their presence felt in every aspect of successful event management resulting in its successful planning and execution in the direction of participant satisfaction. The times have changed and every organisation whether commercial or voluntary or even media must function based on the preferences and opinion of the public. Organisations need to tailor their messages and employ platforms and tools based on the likes and preferences of the masses.

Uses and Gratification Theory is a user centric theory of mass communication. The theory primarily points out that user needs, and satisfaction is the deciding factor behind the usage of media and thus media users deliberately choose media which satisfies their given needs and contributes in enhancing their knowledge, relaxation, entertainment needs, social interactions/companionship or diversion. In times of digital era and the widespread usage of social media, users can communicate instantly with their desired target audiences in real time, and they are the deciding entities regarding which media to use. AI has been like a boon for the organizations as they help the management to better understand their stakeholders and devise a better policy or strategy or content and ensure its better delivery as per the needs and demands of the stakeholders. Therefore, every organization is using AI to reach out to its stakeholders in a better and a more effective manner.

"Uses and Gratifications Theory and New Media" is an extended version of the existing Uses and Gratification Theory talking about the changed gratifications people get through social media in the new age. In today's times people have great control over what media they choose what they interact with, when they interact with it, and more content choices. The theory states that people are very active, and they chose their media as per their needs and satisfaction and in this perspective, they get new types of gratifications from the usage of internet, especially new media. The present new media version of the theory discusses about the gratifications obtained by people through social media platforms. Social media and computer aided AI tools are apt examples of new media tools which have become indispensable for every organization which follows an inclusive approach and operates with user-centric approach. AI technologies enable the organizations to know what the media preferences of the people are and how they are using the media and thus develop a product or content which is as per the likes and tastes of the audience.

Events being one of the most impactful direct marketing tools also needs to deliver its outcome as per the public/client's tastes and preferences to strike their six senses and their overall experience. AI Platforms have provided an easier and more accurate way of knowing the event stakeholders in a better manner and deliver the final event product which is completely customised time and again as per the feedback and demands of event attendees thus helping in getting a complete ROI for the event planners and clients. Social media platforms have been the most widely used tool for connecting with the target audiences and they have been very effective in providing the audiences a place to share their thoughts and opinion about the events with hundreds of people. The platforms have thus made it possible for the attendees to speak out about an event, thus becoming its ambassadors. Social Media Chatbots as a prominent example of AI Tool is widely used by planners to identify event participants at an early point and analyse participant behaviour to develop a better command over future innovative marketing strategies and attendee engagement (Ogle,A. & Lamb, D.J. 2019).

RATIONALE BEHIND THE GROWING UTILITY OF ARTIFICIAL INTELLIGENCE IN EVENT INDUSTRY

In the present times, events are one of the most innovative and appealing image building tools resorted to by the marketers and public relations professionals to reach out to a very close potential target audience in a more authentic and engaging manner. Events by providing a personal and emotional touch to visitor's experiences play a major role in extending the brand personality of the organizations and differentiating it far apart from its competitors in the market by generating a unique and memorable outcome. However, event planning and execution is an intricate task demanding tremendous coordination and flawless knowledge about participants, their attitudes and preferences, likes and dislikes. Contemporary times have witnessed the invasive impact of AI in every sphere and Event Industry is no exception. AI has emerged as a revolutionary tool influencing every aspect of event process ranging from concept creation to canvassing, customization and analysis. The application of innovative AI Tools have enabled the event stakeholders to streamline their tasks in a systematic manner and gain better insights about target market audiences and then market the event accordingly which gives the event planners a competitive edge in the industry. Ergen, F.D. (2021).

Event Planners have been greatly leveraging the benefits of AI enabled software and tools to achieve seamless execution of events as per the likes of target audiences which is the most important requirement of an event. Maybee, M. (2023) discusses about how AI has been immensely useful for event planners in various ways to gather attendee data and execute an event which matches their preferences and expectations thus securing good ROI. Will AI surpass human intelligence, and in which sector of industries can it be applied? AI has immense potential to help business organizations with its immense capabilities which render AI as a promising resource for experiences, especially when it means to know customers in a better manner, track user behaviors, use data in real-time, make suggestions and offer superior value propositions in-context and in real-time – all scenarios, which are particularly extremely relevant for designing high quality events. Neuhofer, B, Magnus, B. & Celuch, K. (2020).

INTEGRATING AI IN THE 5 C'S OF EVENT DESIGN

The entire process of Event Management revolves around the 5 C's of Event Design. The area includes the very innovative aspects of event conceptualisation, understanding client brief, coordinating with stakeholders and staging a successful event. A well laid out event design makes an event impressive and leaves a long-lasting impact on the minds of event attendees. AI tools have benefitted event planners in developing a strong command over each area of event design helping them to get a better insight about client and event attendee expectations and thus contributing significantly in executing an event which has positive attendee engagement.

The 5 C's of Event Design are:

- Conceptualisation
- Costing
- Canvassing
- Customisation
- Carrying Out

The above 5 C's of Event Design are the basic framework and the backbone of executing a master class event delivering utmost satisfaction to the clients and leaving an ever lasting impact on the minds of the people. Advanced and innovative software and technologies as a part of AI have made the tasks related to event design which were earlier mostly manual and very tedious presently very easier for event planners and more participant driven resulting in greater probability of huge success. The entire process of Event Planning stretching from Event Concept making, screening, event registration software, attendee engagement, to seamless carrying out the event ensuring logistics, venue finding checklists, venue security arrangements by the application of AI Tools like facial recognition and biometric attendance, production schedule and workflow charts. (cleproductions.com/)

Technological innovations such as mobile applications for events, portable photo options for events and technologies like event apps for event managers to check out destinations and venues without having to involve physical travel, to name a few have emerged as musts for event managers and their importance would increase multi folds in the coming future. Virtual meetings, teleconferencing, videoconferencing, video, and audio streams are already commonplace today and are being used more and more frequently in training sessions, in-house product launches, briefings, and company presentations (Swayam MOOCs-Event Planning).

Table 1. Benefits offered by AI in the 5 C's of event design

5 Cs of Event Design	Description	Benefits
Conceptualization	Conceptualization- Ideating and framing the most innovative and unique event concept is the most challenging task of the field. The planners analyze a concept based on several factors like societal impact, regulations, risk factor, competition, revenue and expenditure, feasibility and so on. The first step for planning a successful event is the event concept.	AI enabled technology helps in proper utilization of past attendee data- namely attendance, feedback and surveys, attendee behavior and preferences which contributes immensely in the curation of personalized and attendee- centric highly innovative concepts by the event planners which are greatly liked by the attendees. Every event is remembered and differentiated on account of its creative and feasible concept. AI technologies have enabled the event professionals to gather exhaustive data about social media reactions of the people and attendee insights which have provided great direction to the event creative team to think of staging highly appealing events
Costing	Costing is a major area of Event Planning and execution as it influences its every aspect ranging from Concept Screening to stakeholder finalization to the kind of theme and décor to be followed to the extent of execution. The event budget must include detailed information about the items of revenue and expenditure in an event and it is prepared sufficiently ahead of the event so that every action in the event adheres to the budgetary considerations.	Costing is a very differentiating factor influencing every aspect of Event Planning and Execution, strongly influencing the magnitude of activities and the overall reach and impact of events. AI enabled technologies play a very crucial role in maintaining a proper budgetary guideline regarding every area of event planning and guide the event planners in every step to properly manage the event budget and thus helping in their effective channelization towards the right work at the right time. AI tools thus keep a strong check on budgetary expenses and ensure their optimum utilization in the most cost- effective manner.
Canvassing	Canvassing is a major element of event design as it caters to widespread networking by the event planners to identify and finalize the most credible event stakeholders. Canvassing in event management usually involves obtaining sponsorships, raising funds and advertising. Canvassing for clients and seeking sponsors, customers/audience and networking are the most important concerns in successful event management.	The success and the impact of an event is greatly based on the market portfolio of its stakeholders and their efficiency. The right selection of efficient event stakeholders primarily depends upon the quality of canvassing and the pitching out to the right sponsors, vendors, team members volunteers etc. Earlier the task of event canvassing was extremely difficult as the event planners had to exert a lot on the field and manually prepare data of every stakeholder through their field- based research and thus the job was very tedious. AI Technologies have enabled the planners to collect, compile and preserve a very rich and exhaustive data of their stakeholders in a very efficient and systematic manner. Every event leaves a deep imprint on the minds of the attendees on account of the application of AI Technologies. The benefits can range from finding out the right date, time and venue for scheduling an event which ensures that the event delivers optimum output as per the expenditure. Secondly, AI tools also can predict speakers, celebrity as well as vendor availability to avoid any overlap or clash thus helping in proper utilization of resources and right pitching.

5 Cs of Event Design	Description	Benefits
Customization	Customization is the element which encompasses the modifications which are carried out in the event plan right from the conceptualization till the carrying out of the event. In the Customization phase, details regarding the feasibility of Event Concept and Event Plan is examined again and again and changes are incorporated in it, if necessary as per the demands of the clients and event stakeholders to achieve client satisfaction	All the 5 Cs of Event Design are non-linear and iterative in nature as every element of 5 C's can be incorporating changes or suggestions time and again being provided by the event stakeholders, primarily, clients and sponsors . The process of event design commences with the idea generation and the curation of a differentiating and unique event concept. However, event concept also undergoes continuous changes/customization based on the demands of the clients or sponsors till the finalization of all event stakeholders, budgetary considerations, and the final execution of the concept. AI Technologies and ChatGPT has tremendously helped the event professionals to draft customized and personalized event content which can highly appeal to the attendees. AI Tools enable the event professionals to accumulate enormous prior data about the psychographic profile of the attendees which can be used by tools like ChatGPT to create compelling content to which the final customization can be executed by the event planners by tailoring the content and the final output as per their objectives
Carrying Out	Carrying out is the final phase which involves the execution of the entire event plan. The success of an event plan and the unique concept of the event bears fruits only if the event is conducted flawlessly delivering an ever-lasting impact on the minds of event attendees.	Organizing and commencing the preparations of an event is an equally important task as planning and executing an event. AI applications have been immensely useful for the event planners to fix their agendas and event schedules for meetings, brainstorming and begin with the preparations of the event. The carrying out phase of the event is very hectic impacting the work-life balance of the planners. AI Technologies enable the professionals to schedule their meetings properly, keeping track of the issues and deliverables, follow-ups thus delivering an excellent event product to the optimum satisfaction of the clients. AI enabled chatbots are immensely useful to conduct surveys and polls during the event and capture attendee data and take the feedback of the attendees and the resultant data collected can be a significant resource for evaluation of event as a metric and gauge the outcome or ROI value of the event

HARNESSING THE POWER OF VARIOUS ARTIFICIAL INTELLIGENCE APPLICATIONS IN INFLUENCING EVENT PLANNING AND QUALITY OF ATTENDEE ENGAGEMENT

Artificial Intelligence can take on a variety of meanings and applications. However, whether it's witnessing what machine learning can achieve for event design or utilizing digital assistants like Siri or Alexa at events, Al will play an increasingly important part, even if the entire event fraternity is not completely aware of the revolutionary benefits of this technology. Saeed, F. (2020) discusses about how some of the widely used AI Technology Siri, Alexa, Tesla, Cogito, Flying Drones have taken the world by storm since their application and usages provide significant benefits to mankind, whether identifying their behavior or location or providing information. Currently, the most common use of Al in the event parlance is aiding in the selection of innovative concepts and designs to impress and satisfy specific audiences to the highest extent as per their feedback and preferences thus positively transforming event experiences for the attendees and casting a strong impact on attendee engagement level. . The benefits AI has provided to the event industry is numerous. To begin with, AI-ed software, being used by websites such as Eventbrite, helps the event professionals and event entrepreneurs to learn what users have previously loved to and thus effectively direct them to upcoming events that they will be similarly enthused about. The software is complex, but it can collect critical information such as when users are likely to attend events, what current topics they respond to, and even what events their friends are likely to attend. As Al evolves, it will predict what sort of food individuals like, where people's footfall is likely to take them, and even their color preferences.

Communication and coordination is the fundamental building block of every event and as an instance personal events like weddings require keeping in touch with everyone from the client to the groom, bride, vendors, and new consumers. It is a laborious and time- consuming task, especially if done manually. Weddings are the most frequently occurring event in India and economically contribute significantly to the overall revenue pie of event industry and AI has been the biggest boon for this category of personal events. If the number of emails one gets exceeds a certain threshold, AI can help organize them systematically. AI-powered apps, such as Knowmails, may significantly reduce mail reading time by assessing one's reading habits and prioritizing those emails that require the most attention at the top. The program also assists in producing better emails and remembering essential topics. Mittal, V. (2019) talks about the intricacies of planning and executing a wedding event from accounting and scheduling to coordinating with customers. Indian weddings are long-drawn elaborate occasions requiring detail briefing and meticulous minute planning. Whether it's a local wedding or a destination wedding, one needs to schedule hundreds of things as a planner. Wedding planners can oversee more than one wedding event simultaneously. It is critical to ensure that everything is correctly arranged, from photography to food, décor, clothing, invites, etc. In such a case, AI can be of great assistance. Several applications may assist one in sending tailored emails to schedule various occasions. When the system obtains confirmation on the time and date, it will instantly add it to one's calendar. Akinsowon,V. (2023) discusses about how the world of AI in the domain of events have been immensely useful in drafting emails, strategize and plan out systematically the thoughts and ideas of event execution with a great deal of creativity, researching on various vendors and venue providers and drawing project plans etc.

The immense utility of chatbots in the event industry requires no description. Today, AI in chatbots is being employed in virtual hiring events. A chatbot named

Olivia handles some of the very crucial and tedious areas of event execution like application registration, event reminders, and connecting applicants with actual recruiters. Pepper robots and chatbots are examples of natural language processing-based artificial intelligence that have aided the events sector. Aside from conversational robots, event professionals utilize AI to create more immersive, aesthetically appealing, and well- managed events, even some that may have to be done online due to limits prohibiting huge crowds from congregating. Events experts also use AI's machine learning skills to create predictions from massive volumes of data – such as information from participant profiles – to make events more customized which significantly boosts the number of people that attend events.

AI is at the forefront of event management. The numerous benefits which AI tools have offered to event professionals can be witnessed in every phase of event management, especially applications like facial recognition and biometric registration programs. These technologies improve the accuracy with which guests' identities are verified while also eliminating human error and supervision. While AI security solutions may appear to be expensive compared to hiring more employees, the costs can be equivalent or even cheaper in some cases, especially in the context of excellent ROI a event planner gets by the application of AI. These devices are an excellent method to provide additional security for both event employees and spectators. Shortly, AI will make events more tailored for guests with its robust analysis of potential attendee's data while also making organizing tasks easier for businesses. Everyone wants a personalized experience rather than a generic product, and AI is proving to play a significant role in it.

AI for capacity and utilization statistics and emotion recognition are the two most popular usages of AI enabled technologies in the event sector. For example, event organizers employ AI technology at auto exhibitions to track how many people glance at the car or engage with it. This method assists organizations in better understanding audience behavior and adjusting messaging as needed which greatly influences audience satisfaction and engagement. Another widespread application of AI is capacity and usage analytics, which enable event organizers to undertake more effective capacity planning and setup. In the coming years, event companies will utilize AI to customize the event experience for their attendees, such as assigning everyone an AI bot to advise them or link them with individuals who have similar interests.

The amazing and highly advanced flying drones are now delivering goods to clients' homes - albeit in a test mode. They point to a strong machine learning system capable of converting the world into a 3D representation using sensors and video cameras. By connecting the sensors and cameras to the ceiling, the sensors and cameras can detect the location of the drones in the room. The trajectory creation algorithm directs the drone's movement. Using a Wi-Fi system, one can control the drones and utilize them for certain objectives, such as product delivery, video production, or news reporting. Some of the major social festivals celebrated in India like vh1 supersonic, Bacardi nh7, and sunburn have become major landmarks of their respective fields and have attracted a huge number of people and generated enormouseconomic revenues in the event industry. AI enabled advanced safety and security mechanisms have made it very easy for the event professionals to deliver such mega events with more efficiency and success.

ANALYTICAL UNDERSTANDING OF THE APPLICATION OF AI IN THE WORLD OF EVENTS THROUGH THE EYES OF EVENT PROFESSIONALS

As a part of qualitative study to unveil the various spectrums of the field-based realities related to the application of AI in event management and to further substantiate the exhaustive secondary data analysis, the opinion of the real task masters was taken to study the nances of the topic as per their experienced opinion.

Qualitative open-ended telephonic interview was taken of seasoned and highly experienced Events & Festival Directors having a good span of experience of organizing Corporate Events, Artist Management Shows, Music Concerts and Activations. The field-based study was a major eye opener for the researcher as the interviewees disclosed the pros and cons of the emerging new trends in the parlance of Event Management with special reference to the growing application of AI Technology. The respondents opined that AI has been in use for quite some time in the lives of masses, whether it be the entry of calculators or the very popular Spotify's AI Voice Translation or even the Netflix automated AI driven software which does a complete mapping of viewer's likes and preferences and viewing habits and suggests recommendations based on them opening the doors for customized recommendations.

One of the event professionals expressed that ChatGPT is one of the most commonly used AI Technology for the purpose of writing drafts like emails, speeches, and anchoring piece for emcee's, PPT contents for presentation etc. The respondent also discussed the various video and audio editing apps being used by event professionals daily for making engaging content for the target audiences like during product launches or exhibitions. It was also pointed out that without the above AI Technologies, the professionals would have faced a lot of difficulty in preparing rich qualitative content as per the satisfaction of the client and as per the market demands. The interview revealed that attractive image solutions have also been the biggest resort for the event planners to prepare attractive content and presentations. AI Technology is also being used to prepare innovative and highly appealing display layouts for events like product launches or exhibitions which make the event strikingly unique and memorable. The interviewee expressed that certain voice apps have been extremely resourceful for the anchors to learn and produce quality audio content thus adding to the success factor of events.

In the pre-event phase of conceptualization and planning AI tools empower the planners to take a call on which location or artist can be the best option for executing a unique event. The professionals responded that nobody could deny the indispensable benefits that AI has offered to various organizations, citing the example of the collaboration between the reputed AI startup named Niki.ai and Book my Show which has made the ticket booking more customer centric as the software can gauge viewer's cinema venue preferences and book the tickets automatically to the utter most satisfaction of the viewers. One of the interviewees also mentioned the enormous benefits being offered by Zomato AI chatbots too in helping in the booking of orders as per the tastes and preferences of foodies.

The world of AI has been of immense help to event organizers as by availing the premium plans of extremely customized AI Tools they get a plethora of ideas about how events would be done, what are the possible venues, themes, and décor ideas as per the tastes of the client and budgetary considerations. The professional stressed the ever evolving and invasive role of Chat GPT in generating content in seconds as per the pitch deck and the prompt provided and rather in a more detailed and creative manner.

The interviewee pointed out that AI has been a very useful resource for event producers when they need to draft feasible, innovative, and a well explained event proposal. It was expressed that with the right inputs like brand language, brand tonality and theme tonality the event planners can generate the right kind of proposal as per their choice and preferences. A very significant fact pointed out based on the perception study was that it was disclosed that writing has always been a boring task and the present times are characterized by such user friendly AI enabled apps where the user just needs to provide the right prompt and the AI generates very engaging templates providing a good structure as per the tastes and thoughts of the clients and thus the draft gets ready in seconds to give a satisfactory performance.

The success of an event in the perspective of attendee engagement and recall is dependent on various factors primarily event customization as per the tastes and likes of the audiences and the execution of a unique concept with an unforgettable experience. The responses of the interviewees revealed that in the present times of increasing client demands and attendee expectations, collection of valuable attendee data and its compilation acts as a significant resource for the event professionals to conceptualize and design an event which is at par with the expectations of the event stakeholder. In this context it was expressed that customer analytics and feedback study is nowadays the most crucial aspect before designing an event and AI tools have served as boon in this direction. Thus, the valuable insights of the interviewees presented the field-based advantages AI Technology has offered whether it be the free tools like Adobe cloud or the Instagram editing tools or the smartphone editing tools or even the content creating tools which have made the tasks much easier and cheaper for the users and the same applies to event industry too.

ISSUES PROMINENTLY FACED IN THE REALM OF GROWING APPLICATION OF AI IN EVENTS AS PERCEIVED BY EVENT PLANNERS

The world of AI has completely transformed the Event Industry making it more contemporary and as per the needs and demands of the clients. The application of various AI technology in every phase of event management has impacted the quality of event experiences and helped the event planners to reach out to the attendees in a more inclusive and customer-centric manner. "By envisioning events that are highly customized to user preferences, scholars suggest that event organizers will move away from having dedicated event apps to delivering content through messaging platforms via personal event bots (Davidson 2019)". However, the technology besides revitalizing the event design, planning and execution process with the help of pre-set algorithms also sets forth contemplating questions to ponder about and issues to be tacked besides value propositions for the event industry.

The structure of an event company ranges from big event management companies and production houses to party and exhibition planners to event catering companies to professional event organizers. However, the noticeable fact is that every organization in some or the other proportion employs AI technologies either for data analysis or event registrations or AI enable chatbots for personalization of attendee experiences or event apps.

Although the immersive world of AI has transformed the way events are conceptualized, designed, and executed, however their still lie some pertinent challenges and issues which the sunrise industry faces on account of the application of the technology. The primary challenge which emerges is lack of skilled manpower having the knowledge to apply the technologies in the right manner and in the right context. The application has no doubt created a bridge between the physical world and the digital platform as event planners can now collect, analyze, and generate significant outcome and conclusion regarding attendee data in terms of likes and preferences thus delivering a much more impactful experience for the audiences. However, AI means the application of simple as well as complex technologies at various levels and it requires an experienced and trained mindset to feed in and provide the right inputs in order to generate the correct output.

Events are all about creating a unique experience for the attendees and every data on attendee preferences can play a differentiating role in deciding the overall design in specificity to the creative aspect of the event. AI has been like a key to open the lock of past event experiences and participants feedback which has acted like a roadmap to curate the concept of the future events in a stronger manner ranging from finalizing the event activities or the theme or décor or the visit locations or even the catering options.

The qualitative study of the perception of event professionals revealed significant concerns providing food for thought for event managers who have been commonly using AI in their various key tasks whether it be pre-event research and environment scanning or conceptualization and design of an event to the stage of event planning ranging from event registrations to event layout and content generation. The responses highlighted that besides the multiple advantages of AI in events, the need is to introspect the factor of originality and the creative background as somewhere that is dying and fading away. The interviewee further described that something which is original may not have data to substantiate everything. and in the name of AI originality and quality is being compromised at every stage. The study thus draws attention towards the other side of the trend that the present system is so driven by numbers and the number of data points become the base for decision making. The field-based perception study revealed that in the process of over emphasis on quantification and data analytics due to the popular usage of AI Technology, event professionals have stopped reflecting on original quality and such a trend may not work in live events where the performing quality of the artists matter the most and not the data driven inputs. The interviewee cited examples of talented music composers who may not be so popular as per the digital data analytics, however they might be possessing extraordinary talent.

A major challenge faced by event planners in the process of using AI in Event Management was pointed out by one of the interviewees. The respondent expressed that although AI Technologies have made an inroad into event industry but still it is at its very initial stage in terms of widespread application in the Indian perspective. There are many event production companies which either are not using AI Technology or maybe it's usage is very nominal. Secondly, the Event Director revealed that budgetary considerations is a major hindrance in the area of widespread use of AI in events. The interviewee revealed that due to scarcity of financial resources by the clients, the event professionals many a times use free version of AI Apps which lack in terms of number of functionalities as well as outcome generation. The resource crunch imposed by the clients compels the event planners to restrain from the application of high-end AI Apps or tools as most of them are paid versions with more advanced functionalities and overall outcome.

CONCLUSION

Companies in various industries are increasingly investing in "smart" technology. AI applications are expected to be used by 80 percent of enterprises by 2024, and the event planning sector is no exception. It's no surprise that event planners may automate a range of chores and better serve their consumers by utilizing AI technologies in various circumstances. There are few financial or technological impediments to implementing AI-based apps for event planners. They are simple to create or "plug" as a ready-to-use solution, and planners may include them without spending much money. Even better, applications may be used for any size or style of event. AI applications are simple to develop for any event format and business segment. These applications can be swiftly taught to connect with participants and deliver intelligent replies and information. There is no event of any magnitude or type that a well-implemented AI solution cannot enhance.

The benefits that AI technology has provided in the realm of event industry can be noticed in every sphere of event management. AI matching systems may also assist attendees in having a more enjoyable event experience. A huge event may include dozens of presentations, conferences, and quality assurance sessions. It is hard for one participant to attend every session that piques their interest. They can, however, obtain carefully crafted recommendations only for them by employing a matchmaking engine that evaluates their goals, hobbies, social media data, and attendance profile.

It's unusual to find an event with a budget that allows for live, 24-hour assistance. Despite this, questions and concerns continue to occur 24 hours a day, seven days a week. When a vendor, venue management in charge, presenter, attendee, or other important contact has a question or complaint, having them wait for an answer may be extremely inconvenient. Event planners can provide cost- effective extended support without spending money on live support staff by implementing a customer service, AI solution. A well- trained chatbot can answer frequently requested queries, extra contact information, and even escalate situations as required.

There is a huge list of the pros of AI usage in the event industry, however, people engaged in the industry are still reluctant to use AI due to the perception that it might replace humans. It must be accepted somewhere that AI Technologies have already made an influential and impactful entry into the world of events and is slowly-slowly getting integrated into everyday work practices of event professionals assisting them to plan and deliver a much more impactful event with exceptional results.

REFERENCES

Akinsowon, V. (2023). AI Tools for Event Planners: Tips from Meeting Tomorrow's Joey Rodriguez. *Cvent.com Blog*. https://www.cvent.com/en/blog/events/ai-tools-for-event-planners

Bijli, H. K. (2023). *Event Planning-BHC-012. Swayam MOOCs Davidson, R. (2019). Business events*. Routledge.

Ergen, F. D. (2021). *Artificial Intelligence Applications for Event Management and Marketing. Impact of ICTs on Event Management and Marketing*. IGI Global.

EVENTFAQS Bureau. (2023). *Organized live events recovered 129% in 2022: FICCI-EY report*. EVENTFAQs Bureau.: https://www.eventfaqs.com/news/ef-19289/organized-live-events- recovered-129-in-2022-ficci-ey-report

Katz, E, Blumler, J.G. & Gurevitch, M. (1973-74). Uses and Gratifications Research. *The Public Opinion Quaterly, 37*. Oxford University Press

Maybee, M. (2023). *AI for Events: How Artificial Intelligence Improves Efficiency and ROI*. PC Nametag. https://blog.pcnametag.com/event-ai

Mittal, V. (2019). *How Artificial Intelligence Will Improve Things For Wedding Planning Industry in India*. SCelebration. https://scelebration.com/artificial-intelligence-will-improve- things-wedding-planning-industry-india/

Neuhofer, B., Magnus, B., & Celuch, K. (2020). The impact of artificial intelligence on event experiences: A scenario technique approach. [Springer.]. *Electronic Markets, 31*(3), 601–617. doi:10.1007/s12525-020-00433-4 PMID:38624486

Ogle, A., & Lamb, D. J. (2019). *The Role of Robots, Artificial Intelligence, and Service Automation in Events*. ResearchGate. https://www.researchgate.net/publication/336530987_The_Role_of_Robots_Artificial_Intelligence_ and_Service_Automation_in_Events

Indian Events and Activations industry expected to cross Rs 10,000 crore by 2020-21: Report, E. Y. (2017). BestMediaInfo Bureau. Retrived on 20.9.2023 from: www.bestmediainfo.com/2017/09/indian-events-and- activations-industrv-expected-to-cross-rs-10-000-crore-bv-2020-21-ev-report/

Risq, F. (2021). Will AI eventually replace designers or change the way we design? *Medium*. https://uxdesign.cc/human-design-and-artificial-intelligence-f0af52c6ce6

Saeed, F. (2020). *9 powerful examples of artificial intelligence in use today*. IQVIS Inc. https://www.iqvis.com/blog/9-powerful-examples-of- artificial-intelligence-in-use-today/

Schroer, A. (2023). *What is Artificial Intelligence?* Builtin. https://builtin.com/artificial-intelligence

Wilson, C. (2019). Artificial Intelligence is Changing the Event Industry — Here's How. *Swapcard Blog*. https://blog.swapcard.com/artificial-intelligence-and-events

Chapter 13
Development of an Intelligent System for Stock Market Prediction Using Enhanced Deep Learning Technique With Banking Data

B. Manjunatha
New Horizon College of Engineering, India

V. Revathi
https://orcid.org/0000-0002-8583-1916
New Horizon College of Engineering, India

Balasubramanian Prabhu Kavin
https://orcid.org/0000-0001-6939-4683
SRM Institute of Science and Technology, India

Gan Hong Seng
XJTLU Entrepreneur College, Xi'an Jiaotong-Liverpool University, China

ABSTRACT

The future may be unknown and uncertain, but there are still opportunities to make money by anticipating it. The request of AI and ML to stock market prediction is one such opportunity. Artificial intelligence may be used to generate accurate forecasts before investing, even in a dynamic environment like the stock market. The stock market's data is typically not stationary, and its properties are often uncorrelated. The stock market patterns that are traditionally predicted by several STIs may be inaccurate. To study the features of the stock market using STIs and to make profitable trading decisions, a model has been developed. This study presents an enhanced bidirectional gated recurrent neural network (EBGRNN) for detecting stock price trends using STIs. HDFC, Yes Bank, and SBI, three of the most well-known banks, have had their dataset evaluated. It is a real-time snapshot of the national stock exchange (NSE) of India's stock market. The datasets included business days from 11/17/2008 to 11/15/2018.

DOI: 10.4018/979-8-3693-0790-8.ch013

INTRODUCTION

Government expenditure is prioritised in order to boost economies and raise living standards. Large firms are established in the modern economy so that people may take advantage of globalisation and its fast-economic developments (Jiang 2021). Private stock exchanges, open stock exchanges, and mixed ownership stock exchanges are all types of the stock market (Li, & Pan, 2022). Shares in private corporations are traded on the private stock exchange, whereas publicly traded stocks are traded on the open stock exchange. Companies with mixed ownership have stock that can only be traded to a limited extent on public exchanges (Mehtab & Sen 2020). British and American stock exchanges, such as the responsible for their development (Hu et al., 2021).

When a company needs money for things like growth or debt repayment, it can "go public," issuing shares of stock that can be exchanged on the secondary market, also called a stock exchange (Mehtab et al., 2021). The company may avoid the possibility of loss, debt, and interest payments by issuing shares in exchange for financial backing. Second, to generate revenue and profit for the benefit of stockholders (Nabipour et al., 2020). These stockholders, also known as investors, can earn a profit in one of two ways: by receiving dividend payments from the firms in which they invested, or by selling their shares of stock at a price higher than the one at which they were originally acquired. Therefore, persons who interest in trying to anticipate changes in stock prices.

Financial organisations, corporations, and individual investors all confront a difficult dilemma when trying to predict stock prices (Shen & Shafiq 2020). Every economy relies on the stock market, and as the main goals of any investment are to maximise profit while minimising risk, it stands to reason that governments should work to improve their stock markets in order to boost their economies (Ji et al., 2021). Predicting the direction of the stock market is one of the most effective ways to generate a profit because of the potential for rapid returns on stock market investments. The nonlinear nature of stock market prediction makes it more difficult to foresee how a company's shares will perform in a given market (Liu & Long 2020). Therefore, it is necessary for researchers and investors to seek out methods that may produce more reliable outcomes and more revenues.

Stock market prediction refers to any attempt to foretell or anticipate the future value of a stock, market segment, or market as a whole. Many different types of organisations and people (such as traders, market participants, data analysts, computer engineers specialising in ML and AI, etc.) have been fixated on this topic in recent years (Rouf et al., 2021). Due to the fact that the market value of a company's shares is highly dependent on its profits and performance in the marketplace, the value of those shares can fluctuate depending on macroeconomic and microeconomic factors like supply and demand (Mehtab & Sen 2020). An investor may avoid losing money and maximise earnings with the use of such systems and software, which can help them foresee the company's status based on historical and current data, market conditions, etc.

Statistical methods like ARIMA are inferior to traditional models (Jing et al., 2021). However, it has been demonstrated that models such as LSTM are superior to machine learning models such as Regression, and that the deep learning model was detected rather than the machine learning model Support Vector Machine (SVM) (Long et al., 2020). In several cases, deep learning models performed exceptionally well. Due to their capacity to recognise the stock market fluctuations and provide sufficient findings, they shown promise for application in stock market prediction (Ravikumar & Saraf 2020).

The main aims of this paper are obtainable as shadows:

- Examine the results of the supplementary options (High, Open, HiLo, OpSe, etc.).
- Finding STIs that are associated with the closing price.
- Create a technical indicator-based stock market forecasting model based on EBGRNN.
- HM chooses the best weight for the BGRNN. During the scout bee phase, new positions are formed, but the ABCFFA technique does not update the positions with the FFA's replacement. The problems of delayed convergence, and the risk of slipping into the local point that are inherent to ABC have been solved by including FFA's method. A revised search algorithm is used in the worker bee phase to increase the likelihood of finding the better sites; this allows for the replacement of some of the onlooker bee phase's worst placements with plausible ones.
- Provide a practical method that enhances the financier's understanding of sustainable investing.

The break of the paper is developed as shadows: Section 2 offerings the related works and brief explanation of proposed model is given in Section 3. The experimental investigation with its discussion is given in Section 4 and lastly, conclusion with future work is mentioned in Section 5.

RELATED WORKS

When an investor puts money into the stock market, they are demonstrating a desire to make a profit. Investors are looking to the stock market because of cutting-edge applications where predictions can lead to fruitful market forecasting. Accurately predicting the stock market's (Ma et al., 2021) behaviour requires access to relevant data in advance. The appropriate choices may be made with the help of the stock market forecasting tools that are currently available. The stock market has to process a lot of data on industrial stocks that applies to the whole financial system (Ding & Qin 2020). Investors who think about sales and purchases will change these as necessary. The market position can be affected by a number of reasons, such as projections of future revenue, the announcement of recent financial results, management changes, etc. Consequently, better investment decisions may be made with the use of accurate stock market forecast (Rezaei et al., 2021). The investor stands to gain more from high-risk investments using ML approaches.

The price is a subset of market that enables investors to gauge success by comparing present prices to those of the past. The data is then preprocessed to remove noise and other parameters (Yu & Yan 2020) after collection. Then stock market predictions based on preprocessed data might be valuable. From a mountain of data, the feature selection procedures cherry-pick relevant information. The dataset is often separated into "current" and "prediction" information by several data analyst functions or user-friendly applications (Sunny et al., 2020). Better stock market judgements may be made with this information. Alerting investors about the price index follows a decisive action. This alert is valuable to investors since it reveals the current profit or loss for the price index. Traders can make more money by selling more shares if the programme generates a profitable status, and developers can focus more on improving the product if the price index is low (Vijh et al., 2020).

The Dhaka Stock market (DSE) is the largest stock market in Bangladesh, and its future stock price has been predicted using a new machine learning model proposed by (Muhammad et al., 2023). While the transformer model has seen extensive usage in other areas, such as NLP and computer vision, we are unaware of any prior applications to the challenge of predicting stock prices using DSE data. With the advent of time2vec encoding for representing the time series characteristics, the transformer model may now be used for predicting stock prices. The purpose of this study is to use these two powerful methods to learn how to predict the unpredictable DSE stock market. We focus on daily and weekly data from the past for eight different equities traded on the DSE. Our results show promise, with a root-mean-squared error that is tolerable for the majority of stocks. We also show encouraging results when comparing our model to the widely-used ARIMA benchmark for market forecasting.

The optimal feature subset selection has been proposed by (Yun et al., 2023). We also offer piecewise best feature subset selection to account for the time-varying nature of stock price data across a limited time window. Internal are used as input feature sets in the proposed algorithm. In order to choose the most relevant and useful characteristics for our bilateral forecasting scheme, we first expand our feature set using a hybrid genetic algorithm-machine learning regression, then we use a significance score filter to narrow down our features to the most crucial ones. In the end, the most informative subset of features is chosen for further analysis and prediction. The suggested strategy optimises the feature subset for interpretability with a minimal number of characteristics and boosts average forecasting accuracy. The best indicators reduced the Root Mean Squared Error by 13.47%, while the optimal feature set reduced it by 10.42%. In this paper, we apply piecewise optimum curve fitting to investigate each conceivable clustering of external characteristics, therefore improving local interpretability. Using only the best characteristics for each piece of data, the suggested local interpretability method can give a more timely and adaptable price behaviour. The suggested interpretability strategy solves the shortcomings of current feature-importance interpretability approaches by not requiring the use of also a single data point or an entire data period.

Two network models that have been widely utilised to predict stock market values are the Deep Feed-forward Neural Network (used by (Mukherjee et al., 2023)) and the CNN. The models have been used to extrapolate future data values from existing data values. As long as the dataset is correct, this procedure will be repeated repeatedly. The use of deep learning in an effort to improve this prediction has yielded significant outcomes. The accuracy of the CNN model was 98.92%, while that of the ANN model was 97.66%. Predictions are created using 2-D histograms extracted from the quantized dataset at a certain time interval using the CNN model. The examination of such data sets has not before made use of this method. The concept was used to the recent COVID-19 epidemic, which precipitated a precipitous drop in stock prices, as a case study. The study's 91% accuracy is not great, but it's not terrible, either.

A unique hybrid model was presented by (Zhao & Yang 2023). An emotion-enhanced models, and a long short-term memory model (LSTM) are presented to anticipate stock market and simulation trading. First, ECNN was utilised to representation from Internet user comments that were used to supplement stock market data. Second, we use DAE to pull out the most important information from stock market data, which helps with accuracy of predictions. Third, we factor in the timely nature of stock market emotion to create more accurate and trustworthy sentiment indices. The stock market prediction is completed by feeding the LSTM model the most salient elements of the stock data and the sentiment indices. The experimental findings demonstrate that SA-DLSTM provides the most accurate predictions compared to the other replicas used in the study. SA-DLSTM, nevertheless, shows promising results in terms of both return and risk. It can aid investors in making sound choices.

With the use of three fine-tuned deep learning prediction models—a Long Short-Term Memory In order to forecast stock values, (Li et al., 2023) provide a deep learning system that is augmented by clustering. The proposed method employs clustering as a first step in the forecasting process, which can improve the models. We suggest a novel similarity measure, Logistic Weighted to achieve efficient clustering by extending a method to account for the relative importance of return observations while constructing distance matrices. In this case, the WDTW cost weight function using a logistic probability density distribution function. We also employ these three deep learning models to develop a cluster-based forecasting system. Finally, extensive tests on daily US stock that our approach generates remarkable forecasting performance, with the greatest results for the mixture of Logistic WDTW model across 5 separate evaluation system of measurement.

A prediction framework based on emotional analysis has been introduced by BL et al. (BL & BR 2023). Thus, we also consider stock data and news mood data. Features based on technical indicators are derived from the stock market data. These indicators include the the moving average (MA). Meanwhile, processes like (1) pre-processing—during which keywords are extracted and sentiment is categorized—(2) keyword extraction—during which WordNet and sentiment categorization are performed— (3) feature extraction—during which Proposed homotropy based features are extracted—process the news data to ascertain the sentiments. When it comes to step four (classification), a deep neural network is utilised to get an opinionated result (Thirumalraj & Rajesh, 2023). The system trains the NN using the self-improved whale optimisation algorithm (SIWOA) to increase its sentiment prediction accuracy. Finally, an optimised deep belief network (DBN) is employed for stock prediction; this network considers both the characteristics of stock data and the emotional outcomes from news data. The new SIWOA is used to fine-tune the DBN weights in this case.

A Multi-Layer Sequential MLS LSTM model employing the adam optimizer is proposed by (Md et al., 2023) as a novel optimisation strategy for stock price prediction. To further improve prediction accuracy, the MLS LSTM method utilises normalised time series data partitioned into time steps to establish causality among past values and predicted future values. The vanishing neural networks, is also avoided. To make predictions about the stock market index, analysts look at historical data and ongoing trends and patterns. The results show that the MLS LSTM method significantly outperforms existing learning algorithms, with a prediction accuracy of 95.9% on the training data set and 98.1% on the testing data set. When comparing the training set and testing set, we found that the mean absolute percentage error was 1.79% and 2.18%, respectively. The suggested model provides an accurate forecast and is practically viable since it can approximation the stock price with a normalised error of 0.019.

Figure 1. Proposed framework for stock trends forecasting

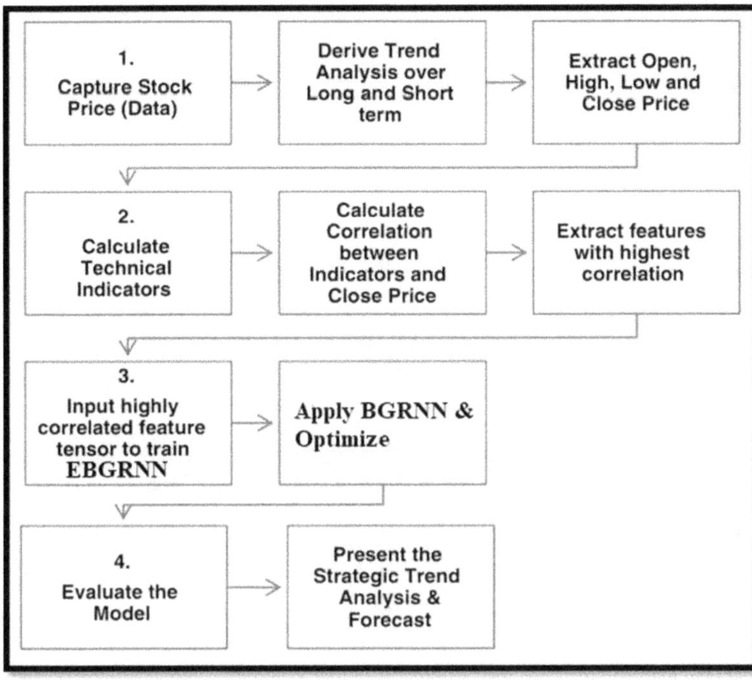

PROPOSED METHODOLOGY

In this research work, three datasets are used for validation, where the stock market technical indicators are predicted by using EGBRNN model and the plan of the research model is exposed in Figure 1.

Pre-Processing the Data

We eliminated the Date/Time axis since it is irrelevant to our forecasting methods. A min-max scaler was used to normalise the data:

$$x^* = (x - min) / (max - min) \tag{1}$$

where min is the smallest value and max is the highest, and x* is the new value. The range [0, 1] is mapped onto x, where [max, min] are the largest and smallest values in the sample, respectively. Next, it is divided into 70% training data, this breakdown is employed to safeguard against overfitting models and provide fair evaluations of those that have been constructed (Al Bashabsheh et al., 2021).

Feature Engineering

The four characteristics used in the first deep learning method for stock prediction were:

- High: identifies the day's highest closing stock price.
- The stock's daily low is denoted by the symbol "Low."
- The term "Open" refers to the stock market's opening price on a certain day.
- The term total number of contracts or shares that have been traded.

The attuned closing price is the stock price after changing the reflect the value of a stock after accounting for any business activities, and these four are the most widely employed in stock price forecast. This study delves into the impact of extending the aforementioned feature set with two new characteristics, HiLo (High-Low) and OpSe (Open-Close), on the original prediction technique.

Correlation-Tensor

Data in a DL model can be represented as numbers or categories, depending on the needs of the algorithm being used. There are primarily two problems with this approach:

a) The word vector can eventually learn as much as the dictionary. Computation is complicated by the size of these vectors and dictionaries.
b) Such a form makes semantic analysis and processing laborious.

When BGRNN is active, neurons multiply and add input variables using the appropriate weights. The model takes in the correlation tensors as input. The BGRNN model can easily and quickly perform computations using the information contained in these tensors, which is stored in STIs. In addition, the model is given time-series data in the form of category ranges rather than individual observations. Tensors can be adequately represented in a space of relatively few dimensions.

Tensor representation for stock trend predictions is applied after correlation vectors are constructed using STIs. Pearson's coefficient of correlation establishes a causal relationship between the quantitative characteristics. This is the best approach since it yields an exact numerical figure for the extent to which a linear relationship can be established between X and Y.

Classification Using Enhanced Bidirectional Gated Recurrent Unit (EBGRNN)

To take sequence data as input, RNN (Lv et al., 2019) recursively follows the sequence's growth direction and all nodes are linked in a chain. Networks was initiated in the 1980s and 1990s, and by the turn of the 21st century, it had become one of the deep learning algorithms. Bidirectional Recurrent Neural Networks are two examples of popular Recurrent Neural Networks. However, issues with gradient disappearance and gradient expansion plague these methods. The issues of gradient vanishing and gradient explosion are addressed in LSTM, an enhanced form of RNN. It excels in the areas of automatic language detection, modelling, and translation. It is also used to any issue that involves time series properties. Bidirectional GRU requires familiarity with GRU. The GRU network is a simplified version of the LSTM network. With only two gates (update and reset), GRU is simpler than LSTM's three (input, forgetting, and output). In LSTM, the update gate serves a purpose comparable to that of the forgetting gate and the input gate. It decides what data should be forgotten and what should be added or updated. In order to determine whether data from the past is irrelevant to the present time calculation, the reset gate is utilised. GRU outperforms LSTM in terms of computation speed since it uses fewer gates. Figure 2 depicts the overall GRU structure. The following is the formula used to determine GRU:

$$z_t = \sigma\left(W_z . \left[h_{t-1}, x_t\right]\right) \tag{2}$$

$$r_t = \sigma\left(W_r . \left[h_{t-1}, x_t\right]\right) \tag{3}$$

$$h_t = \left(1 - z_t\right)^* h_{t-1} + z_t * \tilde{h}_t \tag{4}$$

$$\tilde{h}_t = tanh\left(W . \left[r_t^* h_{t-1}, x_t\right]\right) \tag{5}$$

$$S\left(x\right) = \frac{1}{1 + e^{-x}} \tag{6}$$

Figure 2. GRU structure diagram

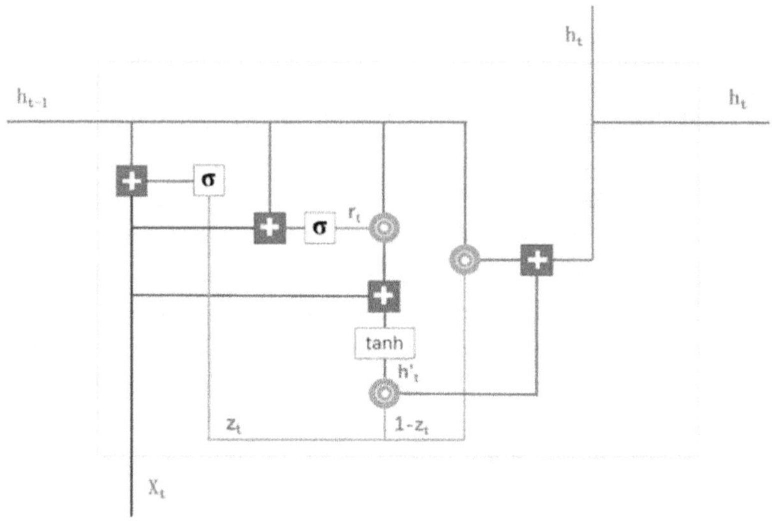

$$S'(x)=\frac{e^{-x}}{\left(1+e^{-x}\right)^2}=S(x)\left(1-S(x)\right) \tag{7}$$

To bandage the output data among 0 and 1, the sigmoid activation function is utilised, denoted by. Formula 6 and formula 7 display and its method of derivation, respectively. The update gate z_t has a weight of W_z, while the reset gate r_t has a weight of W_r. The past is represented by h_(t-1) and the present by h _t; the past is contained in the present by h_t. The current state of knowledge is a function of the current input and h_(t-1). Bidirectional GRU (Chen et al., 2021) is a model with a structure that is quite like the GRU model. One can find both forward-looking and backward-looking time series. The final output is a combination of the results consistent to the end state of the positive results corresponding to the reverse time series. The model may make use of both historical and anticipated data simultaneously. We employ a Bidirectional GRU model in this study. Sub-networks labelled "forward status" and "backward position" in Figure 3 indicate forward and reverse transmission, respectively.

Figure 3 shows that the proposed neural network model has two hidden layers, one for forward propagation and one for backward propagation. Eight GRU cells represent the eight time slices (T1-T8) in each hidden layer. Forward and reverse

Figure 3. BGRNN structure diagram

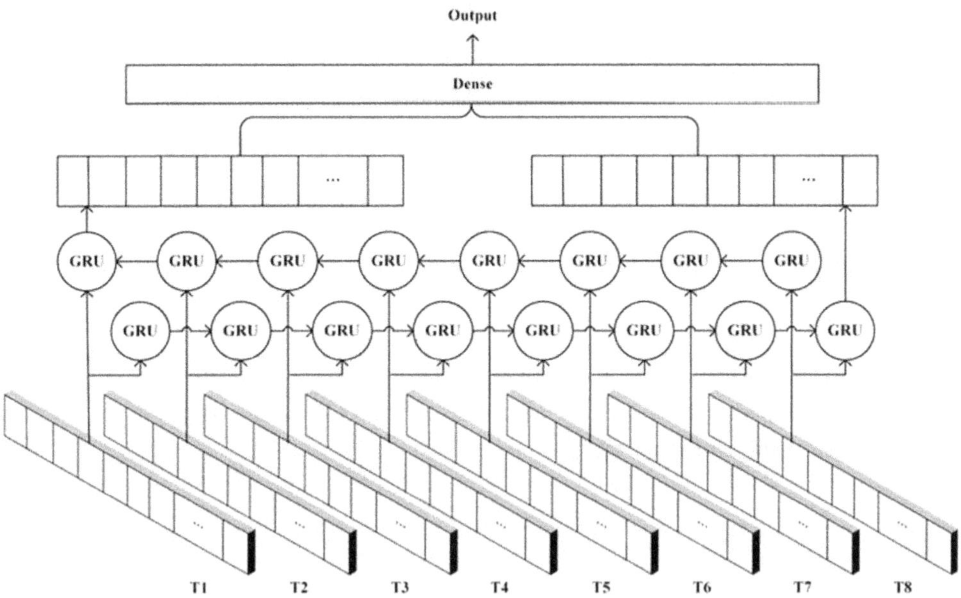

hidden states from the final GRUs are combined and sent to a single neuron in a dense (fully-connected) layer using a sigmoid activation function.

Hyper-Parameter Tuning Using Hybrid Method

The suggested Hybrid Enhanced phase, spectator bee phase, and scout bee phase to determine optimal weights for BGRNN. In order to participate in an efficient topology control process, it is necessary for the worker bee phase to exhaustively seek the effective ideal weights from the whole set of BGRNN. During this stage, each worker bee search agent conducts a thorough search for a new weight by interacting with others. Whenever a potentially useful new weight is discovered during this worker bee search, the search agent replaces the previous weight in memory with the new one. The worker bee phase collects data, and then the observer bee phase is driven to make judgements based on the fitness likelihood computed from that data. During this observer bee stage, a superior weight is selected from the current set so that it may be memorised and updated. The exploitation stage (local search) of this suggested method consists of the worker bee phase and the observer bee phase. Finally, a scout bee with the updated weight of BGRNN that has been determined to be blocked by the worker bee search agent for an extended period of time is used in the subsequent search. This section provides a comprehensive analysis of the suggested method.

Step 1: Initialisation

During this setup phase, we construct the ith weight of BGRNN (worker bee) for each kth weight (food source) using the search equation (8).

$$S_N(i,j) = LT_j + \psi_{i,j}(UT_j - LT_j) \tag{8}$$

However, it is found that the search equation does not promote high-quality solutions, so the search space division technique is used to improve the search equation according to Equation (9).

$$S_N(i,j) = LT_j + \frac{(\psi_{ij} + 2m - 1)(UT_j - LT_j)}{2NS} \tag{9}$$

where “i” signifies the sensor nodes of the system ($1 \leq i \leq NS$), which is examined for its potentiality using “j” likely dimensions ($1 \leq j \leq D$) with NS being the whole set of sensor nodes with a chance sum ψi_j that contents the condition $\psi ij_{\in}$ [−1, 1].

Step 2: Organisational worker bee

To develop a new optimal weight N_(i,j) based on Equation (10), the ith weight of the network communicates with the gth weight (employee bee) of the network.

$$N_{i,j} = \begin{cases} S_N(i,j) + \psi_{ij}(S_N(i,j) - S_N(k,j)) \, j = j^r \\ S_N(i,j) \, j \neq j^r \end{cases} \tag{10}$$

As a result of this analysis, Equation is used to refine the best position approach so that it more efficiently exploits the search space (11)

$$N_{i,j} = \begin{cases} S_N(best,j) + \psi_{ij}(S_N(i,j) - S_N(k,j)) \, j = j^r \\ S_N(i,j) \, j \neq j^r \end{cases} \tag{11}$$

where "k" is a random weight from a set between 1 and NS, and the values of "i" and "j" and "r" are also decided at random from the range between 1 and D. Keep in mind that the only place where N_(i,j) deviates from S_N (i,j) is at the jr component. As part of the process of optimum selection, the new weight potential is weighed against the old weight potential and analysed from many angles before a final decision is made. However, the network only facilitates this process of weight change when the condition $f(N_{i,j})<f(S_N(i,j))$ is satisfied. If the condition does not hold, the previous weight is kept and the number of tests is increased by 1. Trial now improvement on procedure.

Step 3: Onlooker bee stage

The observer bee agent is in charge of prioritising the weights at this stage so that the most optimal weights for topology control may be chosen.

$$PROB\left(SN_{(i)}\right)=\frac{Q-Fit\left(SN_{(i)}\right)}{\sum_{j=1}^{NS}Q-Fit\left(SN_{(i)}\right)} \tag{12}$$

$$Q-Fit\left(SN_{(i)}\right)=\begin{cases}\frac{1}{\left(f\left(S_N\left(i\right)\right)\right)}f\left(S_N\left(i\right)\right)\geq 0\\ 1+\left|f\left(S_N\left(i\right)\right)\right|f\left(S_N\left(i\right)\right)<0\end{cases} \tag{13}$$

Furthermore, based on Equation (14), the weight with low capability is swapped out for the weight with high potential (the weight with the highest fitness value to be elected as the network's optimal weight).

$$S_{N(np)}=H(S_{N(best)}+\psi_{(np)}\left(S_{N(np)}-S_{N(rs1)}+\phi_{(np)}\left(S_{N(np)}-S_{N(rs2)}\right)\right) \tag{14}$$

Step 4: The Scout Bee Phase was mandated by the Firefly Optimisation Algorithm.

The unadjusted coordinates of the new solution are calculated during this scouting phase by applying the modified FFA technique given by Equation (15)

$$E_{n(i)} = \sqrt{\sum_{c=1}^{D} \left(S_{N(i,k)} - S_{N(j,k)} \right)^2} \tag{15}$$

Using Equation (16), we can see how each solution stacks up in terms of how appealing it is to the other solutions.

$$a_{S(i)} = a_0 * e^{-\beta E_{n(i)}^2} \tag{16}$$

In adding, the search equation of the basic ABC is adjusted in accordance with Equation (17), which is used to manage the trade-off between specialisation and generalisation.

$$S_{N(i,j)} = S_{N(i,j)} + \alpha_{S(i)} \left(S_{N(j)} - S_{N(i)} \right) + \left(rand(0,1) - 0.5 \right) \tag{17}$$

In addition, the convergence rate can be increased by using levy flight, as shown in Equation (18).

$$S_{N(i,j)} = S_{N(i,j)} + \alpha_{S(i)} \left(S_{N(j)} - S_{N(i)} \right) + \left(rand(0,1) - 0.5 \right) + Levy(\lambda). \tag{18}$$

The scout bee phase of the proposed HMABC-FFA strategy was designed to maximise the rate of exploration while making weight selections.

Modified Firefly Optimization Algorithm

The dazzling behaviouof fireflies served as inspiration for the Firefly Optimisation Algorithm. This FFA belongs to a subclass of PSOs that is easy to construct and understand throughout the optimisation process. This FFA has developed three possible rules, including (i) all fireflies, regardless of sex, are drawn to one another; (ii) a firefly's brightness determines the strength of its attraction; (iii) a firefly with a lower brightness is drawn to one with a higher brightness;). Fireflies are appealing and brighter the closer they are to one another, and vice versa. For this purpose, we may use Equation (19) to calculate the approximate Cartesian distance between any two fireflies, fi and fj.

$$d_{c(i,j)} = \sqrt{\sum_{m=1}^{D_{SP}} \left(f_{i,m} - f_{j,m} \right)^2} \tag{19}$$

where $f_{i,m}$ and $f_{j,m}$ fireflies f_i and f_j, correspondingly, denote the m-th dimensional spatial coordinate.

At this point, Equation (20) dictates a monotonically decreasing function of brightness for the whole implementation.

$$\beta\left(d_{c(i,j)}\right) = \beta_0 e^{-\gamma^{d^2} c(ij)} \tag{20}$$

More, when the firefly f_i march to the additional firefly f_j based on its advanced attractiveness, then the drive of firefly f_i is strongminded based on Equation (21)

$$f_i^{NEW} = f_i^{OLD} + \beta_0 e^{-\gamma d^2_{c(ij)}} \left(f_i^{OLD} - f_j\right) + a\left(rand - \frac{1}{2}\right) \tag{21}$$

Premature convergence is seen as a weakness of the basic firefly method. To fix the early convergence problem in the firefly method, we can adjust the attractiveness factor and the function that reduces it at each iteration. In this case, the tidal force formula is being evaluated as an alternative to the firefly algorithm's attraction factor. In place of the firefly's attractiveness, we incorporate among them into the tidal formula. Furthermore, the firefly algorithm's coefficient of absorption does not work in the tidal force formula due to the formula's peculiarities. The obtained from the tidal force makes adaptations to the firefly's approach, such as the elimination of the naturally occurring above phenomena. By increasing the sensitivity of firefly behaviour, tidal force helps achieve global optimisation while avoiding premature convergence and keeping the exploitation and exploration in equilibrium.

Inclusion of Tidal Formula

When the Moon, Earth, and Sun all exert their gravitational pull on a body (Tidal water), the resulting effects are known as tides in the field of celestial physics. Newton's universal gravitational law states that the attraction between any two substances is exactly proportional to the product of their masses distance among them. Tides are forces that pull one another due to gravity, and there is only one possible separation between them. Tidal force equation (Td_{Force}) resulting from law of movement is obtainable in Equation (22)

$$Td_{\text{Force}} = \frac{G_C M_m M_{iob}\left(d_{b(ij)} + d_{b(ij)}\right)^2 + G_C M_m M_{iob} d_{b(ij)}^2}{d_{b(ij)}^2 \left(d_{b(ij)} + d_{b(ij)}\right)^2} \tag{22}$$

The simplified and reorganised tidal on Equation (23)

$$Td_{\text{Force}} = \frac{2G_C M_m M_{iob} d_{b(ij)}}{d_{b(ij)}^3} \equiv \frac{G_C M_m M_{iob}}{R_u^2} - \frac{G_C M_m M_{iob}}{R_I^2} withR_u \neq R_I \neq 0 \tag{23}$$

In the new improved formula, the tidal force specified in the above-mentioned Equation (23) is employed to fine-tune the intensity of firefly.

This tidal-force enhanced firefly optimisation can find the global minimum value in a finite amount of peers. When d_(b(ij)) gets smaller as, we say that the intensity is increasing.

$la\frac{1}{d_{b(ij)}}$ the strength of light with a coldness from the basis of light is projected to be equivalent to the brighter light's enhanced intensity. Let the total population, denoted by "n," be. $f = (f1, f2, \ldots, fn)$, then the separate solution of the population is characterized through $f = (f11, f12, \ldots, f1(ds))$ with the goal of selecting appropriate weights taking into account the number of variables or dimensions (ds). Each answer at this point is a reference to the vector that represents the whole weighting information in BGRNN. Each cycle includes a pairwise comparison of the solutions (fireflies). If one solution has a lower fitness value than the other, the present solution is revised taking into account all feasible dimensions. Distance between solutions in the high-selection issue is calculated simply by. of $la\frac{1}{d_{b(ij)}}$ Thus, the matrix "A" obtainable in Equation (24) signifies the comprehensive usual of solutions.

$$A = \begin{bmatrix} f_{11} & f_{12} & \cdots & f_{1n} \\ f_{21} & f_{22} & \cdots & f_{2n} \\ \vdots & \vdots & \cdots & \vdots \\ f_{m1} & f_{m2} & \vdots & f_{mn} \end{bmatrix} \tag{24}$$

Additional, the matrix "B" portrayed in Equation (25) tourist attractions the whole set of keys after the request of $la\frac{1}{d_{b(ij)}}$.

$$B = \begin{bmatrix} \frac{1}{f_{11}} & \frac{1}{f_{12}} & \cdots & \frac{1}{f_{1n}} \\ \frac{1}{f_{21}} & \frac{1}{f_{22}} & \cdots & \frac{1}{f_{23}} \\ \vdots & \vdots & \cdots & \vdots \\ \frac{1}{f_{m1}} & \frac{1}{f_{m2}} & \cdots & \frac{1}{f_{mn}} \end{bmatrix} \tag{25}$$

As seen in Equation (26), here each solution is represented by a single "n"-dimensional vector.

$$S_{Vector} = \left[\frac{1}{f_{11}}\frac{1}{f_{12}}\cdots\cdots\frac{1}{f_{1n}}\right] \tag{26}$$

In addition, the near and distant distances are calculated by comparing the two solution vectors using Equations (27) and (28), respectively.

$$R_I = y = Min\left(S_{vector}\right) \tag{27}$$

$$R_u = z = Max\left(S_{vector}\right) \tag{28}$$

Equation (23) is used to get the attraction factor; from this, Equation (29) is derived to find the tidal force in each dimension.

$$Td_{\text{Force}} = \beta = \frac{G_C M_m M_{iob}}{R_u^2} - \frac{G_C M_m M_{iob}}{R_I^2} \equiv \frac{G_C M_m M_{iob}}{z} - \frac{G_C M_m M_{iob}}{y} \tag{29}$$

Thus, the problem of delayed junction in the standard FFA is avoided by employing tidal force.

Integration of Modified ABC and FFA

To improve exploitation, the bee phases of ABC use a modified version of the FFA algorithm into the optimal weight selection procedure. Additionally, the ABC's scout bee stage has been incorporated for enhanced exploration. As a result, ABC and FFA are used together to create a more optimal balance between specialisation and generalisation.

RESULTS AND DISCUSSION

The approaches presented are tested here and compared to others in the literature. By expanding the standard set of characteristics from four (High, Low, Volume, Open) to six, we can expand the feature set to include an additional six variables enhances the model's performance, with lower loss rates.

Environmental Setup

The Intel Core i3 (2.0 GHz) machine with Windows 10 (64 bit) and 8 GB of RAM is utilised for the experiments. In this study, Python is utilised, and the tested algorithms retain their original key arguments. Google-Colab was used for this study's investigation. In addition, the following libraries were used: pandas, NumPy, Matplotlib, Sklearn, and Keras.

Dataset Description

The NSE datasets of three different banks are used for the implementation; these datasets may be accessible via the NSE website. The financial institutions are either publicly owned or privately operated. Two years' worth of trading data are evaluated (Agrawal et al., 2022)30, beginning on November 16th, 2016 and ending on November 15th, 2018. All numbers, excluding the time stamp, are included in the dataset.

Evaluation Phase

Several tests were been out, and the results are being compared to the best practises now available. Three financial institution datasets are analysed for performance. The intimate price-STI relationship has been the subject of much experimental research. Using MAs, we have shown that we can anticipate stock market patterns with a high degree of accuracy.

Figure 4. HDFC trend investigation over two years

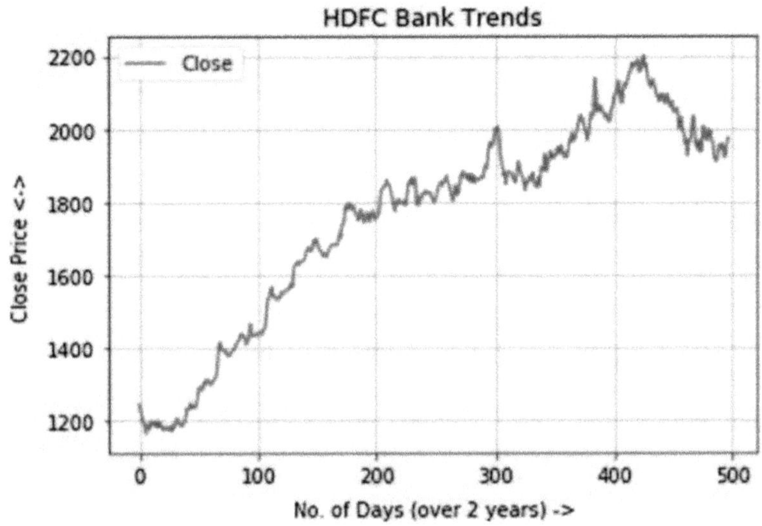

Model Results and Performance

Figure 4–6 displays the results of the experiment for all three stocks. The visualisation makes it clear that the data is not steady, both in the long and short term.

Indicators of various types are analysed here, with Moving Averages coming out on top in terms of correlation. Table 1 displays the relationship between moving averages and the closing price of 3 stocks for a given day.

Considering three distinct day computations, Table 1 displays the relationship among the closing value and moving medians based on three diverse banks:

Evaluation Metrics

MSE and prediction accuracy are used to evaluate the constructed model.

Average Deviation: It is a statistic that calculates the mean squared error over a collection of forecasts.

$$MAE = \frac{1}{n}\sum_{k=1}^{n}\left(y_k - \hat{y}_k\right)^2 \tag{30}$$

where y_k and $\hat{y}_k$ are Actual and Foretold outputs, correspondingly.

Figure 5. Yes, bank trend investigation over two years

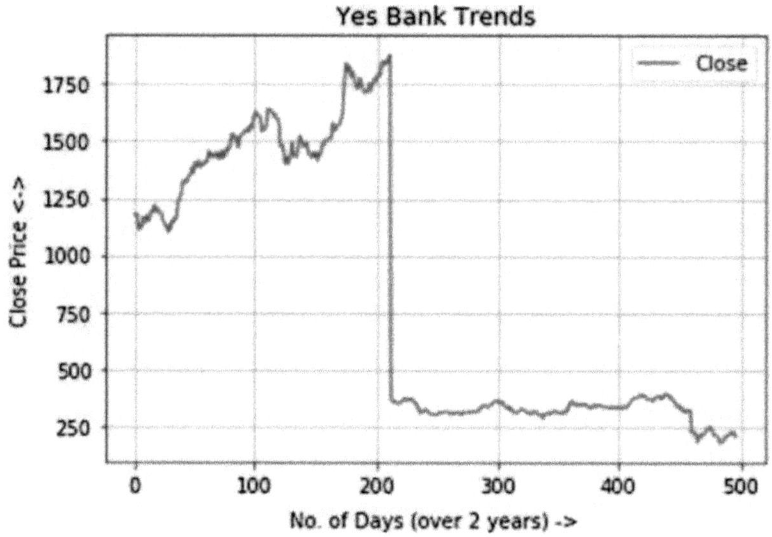

Accuracy in Making Predictions, or PA, is the Rate at Which a System Makes Correct Predictions. When developing classifiers with EBGRNN, we measure

Figure 6. SBI trend investigation over two years

Shen, J., & Shafiq, M. O. (2020). Short-term stock market price trend prediction using a comprehensive deep learning system. *Journal of Big Data*, *7*(1), 1–33. doi:10.1186/s40537-020-00333-6 PMID:32923309

Sunny, M. A. I., Maswood, M. M. S., & Alharbi, A. G. 2020, October. Deep learning-based stock price prediction using LSTM and bi-directional LSTM model. In *2020 2nd novel intelligent and leading emerging sciences conference (NILES)* (pp. 87-92). IEEE.

Thirumalraj, A., & Rajesh, T. (2023). *An Improved ARO Model for Task Offloading in Vehicular Cloud Computing in VANET.*

Vijh, M., Chandola, D., Tikkiwal, V. A., & Kumar, A. (2020). Stock closing price prediction using machine learning techniques. *Procedia Computer Science*, *167*, 599–606. doi:10.1016/j.procs.2020.03.326

Yu, P., & Yan, X. (2020). Stock price prediction based on deep neural networks. *Neural Computing & Applications*, *32*(6), 1609–1628. doi:10.1007/s00521-019-04212-x

Yun, K. K., Yoon, S. W., & Won, D. (2023). Interpretable stock price forecasting model using genetic algorithm-machine learning regressions and best feature subset selection. *Expert Systems with Applications*, *213*, 118803. doi:10.1016/j.eswa.2022.118803

Zhao, Y., & Yang, G. (2023). Deep Learning-based Integrated Framework for stock price movement prediction. *Applied Soft Computing*, *133*, 109921. doi:10.1016/j.asoc.2022.109921

Chapter 14
Ensembled Time Series Deep Learning Framework for Stock Market Prediction

Lakshmipriya Balagourouchetty
Vellore Institute of Technology, Chennai, India

Nidhi Singh
Mount Carmel College, India

S. Jayalakshmy
https://orcid.org/0000-0001-8876-239X
IFET College of Engineering, India

ABSTRACT

Prediction and analysis of Stock Market plays a very important and crucial role in today's economic growth. Understanding the pattern of these financial activity and predicting its transformation and development are the most challenging areas of research in financial sectors and academic sectors. This paper explores the competency of sequential learning elements viz. long short-term memory (LSTM), bidirectional long short-term memory (BiLSTM) and gated recurrent unit (GRU) with different depths and combinations in forecasting the share market trend from the Nifty50 dataset. The experimental assessment elucidates that the ensemble prediction model built using BiLSTM-LSTM and BiLSTM-GRU by the virtue of integrating the merits of BiLSTM and LSTM/GRU layers demonstrate a better performance closer to reality with least error.

DOI: 10.4018/979-8-3693-0790-8.ch014

INTRODUCTION

Forecasting stock market expenditures is a challenging task due to many uncertainties associated and numerous variables that affect the open market valuation on a given day, such as economic conditions, shareholder sentiments toward a particular company, political activities, and so on (Subasi et al., 2021). Along with debt markets, which are generally more imposing but do not trade publicly, the stock market is one of the most important ways for companies to raise money. This enables businesses to go public and raise additional financial capital for expansion by selling shares of ownership in the company on the open market. Stock market prediction is the act of attempting to predict the future values of a company, stock, or other assets. In essence, it is defined as a trial to determine the stock value and provide a solid idea for people to understand and predict the market and stock process (Rouf et al., 2021). It is typically presented using quarterly financial ratios and real-world datasets. Rising stock prices and other related assets have always been an important part of economic activity, influencing the social environment. The stock exchange is widely regarded as the most important indicator of a country's economic strength and development. Rising stock prices are typically associated with an increase in business investment and vice-versa. These share prices have influenced household wealth and consumption, prompting central banks to take strict measures to control and regulate the stock market, as well as to ensure the smooth operation of financial system functions (Vijh et al., 2020). The technology of artificial intelligence with the advent of machine learning and deep learning algorithms is being increasingly deployed to predict the stock market trend well in advance close to reality from the past patterns of the market.

The stock market makes headlines every day and notifies and alerts the public whenever it makes or loses money. The goal is to develop an algorithm that predicts the short-term price of each individual stock, allowing for more efficient business opportunities and stock market investment. Considering the impacts created by stock market prediction and the need to provide accurate prediction closer to reality, this work aims at developing an efficient deep learning framework is proposed to forecast the stock market trend on the recent real world popular business data with high degree of accuracy.

LITERATURE SURVEY

Profits from a successful stock prediction can be enormous for both the seller and the broker. Such processes are well represented by machine and deep learning. (Subasi et al., 2021) proposed a prediction comparison using various classifiers such as

Random Forest, Bagging, AdaBoost, Decision Trees, Support Vector Machine (SVM), K-Nearest Neighbour (KNN), and Artificial Neural Network (ANN). The study compared seven machine learning algorithms on four different stock indices datasets, National Association of Securities Dealers Automated Quotations (NASDAQ), New York Stock Exchange (NYSE), Nikkei 225 Stock Average (NIKKEI), and Financial Times Stock Exchange Group (FTSE), in order to facilitate risk-adjusted investment and found that bagging and random forest with the leaked dataset had the best performance and accuracy for Stock Market Prediction. (Hu et al., 2013). presented a theoretical and empirical framework for using the SVM strategy to predict the stock market data from the Federal Reserve Bank of St. Louis, Big Charts Historical Stock Quotes and reported a performance with accuracy rate of 96.15. (Manojlović & Štajduhar, 2015) presented 5-days-ahead and 10-days-ahead predictive models built with the random forest algorithm on historical data from the CROBEX index as well as a few companies from various sectors that are listed on the Zagreb Stock Exchange and achieved a significant performance accuracy in stock market trend prediction. The study reported a weighted average F-measure for 5-days-ahead models as 0.763, and the average accuracy as 0.765 (76.5%) and for for 10-days-ahead models, the weighted average F-measure was 0.808 (80.8%) and the average accuracy was 0.808. (Miró-Julià et al., 2010) had introduced and evaluated various investment strategies that predict future stock exchanges on Alcoa dataset using decision trees with three and two classes. The 3-class tree yields a 39% accuracy rate and a 118% profit gain, while the 2-class tree yields a 49% accuracy rate and an 88% profit gain. It was observed that the traditional machine learning algorithms were limited in their ability to analyse unstructured data. Deep learning which is capable of performing complex tasks that frequently necessitate extensive feature engineering significantly addresses the short comings of the traditional machine learning algorithms. Deep neural networks' (DNN) multiple layers enable models to become more efficient at learning complex features and performing more intensive computational tasks, i.e., performing many complex operations at the same time. It outperforms machine learning in unstructured dataset machine perception tasks. (Pawar et al., 2019) research focuses on the application of deep learning techniques like Recurrent Neural Network (RNN) and LSTM for stock market prediction. Standard & Poor's (S&P) 500, Google, Tesla, and Apple datasets were used for training, and pre-processing techniques were used and showed that the RNN-LSTM model produce accurate results than traditional machine learning algorithms. With encouraging results, Adil Moghar tried to anticipate future values for both Google (GOOGL) and Nike (NKE) assets by the virtue of LSTM based recurrent neural network (RNN) to estimate adjusted closing prices for a portfolio of assets (Moghar & Hamiche,2020). The research of (Hiransha et al.,2018). focused on techniques such as artificial neural network (ANN), convolution neural network (CNN), multilayer perceptron and RNN for predicting a company's stock price on HCL, Maruti, and Axis Bank datasets from National Stock Exchange of India Ltd (NSE), and Bank of America and Chesapeake Energy datasets from New York Stock Exchange (NYSE) and found that CNN outperformed the other three networks. (Mehtab & Sen 2020) works on deep learning-based regression models for predicting NIFTY 50 index values using encoder-decoder CNN LSTM model with univariate input data performed well in forecasting. (Xu et al.,2018) focused on the RNN, with an LSTM layer, to automatically learn distributed representations of financial entities without any handmade characteristics greatly enhanced the prediction accuracy. In a study proposed by (Mukherjee et al.,2023), two approaches to predict stock market indices and stock prices using ANN and CNN were proposed for NIFTY index dataset and reported that CNN model produced acceptable results, with an average prediction accuracy of 98.92% compared to that of ANN with an accuracy of 97.66% . The study by (Chen & He, 2018), focused on a one-dimensional (1D) CNN model to predict stock prices of China Stock Exchange and proved that the CNN model was robust even for 1D sequential data. (Khare et al., 2017), conducted a comparison study between LSTM model and multi-layer perceptron model on a minute-by-minute stock price data on the NYSE and reported that multi-layer perceptron outperformed the LSTM model. The work by (Singh & Srivastava, 2017) on Google Stock Multimedia data from NASDAQ presented a comparison between DNN with Radial Basis Function Neural Network (RBFNN) and RNN. The goal of (Reddy, V.K.S, 2018, pp. 1033-1035) work was to develop a financial data predictor programme using SVM and radial basis function models on IBM data to reduce the uncertainty associated with investment decisions.The work by (Agrawal et al., 2022) entailed the investigation of popular deep learning architectures and stock technical indicators (STIs). The data was obtained from the NSE for three banking sectors: HDFC, YES Bank, and SBI. The experimental results showed that the evolutionary deep learning approach (EDLA) wass market independent, and can be applied to both stocks and stock market indices.

METHODOLOGY

An experimental trial of deep learning-based regression models for stock market prediction using three different sequential learning elements is presented in this section. Stock market data being a time series data, prediction is performed through regression analysis.

Table 1. Prediction model and result

Reference	Dataset	Prediction Model	Result				
SVM (Subasi et al., 2021)	NASDAQ, NYSE, NIKKEI, FTSE	Random Forest, Bagging, AdaBoost, Decision Trees, SVM, K-NN, and ANN		NASDAQ	NYSE	NIKKEI	FTSE
			Random Forest	54%	52%	53%	32%
			Bagging	50%	52%	53%	39%
			AdaBoost	49%	54%	47%	32%
			Decision Tree	48%	46%	49%	36%
			SVM	67%	62%	56%	21%
			KNN	54%	51%	56%	46%
			ANN	50%	51%	51%	39%
(Hu et al., 2013), (Pawar et al., 2019)	S&P 500, Apple, Google, Tesla	RNN, LSTM	Cells	Layers	Loss (MSE)		
			128 256 512	1	0.0002554		
				2	0.0002835		
				1	0.0002307		
				2	0.0002455		
				1	0.0002080		
				2	0.0002054		
(Manojlović & Štajduhar, 2015), (Moghar & Hamiche,2020).	Google, Nike	RNN, LSTM	Google (Loss)		NKE (Loss)		
			12 Epochs - 0.0011 25 Epochs - 0.001 50 Epochs - 0.00065 100 Epochs - 0.00049		12 Epochs - 0.0019 25 Epochs - 0.0016 50 Epochs - 0.001 100 Epochs - 0.00087		
(Miró-Julià et al., 2010), (Hiransha et al.,2018).	Maruti, Axis Bank, HCL Tech, Bank of America (BoA), Chesapeak Energy	ANN, RNN, LSTM, MLP	MAPE	CNN	RNN	LSTM	MLP
			Maruti	5.36	7.86	6.37	6.29
			Axis Bk	7.94	9.27	8.13	8.10
			HCL	6.42	8.53	6.97	7.38
			Chesapeak	9.18	8.94	8.98	7.85
			BoA	5.31	5.38	6.01	4.82
(Pawar et al., 2019), (Mehtab & Sen 2020)	NIFTY 50	CNN, LSTM	CNN (1)		RMSE - 0.0349		
			CNN (2)		RMSE - 0.0382		
			LSTM (2)		RMSE - 0.0369		
			LSTM & CNN (2)		RMSE - 0.0416		
			Conv LSTM (2)		RMSE - 0.0350		
(Moghar & Hamiche,2020), (Xu et al.,2018)	S&P 500	RCNN, CNN, LSTM	E-CNN		63.44%		
			EB-CNN		64.56%		
			E-CNN-LSTM		65.19%		
			EB-CNN-LSTM		66.31%		

Reference	Dataset	Prediction Model	Result			
(Hiransha et al.,2018), (Mukherjee et al.,2023)	NIFTY	ANN, CNN	CNN - 98.92% ANN - 97.66%			
(Mehtab & Sen 2020),(Chen & He, 2018)	China Stock Exchange	CNN	Iteration	Accuracy		
			25000	73%		
			50000	74.4%		
(Xu et al.,2018),(Khare et al., 2017),	New York Stock Exchange	MLP, LSTM	LSTM (RMSE) - 0.018 MLP (RMSE) - 0.000937			
(Mukherjee et al.,2023),(Singh & Srivastava, 2017)	Google Stock Multimedia	DNN, RNN, RBFNN	DNN is 4.8% more accurate than RBFNN and 15.6% more than RNN.			
(Chen & He, 2018),(Reddy, V.K.S, 2018, pp. 1033-1035)	IBM	SVM, RBF	SVM does not suffer from overfitting while using a large dataset and also provides higher profit compared to other ML models.			
(Agrawal et al., 2022),(Khare et al., 2017),	HDFC, YES Bank, SBI	SVM, EDLA, LSTM		SVM	EDLA	LSTM
			HDFC	51.06%	63.59%	57.2%
			YES Bk	49.64%	56.25%	52.6%
			SBI	55.39%	57.95%	56.8%
(Reddy, V.K.S, 2018, pp. 1033-1035)	Federal Reserve Bank of St Louis, Big Charts	SVM	Accuracy - 96.15%			
(Agrawal et al., 2022)	CROBEX Index, Zagreb Stock Exchange	Random Forest	Accuracy (5 Days) - 76.5% Accuracy (10 Days) - 80.8%			

Data Collection and Pre-Processing

The NSE provided real-time data from which NIFTY-50 dataset was taken

Figure 1. Snapshot of HCL data taken from NIFTY-50 dataset

	Date	Symbol	Series	Prev Close	Open	High	Low	Last	Close	VWAP	Volume	Turnover	Trades	Deliverable Volume	%Deliverble
0	2000-01-11	HCLTECH	EQ	580.00	1550.0	1725.00	1492.00	1560.00	1554.45	1582.72	1192200	1.886915e+14	NaN	NaN	NaN
1	2000-01-12	HCLTECH	EQ	1554.45	1560.0	1678.85	1560.00	1678.85	1678.85	1657.05	344850	5.714349e+13	NaN	NaN	NaN
2	2000-01-13	HCLTECH	EQ	1678.85	1790.0	1813.20	1781.00	1813.20	1813.20	1804.69	53000	9.564880e+12	NaN	NaN	NaN
3	2000-01-14	HCLTECH	EQ	1813.20	1958.3	1958.30	1835.00	1958.30	1958.30	1939.90	270950	5.256169e+13	NaN	NaN	NaN
4	2000-01-17	HCLTECH	EQ	1958.30	2115.0	2115.00	1801.65	1801.65	1801.65	1990.55	428800	8.535473e+13	NaN	NaN	NaN
...	...	...	...	...	...	...	...	...	...	...	...	...	...	...	...
5295	2021-04-26	HCLTECH	EQ	955.65	940.0	954.50	923.05	930.00	928.80	931.70	19619972	1.827997e+15	311431.0	9218486.0	0.4699
5296	2021-04-27	HCLTECH	EQ	928.80	931.0	938.55	923.40	930.30	928.85	928.06	6406825	5.945938e+14	180458.0	3233276.0	0.5047
5297	2021-04-28	HCLTECH	EQ	928.85	931.2	935.85	921.75	925.90	923.80	926.63	6845677	6.343403e+14	228230.0	3890178.0	0.5683
5298	2021-04-29	HCLTECH	EQ	923.80	929.7	929.70	907.10	910.30	909.55	914.34	8588734	7.852988e+14	363122.0	4041614.0	0.4706
5299	2021-04-30	HCLTECH	EQ	909.55	905.0	915.00	895.40	900.10	898.95	904.98	10821664	9.883911e+14	465056.0	6189272.0	0.5667

Figure 2. Process flow diagram

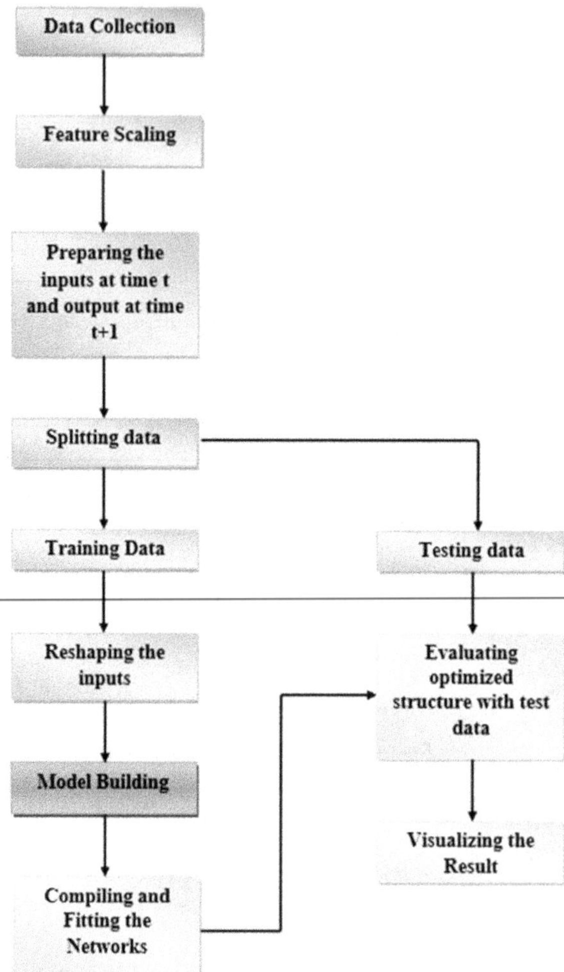

(India,2020). All datasets are on a daily basis, with pricing and trading values distributed across .csv files for each stock, as well as a metadata file containing some macro-information about the stock. The snapshot of the HCL data taken from NIFTY-50 dataset is presented in Figure 1 as a sample. The stock market records of 21 years from January 1, 2000 till April 30 2021 are present in the dataset on a daily basis. Accordingly, 5300 days data were available for every company in the NIFTY-50 dataset.

Since the obtained data is raw and unprocessed, pre-processing using Min Max Normalization followed by imputation to handle null values were done prior to building

Figure 3. Architecture of an LSTM layer

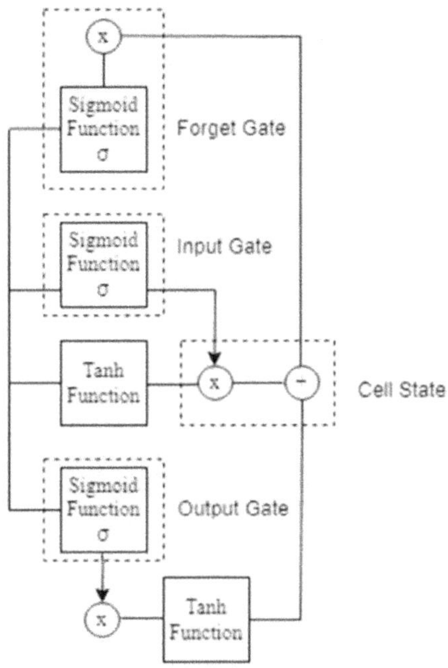

a prediction model. The process flow diagram presented in Figure 2 portraits the different processes involved in building a prediction model for the share market data.

The loss errors were checked, and if they were found to be large, parameter tuning was performed and results were obtained for various network combinations.

Proposed Architecture

Stock market data being time series in nature, it has to be analysed using RNN to extract the time series features from the share market patterns available in the dataset. RNN is a type of neural network in which a set of previous time step's output is fed as input to the network. RNN consists of a hidden layers to leverage in remembering some information about the sequence thereby making a prediction. In this work, recurrent learning-based algorithms like LSTM, BiLSTM and GRU are exploited in the development of share market prediction model.

LSTM networks are the extension of RNN that tend to increase the memory capacity. LSTM layer basically assigns weights to data, allowing the RNN to either let new information in, forget information, or give it enough importance to affect the output. RNN can remember inputs for a long time, as LSTM layers store information in memory, much like a computer's memory. The LSTM has the ability

Figure 4. Architecture of GRU network

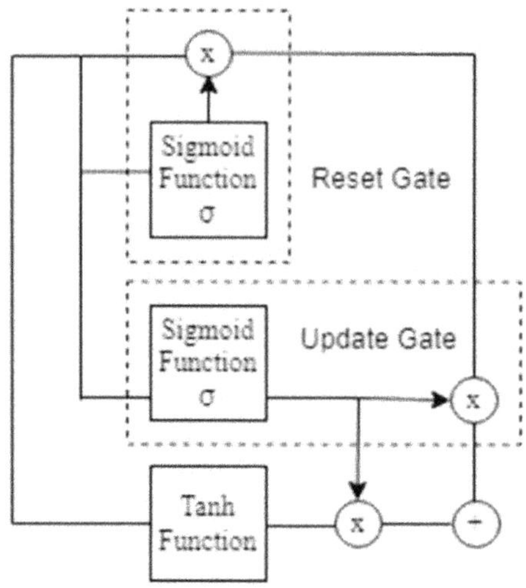

to read, write, and delete data from its memory. The input, forget, and output gates comprise an LSTM network. These gates decide whether to allow new input (input gate), delete the information because it isn't important (forget gate), or let it affect the output at the current timestep (output gate).

BiLSTM is an RNN based sequential learning cell formulated for natural language processing. In contrast to traditional LSTM, in BiLSTM, the input flows in both directions, and it can use data from both sides. It's also useful for simulating the sequential dependencies of words and phrases in both directions. BiLSTM adds an

Figure 5. Architecture of an BiLSTM network

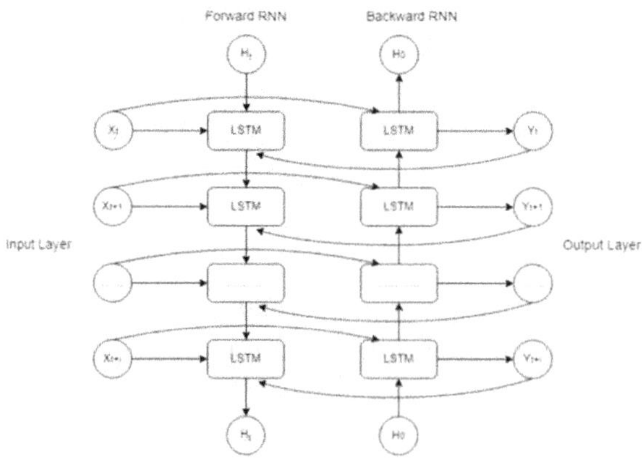

Figure 6. Architecture of the proposed ensemble time series prediction models (a) BiLSTM -LSTM Combination (b) BiLSTM - GRU Combination

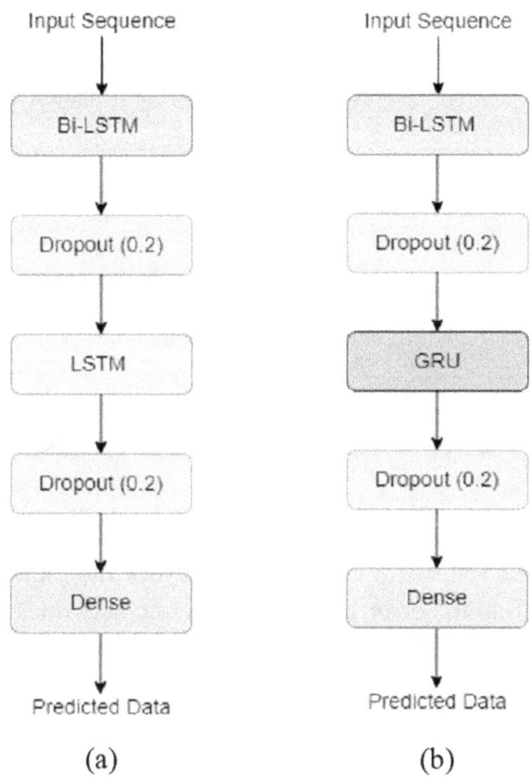

extra LSTM layer that reverses the direction of information flow, which means that the input sequence is reversed in the extra LSTM layer. Both LSTM layers outputs are then combined in a variety of ways, including average, sum, multiplication, and concatenation.

GRU networks are comparable to LSTM networks. GRU is a newer variant of RNN. There are, however, some distinctions between GRU and LSTM. GRU does not have a cell state. It transports data using its hidden states. It has two entrances (Reset and Update Gate). The Update Gate combines the Forget and Input Gates. The forget gate determines which data should be ignored and which should be stored in memory. The Reset gate erases previous data, preventing gradient explosion. The Reset Gate controls how much previous data is erased. GRU outperforms LSTM because it employs fewer tensors and thus runs more quickly. Figures. 3 to 5 shows a functional block diagrams of LSTM, GRU and BiLSTM networks.

Figure 7. Architecture details of the proposed ensemble time series prediction models (a) BiLSTM -LSTM Combination (b) BiLSTM - GRU Combination

```
Model: "sequential"
_________________________________________________________________
Layer (type)                 Output Shape              Param #
=================================================================
bidirectional (Bidirectiona  (None, 50, 100)           21200
l)

dropout (Dropout)            (None, 50, 100)           0

lstm_1 (LSTM)                (None, 50)                30200

dropout_1 (Dropout)          (None, 50)                0

dense (Dense)                (None, 2)                 102

=================================================================
Total params: 51,502
Trainable params: 51,502
Non-trainable params: 0
_________________________________________________________________
```

(a)

```
Model: "sequential_1"
_________________________________________________________________
Layer (type)                 Output Shape              Param #
=================================================================
bidirectional_1 (Bidirectio  (None, 50, 100)           21200
nal)

dropout_2 (Dropout)          (None, 50, 100)           0

gru (GRU)                    (None, 50)                22650

dropout_3 (Dropout)          (None, 50)                0

dense_1 (Dense)              (None, 2)                 102

=================================================================
Total params: 43,952
Trainable params: 43,952
Non-trainable params: 0
_________________________________________________________________
```

(b)

Stock market prediction is experimented in this work using varied number of RNN layers using LSTM, BiLSTM and GRU layers and their performances were analysed by computing the error between the predicted values and the actual data. An attempt to develop a time series prediction model by the ensemble of different sequential learning elements is made in this work for different depths to inherit the advantages of different elements onto a single model. From the performance comparison of variants of ensemble models and models constructed using similar sequential learning elements, it is found that the ensemble models exhibited a greater impact in forecasting the time series data with high degree of accuracy. In particular, two prediction models developed using BiLSTM and LSTM in sequential connection and BiLSTM and GRU connected in series manifested comparatively a better performance with other ensemble models. This is due to the hybridization of BiLSTM and LSTM/GRU layers inheriting the bidirectional data flow onto the

Table 2. Hyperparameter settings

Parameter	Value
Learning rate	10^{-4}
Optimizer	Adam
No. of epochs	50
Metric	Mean absolute error
Loss function	Root mean square error
Training: testing dataset	70:30

Table 3. Validation set error values for varying number of similar layers

	RMSE					MAE				
	HCL	**TCS**	**Wipro**	**Tech Mahindra**	**Maruthi**	**HCL**	**TCS**	**Wipro**	**Tech Mahindra**	**Maruthi**
LSTM 2 layers	0.0233	0.0412	0.0027	0.0087	0.0580	0.1063	0.1608	0.0409	0.0800	0.2025
LSTM 4 layers	0.0315	0.6302	0.0037	0.01621	0.0606	0.119	0.7861	0.0489	0.1137	0.2255
LSTM 6 layers	0.0387	0.0693	0.0044	0.0168	0.0662	0.1452	0.2108	0.0551	0.1142	0.2313
LSTM 8 layers	0.0453	0.0928	0.0055	0.0188	0.0944	0.1561	0.2667	0.0651	0.1157	0.2868
BiLSTM 2 layers	0.0240	0.0393	0.0039	0.0087	0.0693	0.1178	0.1519	0.0450	0.0800	0.2277
BiLSTM 4 layers	0.0252	0.0541	0.0032	0.0173	0.0611	0.1280	0.1975	0.0461	0.1207	0.2161
BiLSTM 6 layers	0.0236	0.0537	0.0033	0.0093	0.0647	0.1074	0.1850	0.0512	0.0838	0.2243
BiLSTM 8 layers	0.0265	0.0652	0.0039	0.0125	0.0744	0.1350	0.2180	0.0532	0.0990	0.2436
GRU 2 layers	0.0175	0.0358	0.0035	0.0365	0.0614	0.1857	0.1421	0.0517	0.0895	0.2339
GRU 4 layers	0.0323	0.0742	0.0037	0.0102	0.1278	0.1592	0.2520	0.0428	0.0899	0.3438
GRU 6 layers	0.0394	0.1134	0.0046	0.01211	0.1471	0.1766	0.3160	0.0581	0.0956	0.3718
GRU 8 layers	0.0408	0.1567	0.0055	0.01903	0.1782	0.1726	0.3814	0.0651	0.1243	0.4112

three or two gated hidden layer structure. The block diagram of the top performing ensemble models for share market prediction is presented in Figure 6. The details of architecture along with the learnable parameters for the two ensemble architectures are presented in Figure 7.

RESULTS AND DISCUSSION

The results of stock market forecasting implemented on Nifty50 dataset using the proposed network models are presented in this section. Every working day record of share market data of five companies viz. HCL, TCS, Wipro, Tech Mahindra and Maruti for the past 21 years from January 2020 till April 2021 are considered for analysis and the experimental validation of the proposed network models. Every dataset has a total of 5300 records in the aforementioned period. The first 70% of the data comprising of 3710 days record are considered for training and the

Table 4. Validation set error values for various combinations of layers

	RMSE					MAE				
	HCL	TCS	Wipro	Tech Mahindra	Maruthi	HCL	TCS	Wipro	Tech Mahindra	Maruthi
LSTM BiLSTM	0.0249	0.0447	0.0033	0.0101	0.2227	0.1074	0.1661	0.0501	0.0872	0.3767
LSTM GRU	0.0219	0.0421	0.0033	0.0087	0.0440	0.0985	0.1576	0.0487	0.0820	0.1817
BiLSTM LSTM	0.0190	**0.0345**	**0.0025**	0.0133	0.0783	0.0987	**0.1357**	**0.0407**	0.1060	0.2335
BiLSTM GRU	**0.0168**	0.0432	0.0036	**0.0039**	**0.0368**	**0.0813**	0.1612	0.0546	**0.0761**	**0.1667**
GRU LSTM	0.0206	0.0466	0.0062	0.0103	0.1552	0.1049	0.1788	0.0723	0.0921	0.7714
GRU BiLSTM	0.0232	0.0497	0.0034	0.008	0.0981	0.1118	0.1769	0.0489	0.0786	0.2672
LSTM (2) BiLSTM (2)	0.0303	0.0632	0.0040	0.0132	0.0618	0.1205	0.2116	0.0547	0.1022	0.2259
LSTM (2) GRU (2)	0.0277	0.0749	0.0040	0.0148	0.0530	0.1127	0.2401	0.0563	0.1093	0.2104
BiLSTM (2) LSTM (2)	0.0196	0.0517	0.0027	0.0110	0.07918	0.0916	0.1898	0.0440	0.0947	0.2697
BiLSTM (2) GRU (2)	0.0201	0.0457	0.0029	0.0096	0.0399	0.0939	0.1784	0.0446	0.0875	0.1839
GRU (2) LSTM (2)	0.0296	0.0635	0.0053	0.0099	0.0686	0.1365	0.2111	0.0631	0.0877	0.2466
GRU (2) BiLSTM (2)	0.0275	0.0915	0.0048	0.0090	0.0681	0.1297	0.2787	0.0646	0.0828	0.2395
LSTM GRU LSTM GRU	0.0263	0.0639	0.0036	0.0149	0.1064	0.1092	0.2105	0.049	0.1095	0.3150
GRU LSTM GRU LSTM	0.0272	0.0637	0.0035	0.0133	0.0525	0.1167	0.2074	0.0508	0.1060	0.2064
LSTM BiLSTM LSTM BiLSTM	0.0242	0.0514	0.0034	0.0116	0.07630	0.1095	0.1823	0.0497	0.0964	0.2379
BiLSTM LSTM BiLSTM LSTM	0.0204	0.0639	0.0047	0.0126	0.0604	0.0913	0.2187	0.0611	0.1042	0.2292

Table 5. Graphs of predicted and actual values by Bi-LSTM – LSTM ensemble architecture

<table>
<tr><th>Dataset</th><th>BiLSTM - LSTM</th></tr>
<tr><td>HCL</td><td>
</td></tr>
<tr><td>TCS</td><td>
</td></tr>
<tr><td>Wipro</td><td>
</td></tr>
</table>

<table>
<tr><td>Tech Mahindra</td><td>
</td></tr>
<tr><td>Maruthi</td><td>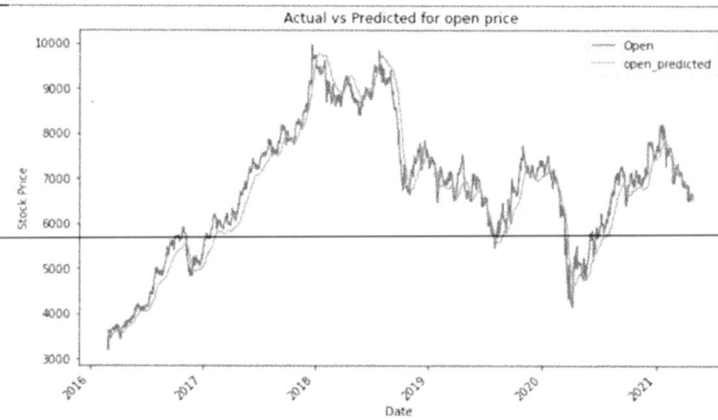
</td></tr>
</table>

Table 6. Graphs of predicted and actual values by Bi-LSTM – GRU ensemble architecture

Dataset	BiLSTM - GRU
HCL	
TCS	
Wipro	

Tech Mahindra	
Maruthi	

trailing 30% data of 1590 days are considered for prediction. The performance of stock market prediction is analysed in terms of root mean square error. The hyper parameter settings for training the prediction model are presented in Table 2. The performance of the proposed combination of prediction models are compared with models realized using different number of LSTM, BiLSTM and GRU layers. In order to perform a fair comparison, the hyper parameter settings are maintained the same for all the network models. The prediction models are implemented using TensorFlow and Keras libraries.

The prediction performance in terms of RMSE and MAE are analysed for different number of LSTM, BiLSTM and GRU layers and also for various combinations of these three layers. The error values obtained for the various network structures with the hyper parameter settings mentioned in Tables 2 are presented in Tables 3 and 4.

From the results presented in Table 3, it is evident that for all three LSTM, BiLSTM and GRU, the prediction performance deteriorates with increase in the number of layers. For a prediction model built with similar layers, model with two layers of sequential element records lowest error resulting in closer to actual value. In the attempt of combining the sequence elements, BiLSTM followed by LSTM and BiLSTM followed by GRU have resulted in a better performance compared to other combinations for the datasets considered in this work. This is presented in Table 4. It is evident from the results presented in Table 4 that the prediction performance is the best with ensemble model built using BiLSTM – LSTM for TCS and Wipro datasets whereas the ensemble model BiLSTM – GRU records lowest error for HCL, Tech Mahindra and Maruthi datasets. The visualization of the prediction made by the proposed combinations of LSTM, BiLSTM and GRU layers for the five datasets considered in the works are presented in Tables 5 and 6.

In the implementation of regression-based prediction models through sequential learning using deep learning framework, with the ensemble of sequential layers, the errors are very less when compared to prediction models constructed using similar sequential learning elements. The fact that BiLSTM contains two LSTMs that can perform both forward and backward propagation, its combination with LSTM/GRU and BiLSTM accomplishes better performance with less error and accurate prediction.

CONCLUSION

An exhaustive experimentation of deep learning models built using LSTM, BiLSTM and GRU with varied depths and combinations for the prediction of stock market trend has been carried out in this work on five datasets taken from Nifty50. The experimental assessment reveals that prediction performance descends with increase in number of sequential layers. Combining sequential learning elements in the prediction models creates a significant impact in the prediction performance. The ensemble model built using BiLSTM – LSTM achieves a phenomenal prediction performance for TCS and Wipro datasets with a lowest RMSE of 0.0345 and 0.0025 respectively. Likewise, the ensemble model built using BiLSTM-GRU results in an exceptional performance with least RMSE values of 0.0168, 0.0039 and 0.0368 respectively for HCL, Tech Mahindra and Maruthi datasets.

REFERENCES

Agrawal, M., Shukla, P. K., Nair, R., Nayyar, A., & Masud, M. (2022). Stock Prediction Based on Technical Indicators Using Deep Learning Model. *Computers, Materials & Continua*, *70*(1), 287–304. doi:10.32604/cmc.2022.014637

Chen, S., & He, H. (2018, November). Stock prediction using convolutional neural network. [). IOP Publishing.]. *IOP Conference Series. Materials Science and Engineering*, *435*, 012026. doi:10.1088/1757-899X/435/1/012026

Hiransha, M., Gopalakrishnan, E. A., Menon, V. K., & Soman, K. P. (2018). NSE stock market prediction using deep-learning models. *Procedia Computer Science*, *132*, 1351–1362. doi:10.1016/j.procs.2018.05.050

Hu, Z., Zhu, J., & Tse, K. (2013, November). Stocks market prediction using support vector machine. In *2013 6th International Conference on Information Management, Innovation Management and Industrial Engineering* (*Vol. 2*, pp. 115-118). IEEE. 10.1109/ICIII.2013.6703096

India, N. (2020). *NSE - National Stock Exchange of India Ltd: Live Share/Stock Market News & Updates, Quotes- Nseindia.com*. NSE India. https://www.nseindia.com/

Khare, K., Darekar, O., Gupta, P., & Attar, V. Z. (2017, May). Short term stock price prediction using deep learning. In *2017 2nd IEEE international conference on recent trends in electronics, information & communication technology (RTEICT)* (pp. 482-486). IEEE. 10.1109/RTEICT.2017.8256643

Manojlović, T., & Štajduhar, I. (2015, May). Predicting stock market trends using random forests: A sample of the Zagreb stock exchange. In *2015 38th International Convention on Information and Communication Technology, Electronics and Microelectronics (MIPRO)* (pp. 1189-1193). IEEE. 10.1109/MIPRO.2015.7160456

Mehtab, S., & Sen, J. (2020, November). Stock price prediction using CNN and LSTM-based deep learning models. In *2020 International Conference on Decision Aid Sciences and Application (DASA)* (pp. 447-453). IEEE. 10.1109/DASA51403.2020.9317207

Miró-Julià, M., Fiol-Roig, G., & Isern-Deyà, A. P. (2010). Decision trees in stock market analysis: construction and validation. In *Trends in Applied Intelligent Systems: 23rd International Conference on Industrial Engineering and Other Applications of Applied Intelligent Systems*. Springer.

Moghar, A., & Hamiche, M. (2020). Stock market prediction using LSTM recurrent neural network. *Procedia Computer Science*, *170*, 1168–1173. doi:10.1016/j.procs.2020.03.049

Mukherjee, S., Sadhukhan, B., Sarkar, N., Roy, D., & De, S. (2023). Stock market prediction using deep learning algorithms. *CAAI Transactions on Intelligence Technology*, *8*(1), 82–94. doi:10.1049/cit2.12059

Pawar, K., Jalem, R. S., & Tiwari, V. (2019). Stock market price prediction using LSTM RNN. In *Emerging Trends in Expert Applications and Security* [Springer Singapore.]. *Proceedings of ICETEAS*, *2018*, 493–503.

Reddy, V. K. S. (2018). Stock market prediction using machine learning. [IRJET]. *International Research Journal of Engineering and Technology*, *5*(10), 1033–1035.

Rouf, N., Malik, M. B., Arif, T., Sharma, S., Singh, S., Aich, S., & Kim, H. C. (2021). Stock market prediction using machine learning techniques: A decade survey on methodologies, recent developments, and future directions. *Electronics (Basel)*, *10*(21), 2717. doi:10.3390/electronics10212717

Singh, R., & Srivastava, S. (2017). Stock prediction using deep learning. *Multimedia Tools and Applications*, *76*(18), 18569–18584. doi:10.1007/s11042-016-4159-7

Subasi, A., Amir, F., Bagedo, K., Shams, A., & Sarirete, A. (2021). Stock market prediction using machine learning. *Procedia Computer Science*, *194*, 173–179. doi:10.1016/j.procs.2021.10.071

Vijh, M., Chandola, D., Tikkiwal, V. A., & Kumar, A. (2020). Stock closing price prediction using machine learning techniques. *Procedia Computer Science*, *167*, 599–606. doi:10.1016/j.procs.2020.03.326

Xu, B., Zhang, D., Zhang, S., Li, H., & Lin, H. (2018). Stock market trend prediction using recurrent convolutional neural networks. In *Natural Language Processing and Chinese Computing: 7th CCF International Conference*. Springer.

Chapter 15
A Smart Innovative Pre-Trained Model-Based QDM for Weed Detection in Soybean Fields

B. Gunapriya
New Horizon College of Engineering, India

Arunadevi Thirumalraj
https://orcid.org/0009-0003-5396-6810
K. Ramakrishnan College of Technology, India

V. S. Anusuya
New Horizon College of Engineering, India

Balasubramanian Prabhu Kavin
https://orcid.org/0000-0001-6939-4683
SRM Institute of Science and Technology, India

Gan Hong Seng
XJTLU Entrepreneur College, Xi'an Jiaotong-Liverpool University, China

ABSTRACT

Precision farming that takes advantage of the internet of things infrastructure now includes weed identification as a core component. Weeds now account for 45 percent of crop losses in farming because of competition with crops. This figure can be lowered with effective weed detecting technology. One of the most important areas of AI, known as deep learning (DL), is revolutionizing weed discovery for site-specific weed management (SSWM). In the past half a decade, DL methods have been used with both ground- and air-based technology for weed documentation in still images and in real time. According to the latest findings in DL-based weed detection, developing methods that aid precision weeding technologies in making informed decisions is a priority. Over the past five years, deep learning algorithms have been successfully incorporated into both ground-based and aerial-based systems for the purpose of weed identification in both still picture and real-time scenarios.

DOI: 10.4018/979-8-3693-0790-8.ch015

INTRODUCTION

Agriculture is a vital aspect of the international economy since it generates substantial income and serves as a critical link in the distribution of food throughout the world. Because of this, agriculture has world's leading economic sectors. The agricultural industry has a major impact on the global economy (Razfar, et al., 2022). The number of linked devices is constantly increasing, and the IoT is rapidly becoming an integral part of our daily lives. Now that digital farming has emerged, farmers and other organisations have access to a streamlined and efficient method for real-time plant monitoring that combines creative tactics with state-of-the-art technology (Osorio, et al., 2020). Smart agriculture aims to reduce resource waste while raising crop yields via the application of technological advancements that augment conventional farming methods. This means that many parts of the production process can benefit from the use of technology on intelligent farms (Islam, et al., 2021). Invasive species are one of the most significant biotic constraints on crop construction. New approaches are being developed as part of an attempt to raise the total amount of soybeans collected by addressing the problem of weeds reducing yields' quality and quantity. The correctness or even the improvement of agro vision systems might be negatively impacted by the poor visibility that happens commonly during hazy or weather schemes (Asad, and Bais, 2020). During some weather patterns, visibility tends to be low.

Weeds in agriculture are defined as reducing crop yields and increasing production costs (Hasan et al., 2021). Weeds aren't usually crop-specific; however, they might share characteristics with annual, biennial, or perennial crops. It is easier to control annual weeds than perennial ones (Veeranampalayam et al., 2020). Plants that germinate from seed, mature for a solo growing season, and then perish are known as annual weeds. One of the most pressing problems that farmers confront today is preventing the spread of weeds (Haq., 2022). It is not uncommon for annual and perennial weeds endemic to Saudi Arabia, adjacent areas. Early detection and control, particularly prior to flowering, is the most effective method for eradicating weeds (Wu et al.,2021). Typically, people use their own eyes to look for weeds. To properly investigate and exert effort to reduce invasive weeds, it is necessary to monitor their spread and activity in near real-time (Shanmugam, et al., 2020).

As a result of its usefulness as a vegan protein source, soybean farming is flourishing. The success of such crops relies on the careful elimination of weeds. To be successful, SSWM must employ a range of weed management techniques, each of which must be tailored to the specific context, population, and density of the weeds in question. The machine's "brain," a vision-based image processing system (Subeesh, et al., 2022), controls the rate at which herbicide is sprayed, allowing for such practises to be carried out with variable rate technology (VRT). One may find mapbased apps and sensorbased applications for VRT right now. A frequent method is map-based, in which a map of a region is created using georeferenced soil or plant samples. Collecting soil samples by hand for subsequent investigation is labor-intensive, time-consuming, and costly. However, sensor-based mapping can gather and interpret data in real time, making the process far more efficient. When using mobile ground or aerial technology in the field, all processing is done in real time through the use of machine learning or deep learning algorithms (Peng et al., 2022).

Before 2015, digital pictures were processed using standard image processing and conventional ML algorithms after being obtained by ground robots. Traditional image processing methods for weed identification among agricultural plants tended to focus on analysing and extracting aspects and textural properties of weed species. Measurements and descriptions of shapes like area, diameter, perimeter, and convexity were used to determine morphological characteristics (Krishnan, and Rajasenbagam, 2021). Whereas, texture was previously understood to refer to the distribution of grayscale pixels in a predetermined region of a digital picture. These values were calculated utilising regularity, roughness, closeness, uniformity, and entropy as the defining statistical and structural traits. As the methods improved, scientists created or built a classifier that could learn from data based on those characteristics. Machine learning-based classifiers were the name given to these devices (Ruigrok, et al., 2020). To distinguish weeds from agricultural plants, popular ML classifiers including sample of photos. These classifiers lacked robustness and stability in an extremely complicated situation with shadows, occlusion, unknown objects, and picture distortion owing to motion blur, in part because of the small sum of training photos provided for training purposes (Espejo-Garcia, et al., 2020). Even fewer studies were able to use machine learning-based classifiers for control. This was primarily because these classifiers lacked the capacity, addressed by DL techniques in the form of bounding boxes, to precisely localise the presence of weeds.

However, agricultural field robots have developed into a crucial part of the production and harvesting of vegetables in the future. They help improve the precision of procedures and the quality of the soil, both of which have a positive effect on productivity. They often have multiple sensors and cameras for mapping, localisation, navigational monitoring, and algorithmic path planning. Digital farming entails the gathering of soil and weather data via ground or aerial-based sensors, the transfer of these data to an essential advisory unit, the analysis and retrieval of info, and the provision of suggestions as well as steps to farmers, field robots, or agro-industrial firms. IoT systems can generate vast amounts of data, despite the fact that the sum of web units may have reached the millions at this moment. This will put a strain on the cloud storage system due to the large amount of data that must be transferred across the Internet (Thirumalraj, et al., 2024).

DL has cleared the ground for SSWM in precision agriculture to get widespread attention and funding from the private sector. The capacity of DL to sort through enormous amounts of unstructured data is a major draw for its adoption by businesses and academics alike (Singh, et al., 2020). The DL algorithm typically performs classification and detection tasks on a uniform distribution of audio, video, and picture data (Jin, et al., 2022). In the realms of IoT and weed detection, image sensors are utilised as data sources to collect the pictures. Weed detection was implemented in agriculture to help eradicate weeds, improve the quality of the agricultural environment, and shed light on issues of sustainability and public health. To accomplish precise weed detection, we propose a vision-based method we call SqueezeNet. As part of an effort to create a comprehensive IoT basis, a RaspberryPi was selected as an edge device to process UAV crop photographs. Validation precision, speed, and latency were used as comparing factors amongst models. The most important findings of this article are as follows.

Using Convolutional Neural Networks (SqueezeNet) to Identify Weeds in Soybeans.
Create a QDMO method for enhancing classification outcomes by careful selection of the model's hyper-parameters.
Using a Raspberry Pi to implement the recommended concept.
Offering analytical comparisons of the many offered models.

In this study, we explore the application of computer vision techniques to design a method for efficiently detecting weeds within a soybean plantation. The article is divided into 5 parts, with Section II focusing on weed identification strategies using learning. The projected models are obtainable in Section III. The experimental evaluation and planning for the projected models are obtainable in Section IV. The entire conclusion, including the top-performing model and recommendations for the future, is presented in Section V.

RELATED WORKS

A novel approach to instance segmentation is described by (Xu, et al., 2023) which makes use of the visible colour index and the encoder/decoder architecture. In areas where both weeds and soybeans are prevalent, this strategy addresses the challenge of pinpointing and removing the former. In addition to improving the accuracy of segmentation through the incorporation of DSASPP in the encoder-decoder architecture, the colour index was developed to emphasise the contrast between plants and soil to mitigate and background. Experimental consequences using real-world field photography demonstrated the higher performance of the proposed approach, with an accuracy of 0.959 and an overall accuracy of 0.978, an IoU score of 0.939, and an accuracy of 0.972. When evaluating the suggested pipeline's performance on weeds and soybeans against Transformer, it was found that all of these methods attained comparable results in terms of time. This research makes a significant addition to precision agriculture by providing a novel tactic to the stimulating problem of weed detection and precise weed control.

(Zhang, et al., 2023) proposed using the Faster R-CNN approach, and it has been tuned specifically for the soybean seedling. A total of 9816 photographs were obtained from various sources to train and distinguish three different weed species, including soybean. Initially, after comparing the classification performance of ResNet50, VGG16, training. In the second portion of the research, the trained Faster R-CNN system was pitted against two traditional target identification algorithms, SSD and Yolov4, for the task of distinguishing between soybeans and weeds in a field setting. To remedy the issue of insufficient focus on the attention target during model training, an attention apparatus was added structure. Testing findings show that soybeans and weeds may be distinguished from complex backgrounds with the use of the Faster R-CNN method employing VGG19-CBAM as network. In comparison to pre-optimization (5.61%), the SSD algorithm (2.24%), and the Yolov4 algorithm (1.24%), the average time required to recognise a single picture is 336 milliseconds, while the regular accuracy is 99.16%.

In order to track down R. pedestris in three different settings (pod filling stage, maturity stage, artificial cage), (Park, et al., 2023) used surveillance technology based on an unmanned ground vehicle (UGV) GoPro CAM. In this work, deep learning technology (MRCNN, YOLOv3, Detectron2) was utilised to create models that could be rapidly challenged (i.e., built with lightweight parameter) via a web application. Images were randomly chosen, tagged, and prepared for annotation to be used in both training and testing. The deep learning algorithm found the R. pedestris persons by using a bounding in the picture data. The model did quite well, as indicated by mAP scores of 0.952, 0.716, and 0.873. The developed model will substantially aid in insect forecasting in the early phases of pest outbreaks in agricultural output by allowing for the identification of R. pedestris in the field.

Using a YOLOv7-based object detection algorithm, (Narayana, & Ramana., 2023) provide a weed detection system. Lastly, we used the YOLOv7 model with a range of parameters for training and testing on the early crop weed dataset and the 4weed dataset. The trial results indicated that the YOLOv7 model achieved values of 99.6, 97.6, 99.8, and 95.5 on the early crop weed dataset and 78.53, 79.83, 86.34, and 74.24 on the 4weed dataset for mAP@0.50, for the bounding boxes, respectively. The YOLOv7 model is quite precise and can aid in the conservation of resources in the agricultural segment.

(Kansal, et al., 2023) have developed an IoT-Fog robotic scheme to categorise weeds and soy plants throughout the foggy season and the regular season. Information on soil, soybeans, grass, and weeds was used to write the article. For the purpose of data image categorization, a deep learning (DL) technique based on a two-dimensional Convolutional Neural Network (2D-CNN) was developed. The dataset used had 150 pixels as its longest side and three channels. The suggested system as a whole is an online server-based classification system for a robotic device connected to the Internet of Things. Edge fog computing enhances reliability of a device in a similar way. Since DL classification works well with IoT and Fog computing, it is a natural fit for the proposed robotic system. A CNN was trained and tested for classification, baseline and test pictures were validated, a dehazing method was employed, and the resulting dehazed image was validated as part of the evaluation of the proposed system. The validation and training parameters guarantee a 97% success rate in a hazy environment when distinguishing between weeds and crops. Finally, it indicates that the dehazing approach can improve classification scores for finding soy fields in bad weather.

(Yang, et al., 2023) suggest using a multi- network to identify crops and weeds. We created MSFCA-Net, an attention network, to employ strip convolutions of variable sizes for crop and weed segmentation in the field. To boost the model's sensitivity towards unique classes and its capacity to learn from hard data. The projected method is trained and tested using datasets consisting of soybeans, sugar beets, carrots, and rice weed. The proposed MSFCA-Net achieves higher MIoU values than conventional semantic segmentation techniques on the aforementioned datasets (92.64%, 89.58%, 79.34%, and 78.12%, respectively). Under the identical experimental conditions and parameter settings, the findings show that the proposed technique excels above its predecessors and has excellent resilience and generalisation ability.

For use with laser weeding robots, (Fatima, et al., 2023) created a lightweight weed detection system. Six separate agricultural landscapes in Pakistan provided the images of weeds. In addition to 9000 images of gourd, the collection also includes images of horseweed, herb paris, grasses, and tiny weeds. We went with the YOLO5 model, a detector that works just once. The selected model predicted numerous true positives (TP) and few false negatives (FN), as indicated by its mAP of 0.88@ IOU 0.5. Despite SSD-ResNet50's mAP of 0.53@IOU 0.5, the model projected less TP with important repercussions like FP or FN. The improved performance of the YOLOv5 perfect made it perfect for classifying weeds and crops in agricultural situations. The perfect was subsequently AGX processor, where it was fine-tuned for maximum computational detection speed and efficiency. The maximum achievable framerate for the model is 27 fps. Accordingly, it pairs well with the laser weeding robot, which can eradicate weeds from an acre of land in around 22 hours and four minutes, moving at a rate of 0.25 feet per second.

Using consistency regularisation and pseudo-labelling as a foundation, (Liu, et al., 2023) enhanced a semi-supervised learning (SSL) system by adding an attention mechanism. The suggested method improved classification accuracy by 16.5%, 17.84%, and 19.67% while using only 100 labelled data per class compared to fully supervised learning (FSL) algorithms on datasets with 200 200-, 300 300-, and 400 400-pixel pictures, respectively. Overall, the suggested strategy resulted in highly accurate machine vision models for weed recognition with significantly fewer labelled training images, saving both time and effort when compared to an FSL algorithm.

PROPOSED SYSTEM

In the present Internet of Things (IoT) devices across platforms can be linked to deliver useful services. The agricultural sector is a fast-growing emergent market where the Internet of Things is having a significant impact. By 2050, there will need to be 70% more nutritious and secure food produced. The decline in natural resources has led to a general decline in crop yields for many of the most important crops, and this is just one of several imminent problems. As a result, there has been a dramatic shift in the agricultural sector, which is now bracing for a drop in its workforce. As a result of these problems, connection approaches have been implemented to foresee a drop in crop yields, identify weeds and other variables that negatively impact crop quality, and ultimately lessen the need for human labour. Precision farming, drones, livestock monitoring and evaluation, and predictive analytics are some of the most prominent Internet of Things applications in the agricultural sector. In order to monitor abnormalities and diseases, crop production readiness, equipment efficiency, and worker performance, precision farming makes use of sensory data. High-precision robotics and autonomous vehicle control system, mobile imaging are all part of the current ecosystem's toolkit. The second major usage for the Internet of Things is in medium- to large-scale aerial and ground-based drone analysis. Monitoring crop health, spraying, planting, and doing preliminary field research are all possible with the help of drones. The monitoring of livestock, for example, involves collecting and analysing information about the health of the species in order to stop the spread of disease.

The last step in smart farming is the incorporation of predictive analytics for the purpose of forecasting crop yields, planning logistics, and evaluating potential hazards. This is accomplished by analysing information gathered from numerous sensors. Soil quality, temperature, the relative humidity index, and precipitation are some of the most important data sets used. The capacity to accurately identify weeds within crops is an important part of precision farming since it allows for the collection of specific data from the plantation. Crop yields and quality are negatively

Figure 1. Sample images

Soy Crop

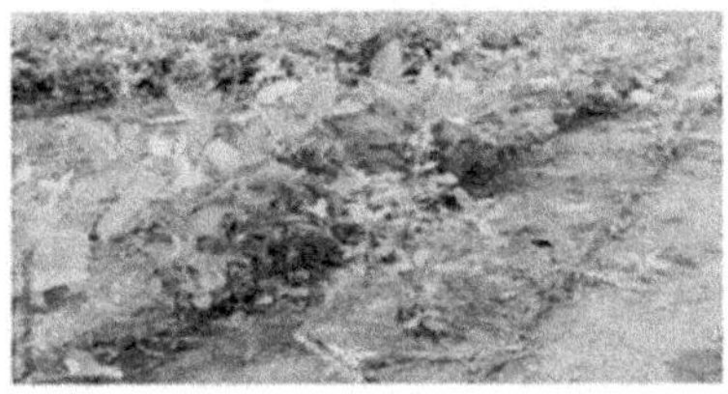

Soy Crop with weed

affected because weeds use valuable resources like water and sunlight. Furthermore, they account for 45% of agriculture's annual losses. Common methods for real-time weed identification have recently adopted deep learning approaches to boost model performance and collective processing resources. Models for machine learning that combine the best features of different approaches are currently in development. In this section, the explanation of dataset, pre-processing and classification using deep learning with architecture diagram are presented.

Data Sources

Early weed detection in soybean crops is crucial because of the economic importance of the crop to a country. The robustness, clarity, and variability of a dataset developed by (dos Santos Ferreira, et al., 2017) were unmatched. The data set was comprised of 400 UAV crop photos. The SLIC super pixel technique was then used to divide those 15336 segments into 3249 soil pixels, 7376 soybean pixels, 3520 grass pixels, and 1191 broadleaf weed pixels. The goal is to recognise grass, broadleaf, and soil weeds in soybean fields. Images of weedy soy fields are shown as examples in Figure 1.

Pre-Processing

The pre-processing algorithm is given access to the raw images. The proposed pre-processing algorithm found that there is a white strip in the upper left and lower right corners of some photos. The skewed area makes it difficult to categorise. About

1% of the top and bottom of the zone is chosen, and the pixel values are reset to zero. The method was designed to handle right-side photos alone, which eliminates the problem of images being upside-down. The image on the left is "seen" using the pixel ratio, and then reversed horizontally to match the right. After histogram equalisation, the resulting image is binarized, with just the bright areas displayed. Morphological operations are used to improve the bright area. The final step is a horizontal scan of the image from left to right until a white pixel is found.

The coordinates (x, y) for each white pixel are saved. The algorithm will continue to scan until either one-third of the image's height has been covered or the white portion has ended. Moreover, the images in the vertical direction are not scanned in order. After each horizontal iteration, the algorithm makes a vertical jump of 10 pixels. These apexes point in the direction of a specific muscle group. After picking several locations along the line, we use the line equation to draw it out to its full extent. We go up and to the left, and to the right. The top right position is known; therefore, we only need the right bottom pixel location from the line equation. The three points are utilised to draw a triangle mask that is then applied to the region to be cropped. After the median filter is applied to the image to reduce noise, the resulting image is binarized. Using the most interconnected components, we can isolate the weedy area. The next step is to round off the weeds, as they have sharp corners. Savitsky Golay is an algorithm used to soften sharp corners. Binary masks may be made with ease thanks to the boundary's rounded corners. Using this binary mask, we can isolate the weed patch from the source image.

Classification Using SqueezeNet Model

At first, the SqueezeNet perfect is used to produce a meaningful set of feature the pre-processed images. SqueezeNet is a convolutional network that is 50 times more efficient than AlexNet while using the same number of input variables. Fifteen layers make up its five distinct types of layers. Figure 2 demonstrations the layered structure of the network.

The filter's receptive arena size is characterized by K×K, the stride size by s, and the length of the feature map by l. The network receives 227×227 dimensional data in the RGB channel as input. Convolution and max pooling are used to generalise an input picture. Weights and smaller regions in an input volume are convoluted in a convolutional layer using a 33 kernel. As part of their supporting evidence, all convolutional layers carry out layer-wise activation functions. The fire layer, which consists of expansion and squeezing phases inside the convolutional layers, is used. Filters of size 11 are used during the squeeze stage, whereas sizes 11 and 33 are used during the expansion step. Squeezing the input tensors H, W, and C produces an initial set of convolutions where C is the square root of four times the

Figure 2. Layered construction of SqueezeNet

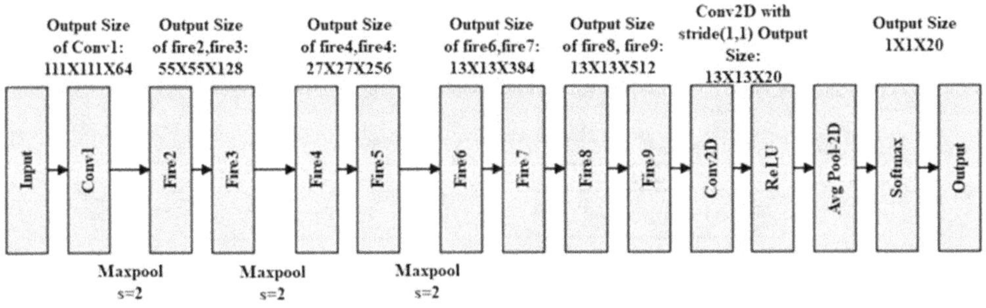

sum of input tensor channels (Ucar & Korkmaz 2020). After that, in the first step, the data undergo an expansion and depth equal to C/2 of the output tensor. Last but not least, the integrating function sorts the expansion's output based on the depth dimension of the input tensors. The workflow of SqueezeNet's fire module is shown in Figure 3. Assuming FM&C choose the feature map and channel, we may write for the kernel w used in the squeeze function's output layer fy:

$$f\{y\} = \sum_{fm1=1}^{FM} \sum_{c=1}^{c} w_c^f x_c^{fm1} \tag{1}$$

Now, $f\{y\} \in \mathbb{R}^N$ and $w \in \mathbb{R}^{C\times 1\times FM2}$. A integration of the feature map of unique tensors might be used to calculate the squeeze output. The global regular pool collapses the class's feature map into a single value, while the max pool layer performs a down-sampling function in the spatial dimension. Multiclass likelihood distribution is then provided by the softmax activation method (Agushaka, et al., 2022).

There are three main advantages that motivated the development of the SqueezeNet framework. The network is very efficient since there are fewer moving parts, and applications built for these networks are portable and need less data transmission, and the module size is less than 5 MB, making embedded system implementation simpler.

QDMO Based Parameter Optimization

To improve the SqueezeNet model's overall performance, we use QDMO to pick the best possible values for the model's hyperparameters. DMO is an example of a stochastic metaheuristic procedure that takes its cues from the social and foraging

Figure 3. Fire module of SqeezeNet

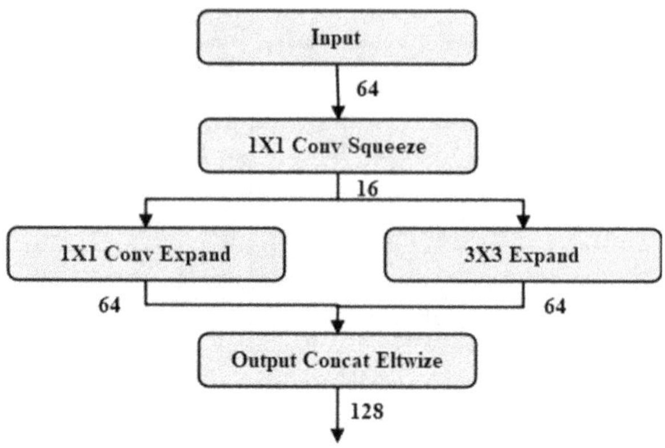

habits of the dwarf mongoose (Helogale). Dwarf mongooses look for food individually, but forage socially. Because of their seminomadic lifestyle, these animals build a sleeping mound close to a food source. The system uses a statistical model of the creature's behaviour to determine the best course of action (Elaziz et al., 2022).

All methods of optimisation that rely on a population have random initialisation processes. After that, the intensification and diversification criteria cause all solutions to converge on the global best optimal. The DMO begins its approach in the same way, by setting up the mongoose's candidate pool. In other words, this population is created at random between the minimum and extreme allowable values for a given situation. In (Hinton, et al., 2012), an MH algorithm called the DMO method was devised to mimic the foraging habits of DM in the wild. There are typically five phases to DMO, beginning with initiation and continuing through the alpha guides exploration of novel territory. The scout group phase begins when the most recently located using information from an earlier SM (i.e., a food source). Initialising the mongoose population (X) is the first step in the DMO method, and the size matrix (nd) is created to r columns.

$$X = \begin{bmatrix} x_{1,1} & x_{1,2} & \cdots & x_{1,d} \\ x_{2,1} & x_{2,2} & \cdots & x_{2,d} \\ \vdots & \vdots & x_{i,j} & \vdots \\ x_{m,1} & x_{n,2} & \cdots & x_{n,d} \end{bmatrix} \quad (2)$$

At the ith population solution, the jth element of the problem's dimensions (denoted by x) can be discovered. In most cases, the value is strongminded by Eq.

(3) as a consistently distributed random integer that falls within the bounds specified by (UB) and (LB).

$$\chi j_{=} \; unifrnd(LB, UB, D) \tag{3}$$

Eq. (4) expresses the procedures involved in calculating all the solutions and determining their likelihood.

$$a = \frac{fit_i}{\sum_{i=1}^{n} fit_i} \tag{4}$$

In Eq. (4), the sum of mongooses n is promoted by Eq. (5):

$$n = n - bs \tag{5}$$

Female alphas employ a unique vocalisation (peep) to communicate with other groups, where bs is the number of babysitters. In order to revise the X_i solution value, the DMO uses Eq. (6).

$$X_{i+1} = X_i + phi \times peep \tag{6}$$

Phi in Eq. (6) represents the random numbers chosen from [1, 1] for each iteration. Eq. (7) also allows the SM to be improved upon.

$$sm_i = \frac{fit_{i+1} - fit_i}{max\{|fit_{i+1}, fit_i|\}} \tag{7}$$

Subsequently computing the regular $SM(\varphi)$, the comparison can be assumed as:

$$\phi = \frac{\sum_{i=1}^{n} sm_i}{n} \tag{8}$$

Nomadic culture dictates that the current SM be neglected during the scouting stage in favour of the new candidate's cuisine or SMs location. The sitters' requirements for exchanging children are met once they have been met while foraging and scouting simultaneously. The explored location for SMs and food is guided using a vector (M), the SM's current position, (rand), as shown below.

$$X_{i+1} = f(x) = \begin{cases} X_i - CP \times phi \times rand \times [X_i - M] \\ \phi_{i+1} > \phi_i \\ X_i + CF \times phi \times rand \times [X_i - M] \\ otherwise \end{cases} \tag{9}$$

The future drive and the afresh created scouted site (X) may be simulated based on the success or failure of the expansion based on the presentation of the group. As seen in Eq. (11), CF determines how far the mongoose (M, specified in Eq. (10)) may go. The parameter facilitates rapid exploration during the search phase, but the focus eventually shifts from finding a novel region to exploiting a fruitful one once all the iterations are used.

$$M = \sum_{i=1}^{n} \frac{X_i \times sm_i}{X_i} \tag{10}$$

$$CF = \left(1 - \frac{iter}{Max_{iier}}\right)^{\left(\frac{2 \times iter}{Max_{iter}}\right)} \tag{11}$$

In the late afternoon and initial evening, when the alpha group traded shifts with the babysitters, they had a good look at the developing colony. Caregiver-to-forager mongoose ratios fluctuate depending on population sizes. To simulate the trading process after work or lunch, use Eq. (12).

$$phase = \begin{cases} Scout, C < L \\ Babysitting, C \geq L \end{cases} \tag{12}$$

The data composed by the prior foraging collections is cleared and reset to zero until the counter (C) surpasses the exchange principles. From the initial reconnaissance phase on, the alpha remains (Hinton, et al., 2012). To ensure a decrease in the mean of alpha-group weights, the babysitter's main weight was set to 0. After a certain number of repetitions, the DMO procedure stops and returns the improved result.

Specifically, a quantum-based optimisation (QBO) method is used to create the QDMO algorithm. In this case, a binary integer between 0 and 1 might stand in for the feature's potential deselection or selection. Quantum bits (Qbit(q)) are used to describe every aspect of QBO, with q denoting the superposition of the binary values 0 and 1. The mathematical model Q-bit(q) may be constructed using the following formula.

$$q = a + i\beta = e^{i\theta}, |a|^2 + |\beta|^2 \tag{13}$$

where 0 and 1 signify the two possible values for the Q-bit's probability. The parameter represents the angle q, and its value is improved by tan1(/).

QBO's major objective is to ascertain the shift in q's value, and this may be stated as:

$$q(t+1) = q(t) \times R(\theta) = \left[a(t)\beta(t)\right] \times R(\theta) \tag{14}$$

$$R(\theta) = \begin{bmatrix} \cos(\theta) - sin(\theta) \\ sin(\theta) - \cos(\theta) \end{bmatrix} \tag{15}$$

In Eq. (15), represents the angular velocity with which the ith bit of the jth Q-solution rotates. QBO was used to improve DMA's potential for balancing exploration with exploitation while still locating the optimal solution. QDMO, a newly developed FS method, uses 30% and 70% of the total data, respectively, for its testing and training subsets. Then, using the sample data, fitness is calculated for each population. After that, the lowest-fitness agents are given the tasks that need the best performance. The DMO operator will then implement the solution during the exploitation phase. The process of updating each person proceeds until the termination condition is met. Then, the QDMO as FS was applied, and the testing set dimensions were reduced depending on the superior solution, all while being evaluated using a variety of metrics. The N agents on behalf of the populace are created first. Q-bits and D-features are present in every answer. In Eq. (16), the solution formula is X_i, as shown below:

$$X_i = \left[q_{i1} \mid q_{i2}\right] \ldots \mid q_{iD} = \left[\theta_{i1} \mid \theta_{i2} \ldots \theta_{iD}\right], i = 1, 2, \ldots, N \tag{16}$$

The feature's probability distribution, represented as X_i, is a set of superpositions.

In this phase of the QDMO, updating the agent until it satisfies the stopping disorder is the primary goal. Calculating the binary representation of each distinct X_i using Eq:

$$BX_{i,j} = \begin{cases} 1 if rand < |\beta|^2 \\ 0 otherwise \end{cases} \tag{17}$$

where is found by solving Eq. (13). The range of possible values for rand is [0, 1]. The second step is to determine the fitness values displayed below by training the classifiers using the feature from BX_(i,j):

$$Fit_i = \rho \times \gamma + (1-\rho) \times \left(\frac{|BX_{i,j}|}{D} \right) \tag{18}$$

In the aforementioned equation, $|BX_{i,j}|$ characterizes the entire sum of features picked, while denotes the error classification made when employing the classifier (relevant feature). The factor (0, 1) is the fitness value balancer between the two halves.

The following step is to identify agent X_b that has a lower Fit_i value. Last but not least, we reduce the size of the testing set by picking a feature that is identical to the binary X_b variant. Afterward, the trained classifier may make predictions about the output. The quality of the final product is then evaluated using several standards. Figure 4 displays some example results from the proposed approach, with the weeds in the study indicated by colour.

RESULTS AND DISCUSSION

Initially, a Core i5 2.5 GHz CPU were used to run the proposed SqueezeNet model. The model was then put through its paces on the cloud stage using a 12 GB NVIDIA Tesla K80 to evaluate processing time with GPU assistance. This study made use of Python 3.8, the Keras 2.3.0 API, and the TensorFlow 2.0 backend, together with the NumPy, matplotlib, cv2, sklearn, and glob libraries (Gunapriya et al., 2023).

Implementation Details

Initially, a Core i5 2.5 GHz CPU and a 1 GB graphics were used to run the proposed SqueezeNet model. The model was then put through its paces on the cloud stage using a 12 GB NVIDIA Tesla K80 to evaluate processing time with GPU assistance. This study made use of Python 3.8, the Keras 2.3.0 API, and the TensorFlow 2.0 backend, together with the NumPy, matplotlib, cv2, sklearn, and glob libraries.

Figure 4. Sample output detection of weeds

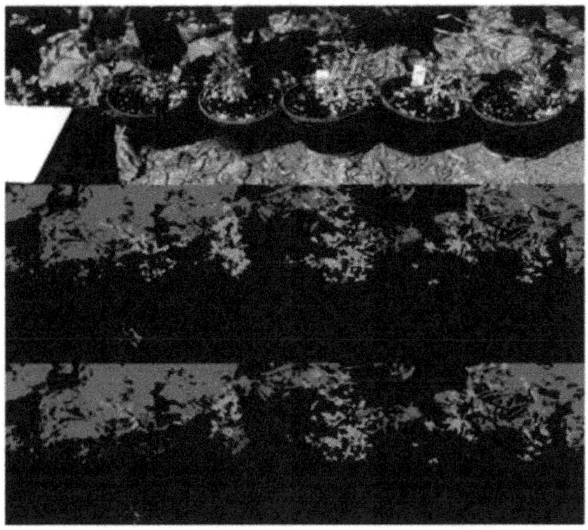

Evaluation Metrics

Our method's categorization performance and position in the rankings are evaluated using ranking metrics. Specificity, sensitivity, and accuracy are three measures of categorization quality. The standards of performance are as follows:

$$SE = \frac{tp}{tp + fn} \tag{19}$$

$$SP = \frac{tn}{tn + fp} \tag{20}$$

$$\mathrm{AC} = \frac{tp + tn}{tp + fp + tn + fn} \tag{21}$$

Where *tp, tn, fp,* and *fn* signify the summation of a *true positive, true negative, false positive,* and *false negative*. Figure 5 provides the accuracy and loss of the projected model.

Figure 5. Validation analysis of proposed model

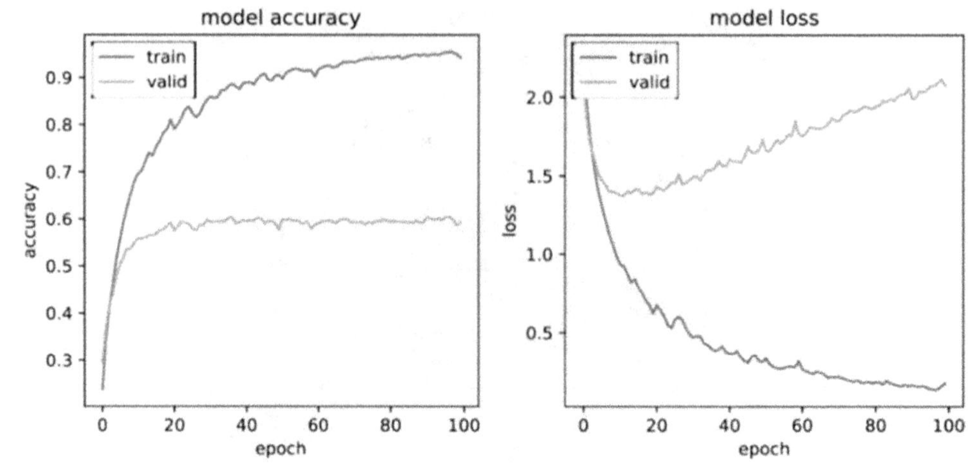

Validation Analysis of Projected Model

Table 1 above depicts the experimental analysis without the use of QDMO. The accuracy, sensitivity, and specificity of the ResNet model in the analysis were 82.00, 72.00, and 91.00, respectively. Another typical result came from the VGGNet model, which achieved accuracy of 84.54, sensitivity of 76.65, and specificity of 92.64. Another typical result came from the AlexNet model, which achieved accuracy of 86.02, sensitivity of 78.95, and specificity of 95.88. Another typical example is when the DenseNet model achieved accuracy of 91.25, sensitivity of 81.56, and specificity of 96.12, respectively. Another common model, the SquuezeNet model, achieved accuracy of 3.65, sensitivity of 86.78, and specificity of 97.24 respectively.

Indicated in the above table is the experimental analysis using QDMO. We employed a different process for the analysis to determine the performance evaluation. In the ResNet model, the accuracy was 87.91, the sensitivity was 77.26, and the

Table 1. Experimental analysis without QDMO

Method	ACC (%)	SE (%)	SP (%)
ResNet	82.00	72.00	91.00
VGGNet	84.54	76.65	92.64
AlexNet	86.02	78.95	95.88
DenseNet	91.25	81.56	96.12
SquuezeNet	93.65	86.78	97.24

Table 2. Experimental analysis with QDMO

Method	ACC (%)	SE (%)	SP (%)
ResNet	87.91	77.26	97.98
VGGNet	91.03	81.35	98.01
AlexNet	93.30	83.12	98.34
DenseNet	95.00	85.61	98.69
SquuezeNet	96.93	90.94	99.12

specificity was 97.98. Another example result came from the VGGNet model, which achieved accuracy of 91.03, sensitivity of 81.35, and specificity of 98.01, respectively. Another typical result came from the AlexNet model, which achieved accuracy of 93.30, sensitivity of 83.12, and specificity of 98.34. Another noteworthy example is the DenseNet model, which achieved accuracy of 95.00, sensitivity of 85.61, and specificity of 98.69. Another good example is when the SquuezeNet model achieved accuracy of 96.93, sensitivity of 90.94, and specificity of 99.12, respectively. Figure 6 to 8 offerings the graphical investigation of projected model with existing procedures in terms of three different metrics.

Analysis of Proposed Model With Existing Procedures in Terms of Learning Rate

Table 3 provides the learning rate analysis for various pre-trained models, where Figure 9 presents the graphical comparison of the proposed model.

The purpose for better performance of proposed perfect is that QDMO is used for optimize the learning rate.

CONCLUSION

Since weeds consume a variety of nutrients and water that could otherwise be used by the crops, detecting weeds has become an important area of study in agriculture. Many techniques, ranging from human observation to automated visual analysis, have been developed to combat this problem. Since soy is a great plant-based protein source, its cultivation has increased in recent years. Careful eradication of weeds is essential to the effective production of such crops. It might be difficult to tell if a farm's land is occupied by crops or weeds. The complexity of the categorization increases dramatically if it must be done in less-than-ideal circumstances. This piece's focus is on identifying weeds among soybean crops. This article delves into

Figure 6. Graphical illustration of projected model

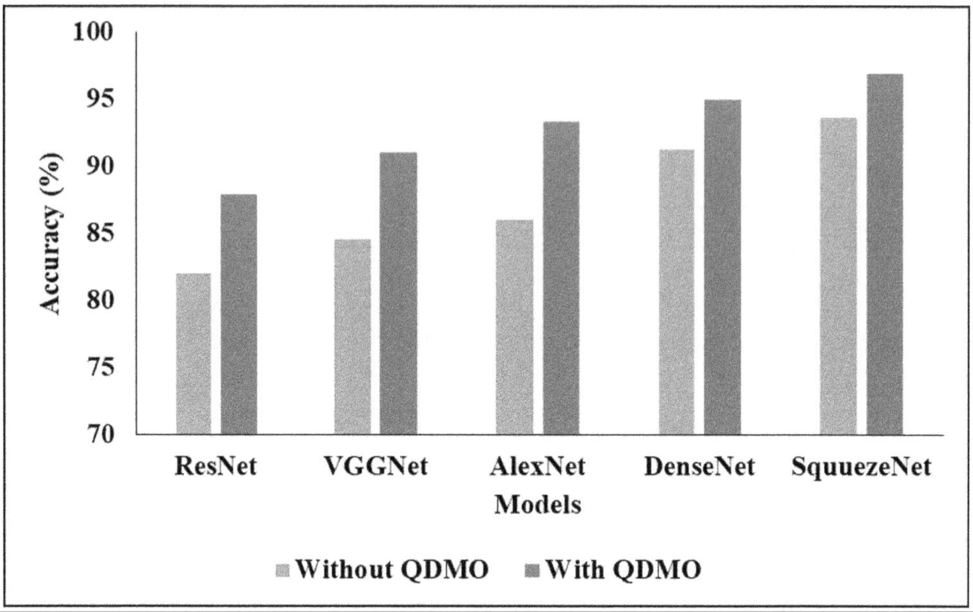

the use of picture datasets and an edge-based vision system for weed detection in a soybean field. To successfully categorise weeds, researchers investigated a variety

Figure 7. Investigation of various pre-trained models

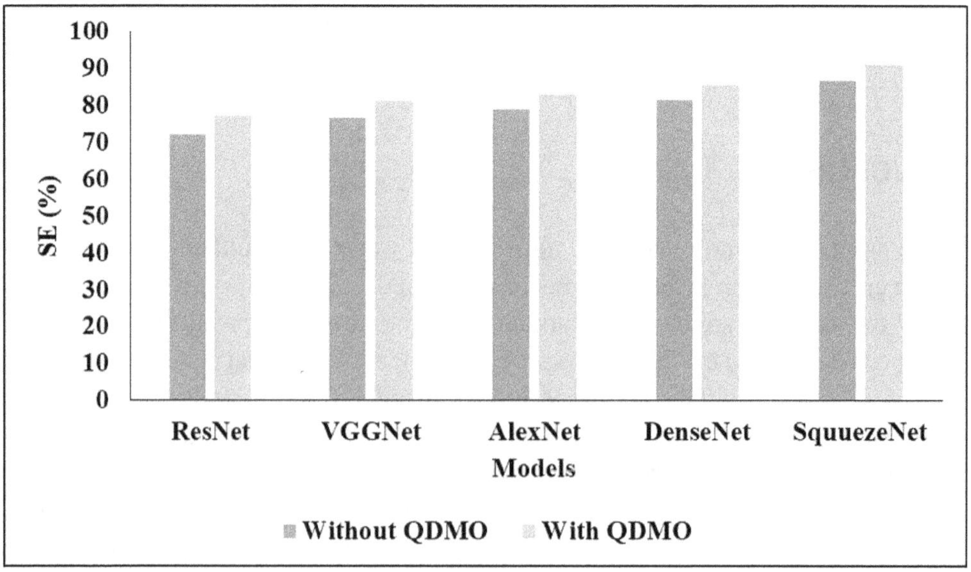

Figure 8. Comparative analysis of projected model with and without hyper-parameter tuning

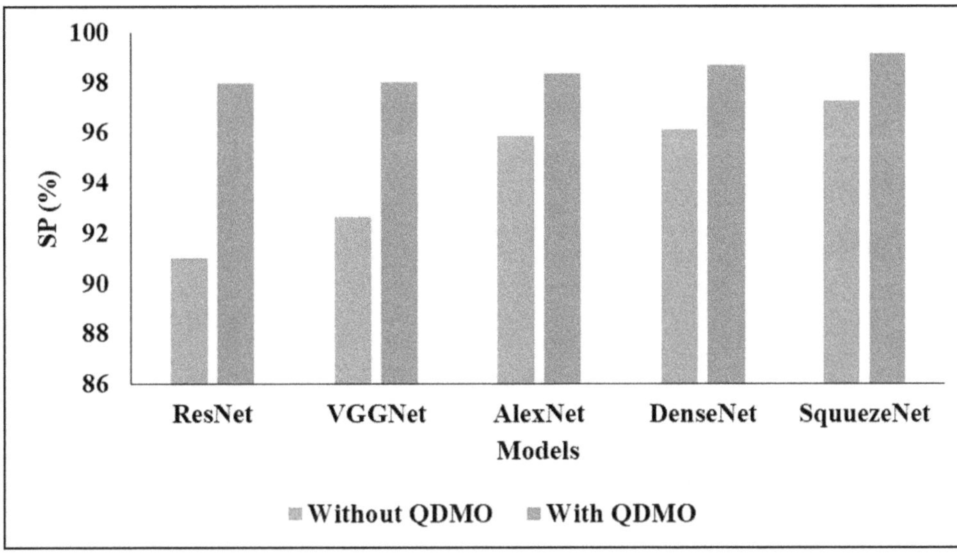

of CNN designs. SqueezeNet is the primary method, and the QDMO algorithm is used to find the best possible values for the model's parameters. Based on the consequences of the experiments, it is clear that the recommended model achieves 93% accuracy without QDMO and 96.93% accuracy with it. The next step for this investigation will be to gather more photographs from other locations. Although the new algorithm outperforms previous research on weed categorization, further progress may be made by in-field testing. The present model relies on processed data collected in a lab setting.

Table 3. Learning rate analysis

Learning Rate	Pre-trained Techniques				
	Proposed	DenseNet	AlexNet	VGGNet	ResNet
0.01	96.27	72.45	76.34	72.5	72.45
0.001	95.67	87.91	78.75	76.25	78.35
0.0001	93.78	88.27	82.51	79.44	89.2
0.00001	90.87	89.26	87.98	83.05	84.64

Figure 9. Learning rate analysis on different pre-trained models of CNN

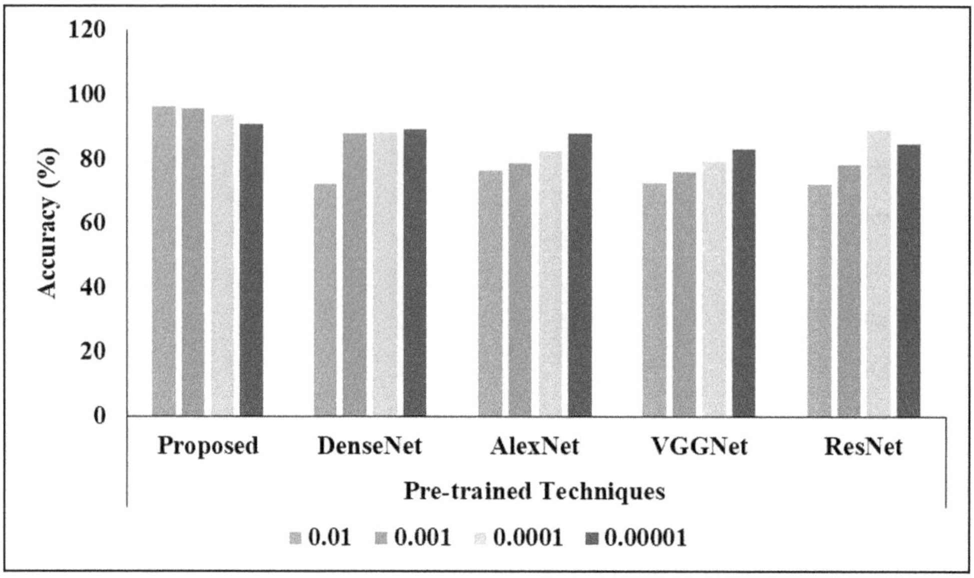

REFERENCES

Agushaka, J. O., Ezugwu, A. E., & Abualigah, L. (2022). Dwarf mongoose optimization algorithm. *Computer Methods in Applied Mechanics and Engineering*, *391*(Mar), 114570. doi:10.1016/j.cma.2022.114570

Asad, M. H., & Bais, A. (2020). Weed detection in canola fields using maximum likelihood classification and deep convolutional neural network. *Information Processing in Agriculture*, *7*(4), 535–545. doi:10.1016/j.inpa.2019.12.002

dos Santos Ferreira, A., Freitas, D. M., da Silva, G. G., Pistori, H., & Folhes, M. T. (2017). Weed detection in soybean crops using convnets. *Computers and Electronics in Agriculture*, *143*, 314–324. doi:10.1016/j.compag.2017.10.027

Elaziz, M. A., Ewees, A. A., Al-qaness, M. A. A., Alshathri, S., & Ibrahim, R. A. (2022, December). Feature selection for high dimensional datasets based on quantum-based dwarf mongoose optimization. *Mathematics*, *10*(23), 4565. doi:10.3390/math10234565

Espejo-Garcia, B., Mylonas, N., Athanasakos, L., Fountas, S., & Vasilakoglou, I. (2020). Towards weeds identification assistance through transfer learning. *Computers and Electronics in Agriculture*, *171*, 105306. doi:10.1016/j.compag.2020.105306

Fatima, H. S., ul Hassan, I., Hasan, S., Khurram, M., Stricker, D., & Afzal, M. Z. (2023). Formation of a Lightweight, Deep Learning-Based Weed Detection System for a Commercial Autonomous Laser Weeding Robot. *Applied Sciences (Basel, Switzerland)*, *13*(6), 3997. doi:10.3390/app13063997

Gunapriya, B., Rajesh, T., Thirumalraj, A., & Manjunatha, B. (2023). LW-CNN-based extraction with optimized encoder-decoder model for detection of diabetic retinopathy. *Journal of Autonomous Intelligence*, *7*(3). doi:10.32629/jai.v7i3.1095

Haq, M. A. (2022). CNN Based Automated Weed Detection System Using UAV Imagery. *Computer Systems Science and Engineering*, *42*(2).

Hasan, A. M., Sohel, F., Diepeveen, D., Laga, H., & Jones, M. G. (2021). A survey of deep learning techniques for weed detection from images. *Computers and Electronics in Agriculture*, *184*, 106067. doi:10.1016/j.compag.2021.106067

Hinton, G., Srivastava, N., Krizhevsky, A., & Sutskever, I. R. (2012). Salakhutdinov, Improving neural networks by preventing co-adaptation of feature detectors. arXiv preprint, vol. arXiv 07.

Islam, N., Rashid, M. M., Wibowo, S., Xu, C. Y., Morshed, A., Wasimi, S. A., Moore, S., & Rahman, S. M. (2021). Early weed detection using image processing and machine learning techniques in an Australian chilli farm. *Agriculture*, *11*(5), 387. doi:10.3390/agriculture11050387

Jin, X., Sun, Y., Che, J., Bagavathiannan, M., Yu, J., & Chen, Y. (2022). A novel deep learning-based method for detection of weeds in vegetables. *Pest Management Science*, *78*(5), 1861–1869. doi:10.1002/ps.6804 PMID:35060294

Kansal, I., Khullar, V., Verma, J., Popli, R., & Kumar, R. (2023). IoT-Fog-enabled robotics-based robust classification of hazy and normal season agricultural images for weed detection. *Paladyn : Journal of Behavioral Robotics*, *14*(1), 20220105. doi:10.1515/pjbr-2022-0105

Krishnan, G. H., & Rajasenbagam, T. (2021). A comprehensive survey for weed classification and detection in agriculture lands. *Journal of Information Technology*, *3*(4), 281–289.

Liu, T., Jin, X., Zhang, L., Wang, J., Chen, Y., Hu, C., & Yu, J. (2023). Semi-supervised learning and attention mechanism for weed detection in wheat. *Crop Protection (Guildford, Surrey)*, *174*, 106389. doi:10.1016/j.cropro.2023.106389

Narayana, C. L., & Ramana, K. V. (2023). An Efficient Real-Time Weed Detection Technique using YOLOv7. *International Journal of Advanced Computer Science and Applications*, *14*(2). Advance online publication. doi:10.14569/IJACSA.2023.0140265

Osorio, K., Puerto, A., Pedraza, C., Jamaica, D., & Rodríguez, L. (2020). A deep learning approach for weed detection in lettuce crops using multispectral images. *AgriEngineering*, *2*(3), 471–488. doi:10.3390/agriengineering2030032

Park, Y. H., Choi, S. H., Kwon, Y. J., Kwon, S. W., Kang, Y. J., & Jun, T. H. (2023). Detection of Soybean Insect Pest and a Forecasting Platform Using Deep Learning with Unmanned Ground Vehicles. *Agronomy (Basel)*, *13*(2), 477. doi:10.3390/agronomy13020477

Peng, H., Li, Z., Zhou, Z., & Shao, Y. (2022). Weed detection in paddy field using an improved RetinaNet network. *Computers and Electronics in Agriculture*, *199*, 107179. doi:10.1016/j.compag.2022.107179

Razfar, N., True, J., Bassiouny, R., Venkatesh, V., & Kashef, R. (2022). Weed detection in soybean crops using custom lightweight deep learning models. *Journal of Agriculture and Food Research*, *8*, 100308. doi:10.1016/j.jafr.2022.100308

Ruigrok, T., van Henten, E., Booij, J., Van Boheemen, K., & Kootstra, G. (2020). Application-specific evaluation of a weed-detection algorithm for plant-specific spraying. *Sensors (Basel)*, *20*(24), 7262. doi:10.3390/s20247262 PMID:33352873

Shanmugam, S., Assunção, E., Mesquita, R., Veiros, A., & Gaspar, P. D. (2020). *Automated weed detection systems: A review*. KnE Engineering.

Singh, V., Rana, A., Bishop, M., Filippi, A. M., Cope, D., Rajan, N., & Bagavathiannan, M. (2020). Unmanned aircraft systems for precision weed detection and management: Prospects and challenges. *Advances in Agronomy*, *159*, 93–134. doi:10.1016/bs.agron.2019.08.004

Subeesh, A., Bhole, S., Singh, K., Chandel, N. S., Rajwade, Y. A., Rao, K. V. R., Kumar, S. P., & Jat, D. (2022). Deep convolutional neural network models for weed detection in polyhouse grown bell peppers. *Artificial Intelligence in Agriculture*, *6*, 47–54. doi:10.1016/j.aiia.2022.01.002

Thirumalraj, A., Anusuya, V. S., & Manjunatha, B. (2024). Detection of Ephemeral Sand River Flow Using Hybrid Sandpiper Optimization-Based CNN Model. In *Innovations in Machine Learning and IoT for Water Management* (pp. 195–214). IGI Global.

Ucar, F., & Korkmaz, D. (2020). COVIDiagnosis-Net: Deep Bayes-SqueezeNet based diagnosis of the coronavirus disease 2019 (COVID-19) from X-ray images. *Medical Hypotheses*, *140*, 109761. doi:10.1016/j.mehy.2020.109761 PMID:32344309

Veeranampalayam Sivakumar, A.N., Li, J., Scott, S., Psota, E., & Jhala, J., A., Luck, J.D. and Shi, Y. (. (2020). Comparison of object detection and patch-based classification deep learning models on mid-to late-season weed detection in UAV imagery. *Remote Sensing*, *12*(13), 2136. doi:10.3390/rs12132136

Wu, Z., Chen, Y., Zhao, B., Kang, X., & Ding, Y. (2021). Review of weed detection methods based on computer vision. *Sensors (Basel)*, *21*(11), 3647. doi:10.3390/s21113647 PMID:34073867

Xu, B., Fan, J., Chao, J., Arsenijevic, N., Werle, R., & Zhang, Z. (2023). Instance segmentation method for weed detection using UAV imagery in soybean fields. *Computers and Electronics in Agriculture*, *211*, 107994. doi:10.1016/j.compag.2023.107994

Yang, Q., Ye, Y., Gu, L., & Wu, Y. (2023). MSFCA-Net: A Multi-Scale Feature Convolutional Attention Network for Segmenting Crops and Weeds in the Field. *Agriculture*, *13*(6), 1176. doi:10.3390/agriculture13061176

Zhang, X., Cui, J., Liu, H., Han, Y., Ai, H., Dong, C., Zhang, J., & Chu, Y. (2023). Weed Identification in Soybean Seedling Stage Based on Optimized Faster R-CNN Algorithm. *Agriculture*, *13*(1), 175. doi:10.3390/agriculture13010175

Compilation of References

Aarif, K. O., & Sivakumar, P. (2022). Multi-Domain Deep Convolutional Neural Network for Ancient Urdu Text Recognition System. *Intelligent Automation & Soft Computing*, *33*(1).

Agosto, A., & Giudici, P. (2020). COVID-19 contagion and digital finance. *Digital Finance*, *2*(1), 159–167. doi:10.1007/s42521-020-00021-3 PMID:33179008

Agrawal, M., Shukla, P. K., Nair, R., Nayyar, A., & Masud, M. (2022). Stock Prediction Based on Technical Indicators Using Deep Learning Model. *Computers, Materials & Continua*, *70*(1), 287–304. doi:10.32604/cmc.2022.014637

Aguilar, R. M., Munoz, V., Noda, M., Bruno, A., & Moreno, L. (2010). Teacher Strategies Simulation by Using Fuzzy Systems. *Computer Applications in Engineering Education*, *18*(1), 183–192. doi:10.1002/cae.20128

Agushaka, J. O., Ezugwu, A. E., & Abualigah, L. (2022). Dwarf mongoose optimization algorithm. *Computer Methods in Applied Mechanics and Engineering*, *391*(Mar), 114570. doi:10.1016/j.cma.2022.114570

Ahmad, S., Miskon, S., Alkanhal, T. A., & Tlili, I. (2020). Modeling of business intelligence systems using the potential determinants and theories with the lens of individual, technological, organizational, and environmental contexts-a systematic literature review. *Applied Sciences (Basel, Switzerland)*, *10*(9), 3208. doi:10.3390/app10093208

Ahmed, G., Alyas, T., Iqbal, M. W., Ashraf, M. U., Alghamdi, A. M., Bahaddad, A. A., & Almarhabi, K. A. (2022). Recognition of Urdu Handwritten Alphabet Using Convolutional Neural Network (CNN). *Computers, Materials & Continua*, *73*(2), 2967–2984. doi:10.32604/cmc.2022.029314

Akinsowon, V. (2023). AI Tools for Event Planners: Tips from Meeting Tomorrow's Joey Rodriguez. *Cvent.com Blog*. https://www.cvent.com/en/blog/events/ai-tools-for-event-planners

Al Bashabsheh, E., & Alasal, S. A. (2021). ES-JUST at SemEval-2021 Task 7: Detecting and Rating Humor and Offensive Text Using Deep Learning. In Proceedings of the 15th International Workshop on Semantic Evaluation (SemEval-2021). *Online (Bergheim)*, *5–6*(August), 1102–1107.

Al Suwaidi, F., Alshurideh, M., Al Kurdi, B., & Salloum, S. A. (2020, September). The impact of innovation management in SMEs performance: A systematic review. In *International conference on advanced intelligent systems and informatics* (pp. 720-730). Cham: Springer International Publishing.

Albescu, F., Pugna, I., & Paraschiv, D. (2008). Business intelligence & knowledge management–Technological support for strategic management in the knowledge based economy. *Revista Informatica Economică*, *4*(48), 5–12.

Almazrouei, F. A., Alshurideh, M., Al Kurdi, B., & Salloum, S. A. (2021). Social media impact on business: a systematic review. In *Proceedings of the International Conference on Advanced Intelligent Systems and Informatics 2020* (pp. 697-707). Springer International Publishing. 10.1007/978-3-030-58669-0_62

Alqahtani, M. (2023). Artificial intelligence and entrepreneurship education: A paradigm in Qatari higher education institutions after covid-19 pandemic. *International Journal of Data and Network Science*, *7*(2), 695–706. doi:10.5267/j.ijdns.2023.3.002

Anand, A., Argade, P., Barkemeyer, R., & Salignac, F. (2021). Trends and patterns in sustainable entrepreneurship research: A bibliometric review and research agenda. *Journal of Business Venturing*, *36*(3), 106092. doi:10.1016/j.jbusvent.2021.106092

AngelJ. (2021). Gamestonk: What Happened and What to Do about It. Available at SSRN 3782195. doi:10.2139/ssrn.3782195

Annan-Diab, F., & Molinari, C. (2017). Interdisciplinarity: Practical approach to advancing education for sustainability and for the Sustainable Development Goals. *International Journal of Management Education*, *15*(2), 73–83. doi:10.1016/j.ijme.2017.03.006

Anuradha, J., Tisha, Ramachandran, V., Arulalan, K.V., & Tripathy, B.K. (2010). Diagnosis of ADHD using SVM algorithm. In: *Proceedings of the Third Annual ACM Bangalore Conference*. ACM. 10.1145/1754288.1754317

Arafat, S. Y., Ashraf, N., Iqbal, M. J., Ahmad, I., Khan, S., & Rodrigues, J. J. (2022). Urdu signboard detection and recognition using deep learning. *Multimedia Tools and Applications*, *81*(9), 1–23. doi:10.1007/s11042-020-10175-2

Arora, A., Bansal, S., & Singh, S. (2019). A review of industrial applications of artificial intelligence. *Journal of Advanced Research in Dynamical and Control Systems*, *11*(2), 872–881.

Asad, M. H., & Bais, A. (2020). Weed detection in canola fields using maximum likelihood classification and deep convolutional neural network. *Information Processing in Agriculture*, *7*(4), 535–545. doi:10.1016/j.inpa.2019.12.002

Audretsch, D. B., & Thurik, A. R. (2001). What's new about the new economy? Sources of growth in managed and entrepreneurial economies. *Industrial and Corporate Change*, *10*(1), 267–315. doi:10.1093/icc/10.1.267

Azuma, R., Baillot, Y., Behringer, R., Feiner, S., Julier, S., & MacIntyre, B. (2001). Recent advances in augmented reality. *IEEE Computer Graphics and Applications*, *21*(6), 34–47. doi:10.1109/38.963459

B L, S., & B R, S. (2023). Combined deep learning classifiers for stock market prediction: Integrating stock price and news sentiments. *Kybernetes*, *52*(3), 748–773. doi:10.1108/K-06-2021-0457

Baig, A. S., Butt, H. A., Haroon, O., & Rizvi, S. A. R. (2021). Deaths, panic, lockdowns and US equity markets: The case of COVID-19 pandemic. *Finance Research Letters*, *38*, 101701. doi:10.1016/j.frl.2020.101701 PMID:32837381

Bajdor, P., Pawełoszek, I., & Fidlerova, H. (2021). Analysis and Assessment of Sustainable Entrepreneurship Practices in Polish Small and Medium Enterprises. *Sustainability (Basel)*, *13*(7), 3595. doi:10.3390/su13073595

Baker, T., & Smith, L. (2019). *Educ-AI-tion rebooted? Exploring the future of artificial intelligence in schools and colleges*. Nesta Foundation. https://media.nesta.org.uk/documents/Future_of_AI_and_education_v5_WEB.pdf

Balakrishnan, R. (2021). *Women Entrepreneurs*. YourStory. https://yourstory.com/herstory/2021/09/women-entrepreneurs-leveraged-facebook-instagram-whatsapp-covid19/amp

Balasubramanian, N., Ye, Y., & Xu, M. (2022). Substituting human decision-making with machine learning: Implications for organizational learning. *Academy of Management Review*, *47*(3), 448–465. doi:10.5465/amr.2019.0470

Baseer, K. (2020). Internet of Things:A Product Development Cycle for the Entrepreneurs. Helix, 10(2).

Baseer, K. K., Jaya Naga Varma, B., Harish, B., Sravani, E., Kumar, K. Y., & Varshitha, K. (2023). Design and Implementation of Electronic Health Records using Ethereum Blockchain. *2023 Second International Conference on Electronics and Renewable Systems (ICEARS)*, Tuticorin, India. 10.1109/ICEARS56392.2023.10085012

Beddington, J. R., Asaduzzaman, M., Bremauntz, F. A., Clark, M. E., Guillou, M., Jahn, M. M., Erda, L., Mamo, T., Van Bo, N., & Nobre, C. A. (2012). *Achieving food security in the face of climate change: Final report from the Commission on Sustainable Agriculture and Climate Change*.

Behrendt, S., Peter, F. J., & Zimmermann, D. J. (2020). An encyclopedia for stock markets? Wikipedia searches and stock returns. *International Review of Financial Analysis*, *72*, 101563. doi:10.1016/j.irfa.2020.101563

Bentley, D. (2017). *Business Intelligence and Analytics*. PDF Drive. https://www.pdfdrive.com/business-intelligence-and-analytics-e56416503.html.

Berger, E. S. C., von Briel, F., Davidsson, P., & Kuckertz, A. (2021). Digital or not – The future of entrepreneurship and innovation. *Journal of Business Research, 125*, 436–442. doi:10.1016/j.jbusres.2019.12.020

Bestaieva, D. (2022). *The full Guide on Business Intelligence Implementation in 2022.* Clever Road.

Bhatti, A., Arif, A., Khalid, W., Khan, B., Ali, A., Khalid, S., & Rehman, A. U. (2023). Recognition and classification of handwritten urdu numerals using deep learning techniques. *Applied Sciences (Basel, Switzerland), 13*(3), 1624. doi:10.3390/app13031624

Bijli, H. K. (2023). *Event Planning-BHC-012. Swayam MOOCs Davidson, R. (2019). Business events*. Routledge.

Black, F. (1976) Studies in stock price volatility changes. In: *Proceedings of the 1976 Meeting of the Business and Economic Statistics Section.* American Statistical Association.

Bollen, J., & Mao, H. (2011). Twitter mood as a stock market predictor. *Computer, 44*(10), 91–94. doi:10.1109/MC.2011.323

Brammer, S., Hoejmose, S., & Marchant, K. (2012). Environmental management in SME s in the UK: Practices, pressures and perceived benefits. *Business Strategy and the Environment, 21*(7), 423–434. doi:10.1002/bse.717

Brush, C. G., Henry, C., & Gatewood, J. E. (2010). Women Entrepreneurs and the Global Environment for Growth. Edward Elgar.

Brush, K. (2019, December 30). *What is a learning management system (LMS) and what is it used for?* SearchCIO. https://www.techtarget.com/searchcio/definition/learning-management-system

Brynjolfsson, E., & McAfee, A. (2014). *The Second Machine Age: Work, Progress, and Prosperity in a Time of Brilliant Technologies.* W. W. Norton & Company.

Bullen, C. V., & Rockart, J. F. (1981). *A primer on critical success factors.* MIT Press. https://dspace.mit.edu/bitstream/handle/1721.1/1988/SWP-1220-08368993-CISR-069.pdf?sequen.

Bustamante, A., Sebastia, L., & Onaindia, E. (2020). BITOUR: A Business Intelligence Platform for Tourism Analysis. *ISPRS International Journal of Geo-Information, 9*(11), 671. doi:10.3390/ijgi9110671

Butt, M. A., Ul-Hasan, A., & Shafait, F. 2022, May. Traffsign: Multilingual traffic signboard text detection and recognition for urdu and english. In *International Workshop on Document Analysis Systems* (pp. 741-755). Cham: Springer International Publishing. 10.1007/978-3-031-06555-2_50

Cantele, S., Vernizzi, S., & Campedelli, B. (2020). Untangling the Origins of Sustainable Commitment: New Insights on the Small vs. Large Firms' Debate. *Sustainability (Basel), 12*(2), 671. doi:10.3390/su12020671

Careerera. (2023, January). *What are the advantages and disadvantages of AI in education?* Careerera. https://www.careerera.com/blog/advantages-and-disadvantages-of-ai-in-education

Carr, S. (2010). *Personalisation: A rough guide* (rev. ed). Social Care Institute for Excellence.

CGI. (1986). *Simulation Craft*. Carnegie Group Inc., Commerce Court at Station Square.

Chakraborti, J., Dasgupta, M., & Jana, B. (2002). *How Women Entrepreneurs are Reshaping the Beauty and Wellness Business in India*. Emerald Publishing Limited.

Chalmers, D., MacKenzie, N. G., & Carter, S. (2021). AI and entrepreneurship: Implications for venture creation in the fourth Industrial Revolution. *Entrepreneurship Theory and Practice*, *45*(5), 1028–1053. doi:10.1177/1042258720934581

Chandio, A. A., Asikuzzaman, M. D., Pickering, M. R., & Leghari, M. (2022). Cursive text recognition in natural scene images using deep convolutional recurrent neural network. *IEEE Access : Practical Innovations, Open Solutions*, *10*, 10062–10078. doi:10.1109/ACCESS.2022.3144844

Chassignol, M., Khoroshavin, A., Klimova, A., & Bilyatdinova, A. (2018). Artificial intelligence trends in education: A narrative overview. *Procedia Computer Science*, *136*, 16–24. doi:10.1016/j.procs.2018.08.233

Chatterjee, U., & French, J. J. (2022). A note on tweeting and equity markets before and during the Covid-19 pandemic. *Finance Research Letters*, *46*, 102224. doi:10.1016/j.frl.2021.102224 PMID:35431675

Chee, T., Chan, L. K., Chuah, M. H., Tan, C. S., Wong, S. F., & Yeoh, W. (2009). Business intelligence systems: state-of-the-art review and contemporary applications. *In Symposium on progress in information and communication technology*. IEEE.

Chen, X., Williams, B. M., Vallabhaneni, S. R., Czanner, G., Williams, R., & Zheng, Y. (2019). Learning active contour models for medical image segmentation. *Proc. IEEE/CVF Conf. Comput. Vis. Pattern Recognit. (CVPR)*. IEEE. 10.1109/CVPR.2019.01190

Chen, D. Q., Yan, X. D., Liu, X. B., Li, S., Wang, L. W., & Tian, X. M. (2021). A multiscale-Grid-Based Stacked Bidirectional GRU Neural Network Model for Predicting Traffic Speeds of Urban Expressways [J]. *IEEE Access : Practical Innovations, Open Solutions*, *9*, 1321–1337. doi:10.1109/ACCESS.2020.3034551

Chen, S., & He, H. (2018, November). Stock prediction using convolutional neural network. []). IOP Publishing.]. *IOP Conference Series. Materials Science and Engineering*, *435*, 012026. doi:10.1088/1757-899X/435/1/012026

Chesbrough, H. (2006). *Open Innovation: The New Imperative for Creating and Profiting from Technology*. Harvard Business Press. doi:10.1093/oso/9780199290727.001.0001

Chien, C. F., Wang, H. K., & Fu, W. H. (2018). Industry 3.5 framework of an advanced intelligent manufacturing system: Case studies from semiconductor intelligent manufacturing. *Management Review*, *37*(3), 105–121.

Chiliya, N. (2016). *Towards Sustainable Development in Small, Micro and Medium Adventure Tourism Enterprises*. University of Johannesburg.

Chistov, V., Tanwar, S., & Yadav, C. (2021). Sustainable Entrepreneurship and Innovation. *Addressing the Grand Challenges through Radical Change and Open Innovation.*

ChoK.van MerrienboerB.GulcehreC.BahdanauD.BougaresF.SchwenkH.BengioY. (2014). *Learning phrase representations using RNN encoder-decoder for statistical machine translation.* arXiv:1406.1078. http://arxiv.org/abs/1406.1078 doi:10.3115/v1/D14-1179

Chollet, F. (2017). Xception: Deep learning with depthwise separable convolutions. *Proc. IEEE Conf. Comput. Vis. Pattern Recognit. (CVPR)*. IEEE. 10.1109/CVPR.2017.195

Crossley, R. M., Elmagrhi, M. H., & Ntim, C. G. (2021). Sustainability and legitimacy theory: The case of sustainable social and environmental practices of small and medium-sized enterprises. *Business Strategy and the Environment*, *30*(8), 3740–3762. doi:10.1002/bse.2837

Daneshvar Kakhki, M. & Palvia, P. (2016). Effect of business intelligence and analytics on business performance. *AIS Electronic Library* (AISeL), 1-10.

Daradkeh, M. (2022). Innovation in Business Intelligence Systems: The Relationship Between Innovation Crowdsourcing Mechanisms and Innovation Performance. [IJISSS]. *International Journal of Information Systems in the Service Sector*, *14*(1), 1–25. doi:10.4018/IJISSS.302885

Davenport, T. H., & Harris, J. (2007). *Competing on Analytics: The New Science of Winning*. Harvard Business Review Press.

Davidsson, P. (2016). What Is Entrepreneurship? *International Studies in Entrepreneurship*, *33*, 1–19. doi:10.1007/978-3-319-26692-3_1

Decker, S., & Schmitz, H. (2016). Health shocks and risk aversion. *Journal of Health Economics*, *50*, 156–170. doi:10.1016/j.jhealeco.2016.09.006 PMID:27792902

Delavarian, M., Towhidkhah, F., Dibajnia, P., & Gharibzadeh, S. (2010). Designing a decision support system for distinguishing ADHD from similar children behavioral disorders. *Journal of Medical Systems*, *36*(3), 1335–1343. doi:10.1007/s10916-010-9594-9 PMID:20878211

Dhameja, S. (2002). *Women Entrepreneurs Opportunities, Performance and Problems*. Deep & Deep Publications.

Dias, S. B., Hadjileontiadou, S. J., Hadjileontiadis, L. J., & Diniz, J. A. (2015). Fuzzy cognitive mapping of LMS users' quality of interaction within higher education blended-learning environment. *Expert Systems with Applications*, *42*(21), 7399–7423. doi:10.1016/j.eswa.2015.05.048

Ding, G., & Qin, L. (2020). Study on the prediction of stock price based on the associated network model of LSTM. *International Journal of Machine Learning and Cybernetics*, *11*(6), 1307–1317. doi:10.1007/s13042-019-01041-1

Dinh, T. N., & Thai, M. T. (2018). AI and blockchain: A disruptive integration. *Computer*, *51*(9), 48–53. doi:10.1109/MC.2018.3620971

dos Santos Ferreira, A., Freitas, D. M., da Silva, G. G., Pistori, H., & Folhes, M. T. (2017). Weed detection in soybean crops using convnets. *Computers and Electronics in Agriculture*, *143*, 314–324. doi:10.1016/j.compag.2017.10.027

Drigas, A. S., & Ioannidou, R.-E. (2012). Artificial intelligence in special education: A decade review. *International Journal of Engineering Education*, *28*(6), 1366–1372.

Drucker, P. F. (1985). *Innovation and Entrepreneurship: Practice and Principles*. Harper & Row.

E-commerce Fastlane. (2023). *The impact of AI on business opportunities and challenges for entrepreneurs*. Retrieved from https://ecommercefastlane.com/the-impact-of-ai-on-business-opportunities-and-challenges-for-entrepreneurs/

Economic commission for, A. (2012). Economic Report on Africa 2012: Unleashing Africa's Potential as a Pole of Global Growth. *Economic commission for Africa.*

EE-HUB. (2017, APRIL). *Policy Recommendation*. The European Entrepreneurship Education Network. http://ee-hub.eu/component/attachments/?task=download&id=492:EE-HUB-Policy-Recommendations-web

El-Adaileh, N. A., & Foster, S. (2019). Successful business intelligence implementation: A systematic literature review. *Journal of Work-Applied Management*, *11*(2), 121–132. doi:10.1108/JWAM-09-2019-0027

Elaziz, M. A., Ewees, A. A., Al-qaness, M. A. A., Alshathri, S., & Ibrahim, R. A. (2022, December). Feature selection for high dimensional datasets based on quantum-based dwarf mongoose optimization. *Mathematics*, *10*(23), 4565. doi:10.3390/math10234565

Elia, G., Margherita, A., & Passiante, G. (2020). Digital entrepreneurship ecosystem: How digital technologies and collective intelligence are reshaping the entrepreneurial process. *Technological Forecasting and Social Change*, *150*, 119791. Advance online publication. doi:10.1016/j.techfore.2019.119791

Ellison, N., Steinfield, C., & Lampe, C. (2008). The benefits of Facebook "friends:" Social capital and college students' use of online social network sites. *Journal of Computer-Mediated Communication*, *12*(4), 1143–1168. doi:10.1111/j.1083-6101.2007.00367.x

Elsobeihi, M., & Naser, S. (2017). Effects of Mobile Technology on Human Relationships. *International Journal of Engineering and Information Systems*, *1*(5), 110–125. https://www.researchgate.net/publication/319212701_Effects_of_Mobile_Technology_on_Human_Relationship

Ergen, F. D. (2021). *Artificial Intelligence Applications for Event Management and Marketing. Impact of ICTs on Event Management and Marketing*. IGI Global.

Espejo-Garcia, B., Mylonas, N., Athanasakos, L., Fountas, S., & Vasilakoglou, I. (2020). Towards weeds identification assistance through transfer learning. *Computers and Electronics in Agriculture, 171*, 105306. doi:10.1016/j.compag.2020.105306

EVENTFAQS Bureau. (2023). *Organized live events recovered 129% in 2022: FICCI-EY report*. EVENTFAQs Bureau.: https://www.eventfaqs.com/news/ef-19289/organized-live-events-recovered-129-in-2022-ficci-ey-report

Fatima, H. S., ul Hassan, I., Hasan, S., Khurram, M., Stricker, D., & Afzal, M. Z. (2023). Formation of a Lightweight, Deep Learning-Based Weed Detection System for a Commercial Autonomous Laser Weeding Robot. *Applied Sciences (Basel, Switzerland), 13*(6), 3997. doi:10.3390/app13063997

Femenia-Serra, F., Alzua-Sorzabal, A., & Pousa-Unanue, A. (2022). Business intelligence and the public management of destinations: The view of DMOs. In *Information and Communication Technologies in Tourism 2022: Proceedings of the ENTER 2022 eTourism Conference*, (pp. 417-422). Springer International Publishing.

Fernando, Y., Chiappetta Jabbour, C. J., & Wah, W.-X. (2019). Pursuing green growth in technology firms through the connections between environmental innovation and sustainable business performance: Does service capability matter? *Resources, Conservation and Recycling, 141*, 8–20. doi:10.1016/j.resconrec.2018.09.031

Frąckiewicz, M. (2023, May 3). *The potential of AI in special education*. TS2 SPACE. https://ts2.space/en/the-potential-of-ai-in-special-education/

Fuchs, M., Höpken, W., & Lexhagen, M. (2014). Applying business intelligence for knowledge generation in tourism destinations–A case study from Sweden. In *Tourism and leisure: Current issues and perspectives of development* (pp. 161–174). Springer Fachmedien Wiesbaden.

Garg, S., & Sharma, S. (2020). Impact of artificial intelligence in Special need education to promote inclusive pedagogy. *International Journal of Information and Education Technology (IJIET), 10*(7), 523–527. doi:10.18178/ijiet.2020.10.7.1418

Gascoigne, B. (2019). *History of communication*. History World. http://www.historyworld.net/wrldhis/PlainTextHistories.asp?historyid=aa93

Ghosh, S. (2022, July 29). AIIMS' AI-based website for dyslexia offers fresh hope | Delhi news - Times of India. *The Times of India*. https://timesofindia.indiatimes.com/city/delhi/aiims-ai-based-website-for-dyslexia-offers-fresh-hope/articleshow/93196612.cms

Ghosh, S., & Das, N. (2022). Corporate Social Responsibility in the Time of Pandemic: An Indian Overview. In COVID-19, the Global South and the Pandemic's Development Impact (pp. 77-92). Bristol University Press.

Giuggioli, G., & Pellegrini, M. M. (2023). Artificial intelligence as an enabler for entrepreneurs: A systematic literature review and an agenda for future research. *International Journal of Entrepreneurial Behaviour & Research*, *29*(4), 816–837. doi:10.1108/IJEBR-05-2021-0426

Glorot, X., Bordes, A., & Bengio, Y. (2011). Deep sparse rectifier neural networks. *Proc. 14th Int. Conf. Artif. Intell. Statist.*

Glosten, L. R., Jagannathan, R., & Runkle, D. E. (1993). On the relation between the expected value and the volatility of the nominal excess return on stocks. *The Journal of Finance*, *48*(5), 1779–1801. doi:10.1111/j.1540-6261.1993.tb05128.x

Gómez-Martínez, R., Orden-Cruz, C., & Martínez-Navalón, J. G. (2022). Wikipedia pageviews as investors' attention indicator for Nasdaq. *International Journal of Intelligent Systems in Accounting Finance & Management*, *29*(1), 41–49. doi:10.1002/isaf.1508

Gregori, P., & Holzmann, P. (2020). Digital sustainable entrepreneurship: A business model perspective on embedding digital technologies for social and environmental value creation. *Journal of Cleaner Production*, *272*, 122817. doi:10.1016/j.jclepro.2020.122817

Guild. (2015). *Why Do Consulting Engagements Fail?* Guild. https://blog.guild.im/why-do-consulting-engagements-fail-dab 33a471b29

Gunapriya, B., Rajesh, T., Thirumalraj, A., & Manjunatha, B. (2023). LW-CNN-based extraction with optimized encoder-decoder model for detection of diabetic retinopathy. *Journal of Autonomous Intelligence*, *7*(3). doi:10.32629/jai.v7i3.1095

Gupta, U. (2018). *Story of the beauty entrepreneur Falguni Nayar*. Kindle Edition.

Hahn, R., Spieth, P., & Ince, I. (2018). Business model design in sustainable entrepreneurship: Illuminating the commercial logic of hybrid businesses. *Journal of Cleaner Production*, *176*, 439–451. doi:10.1016/j.jclepro.2017.12.167

Hakoama, M., & Hakoyama, S. (2011). The Impact of Cell Phone Use on Social Networking and Development among College Students. *The AABSS Journal*, *15*, 1–20.

Haq, M. A. (2022). CNN Based Automated Weed Detection System Using UAV Imagery. *Computer Systems Science and Engineering*, *42*(2).

Hasan, A. M., Sohel, F., Diepeveen, D., Laga, H., & Jones, M. G. (2021). A survey of deep learning techniques for weed detection from images. *Computers and Electronics in Agriculture*, *184*, 106067. doi:10.1016/j.compag.2021.106067

Hernandez, J. (2009). Learning difficulties diagnosis for children's basic education using expert systems. *WSEAS Transactions on Information Science and Applications*, *6*(7), 1206–1215.

Hinton, G., Srivastava, N., Krizhevsky, A., & Sutskever, I. R. (2012). Salakhutdi- nov, Improving neural networks by preventing co-adaptation of feature detectors. arXiv preprint, vol. arXiv 07.

Hiransha, M., Gopalakrishnan, E. A., Menon, V. K., & Soman, K. P. (2018). NSE stock market prediction using deep-learning models. *Procedia Computer Science*, *132*, 1351–1362. doi:10.1016/j.procs.2018.05.050

Hočevar, B., & Jaklič, J. (2010). Assessing benefits of business intelligence systems–a case study. *Management*, *15*(1), 87–119.

Hoejmose, S. U., & Adrien-Kirby, A. J. (2012). Socially and environmentally responsible procurement: A literature review and future research agenda of a managerial issue in the 21st century. *Journal of Purchasing and Supply Management*, *18*(4), 232–242. doi:10.1016/j.pursup.2012.06.002

Holzinger, A., Haibe-Kains, B., & Jurisica, I. (2019). Why imaging data alone is not enough: AI-based integration of imaging, omics, and clinical data. *European Journal of Nuclear Medicine and Molecular Imaging*, *46*(13), 2722–2730. doi:10.1007/s00259-019-04382-9 PMID:31203421

Höpken, W., & Fuchs, M. (2022). Business Intelligence in Tourism. In *Handbook of e-Tourism* (pp. 497–527). Springer International Publishing. doi:10.1007/978-3-030-48652-5_3

Horakova, M. & Skalska, H. (2013). Business Intelligence and Implementation in a Small Enterprise. *Journal of Systems Integration* (1804-2724), *4*(2), 50-61.

Hsu, C., Lee, J. N., Fang, Y., Straub, D. W., Su, N., & Ryu, H. S. (2022). The role of vendor legitimacy in IT outsourcing performance: Theory and evidence. *Information Systems Research*, *33*(1), 337–361. doi:10.1287/isre.2021.1059

Hu, Z., Zhu, J., & Tse, K. (2013, November). Stocks market prediction using support vector machine. In *2013 6th International Conference on Information Management, Innovation Management and Industrial Engineering* (*Vol. 2*, pp. 115-118). IEEE. 10.1109/ICIII.2013.6703096

Huang, M. Y., Rojas, R. R., & Convery, P. D. (2020). Forecasting stock market movements using Google Trend searches. *Empirical Economics*, *59*(6), 2821–2839. doi:10.1007/s00181-019-01725-1

Huang, Z., & Cao, L. (2020). Bicubic interpolation and extrapolation iteration method for high resolution digital holographic reconstruction. *Optics and Lasers in Engineering*, *130*(Jul), 106090. doi:10.1016/j.optlaseng.2020.106090

Hui, L., Wang, G., & Yu, S. (2019). AI-enabled intelligent manufacturing: A state-of-the-art survey. *Journal of Manufacturing Systems*, *50*, 59–68.

Hutson, J., Jeevanjee, T., Graaf, V. V., Lively, J., Weber, J., Weir, G., Arnone, K., Carnes, G., Vosevich, K., Plate, D., Leary, M., & Edele, S. (2022). Artificial intelligence and the disruption of higher education: Strategies for integrations across disciplines. *Creative Education*, *13*(12), 3953–3980. doi:10.4236/ce.2022.1312253

Hu, Z., Zhao, Y., & Khushi, M. (2021). A survey of forex and stock price prediction using deep learning. *Applied System Innovation*, *4*(1), 9. doi:10.3390/asi4010009

Iansiti, M., & Lakhani, K. (2020). *Competing in the age of AI: Strategy and leadership when algorithms and networks run the world.* Harvard Business Review Press.

Iberdrola. (2020). Educational robotics: Definition, advantages, and examples. *Iberdrola.* https://www.iberdrola.com/innovation/educational-robots

Illia, L., Colleoni, E., & Zyglidopoulos, S. (2023). Ethical implications of text generation in the age of artificial intelligence. *Business Ethics, the Environment & Responsibility, 32*(1), 201–210. doi:10.1111/beer.12479

Immersionvr. (2020, January 2). *VR for education.* Immersionvr. https://immersionvr.co.uk/about-360vr/vr-for-education/

Inamdar, S. R., & Gursoy, K. (2019). *Cloud hosted business-data driven BI platforms.* Availabe at: https://scholarship.libraries.rutgers.edu/discovery/delivery/01RUT_INST:ResearchRepository/12643384890004646?l#136435357
70004646

Inclusive Minds. (2023, May 16). Unraveling the latest trends in special education technology. *Inclusive Minds.* https://inclusiveminds.org/unraveling-the-latest-trends-in-special-education-technology/

India, N. (2020). *NSE - National Stock Exchange of India Ltd: Live Share/Stock Market News & Updates, Quotes- Nseindia.com.* NSE India. https://www.nseindia.com/

Indian Events and Activations industry expected to cross Rs 10,000 crore by 2020-21: Report, E. Y. (2017). BestMediaInfo Bureau. Retrived on 20.9.2023 from: www.bestmediainfo.com/2017/09/indian-events-and- activations -industrv-expected-to- cross-rs-10-000-crore-bv-2020-21-ev-report/

Islam, N., Rashid, M. M., Wibowo, S., Xu, C. Y., Morshed, A., Wasimi, S. A., Moore, S., & Rahman, S. M. (2021). Early weed detection using image processing and machine learning techniques in an Australian chilli farm. *Agriculture, 11*(5), 387. doi:10.3390/agriculture11050387

Jackblackwell. (2023, January 27). *10 best AI tools for people with disabilities (Free and paid). Pure Future AI - Unlock the Possibilities of Open-Source and Public API AI: Resources and Insight at Your Fingertips!* Pure Future. https://purefuture.net/2023/01/27/10-best-ai-tools-for-people-with-disabilities-free-and-paid/#google_vignette

Jain, K., Manghirmalani, P., Dongardive, J., & Abraham, S. (2009). Computational Diagnosis of Learning Disability. *International Journal of Recent Trends in Engineering, 2*(3).

Jiang, W. (2021). Applications of deep learning in stock market prediction: Recent progress. *Expert Systems with Applications, 184*, 115537. doi:10.1016/j.eswa.2021.115537

Jing, N., Wu, Z., & Wang, H. (2021). A hybrid model integrating deep learning with investor sentiment analysis for stock price prediction. *Expert Systems with Applications, 178*, 115019. doi:10.1016/j.eswa.2021.115019

Jin, X., Sun, Y., Che, J., Bagavathiannan, M., Yu, J., & Chen, Y. (2022). A novel deep learning-based method for detection of weeds in vegetables. *Pest Management Science*, *78*(5), 1861–1869. doi:10.1002/ps.6804 PMID:35060294

Ji, X., Wang, J., & Yan, Z. (2021). A stock price prediction method based on deep learning technology. *International Journal of Crowd Science*, *5*(1), 55–72. doi:10.1108/IJCS-05-2020-0012

Johnson, C. (2007). *National School Debate: Banning Cell Phones on Public School Campuses in America*. Semantic Scholar.

Johnson, M. P. (2017). Knowledge acquisition and development in sustainability-oriented small and medium-sized enterprises: Exploring the practices, capabilities and cooperation. *Journal of Cleaner Production*, *142*, 3769–3781. doi:10.1016/j.jclepro.2016.10.087

Joseph, B. M., & Baseer, K. K. (2023). IoT-Sensed Data for Data Integration Using Intelligent Decision-Making Algorithm Through Fog Computing. In H. Sharma, V. Shrivastava, K. K. Bharti, & L. Wang (Eds.), *Communication and Intelligent Systems. ICCIS 2022. Lecture Notes in Networks and Systems* (Vol. 689). Springer., doi:10.1007/978-981-99-2322-9_34

Joshi, S., Rambola, R. K., & Churi, P. (2021). Evaluating artificial intelligence in education for the next generation. *Journal of Physics: Conference Series*, *1714*(1), 012039. doi:10.1088/1742-6596/1714/1/012039

Jussupow, E., Spohrer, K., Heinzl, A., & Gawlitza, J. (2021). Augmenting medical diagnosis decisions? An investigation into physicians' decision-making process with artificial intelligence. *Information Systems Research*, *32*(3), 713–735. doi:10.1287/isre.2020.0980

Kansal, I., Khullar, V., Verma, J., Popli, R., & Kumar, R. (2023). IoT-Fog-enabled robotics-based robust classification of hazy and normal season agricultural images for weed detection. *Paladyn : Journal of Behavioral Robotics*, *14*(1), 20220105. doi:10.1515/pjbr-2022-0105

Kashif, M. (2021). *Urdu Handwritten Text Recognition Using ResNet18*. arXiv preprint arXiv:2103.05105.

Katz, E, Blumler, J.G. & Gurevitch, M. (1973-74). Uses and Gratifications Research. *The Public Opinion Quaterly, 37*. Oxford University Press

Khan, A. (2020, February 18). 8 benefits of chatbots in the education industry. *Botsify*. https://botsify.com/blog/education-industry-chatbot/

Khan, H. (2021). *COVID-19 in South Africa: An Intersectional Perspective based on Socio-economic Modeling and Indigenous Knowledge Base*.

Khan, H. R., Hasan, M. A., Kazmi, M., Fayyaz, N., Khalid, H., & Qazi, S. A. (2021). A holistic approach to Urdu language word recognition using deep neural networks. Engineering, Technology &. *Applied Scientific Research*, *11*(3), 7140–7145.

Khare, K., Darekar, O., Gupta, P., & Attar, V. Z. (2017, May). Short term stock price prediction using deep learning. In *2017 2nd IEEE international conference on recent trends in electronics, information & communication technology (RTEICT)* (pp. 482-486). IEEE. 10.1109/RTEICT.2017.8256643

Kim, Y., & Baylor, A. L. (2016). based design of pedagogical agent roles: A review, progress, and recommendations. *International Journal of Artificial Intelligence in Education*, *26*(1), 160–169. doi:10.1007/s40593-015-0055-y

Knoppen, D., & Knight, L. (2022). Pursuing sustainability advantage: The dynamic capabilities of born sustainable firms. *Business Strategy and the Environment*, *31*(4), 1789–1813. doi:10.1002/bse.2984

Kolk, A. (2016). The social responsibility of international business: From ethics and the environment to CSR and sustainable development. *Journal of World Business*, *51*(1), 23–34. doi:10.1016/j.jwb.2015.08.010

Korreck, S. (2019, September 25). *ORF*. ORF Online. https://www.orfonline.org/research/women-entrepreneurs-in-in dia-what-is-holding-them-back-55852/

Kraus, S., Clauss, T., Breier, M., Gast, J., Zardini, A., & Tiberius, V. (2020). The economics of COVID-19: Initial empirical evidence on how family firms in five European countries cope with the corona crisis. *International Journal of Entrepreneurial Behaviour & Research*, *26*(5), 1067–1092. doi:10.1108/IJEBR-04-2020-0214

Krishnan, G. H., & Rajasenbagam, T. (2021). A comprehensive survey for weed classification and detection in agriculture lands. *Journal of Information Technology*, *3*(4), 281–289.

Kristoufek, L. (2013). BitCoin meets Google Trends and Wikipedia: Quantifying the relationship between phenomena of the Internet era. *Scientific Reports*, *3*(1), 1–7. doi:10.1038/srep03415 PMID:24301322

Kristoufek, L. (2015). Power-law correlations in finance-related Google searches, and their cross-correlations with volatility and traded volume: Evidence from the Dow Jones Industrial components. *Physica A*, *428*, 194–205. doi:10.1016/j.physa.2015.02.057

Kulik, J. A., & Fletcher, J. D. (2016). Effectiveness of intelligent tutoring systems: A meta-analytic review. *Review of Educational Research*, *86*(1), 42–78. doi:10.3102/0034654315581420

Kumar, P. (2016). *Indian Women as Entrepreneurs: An Exploration of Self-Identity*. Palgrave Macmillan. doi:10.1057/978-1-137-60259-6

Kumar, V., & Garg, M. L. (2018). Predictive analytics: A review of trends and techniques. *International Journal of Computer Applications*, *182*(1), 31–37. doi:10.5120/ijca2018917434

Kunduru, A. R. (2023). Effective Usage of Artificial Intelligence in Enterprise Resource Planning Applications. *International Journal of Computer Trends and Technology*, *71*(4), 73–80. doi:10.14445/22312803/IJCTT-V71I4P109

Kurzweil, R. (2005). *The Singularity Is Near: When Humans Transcend Biology*. Penguin.

Laasch, O., Ryazanova, O., & Wright, A. L. (2022). Lingering covid and looming grand crises: Envisioning business schools' business model transformations. *Academy of Management Learning & Education, 21*(1), 1–6. doi:10.5465/amle.2022.0035

Lapa, J., Bernardino, J., & Figueiredo, A. (2014). A comparative analysis of open source business intelligence platforms. *In Proceedings of the International Conference on Information Systems and Design of Communication*, (pp. 86-92). ACM. 10.1145/2618168.2618182

Leonidou, L. C., Fotiadis, T. A., Christodoulides, P., Spyropoulou, S., & Katsikeas, C. S. (2015). Environmentally friendly export business strategy: Its determinants and effects on competitive advantage and performance. *International Business Review*, *24*(5), 798–811. doi:10.1016/j.ibusrev.2015.02.001

Lévesque, M., Obschonka, M., & Nambisan, S. (2022). Pursuing impactful entrepreneurship research using artificial intelligence. *Entrepreneurship Theory and Practice*, *46*(4), 803–832. doi:10.1177/1042258720927369

Li, M., Zhu, Y., Shen, Y., & Angelova, M. (2023). Clustering-enhanced stock price prediction using deep learning. *World Wide Web (Bussum)*, *26*(1), 207–232. doi:10.1007/s11280-021-01003-0 PMID:35440889

Lin, T.-Y., Dollar, P., Girshick, R., He, K., Hariharan, B., & Belongie, S. (2017). Feature pyramid networks for object detection. *Proc. IEEE Conf. Comput. Vis. Pattern Recognit. (CVPR)*. IEEE. 10.1109/CVPR.2017.106

Lindebaum, D., Vesa, M., & Den Hond, F. (2020). Insights from "The Machine Stops " to Better Understand Rational Assumptions in Algorithmic Decision Making and Its Implications for Organizations. *Academy of Management Review*, *45*(1), 247–263. doi:10.5465/amr.2018.0181

Ling, R. (2004). *The Mobile Connection: The Cell Phone's Impact on Society*. Elsevier., doi:10.1145/1029383.1029381

Liu, M., Chen, C., & Wei, H. (2021). *A systematic review of artificial intelligence applications.*

Liu, B. (2020). *Sentiment analysis: Mining opinions, sentiments, and emotions*. Cambridge university press. doi:10.1017/9781108639286

Liu, H., & Long, Z. (2020). An improved deep learning model for predicting stock market price time series. *Digital Signal Processing*, *102*, 102741. doi:10.1016/j.dsp.2020.102741

Liu, T., Jin, X., Zhang, L., Wang, J., Chen, Y., Hu, C., & Yu, J. (2023). Semi-supervised learning and attention mechanism for weed detection in wheat. *Crop Protection (Guildford, Surrey)*, *174*, 106389. doi:10.1016/j.cropro.2023.106389

Li, Y., & Pan, Y. (2022). A novel ensemble deep learning model for stock prediction based on stock prices and news. *International Journal of Data Science and Analytics*, *13*(2), 1–11. doi:10.1007/s41060-021-00279-9 PMID:34549080

Loi, D., Wolf, C. T., Blomberg, J. L., Arar, R., & Brereton, M. (2019). *Co-designing AI futures. Companion Publication of the 2019 on Designing Interactive Systems Conference 2019 Companion*. doi:10.1145/3301019.3320000

Long, D., & Magerko, B. (2020). What is AI literacy? Competencies and design considerations. In *Proceedings of the 2020 CHI Conference on Human Factors in Computing Systems* (pp. 1–16). ACM. 10.1145/3313831.3376727

Long, J., Chen, Z., He, W., Wu, T., & Ren, J. (2020). An integrated framework of deep learning and knowledge graph for prediction of stock price trend: An application in Chinese stock exchange market. *Applied Soft Computing*, *91*, 106205. doi:10.1016/j.asoc.2020.106205

Lönnqvist, A., & Pirttimäki, V. (2006). The measurement of business intelligence. *Information Systems Management*, *23*(1), 32–40. doi:10.1201/1078.10580530/45769.23.1.20061201/91770.4

Luckin, R., Holmes, W., Griffiths, M., & Forcier, L. B. (2016). *Intelligence Unleashed: An argument for AI in education.* UCL. https://discovery.ucl.ac.uk/1475756/

Luhn, H. P. (1958). A business intelligence system. *IBM Journal of Research and Development*, *2*(4), 314–319. doi:10.1147/rd.24.0314

Lv, Y. F., Zhang, X. H., Xiong, W., Cui, Y. Q., & Cai, M. (2019). An End-to-End Local-Global-Fusion Feature Extraction Network for Remote Sensing image Scene Classification [J]. *Remote Sensing (Basel)*, *11*(24), 3006. doi:10.3390/rs11243006

Lynch, M. (2023, March 24). How artificial intelligence is improving assistive technology. *The Tech Edvocate*. https://www.thetechedvocate.org/how-artificial-intelligence-is-improving-assistive-technology/

M.Rezvani, M. L. (2018). organisational entrepreneurial alaertness framework in opportunity discovery. *academy of entrepreneurship journal*.

Mackay, M. M & Weidlich O. (2007). Australian Mobile Phone Lifestyle Index (3rd ed.). Special Topic: Advertising on the Mobile Phone. Australian Interactive Media Industry Association.

Madyatmadja, E. D., Adiba, C. N. A., Sembiring, D. J. M., Pristinella, D., & Putra, A. M. (2021). The Positive Impact of Implementation Business Intelligence and Big Data in Hospitality and Tourism Sector. *International Journal of Emerging Technology and Advanced Engineering*, *11*(6), 59–71. doi:10.46338/ijetae0621_07

Magaireah, A. I., Sulaiman, H., & Ali, N. (2019). Identifying the most critical factors to business intelligence implementation success in the public sector organizations. *The Journal of Social Sciences Research*, *5*(2), 450–462. doi:10.32861/jssr.52.450.462

Malarvizhi, P., & Yadav, S. (2008). Corporate environmental disclosures on the internet: An empirical analysis of Indian companies. *Issues in Social & Environmental Accounting*, *2*(2), 211–232. doi:10.22164/isea.v2i2.33

Manojlović, T., & Štajduhar, I. (2015, May). Predicting stock market trends using random forests: A sample of the Zagreb stock exchange. In *2015 38th International Convention on Information and Communication Technology, Electronics and Microelectronics (MIPRO)* (pp. 1189-1193). IEEE. 10.1109/MIPRO.2015.7160456

Marwala, T., & Hurwitz, E. (2019). *Artificial intelligence and the fourth industrial revolution.* Wiley.

Masa'Deh, R. E., Obeidat, Z., Maqableh, M., & Shah, M. (2021). The impact of business intelligence systems on an organization's effectiveness: The role of metadata quality from a developing country's view. *International Journal of Hospitality & Tourism Administration*, *22*(1), 64–84. doi:10.1080/15256480.2018.1547239

Masarira, S. K. (2014). *An analysis of small business social responsibility practices in South Africa*. University of South Africa.

Ma, Y., Han, R., & Wang, W. (2021). Portfolio optimization with return prediction using deep learning and machine learning. *Expert Systems with Applications*, *165*, 113973. doi:10.1016/j.eswa.2020.113973

Maybee, M. (2023). *AI for Events: How Artificial Intelligence Improves Efficiency and ROI*. PC Nametag. https://blog.pcnametag.com/event-ai

McKeown, P. (2017). *Competitive Intelligence Advantage: How to Minimize Risk, Avoid Surprises, and Grow Your Business in a Changing World.* John Wiley & Sons.

Md, A. Q., & Kapoor, S., AV, C. J., Sivaraman, A. K., Tee, K. F., Sabireen, H., & Janakiraman, N. (. (2023). Novel optimization approach for stock price forecasting using multi-layered sequential LSTM. *Applied Soft Computing*, *134*, 109830. doi:10.1016/j.asoc.2022.109830

Mehtab, S., Sen, J., & Dutta, A. (2021). Stock price prediction using machine learning and LSTM-based deep learning models. In *Machine Learning and Metaheuristics Algorithms, and Applications: Second Symposium, SoMMA 2020*, (pp. 88-106). Springer Singapore.

Mehtab, S., & Sen, J. (2020). A time series analysis-based stock price prediction using machine learning and deep learning models. *International Journal of Business Forecasting and Marketing Intelligence*, *6*(4), 272–335. doi:10.1504/IJBFMI.2020.115691

Mehtab, S., & Sen, J. 2020, November. Stock price prediction using CNN and LSTM-based deep learning models. In *2020 International Conference on Decision Aid Sciences and Application (DASA)* (pp. 447-453). IEEE. 10.1109/DASA51403.2020.9317207

Meissner, P., & Keding, C. (2021). The human factor in AI-based decision-making. *MIT Sloan Management Review*, *63*(1), 1–5.

Miró-Julià, M., Fiol-Roig, G., & Isern-Deyà, A. P. (2010). Decision trees in stock market analysis: construction and validation. In *Trends in Applied Intelligent Systems: 23rd International Conference on Industrial Engineering and Other Applications of Applied Intelligent Systems*. Springer.

Misgar, M. M., Mushtaq, F., Khurana, S. S., & Kumar, M. (2023). Recognition of offline handwritten Urdu characters using RNN and LSTM models. *Multimedia Tools and Applications*, *82*(2), 2053–2076. doi:10.1007/s11042-022-13320-1

Mitra, S. (2008). *Entrepreneur Journeys*. Createspace Independent Pub.

Mittal, V. (2019). *How Artificial Intelligence Will Improve Things For Wedding Planning Industry in India*. SCelebration. https://scelebration.com/artificial-intelligence-will-improve- things-wedding-planning-industry-india/

Moghar, A., & Hamiche, M. (2020). Stock market prediction using LSTM recurrent neural network. *Procedia Computer Science*, *170*, 1168–1173. doi:10.1016/j.procs.2020.03.049

Mohan, P. (2021, December 10). Artificial intelligence in education. *Times of India Blog*. https://timesofindia.indiatimes.com/readersblog/newtech/artificial-intelligence-in-education-39512/

Morrison, C., Cutrell, E., Dhareshwar, A., Doherty, K., Thieme, A., & Taylor, A. (2017). Imagining artificial intelligence applications with people with visual disabilities using tactile ideation. *Proceedings of the 19th International ACM SIGACCESS Conference on Computers and Accessibility*. ACM. 10.1145/3132525.3132530

Moss, L., & Hoberman, S. (2004). *The importance of data modeling as a foundation for business insight*. Design.

Muhammad, T., Aftab, A. B., Ibrahim, M., Ahsan, M. M., Muhu, M. M., Khan, S. I., & Alam, M. S. (2023). Transformer-based deep learning model for stock price prediction: A case study on Bangladesh stock market. *International Journal of Computational Intelligence and Applications*, *22*(3), 2350013. doi:10.1142/S146902682350013X

Mukherjee, S., Sadhukhan, B., Sarkar, N., Roy, D., & De, S. (2023). Stock market prediction using deep learning algorithms. *CAAI Transactions on Intelligence Technology*, *8*(1), 82–94. doi:10.1049/cit2.12059

Mungree, D., Rudra, A., & Morien, D. (2013). *A framework for understanding the critical success factors of enterprise business intelligence implementation. Proceedings of the Nineteenth Americas Conference on Information Systems*, Chicago, Illinois.

Muntean, M. (2018). Business intelligence issues for sustainability projects. *Sustainability (Basel)*, *10*(2), 335. doi:10.3390/su10020335

Nabipour, M., Nayyeri, P., Jabani, H., Mosavi, A., Salwana, E., & S, S. (2020). Deep learning for stock market prediction. *Entropy (Basel, Switzerland)*, *22*(8), 840. doi:10.3390/e22080840 PMID:33286613

Nagma, M. (2021, July 26). Tales of Grit and Courage. *ETNOWNEWS*. https://www.timesnownews.com/business-economy/economy/article/tales-of-grit-and-courage-the-journey-of-women-entrepreneurs-in-india-during-covid/780697

Nanda, A., Gupta, S., & Vijrania, M. (2019). A comprehensive survey of OLAP: recent trends. *In 2019 3rd International Conference on Electronics, Communication and Aerospace Technology (ICECA), IEEE,* (pp. 425-430). IEEE.

Narayana, C. L., & Ramana, K. V. (2023). An Efficient Real-Time Weed Detection Technique using YOLOv7. *International Journal of Advanced Computer Science and Applications*, *14*(2). Advance online publication. doi:10.14569/IJACSA.2023.0140265

Narwani, K., Lin, H., Pirbhulal, S., & Hassan, M. (2022). Towards AI-enabled approach for urdu text recognition: A legacy for urdu image apprehension. *IEEE Access : Practical Innovations, Open Solutions*.

Nasab, S. S., Selamat, H., & Masrom, M. (2015). A delphi study of the important factors for BI system implementation in the public sector organizations. *Jurnal Teknologi*, *77*(19), 113–120. doi:10.11113/jt.v77.6539

Nasir, T., Malik, M. K., & Shahzad, K. (2021). MMU-OCR-21: Towards end-to-end Urdu text recognition using deep learning. *IEEE Access : Practical Innovations, Open Solutions*, *9*, 124945–124962. doi:10.1109/ACCESS.2021.3110787

Nayomi, B. (2023). *A Framework for Processing and Analysing Real-Time data in e-Commerce Applications*. 2023 8th International Conference on Communication and Electronics Systems (ICCES), Coimbatore, India. doi:10.1109/ICCES57224.2023.10192771

Nebeker, C., Harlow, J., Espinoza Giacinto, R., Orozco-Linares, R., Bloss, C. S., & Weibel, N. (2017). Ethical and regulatory challenges of research using pervasive sensing and other emerging technologies: IRB perspectives. *AJOB Empirical Bioethics*, *8*(4), 266–276. doi:10.1080/23294515.2017.1403980 PMID:29125425

Negash, S., & Gray, P. (2008). Business intelligence. In *Handbook on decision support systems 2* (pp. 72–80). Springer. doi:10.1007/978-3-540-48716-6_9

Nespeca, A., & Chiucchi, M. S. (2018). The impact of business intelligence systems on management accounting systems: The consultant's perspective. In *Network, Smart and Open: Three Keywords for Information Systems Innovation* (pp. 283–297). Springer International Publishing. doi:10.1007/978-3-319-62636-9_19

Neuhofer, B., Magnus, B., & Celuch, K. (2020). The impact of artificial intelligence on event experiences: A scenario technique approach. [Springer.]. *Electronic Markets*, *31*(3), 601–617. doi:10.1007/s12525-020-00433-4 PMID:38624486

Nhemachena, C. (2017). *Motivations of sustainable entrepreneurship in Gauteng province*.

Nickolas, J. D. (2000). *Flattening the Military Force Structure*. Army Command and General Staff Coll Fort Leavenworth Ks School of Advanced Military Studies.

Nyanga, C., Pansiri, J., & Chatibura, D. (2019). Enhancing competitiveness in the tourism industry through the use of business intelligence: A literature review. *Journal of Tourism Futures*, *6*(2), 139–151. doi:10.1108/JTF-11-2018-0069

O'Leary, D. E., & Storey, V. C. (2020). A Google Wikipedia Twitter model as a leading indicator of the numbers of coronavirus deaths. *International Journal of Intelligent Systems in Accounting Finance & Management*, *27*(3), 151–158. doi:10.1002/isaf.1482

Ogle, A., & Lamb, D. J. (2019). *The Role of Robots, Artificial Intelligence, and Service Automation in Events*. ResearchGate. https://www.researchgate.net/publication/336530987_The_Role_of_Robots_Artificial_Intelligence_ and_Service_Automation_in_Events

Olszak, C. M., & Ziemba, E. (2007). Approach to building and implementing business intelligence systems. *Interdisciplinary Journal of Information, Knowledge, and Management*, *2*(1), 135–148. doi:10.28945/105

Osorio, K., Puerto, A., Pedraza, C., Jamaica, D., & Rodríguez, L. (2020). A deep learning approach for weed detection in lettuce crops using multispectral images. *AgriEngineering*, *2*(3), 471–488. doi:10.3390/agriengineering2030032

Özdemir, V. (2019). Not all intelligence is artificial: Data science, automation, and AI meet HI. *OMICS: A Journal of Integrative Biology*, *23*(2), 67–69. doi:10.1089/omi.2019.0003 PMID:30707659

Oztemel, E., & Gursev, S. (2020). Literature review of Industry 4.0 and related technologies. *Journal of Intelligent Manufacturing*, *31*(1), 127–182. doi:10.1007/s10845-018-1433-8

Pai, S. &. (2021, December). NYKAA: A Comprehensive Analysis of a Leading Indian E- Commerce Cosmetic Agency. *International Journal of Case Studies in Business, IT and Education, 5*(2).

Papakostas, G. A., Sidiropoulos, G. K., Papadopoulou, C. I., Vrochidou, E., Kaburlasos, V. G., Papadopoulou, M. T., Holeva, V., Nikopoulou, V., & Dalivigkas, N. (2021). Social robots in special education: A systematic review. *Electronics (Basel)*, *10*(2), 1398. doi:10.3390/electronics10121398

Paranjape, K., Schinkel, M., Nannan Panday, R., Car, J., & Nanayakkara, P. (2019). Introducing artificial intelligence training in medical education. *JMIR Medical Education*, *5*(2), e16048. doi:10.2196/16048 PMID:31793895

Parasuraman, R., Sheridan, T., Wickens, C. (2000). A model for types and levels of human interaction with automation. *IEEE transactions on systems, man, and cybernetics*. IEEE. DOI:. doi:10.1109/3468.844354

Park, Y. H., Choi, S. H., Kwon, Y. J., Kwon, S. W., Kang, Y. J., & Jun, T. H. (2023). Detection of Soybean Insect Pest and a Forecasting Platform Using Deep Learning with Unmanned Ground Vehicles. *Agronomy (Basel)*, *13*(2), 477. doi:10.3390/agronomy13020477

Pasha, M. (2022). IoT Technology Enabled Multi-Purpose Chair to Control the Home/Office Appliance. *Journal of Algebraic Statistics, 13*(1).

Pawar, K., Jalem, R. S., & Tiwari, V. (2019). Stock market price prediction using LSTM RNN. In *Emerging Trends in Expert Applications and Security* [Springer Singapore.]. *Proceedings of ICETEAS, 2018*, 493–503.

Pearson, A. W. (2018). *The predictive airliner*. Intelligencia Publishing.

Peng, H., Li, Z., Zhou, Z., & Shao, Y. (2022). Weed detection in paddy field using an improved RetinaNet network. *Computers and Electronics in Agriculture*, *199*, 107179. doi:10.1016/j.compag.2022.107179

Pertus, S. (2017, August 4). *How Equadex used cognitive services to help people with language disorders*. Microsoft Technical Case Studies. https://microsoft.github.io/techcasestudies/cognitive%20services/2017/08/04/equadexcognitives.html

Pham, N. T., Chiappetta Jabbour, C. J., Vo-Thanh, T., Huynh, T. L. D., & Santos, C. (2020). Greening hotels: Does motivating hotel employees promote in-role green performance? The role of culture. *Journal of Sustainable Tourism*, 1–20.

Pirttimäki, V., Lönnqvist, A., & Karjaluoto, A. (2006). Measurement of Business Intelligence in a Finnish Telecom-munications Company. *Electronic Journal of Knowledge Management*, *4*(1), 83–90.

Poddar, A., Narula, S. A., & Zutshi, A. (2019). A study of corporate social responsibility practices of the top Bombay Stock Exchange 500 companies in India and their alignment with the Sustainable Development Goal s. *Corporate Social Responsibility and Environmental Management*, *26*(6), 1184–1205. doi:10.1002/csr.1741

Popovič, A., Puklavec, B., & Oliveira, T. (2019). Justifying business intelligence systems adoption in SMEs: Impact of systems use on firm performance. *Industrial Management & Data Systems*, *119*(1), 210–228. doi:10.1108/IMDS-02-2018-0085

Preis, T., Moat, H. S., & Stanley, H. E. (2013). Quantifying trading behavior in financial markets using Google Trends. *Scientific Reports*, *3*(1), 1–6. doi:10.1038/srep01684 PMID:23619126

Prescott, J. E. (1995). The evolution of competitive intelligence. *International review of strategic management, 6,* 71-90.

Presence. (2023, March 1). 5 special education technology trends SPED directors must know about. *Presence*. https://presence.com/insights/special-ed-tech-trends-sped-directors-must-know/

Puppim de Oliveira, J. A., & Jabbour, C. J. C. (2017). Environmental management, climate change, CSR, and governance in clusters of small firms in developing countries: Toward an integrated analytical framework. *Business & Society*, *56*(1), 130–151. doi:10.1177/0007650315575470

PwC. (2023). 54 of the companies have implemented AI for business PwC India Survey. Retrieved from https://www.pwc.in/press-releases/2023/54-of-the-companies-have-implemented-ai-for-business-pwc-india-survey.html

Qian, Z., & Liao, W. (2021). Artificial intelligence for smart manufacturing: A review. *Robotics and Computer-integrated Manufacturing*, *68*, 101986.

Rahman, A., Ghosh, A., & Arora, C. (2023). UTRNet: High-Resolution Urdu Text Recognition In Printed Documents. arXiv preprint arXiv:2306.15782. doi:10.1007/978-3-031-41734-4_19

Rai, R. (2019). The Contribution of Women Entrepreneirs in the Economic Development of India. *Journal of Global Values,* (10).

Raisch, S., & Krakowski, S. (2021). Artificial intelligence and management: The automation-augmentation paradox. *Academy of Management Review*, *46*(1), 192–210. doi:10.5465/amr.2018.0072

Raja, A. K. (2022). *Girls from Delhi use AI for aiding children fighting cerebral palsy*. INDIAai. https://indiaai.gov.in/article/girls-from-delhi-use-ai-for-aiding-children-fighting-cerebral-palsy

Ramlal, N., & Chiweshe, N. (2022). An Interrogation of Entrepreneur Perspectives on the Nexus of Sustainability and Entrepreneurship: Sustainable Entrepreneurship. In Institutions, Resilience, and Dynamic Capabilities of Entrepreneurial Ecosystems in Emerging Economies (pp. 139-157). IGI Global.

Ransbotham, S., Khodabandeh, S., Kiron, D., Candelon, F., Chu, M., & LaFountain, B. (2020). *Expanding AI's impact with organizational learning*. MIT Sloan Management Review and Boston Consulting Group. Retrieved from http://dln.jaipuria.ac.in:8080/jspui/bitstream/123456789/10852/1/MITSMR-BCG-Report-2020-Expanding%20AI%20impact%20with.pdf

Rashid, D., & Kumar Gondhi, N. (2022). Scrutinization of Urdu handwritten text recognition with machine learning approach. In *International Conference on Emerging Technologies in Computer Engineering* (pp. 383-394). Cham: Springer International Publishing. 10.1007/978-3-031-07012-9_33

Ravasan, A. Z., & Savoji, S. R. (2014). An investigation of BI implementation critical success factors in Iranian context. [IJBIR]. *International Journal of Business Intelligence Research*, *5*(3), 41–57. doi:10.4018/ijbir.2014070104

Ravikumar, S., & Saraf, P. (2020). Prediction of stock prices using machine learning (regression, classification) Algorithms. In *2020 International Conference for Emerging Technology (INCET)* (pp. 1-5). IEEE. 10.1109/INCET49848.2020.9154061

Razfar, N., True, J., Bassiouny, R., Venkatesh, V., & Kashef, R. (2022). Weed detection in soybean crops using custom lightweight deep learning models. *Journal of Agriculture and Food Research*, *8*, 100308. doi:10.1016/j.jafr.2022.100308

Reddy, V. K. S. (2018). Stock market prediction using machine learning. [IRJET]. *International Research Journal of Engineering and Technology*, *5*(10), 1033–1035.

Rehman, A., Ul-Hasan, A., & Shafait, F. (2021). High performance Urdu and Arabic video text recognition using convolutional recurrent neural networks. In *Document Analysis and Recognition–ICDAR 2021 Workshops: Lausanne, Switzerland*. Springer International Publishing.

Rezaei, H., Faaljou, H., & Mansourfar, G. (2021). Stock price prediction using deep learning and frequency decomposition. *Expert Systems with Applications*, *169*, 114332. doi:10.1016/j.eswa.2020.114332

Riaz, N., Arbab, H., Maqsood, A., Nasir, K., Ul-Hasan, A., & Shafait, F. (2022). Conv-transformer architecture for unconstrained off-line Urdu handwriting recognition. [IJDAR]. *International Journal on Document Analysis and Recognition*, *25*(4), 373–384. doi:10.1007/s10032-022-00416-5

Riedl, M., Arriaga, R., Boujarwah, F., Hong, H., Isbell, J., & Heflin, L. J. (2007). Graphical Social Scenarios: Toward Intervention and Authoring for Adolescents with High Functioning Autism. *Virtual Healthcare Interaction, Papers from the AAAI Fall Symposium.*

Ries, E. (2011). *The Lean Startup: How Today's Entrepreneurs Use Continuous Innovation to Create Radically Successful Businesses.* USA: Crown Currency; Illustrated edition.

Ripberger, J. T. (2011). Capturing curiosity: Using internet search trends to measure public attentiveness. *Policy Studies Journal: the Journal of the Policy Studies Organization*, *39*(2), 239–259. doi:10.1111/j.1541-0072.2011.00406.x

Risq, F. (2021). Will AI eventually replace designers or change the way we design? *Medium.* https://uxdesign.cc/human-design-and-artificial-intelligence-f0af52c6ce6

Roach, J. (2018, May 11). AI technology helps students who are deaf learn. *The AI Blog*. https://blogs.microsoft.com/ai/ai-powered-captioning/

Rojas, A., & Tuomi, A. (2022). Reimagining the sustainable social development of AI for the service sector: The role of startups. *Journal of Ethics in Entrepreneurship and Technology*, *2*(1), 39–54. doi:10.1108/JEET-03-2022-0005

Rostami, N. A. (2014). Integration of Business Intelligence and Knowledge Management–A literature review. *Journal of Intelligence Studies in Business*, *4*(2), 30–40. doi:10.37380/jisib.v4i2.95

Rouf, N., Malik, M. B., Arif, T., Sharma, S., Singh, S., Aich, S., & Kim, H. C. (2021). Stock market prediction using machine learning techniques: A decade survey on methodologies, recent developments, and future directions. *Electronics (Basel)*, *10*(21), 2717. doi:10.3390/electronics10212717

Rouhani, S., Ashrafi, A., Ravasan, A. Z., & Afshari, S. (2016). The impact model of business intelligence on decision support and organizational benefits. *Journal of Enterprise Information Management*, *29*(1), 19–50. doi:10.1108/JEIM-12-2014-0126

Roundy, P. T. (2022). Artificial intelligence and entrepreneurial ecosystems: Understanding the implications of algorithmic decision-making for startup communities. *Journal of Ethics in Entrepreneurship and Technology*, *2*(1), 23–38. doi:10.1108/JEET-07-2022-0011

ROYBI. (2022, May 20). *Artificial intelligence in special education.* ROYBI Robot. https://roybirobot.com/blogs/news/artificial-intelligence-in-special-education

Rubbaniy, G., Khalid, A. A., Syriopoulos, K., & Samitas, A. (2021). Safe-haven properties of soft commodities during times of COVID-19. *Journal of Commodity Markets, 100223.*

Ruigrok, T., van Henten, E., Booij, J., Van Boheemen, K., & Kootstra, G. (2020). Application-specific evaluation of a weed-detection algorithm for plant-specific spraying. *Sensors (Basel), 20*(24), 7262. doi:10.3390/s20247262 PMID:33352873

Saeed, F. (2020). *9 powerful examples of artificial intelligence in use today*. IQVIS Inc. https://www.iqvis.com/blog/9-powerful-examples-of- artificial-intelligence-in-use-today/

Sarangi, G. K. (2021). *Resurgence of ESG investments in India: Toward a sustainable economy.*

Schlick, J., Stephan, P., Loskyll, M., & Lappe, D. (2014). Industrie 4.0 in der praktischen Anwendung. Industrie 4.0 in Produktion, Und Logistik, A. Anwendung·Technologien·Migration (pp. 57–84).

Schroer, A. (2023). *What is Artificial Intelligence?* Builtin. https://builtin.com/artificial-intelligence

Shafi, M., & Zia, K. (2021). Urdu character recognition: A systematic literature review. *International Journal of Applied Pattern Recognition*, *6*(4), 283–307. doi:10.1504/IJAPR.2021.118914

Shane, S. (2008). *The Illusions of Entrepreneurship: The Costly Myths That Entrepreneurs, Investors, and Policy Makers Live By*. Yale University Press.

Shanmugam, S., Assunção, E., Mesquita, R., Veiros, A., & Gaspar, P. D. (2020). *Automated weed detection systems: A review*. KnE Engineering.

Shaw, T. (2004). *Shaku Atre Interview: What is Business Intelligence?* DSS Resources. http://dssresources.com/interviews/atre/atre07092004.html

Shen, J., & Shafiq, M. O. (2020). Short-term stock market price trend prediction using a comprehensive deep learning system. *Journal of Big Data*, *7*(1), 1–33. doi:10.1186/s40537-020-00333-6 PMID:32923309

Shollo, A., & Kautz, K. (2010). Towards an understanding of business intelligence. *ACIS 2010 Proceedings, 86*. https://aisel.aisnet.org/acis2010/86

Singh, A. K., & Taterh, S. (2023). Exploring the Significance and Obstacles of Adopting Futuristic Technology Perspectives for Entrepreneurship and Sustainable Innovation. In Futuristic Technology Perspectives on Entrepreneurship and Sustainable Innovation (pp. 1-10). IGI Global. doi:10.4018/978-1-6684-5871-6.ch001

Singh, A. K., Taterh, S., & Mitra, U. (2023). An Efficient Tactic for Analysis and Evaluation of Malware Dump File Using the Volatility Tool. *SN Computer Science*, *4*(5), 457. doi:10.1007/s42979-023-01844-8

Singh, R., & Srivastava, S. (2017). Stock prediction using deep learning. *Multimedia Tools and Applications*, *76*(18), 18569–18584. doi:10.1007/s11042-016-4159-7

Singh, V., Rana, A., Bishop, M., Filippi, A. M., Cope, D., Rajan, N., & Bagavathiannan, M. (2020). Unmanned aircraft systems for precision weed detection and management: Prospects and challenges. *Advances in Agronomy*, *159*, 93–134. doi:10.1016/bs.agron.2019.08.004

Skyrius, R. (2021). *Business Intelligence*. Springer International Publishing. doi:10.1007/978-3-030-67032-0

Stanberry, K., & Raskind, M. H. (2022, January 17). *Assistive technology for kids with learning disabilities: An overview*. Reading Rockets. https://www.readingrockets.org/article/assistive-technology-kids-learning-disabilities-overview

Subasi, A., Amir, F., Bagedo, K., Shams, A., & Sarirete, A. (2021). Stock market prediction using machine learning. *Procedia Computer Science*, *194*, 173–179. doi:10.1016/j.procs.2021.10.071

Subeesh, A., Bhole, S., Singh, K., Chandel, N. S., Rajwade, Y. A., Rao, K. V. R., Kumar, S. P., & Jat, D. (2022). Deep convolutional neural network models for weed detection in polyhouse grown bell peppers. *Artificial Intelligence in Agriculture*, *6*, 47–54. doi:10.1016/j.aiia.2022.01.002

Sunny, M. A. I., Maswood, M. M. S., & Alharbi, A. G. 2020, October. Deep learning-based stock price prediction using LSTM and bi-directional LSTM model. In *2020 2nd novel intelligent and leading emerging sciences conference (NILES)* (pp. 87-92). IEEE.

Swetha, K., Shareef, C. I., Sreenivasulu, G., Baseer, K. K., & Pasha, M. J. (2023). *Study on Implementation of Electronic Health Records using Blockchain Technology*. 2023 4th International Conference on Electronics and Sustainable Communication Systems (ICESC), Coimbatore, India. 10.1109/ICESC57686.2023.10192992

Taherdoost, H., & Madanchian, M. (2023). Artificial Intelligence and Knowledge Management: Impacts, Benefits, and Implementation. *Computers*, *12*(4), 72. doi:10.3390/computers12040072

Tapscott, D., & Williams, A. D. (2006). *Wikinomics: How Mass Collaboration Changes Everything*. Penguin.

TCS. (2024). TCS' AI speech device helps kids who have cerebral palsy. *Tata Consultancy Services: Driving Innovation and Building on Belief*. https://www.tcs.com/what-we-do/pace-innovation/case-study/assistive-technology-celebral-palsy

Teece, D. J. (2010). Business Models, Business Strategy and Innovation. *Long Range Planning*, *43*(2-3), 172–194. doi:10.1016/j.lrp.2009.07.003

Tetlock, P. C. (2015). The role of media in finance. Handbook of media Economics, 1, 701-721. doi:10.1016/B978-0-444-63685-0.00018-8

Thirumalraj, A., & Rajesh, T. (2023). *An Improved ARO Model for Task Offloading in Vehicular Cloud Computing in VANET*.

Thirumalraj, A., Asha, V., & Kavin, B. P. (2023). An Improved Hunter-Prey Optimizer-Based DenseNet Model for Classification of Hyper-Spectral Images. In AI and IoT-Based Technologies for Precision Medicine (pp. 76-96). IGI Global. doi:10.4018/979-8-3693-0876-9.ch005

Thirumalraj, A., Anusuya, V. S., & Manjunatha, B. (2024). Detection of Ephemeral Sand River Flow Using Hybrid Sandpiper Optimization-Based CNN Model. In *Innovations in Machine Learning and IoT for Water Management* (pp. 195–214). IGI Global.

Tian, Z., He, T., Shen, C., & Yan, Y. (2019). Decoders matter for semantic segmentation: Data-dependent decoding enables flexible feature aggregation. *Proc. IEEE/CVF Conf. Comput. Vis. Pattern Recognit. (CVPR).* IEEE. 10.1109/CVPR.2019.00324

Tikly, L., Joubert, M., Barrett, A. M., Bainton, D., Cameron, L., & Doyle, H. (2018). *Supporting secondary school STEM education for sustainable development in Africa.* University of Bristol, Bristol Working Papers in Education Series.

Toppr. (2019). *Uses of Mobile Phones Essay for Students.* Toppr. https://www.toppr.com/guides/essays/uses-of-mobile-phones-es say/

Townsend, D. M. D. M., & Hunt, R. A. (2019). Entrepreneurial action, creativity, and judgment in the age of artificial intelligence. *Journal of Business Venturing Insights*, *11*, e00126. doi:10.1016/j.jbvi.2019.e00126

Treiblmaier, H. (2018). The impact of the blockchain on the supply chain: A theory-based research framework and a call for action. *Supply Chain Management*, *23*(6), 545–559. doi:10.1108/SCM-01-2018-0029

Turban, E. (2011). *Decision support and business intelligence systems.* Pearson Education India.

Turktarhan, G., Gopalan, R. & Ozkul, E. (2021). Big Data and Business Intelligence in Hospitality and Tourism. *University of South Florida M3 Center Publishing*, *17*(9781732127593), 5.

Ucar, F., & Korkmaz, D. (2020). COVIDiagnosis-Net: Deep Bayes-SqueezeNet based diagnosis of the coronavirus disease 2019 (COVID-19) from X-ray images. *Medical Hypotheses*, *140*, 109761. doi:10.1016/j.mehy.2020.109761 PMID:32344309

UghuluD. J. (2022). The role of Artificial intelligence (AI) in Starting, automating and scaling businesses for Entrepreneurs. *ScienceOpen* preprints.

Uhlenbrock, L., Sixt, M., Tegtmeier, M., Schulz, H., Hagels, H., Ditz, R., & Strube, J. (2018). Natural Products Extraction of the Future—Sustainable Manufacturing Solutions for Societal Needs. *Processes (Basel, Switzerland)*, *6*(10), 177–177. doi:10.3390/pr6100177

UIS-UNESCO (UNESCO Institute for Statistics). (n.d.). *Special needs education.* In: Glossary. UIS-UNESCO. https://uis.unesco.org/en/glossary-term/special-needs-educat ion

Umair, M., Zubair, M., Dawood, F., Ashfaq, S., Bhatti, M. S., Hijji, M., & Sohail, A. (2022). A Multi-Layer Holistic Approach for Cursive Text Recognition. *Applied Sciences (Basel, Switzerland)*, *12*(24), 12652. doi:10.3390/app122412652

Umar, Z., Gubareva, M., Yousaf, I., & Ali, S. (2021). A tale of company fundamentals vs sentiment driven pricing: The case of GameStop. *Journal of Behavioral and Experimental Finance*, *30*, 100501. doi:10.1016/j.jbef.2021.100501

UNESCO. (2017). *A guide for ensuring inclusion and equity in education*. Paris: UNESCO. https://unesdoc.unesco.org/images/0024/002482/248254e.pdf

USwitch. (2020). *History of mobile phones: What was the first mobile phone?* U Switch. https://www.uswitch.com/mobiles/guides/history-of-mobilephones/#:~:text=Mobile%20phones%20were%20invented%20as. • https://www.forbes.com/sites/bernardmarr/2023/02/28/beyond-chatgpt-14-mind-blowing-ai-tools-everyone-should-be-trying-out-now/?sh=21831bdd7a1b

Vajirakachorn, T., & Chongwatpol, J. (2017). Application of business intelligence in the tourism industry: A case study of a local food festival in Thailand. *Tourism Management Perspectives*, *23*, 75–86. doi:10.1016/j.tmp.2017.05.003

Van Aelst, P., Toth, F., Castro, L., Štětka, V., Vreese, C. D., Aalberg, T., Cardenal, A. S., Corbu, N., Esser, F., Hopmann, D. N., Koc-Michalska, K., Matthes, J., Schemer, C., Sheafer, T., Splendore, S., Stanyer, J., Stępińska, A., Strömbäck, J., & Theocharis, Y. (2021). Does a crisis change news habits? A comparative study of the effects of COVID-19 on news media use in 17 European countries. *Digital Journalism (Abingdon, England)*, *9*(9), 1208–1238. doi:10.1080/21670811.2021.1943481

Vasileiou, E. (2021a). Behavioral finance and market efficiency in the time of the COVID-19 pandemic: Does fear drive the market? *International Review of Applied Economics*, *35*(2), 224–241. doi:10.1080/02692171.2020.1864301

Vasileiou, E. (2021b). Explaining stock markets' performance during the COVID-19 crisis: Could Google searches be a significant behavioral indicator? *International Journal of Intelligent Systems in Accounting Finance & Management*, *28*(3), 173–181. doi:10.1002/isaf.1499

Vasileiou, E. (2021c). Does the short squeeze lead to market abnormality and antileverage effect? Evidence from the Gamestop case. *Journal of Economic Studies (Glasgow, Scotland)*.

Vasileiou, E., Samitas, A., Karagiannaki, M., & Dandu, J. (2021). Health risk and the efficient market hypothesis in the time of COVID-19. *International Review of Applied Economics*, *35*(2), 210–223. doi:10.1080/02692171.2020.1864299

Veeranampalayam Sivakumar, A.N., Li, J., Scott, S., Psota, E., & Jhala, J., A., Luck, J.D. and Shi, Y. (. (2020). Comparison of object detection and patch-based classification deep learning models on mid-to late-season weed detection in UAV imagery. *Remote Sensing*, *12*(13), 2136. doi:10.3390/rs12132136

Venkatraman, N. (1997). The Concept of Fit in Strategy Research: Toward Verbal and Statistical Correspondence. *Academy of Management Review*, *22*(4), 853–854.

Vijh, M., Chandola, D., Tikkiwal, V. A., & Kumar, A. (2020). Stock closing price prediction using machine learning techniques. *Procedia Computer Science*, *167*, 599–606. doi:10.1016/j.procs.2020.03.326

Viviers, S. (2009). Going green: An SMME perspective. *The Southern African Journal of Entrepreneurship and Small Business Management*, *2*(1), 30–49. doi:10.4102/sajesbm.v2i1.18

Vosen, S., & Schmidt, T. (2011). Forecasting private consumption: Survey-based indicators vs. Google trends. *Journal of Forecasting*, *30*(6), 565–578. doi:10.1002/for.1213

Wagman-Geller, M. (2018). *Women Who Launch: The Women Who Shattered Glass Ceilings*. Mango.

Wang, K., Wan, J., Li, D., Zhang, C., & Zhang, H. (2021). Intelligent manufacturing in the era of artificial intelligence: A review. *Journal of Intelligent Manufacturing*, *32*(1), 153–174.

Wang, Y., & Wang, J. (2021). Research on the application of artificial intelligence technology in the field of intelligent manufacturing. In *2021 International Conference on Mechanical and Electrical Engineering, Automation and Information Engineering (MEAI)* (pp. 276-279). IEEE

Watson, H. J., & Wixom, B. H. (2007). The current state of business intelligence. *Computer*, *40*(9), 96–99. doi:10.1109/MC.2007.331

Wieder, B., Ossimitz, M., & Chamoni, P. (2012). The impact of business intelligence tools on performance: A user satisfaction paradox? *International Journal of Economic Sciences and Applied Research*, *5*(3), 7–32.

Wilson, C. (2019). Artificial Intelligence is Changing the Event Industry — Here's How. *Swapcard Blog*. https://blog.swapcard.com/artificial-intelligence-and-events

Wixom, B., & Watson, H. (2010). The BI-based organization. [IJBIR]. *International Journal of Business Intelligence Research*, *1*(1), 13–28. doi:10.4018/jbir.2010071702

Wójcik, D., & Ioannou, S. (2020). COVID-19 and finance: Market developments so far and potential impacts on the financial sector and centres. *Tijdschrift voor Economische en Sociale Geografie*, *111*(3), 387–400. doi:10.1111/tesg.12434 PMID:32836484

World Health Organization. (2023). *Assistive technology*. World Health Organization. https://www.who.int/news-room/fact-sheets/detail/assistive-technology

World Health Organization. (2023). *Disability and health*. WHO. https://www.who.int/news-room/fact-sheets/detail/disability-and-health#:~:text=Key%20facts,earlier%20than%20those%20without%20disabilities

Worthington, I., & Patton, D. (2005). Strategic intent in the management of the green environment within SMEs: An analysis of the UK screen-printing sector. *Long Range Planning*, *38*(2), 197–212. doi:10.1016/j.lrp.2005.01.001

Wu, Z., Chen, Y., Zhao, B., Kang, X., & Ding, Y. (2021). Review of weed detection methods based on computer vision. *Sensors (Basel)*, *21*(11), 3647. doi:10.3390/s21113647 PMID:34073867

Wyness, L., Jones, P., & Klapper, R. (2015). Sustainability: What the entrepreneurship educators think. *Education + Training*, *57*(8/9), 834–852. doi:10.1108/ET-03-2015-0019

Xu, B., Fan, J., Chao, J., Arsenijevic, N., Werle, R., & Zhang, Z. (2023). Instance segmentation method for weed detection using UAV imagery in soybean fields. *Computers and Electronics in Agriculture*, *211*, 107994. doi:10.1016/j.compag.2023.107994

Xu, B., Zhang, D., Zhang, S., Li, H., & Lin, H. (2018). Stock market trend prediction using recurrent convolutional neural networks. In *Natural Language Processing and Chinese Computing: 7th CCF International Conference*. Springer.

Xu, S. X., & Zhang, X. (2013). Impact of Wikipedia on market information environment: Evidence on management disclosure and investor reaction. *Management Information Systems Quarterly*, *37*(4), 1043–1068. doi:10.25300/MISQ/2013/37.4.03

Yadav, N., Gupta, K., Rani, L., & Rawat, D. (2018). Drivers of sustainability practices and SMEs: A systematic literature review. *European Journal of Sustainable Development*, *7*(4), 531–531. doi:10.14207/ejsd.2018.v7n4p531

Yang, Q., Ye, Y., Gu, L., & Wu, Y. (2023). MSFCA-Net: A Multi-Scale Feature Convolutional Attention Network for Segmenting Crops and Weeds in the Field. *Agriculture*, *13*(6), 1176. doi:10.3390/agriculture13061176

Yang, X., & Jiang, X. (2020, January). A hybrid active contour model based on new edgestop functions for image segmentation. *International Journal of Ambient Computing and Intelligence*, *11*(1), 87–98. doi:10.4018/IJACI.2020010105

Yellow.ai. (2022, September 9). 10 powerful use cases of educational chatbots in 2022. *Yellow.ai*. https://yellow.ai/chatbots/use-cases-of-chatbots-in-education-industry

Yeoh, W., & Koronios, A. (2010). Critical success factors for business intelligence systems. *Journal of Computer Information Systems*, *50*(3), 23–32.

Yiu, L. D., Yeung, A. C., & Cheng, T. E. (2021). The impact of business intelligence systems on profitability and risks of firms. *International Journal of Production Research*, *59*(13), 3951–3974. doi:10.1080/00207543.2020.1756506

Yun, K. K., Yoon, S. W., & Won, D. (2023). Interpretable stock price forecasting model using genetic algorithm-machine learning regressions and best feature subset selection. *Expert Systems with Applications*, *213*, 118803. doi:10.1016/j.eswa.2022.118803

Yu, P., & Yan, X. (2020). Stock price prediction based on deep neural networks. *Neural Computing & Applications*, *32*(6), 1609–1628. doi:10.1007/s00521-019-04212-x

Zafary, F. (2020). Implementation of business intelligence considering the role of information systems integration and enterprise resource planning. *Journal of intelligence studies in business*, *10*(1), 59-74.

Zahid, H., Rashid, M., Hussain, S., Azim, F., Syed, S. A., & Saad, A. (2022). Recognition of Urdu sign language: A systematic review of the machine learning classification. *PeerJ. Computer Science*, *8*, e883. doi:10.7717/peerj-cs.883 PMID:35494799

Zapata-Caceres, M., & Martin-Barroso, E. (2021). Applying game learning analytics to a voluntary video game: Intrinsic motivation, persistence, and rewards in learning to program at an early age. *IEEE Access : Practical Innovations, Open Solutions*, *9*, 123588–123602. doi:10.1109/ACCESS.2021.3110475

ZargarH.KóczyL. T. (2023). Handwritten Urdu Character Recognition and Comparative Analysis with Popular Machine Learning Algorithms. Available at SSRN 4461891. doi:10.2139/ssrn.4461891

Zeng, F. (2017). A new landscape for hearing aids. *The Hearing Journal*, *70*(12), 6. doi:10.1097/01.HJ.0000527871.60334.ad

Zhang, Y., Tian, Y., Kong, Y., Zhong, B., & Fu, Y. (2018). Residual dense network for image super-resolution. *Proc. IEEE/CVF Conf. Comput. Vis. Pattern Recognit*. IEEE. 10.1109/CVPR.2018.00262

Zhang, H., Gao, S., & Zhou, P. (2023). Role of digitalization in energy storage technological innovation: Evidence from China. *Renewable & Sustainable Energy Reviews*, *171*, 113014. doi:10.1016/j.rser.2022.113014

Zhang, L., Wang, S., & Liu, B. (2018). Deep learning for sentiment analysis: A survey. *Wiley Interdisciplinary Reviews. Data Mining and Knowledge Discovery*, *8*(4), e1253. doi:10.1002/widm.1253

Zhang, X., Cui, J., Liu, H., Han, Y., Ai, H., Dong, C., Zhang, J., & Chu, Y. (2023). Weed Identification in Soybean Seedling Stage Based on Optimized Faster R-CNN Algorithm. *Agriculture*, *13*(1), 175. doi:10.3390/agriculture13010175

Zhang, Z., Wu, C., Coleman, S., & Kerr, D. (2020). DENSE-INception U-net for medical image segmentation. *Computer Methods and Programs in Biomedicine*, *192*(Aug), 105395. doi:10.1016/j.cmpb.2020.105395 PMID:32163817

Zhao, Y., & Yang, G. (2023). Deep Learning-based Integrated Framework for stock price movement prediction. *Applied Soft Computing*, *133*, 109921. doi:10.1016/j.asoc.2022.109921

Zia, S., Azhar, M., Lee, B., Tahir, A., Ferzund, J., Murtaza, F., & Ali, M. (2023). Recognition of printed Urdu script in Nastaleeq font by using CNN-BiGRU-GRU Based Encoder-Decoder Framework. *Intelligent Systems with Applications*, *18*, 200194. doi:10.1016/j.iswa.2023.200194

Zubair, M., Umair, M., Alhussein, M., Hussain, H. A., Aurangzeb, K., & Asghar, M. N. (2023). *Scene Character Recognition from Cursive Text Using Deep Learning Models.*

About the Contributors

Sanjay Misra, a Sr. member of IEEE and ACM Distinguished Lecturer, is a Senior Scientist at the Institute for Energy Technology(IFE), Halden, Norway. Before joining IFE, he was associated with the Computer Science and Communication department of Østfold University College, Halden, Norway, and was a Full Professor (since Jan 2010) of Computer (Software) Engineering at Covenant University (400-500 ranked by THE(2019)) since 2012 yrs. He holds PhD. in Information & Knowledge Engg(Software Engg)from the University of Alcala, Spain & M.Tech. (Software Engg) from MLN National Institute of Tech, India.As per SciVal (SCOPUS- Elsevier) analysis (on 01.12.2021). He has been the most productive researcher (Number 1) in Nigeria since 2017 (in all disciplines), in computer science no 1 in the country & no 2 in the whole of Africa. Total around 700 articles (SCOPUS/WoS) with 500 coauthors worldwide (-150 JCR/SCIE) in the core & appl. area of Software Engineering, Web engineering, Health Informatics, Cybersecurity,Intelligent systems,AI,etc. He has been amongst the top 2% of scientists in the world (published by Standford University) for last 3 years.

Amit Kr. Jain is Director / Professor / Advisor as well as Founder Director of various Centre / Institutions. He has had an outstanding academic record and is a product of prestigious system throughout. He obtained Ph. D, M. Tech & B.Tech in Electronics & Communication Engineering. Also, had a Ph. D (Management) from AMITY University, Noida & MBA (IMT Ghaziabad). Published more than 81 Research Papers in reputed Journals and International and National Conferences and authored eight books.

Manju Kaushik presently working as an Associate Professor-AIIT, President, IIC, Amity University Rajasthan. Head Amity Innovation Incubator, E-Cell,IEEE, ACM Branch Counselor &Coordinator Tech. Clubs,AUR.She has more than 17 years of experience in the field of teaching &research.She was awarded Ph.D. from the Mohan Lal Sukhadia University, Udaipur, Raj. Her research papers have been published in various journals and conferences of National and International repute like IEEE, springer, Elsevier, and Scopus indexed. She has organized International conference and more than 60 events (workshop, webinars, FDPs, awareness programs) two research scholars have successfully awarded with Ph.D. under her supervision. Currently She is Guiding 06 Ph.D scholars, Guided more than 100 PG Level students (MCA, M.tech.). She has appointed as paper setter and an external examiner for the viva-voce exams of post graduate students, Ph.D Students of various Universities. She is an active reviewer of different indexed journals. Presently, she is the executive member at Rajasthan sub-section of IEEE & Member of ACM, life member of ISTE and CSI. She has published 02 Patents & editor of 02 Books.

Chitresh Banerjee is a Science Graduate (B.Sc.), he holds a Masters Degree in Computer Science (M.Tech.), Masters Degree in Computer Applications (MCA) with GNIIT (3 years) program from NIIT Ltd. He is Ph.D. CS from Pacific University, Udaipur, Rajasthan, India. He has a rich academic experience of about 19+ years in the field of Computer Applications / Science / IT. He is currently working as Assistant Professor (AP-III), Amity Institute of Information Technology, Amity University, Jaipur. He has also worked as Executive Officer in the Board of Studies, The Institute of Chartered Accountants of India (Set up by an Act of Parliament), New Delhi. He is also a member of management committee of Jaipur Chapter of CSI (Computer Society of India) for the year 2011-12 & 2012-13. In addition, he is also member in 15 International Societies/Associations. He has an excellent academic background with a very sound academic and research experience. Under the Institute-Industry linkage programme, he delivers expert lectures on varied themes pertaining to IT. As a prolific writer in the arena of Computer Sciences and Information Technology, he penned down a number of books/learning material on Multimedia Systems, Information Technology, Software Engineering, E-banking Security Transactions, System Analysis and Design, Web Technologies, etc. He has contributed 64 research papers/chapters/articles in the conferences / journals / seminar / publications of international and national repute. He also provides consultancy in the area of software and project management to a no. of IT companies. He has acted as Editor in five International Journals and in two International Convention of Climate Change and Water (during 2012 & 2013). He has organized 7 National and International Conference. He is also Reviewer of 7 International Journals. He is Guest Editor in 6 International Journal of Inderscience Publisher and IGI Global. His area of interest includes software security, software engineering, and e-learning.

***

Mahsa Amiri has a master's degree in Management of Tourism Organizations from the University of the Algarve, and has knowledge in the area of Business Intelligence.

Aikaterini Chalkiadaki is a graduate of the Department of Financial and Management Engineering (University of the Aegean) and she is working in the financial sector.

Nigel Chiweshe is a lecturer at the University of KwaZulu-natal. He is currently pursuing Doctoral studies specialising in Marketing with a focus on motivations for luxury brand consumption by deluxe aspirers. He also lectures Responsible & Sustainable Management Principles, Technology Management at the undergraduate level and Entrepreneurship Innovation and Venture Creation, at the Honours level and Contemporary Marketing at the Masters level. Through his engagement with the disciplines of management, marketing and entrepreneurship, Nigel has developed a keen interest in social enterprises, sustainability practices in SMMEs and luxury branding. He is currently involved in mentoring youth entrepreneurs, communities of practice in youth entrepreneurship, book editorship and research in social enterprises in the 4th Industrial Revolution.

Vasileiou Evangelos is an Assistant Professor of finance in the Department of Financial and Management Engineering at the University of the Aegean, Greece. He holds a Bachelor degree in Economics (University of Piraeus), a MSc degree in Financial Analysis (Department of Banking and Financial Management, University of Piraeus), and a PhD in Finance (Department of Business Administration, University of the Aegean). He is a certified financial analyst, and he has working experience in banking and asset management industry. His main research areas are: financial economics, economic modelling, behavioral finance, financial risk, market efficiency.

K. Madhu Kishore Raghunath has obtained his Ph.D. in Management from the National Institute of Technology-Warangal and he is currently working as an Assistant Professor in the Department of Finance, GITAM institute of management, in GITAM (Deemed to be University) Visakhapatnam Campus. He has a Post-graduate degree in Management with Finance and Marketing specializations from Jawaharlal Nehru Technological University and has over 5 years of teaching experience in higher education along with CBSE-NET & AP & TS- SLET qualification. His research interests include subjects like Finance, Marketing, Risk Management, and Supply Chain Management.

Pallavi Mishra is working as an Associate Professor at Amity School of Communication, Amity University Rajasthan, Jaipur, India. Apart from the Academic contribution she is engaged in creative writing. Represented India Internationally and was felicitated with "Antarashtriya Hindi Sahitya Samman" at International Hindi Secreteriat, Mauritius. Actively working as the Convener of Amity's Institution's Innovation Council and Entrepreneurship cell wherein she trains budding entrepreneurs to develop their business models and groom their entrepreneurship skills with a purpose of systematically fostering the culture of Innovation in all Higher Education Institutions. Awarded with the Junior Research Fellowship by the University Grant Commission, Government of India. Awarded with a meritorious award of Second Topper in Master of Mass Communication from the University of Lucknow. As a mark of academic excellence, she has bagged many awards of high esteem. With a rigorous thinking and thorough understanding of academics cultivated student's involvement through capturing their interest in training, support, and guidance and Awarded with ASIAN EDUCATION AWARDS 2021 for the Contribution to Student Development and Excellence in Education. Awarded with Young Achiever Award 2021 for my Research Publication and received multiple awards for Best Research Paper. My academic account is credited with various research papers and chapter publications. Awarded with Best Paper Award for her Research Paper Award titled "Persuading Consumers through Scientific Claims: A study on Pseudo-Scientific claims in Advertisements" at 6th International Conference held on April 23, 2021, organized by Maharaja Agrasen Institute of Management in association with Waljat College of Applied Sciences Rusayi Oman & Thammasat Universsity ECON, BKK, Thailand. Awarded with Young Achiever Award 2021 for her Research Publication "Restructuring Mainstream Journalism: A Comparative Study of Traditional and New Media Concepts" in Journal of Critical Reviews May 2020. Awarded with "Best Research Paper Award" for my Research Paper titled "Netnographic Analysis: Understanding Cyber Psychology in Adolescence through social media posts" at 3rd International Conference on Recent Trends in Multi-disciplinary Research (ICRT-MDR-20) organized by Institute for Engineering Research and Publication (IFERP) in association with Cyryx College, Avid College, MI College, Maldives &Dep of CSE A.P.C Mahalaxmi College for Women, Maldives held at Maldives. Prior to this she has worked as an Assistant Professor at the Department of Journalism & Mass Communication, Banasthali Vidyapith, Rajasthan. She has served at the University of Lucknow as Teaching Assistant. Before this she worked as an Assistant Professor at Aizaz Rizvi College of Journalism and Mass Communication. She has served at Hindustan Times a leading English newspaper as a Sub-editor and also worked as a Public Relation Officer at an Industry Trade Board of Minority Society. Remarkably, at the same time, she contributes with her write-ups/poetries for various newspapers and magazines and served as a media educator at EduCoach, New Delhi. Presently she is also responsible for handling various key academic and administrative tasks of the department like, NAAC Coordinator, University Newsletter Coordinator, Public Relations & Media Committee Coordinator, KAPILA Coordinator, Entrepreneurship Cell Coordinator, Publications Board Member. As a mark of Academic Excellence, she has been the Chief Coordinator of Curriculum and Syllabus making/revision of all Professional Programmes of Amity School of Communication. She has delivered impressive research papers at national and international conferences and served as a session chair at international conferences. She has also produced a significant number of research papers in reputable national and international journals, as well as book chapters, Edited book and books of conference proceedings. She also serves as a member of the editorial board and a journal reviewer. She is a Life-Time Member of Indian Society for Training and Development (ISTD), Jaipur.

Tanushri Mukherjee is a top-performing, self-motivated and result-oriented teaching professional with a rich teaching experience of 17.8 years. Highly experienced in teaching Undergraduate as well as Post Graduate Students of Journalism and Mass Communication and students of Business School (BBA & Executive MBA) specialized subjects like Public Relations, Corporate Communication and Event Management, Design Thinking & Innovation. Has done Ph.D in Public Relations from Amity University Rajasthan in the field of Mass Communication in the Faculty of Humanities and Social Sciences in 2016. She is also UGC NET Qualified. As a mark of academic excellence, she has bagged many awards of high repute like featured in the July, 2021 edition of the renowned " IMPACT" Magazine under " Top 50 Women Leaders in PR and Corporate Communication, Distinguished Associate Professor Award, Educator of the Year Award by Exchange4media Group, Distinguished Teacher for Holistic Development of Students Award by International Centre for Excellence in Education (INCEED) and SPACE (India) {Society for Perpetuation of Art, Culture & Education), Teaching Excellence Award in "PR and Communication" from Public Relations Society of India, Jaipur Chapter, Media Innovation Award on the occasion of All India Media Conference, Women's Excellence Award, Empowered Women Award, Certificate of Excellence in EET CRS 2ND Faculty Branding Awards" and has also bagged Medal, Citation & Certificate of Merit in the "Gold Medallion National Award for the Best PR Case Study by PRSI, Hyderabad Chapter. Presently she is Deputy Director Outcome, Amity University Rajasthan. Responsible for handling various key academic and administrative tasks of the department like, NAAC Coordinator, IQAC Coordinator, Alumni Affairs Coordinator, Ph.D Coordinator, Exam Coordinator etc. As a mark of Academic Excellence, she has been the Chief Coordinator of Curriculum and Syllabus making/revision of all Professional Programmes of Amity School of Communication. Has presented quality Research Papers at various National & International Conferences.

Has been Session Chair & Guest of Honor in various International Conferences and has a good number of Research Papers published in various reputed National and International Journals along with Publications in Book of Conference Proceedings, Book Chapters, Souvenir, Newsletters etc to her credit. As a mark of excellence in the field of research, she is also Member of Editorial Board as well as Reviewer of Eminent Journals. She is also in the panel of External Examiner for judging Practical Projects of leading Jaipur based Universities and is also an eminent Paper Setter & Examiner for various courses of her specialization area in reputed Universities. She, besides being convener of Board of Studies (Film & Animation) of Amity School of Communication, is also an eminent member of Board of Studies in the area of Public Relations of reputed Universities. She is an active member of various Professional Bodies like Lifetime Member of Public Relations Society of India, Member of Jaipur Management Association, Standard Member of All India Communication and Media Association (AICMA) and Life-Time Member of Indian Society for Training and Development (ISTD), Jaipur.

Chandra Sekhar Patro is currently serving as Assistant Professor at Gayatri Vidya Parishad College of Engineering (Autonomous), Visakhapatnam, India. He has PhD in Faculty of Commerce and Management Studies from Andhra University, India. He has a post-graduate degree in Management (MBA) from JNT University, Commerce (M.Com.) from Andhra University, and Financial Management (MFM) from Pondicherry University. Dr. Patro has more than 13 years of experience in teaching and research in the area of Commerce and Management Studies. His teaching interests include marketing management, financial management, and human resource management. His research interests include marketing especially e-marketing, consumer behavior and HR management. Dr. Patro has published 42 articles in reputed national and international journals, 41 chapters in edited books and 3 books. He has been associated with various social bodies as a member and life member of these associations.

Thembelihle Pita, is an emerging scholar in the field of sustainability in small to medium enterprises, with a passion for understanding and promoting sustainable business practices. Thembelihle holds a Master's degree from the University of KwaZulu-Natal (UKZN), where she conducted extensive research on factors influencing the engagement in sustainable practices within SMMEs, specifically in the city of Pietermaritzburg.

Célia M. Q. Ramos graduated in Computer Engineering from the University of Coimbra, obtained her Master in Electrical and Computers Engineering from the Higher Technical Institute, Lisbon University, and the PhD in Econometrics in the University of the Algarve (UALG), Faculty of Economics, Portugal. She is Associate Professor at School for Management, Hospitality and Tourism, also in the UALG, where she lectures computer science. Areas of research and special interest include conception and development of information systems, tourism information systems, big data, etourism, econometric modeling and panel-data models. Célia Ramos has published in the fields of information systems and tourism, namely, she has authored a book, six book chapters, conference papers and journal articles. At the level of applied research, she has participated in several funded projects.

Suyesha Singh is an Assistant Professor (Senior) in Department of Psychology, Manipal University Jaipur. She has an experience of over 13 years in teaching, research and Life Skills Training. Her research interests include Clinical Psychology, Applied Psychology, Counselling and Psychotherapy, Health Psychology & Organizational Behaviour. She is Certified Counsellor and an Art Analyst.

Swapnesh Taterh currently serving as Professor & Head, Amity Institute of Information Technology, Amity University Rajasthan, Jaipur, India. Experienced Researcher and Professor with 20 years of rich experience in teaching and research. As an ingenious researcher, had presented several research papers at national and international conferences and published more than 45 research papers in international journals. His doctoral thesis work focuses on security of software. He holds two master degrees in computer science and a bachelor degree in science. His current and prospective research & academic interests include Cryptography, Information Security, Data Analytics, and Open-Source software. He Filled Patents and published research paper in reputed Indexed journals with Impact Factor 13.473, ranking it 2 out of 162 in Computer Science Journal, SCIE, 2021. Besides these he also participated in UGC sponsored Orientation & Refresher Course, Awarded with A+ Grade and associates as a Chief Editor, Guest Editor, and Reviewer of International and National Journal of repute including IGI and InderScience

Arunadevi Thirumalraj did her BE in Computer Science Engineering in Government college of Engineering, Bodinayakanur and she has worked as a Research associate in various industrial and academic research institutes for past 6 years. Now she is pursing ME Computer Science Engineering in K.Ramakrishnan College of Technology, (KRCT), Tiruchirappalli. She is actively involved in the field of innovative teaching and Learning. She has publishing a good number of papers in indexed journals.

V. Asha completed her Master and PhD degrees in Computer Science from University of Mysore. Her research areas of interest include Image Analysis, Pattern

Recognition, Data Mining, etc. She has several publications in reputed journals and is serving as referee for various journals such as Pattern Recognition. Currently, she is Professor and Head of the Department – Master of Computer Applications, New Horizon College of Eng., Bangalore.

Index

T

U

W

Z

Ensure Quality Research is Introduced to the Academic Community

Become a Reviewer for IGI Global Authored Book Projects

The overall success of an authored book project is dependent on quality and timely manuscript evaluations.

Applications and Inquiries may be sent to:

development@igi-global.com

Applicants must have a doctorate (or equivalent degree) as well as publishing, research, and reviewing experience. Authored Book Evaluators are appointed for one-year terms and are expected to complete at least three evaluations per term. Upon successful completion of this term, evaluators can be considered for an additional term.

If you have a colleague that may be interested in this opportunity, we encourage you to share this information with them.

www.ingramcontent.com/pod-product-compliance
Lightning Source LLC
LaVergne TN
LVHW080637011026
849160LV00014B/1244